THE OBEDIENCE OF FAITH

"Dr. Yuille expresses his desire in writing this study in Romans as follows: 'It's my prayer that our appreciation of God's grace toward us in Christ might cause our hearts to burn with zeal for God's glory in the proclamation of his gospel.' The riches and treasure of Romans are uncovered and presented in this easy to read, concise, yet theologically deep, study on Romans. I highly recommend this book for all who wish to gain a deeper understanding of God's revealed truth and develop a greater zeal for God's glory."

Norm Millar
Senior Pastor, Redemption Bible Chapel,
London, ON

"In listening to Stephen Yuille preach through Romans verse by verse, our congregation's grasp of difficult doctrines was strengthened and lives were deeply transformed. As we entered the courtroom of God, I personally shed tears over conviction of sin as well as tears of joy in being taken by the hand and escorted into the depths of the gospel and its glorious implications for all of life. This book will quickly become a favourite for personal and family devotions, small group studies, sermon preparation, and biblical counselling."

Bryan Gaines
Pastor of Leadership and Discipleship,
Grace Community Church of Glen Rose, TX

"For centuries, believers have been helped by books of sermons. Dr. Stephen Yuille has given us a collection of his sermons from Romans that speak with orthodox clarity and pastoral warmth. This is how Romans ought to be known and these sermons can guide you in that great pursuit: the obedience of faith."

Clint Humfrey
Senior Pastor, Calvary Grace Church,
Calgary, AB

"I heartily recommend *Obedience of Faith* to a wide readership. It is scholarly yet pastoral, historical yet contemporary, reformational yet accessible, and exegetical yet homiletical. Though new Christians (or those exploring the gospel) will find spiritual nourishment in these pages, seasoned Christians will no doubt discover new depths that will build them up and spur them on in Christ. Pastors would also do well to include it in their reading list as they preach through this great epistle."

Ian J. Vaillancourt
Associate Professor of Old Testament and Hebrew,
Heritage Theological Seminary,
Cambridge, ON

In memory of Mark Phillips (1966–2020)

husband, father, friend, ambassador of Christ

THE OBEDIENCE OF FAITH

Paul's Epistle to the Romans

J. STEPHEN YUILLE

The Obedience of Faith

Copyright © 2021 J. Stephen Yuille

Unless otherwise indicated, all Scripture quotations are from The ESV® Bible (The Holy Bible, English Standard Version®), copyright © 2001 by Crossway, a publishing ministry of Good News Publishers. Used by permission. All rights reserved.

All rights reserved. This book or any portion thereof may not be reproduced or used in any manner whatsoever without the express written permission of the publisher except for the use of brief quotations in a book review.

Published by: H&E Publishing, Peterborough, Ontario, Canada
www.hesedandemet.com

Cover design by Chance Faulkner

Paperback ISBN: 978-1-989174-82-1
Ebook ISBN: 978-1-989174-83-8

Contents

Preface 1

Introduction (1:1-17)

1. Paul's Greeting (1:1-7) 5
2. The Gospel of God: Part 1 (1:1-7) 11
3. The Gospel of God: Part 2 (1:8-17) 15
4. The Power of the God (1:14-17) 21

Section 1: Condemnation (1:18-3:20)

5. The Wrath of God (1:18) 29
6. A Dreadful Exchange (1:19-32) 35
7. A Christian Worldview (1:18-32) 41
8. No Excuse (2:1-5) 49
9. Saved by Works (2:6-11) 53
10. The Secrets of Men (2:12-16) 57
11. Relying on Religious Obedience (2:17-24) 61
12. Relying on Religious Observance (2:25-29) 67
13. The Objections (3:1-8) 73
14. The Verdict (3:9-20) 77

Section 2: Justification (3:21-5:21)

15. Reformation Day (3:24) 85
16. Righteousness Revealed (3:21-26) 91
17. The Doctrine of Justification (3:23-26) 97
18. Deductions (3:27-31) 103
19. Father Abraham (4:1-8) 109
20. Timing Is Everything (4:9-12) 115
21. Guaranteed (4:13-17) 119
22. In Hope against Hope (4:18-22) 123
23. Believing God (4:23-25) 129
24. The Benefits of Justification (5:1-5) 133
25. Much More (5:6-11) 139
26. The Tale of Two Adams (5:12-19) 143
27. The Reign of Death (5:13-17) 147
28. Super Abounding Grace (5:20-21) 151
29. The Struggle of Two Kingdoms (5:21) 159

Section 3: Sanctification (6:1-8:39)

30. Union with Christ (6:1-23) 167
31. A Death Certificate (6:1-10) 173
32. A Moral Imperative (6:11-14) 179
33. Two Masters: Part 1 (6:15-18) 183
34. Two Masters: Part 2 (6:19-23) 189
35. Two Marriages (7:1-6) 193
36. Holy & Righteous & Good (7:7-12) 199
37. Sold Under Sin (7:13-25) 205
38. No Condemnation (8:1-4) 211
39. Walking by the Spirit (8:5-13) 217
40. The Climax of the Bible (8:14-17) 223
41. Future Glory (8:18) 229
42. The Creation's Groaning (8:19-25) 233
43. The Believer's Groaning (8:26-27) 237
44. Glorified (8:28-30) 241
45. Justified (8:28-30) 245
46. Called (8:28-30) 249
47. Predestined (8:28-30) 253
48. Foreknown (8:28-30) 257
49. All Things for Good (8:28-30) 261
50. Divine Sovereignty (8:28-30) 267
51. Victory: Part 1 (8:31-39) 273
52. Victory: Part 2 (8:31-39) 279

Section 4: Election (9:11-11:36)

53. Great Sorrow (9:1-6) 285
54. God's Purpose of Election (9:6-13) 291
55. The Objections: Part 1 (9:14-23) 297
56. The Objections: Part 2 (9:14-23) 303
57. God's People (9:24-29) 311
58. A Stone of Stumbling (9:30-10:3) 317
59. Abounding in Riches (10:4-13) 323
60. Hearing the Word (10:14-21) 327
61. Chosen by Grace (11:1-6) 333
62. When Grace Isn't Grace (11:7-10) 339
63. A Remnant, Chosen by Grace (11:11-24) 345
64. A Mystery (11:25-32) 351
65. The Depth of God's Knowledge (11:33-36) 355
66. The Depth of God's Wisdom (11:33-36) 359
67. The Depth of God's Sovereignty: Part 1 (11:36) 365
68. The Depth of God's Sovereignty: Part 2 (11:36) 371

Section 5: Application (12:1-15:13)

69. A Living Sacrifice (12:1) 379
70. A Renewed Mind (12:2) 385
71. Sober Judgment (12:3-8) 391
72. Genuine Love (12:9-16) 397
73. Active Compassion (12:17-21) 403
74. Grateful Submission (13:1-7) 409
75. Glorifying the King (13:1-7) 415
76. Fulfilling the Law (13:8-14) 419
77. Keeping the Peace (14:1-15:12) 425
78. Remedy 1: Don't Judge! Welcome! (14:1-12) 431
79. Remedy 2: Don't Destroy! Edify! (14:13-23) 435
80. The Kingdom of God (14:17) 439
81. Remedy 3: Don't Ignore! Honour! (15:1-12) 443
82. Abounding in Hope (15:13) 449

Conclusion (15:14-16:27)

83. A Healthy Christian (15:14-16) 459
84. Holy Ambition (15:17-21) 463
85. Fullness of Blessing (15:22-33) 467
86. Striving in Prayer (15:30-33) 471
87. Final Greetings (16:1-24) 475
88. Doctrinal Discernment (16:17-20) 481
89. The Only Wise God (16:25-27) 485

About the Author 489
Bibliography 491
Scripture Index 497

Preface

In reference to Paul's epistle to the Romans, John Calvin penned, "When anyone understands this epistle, he has a passage opened to him to the whole Scriptures."[1] I have shared Calvin's conviction for many years now, and I have found that no other book unlocks the depths of God's Word, unfolds the wonders of Christian theology, nor establishes the pillars of Evangelical piety, quite like Paul's epistle to the Romans. It has been my privilege to preach through it on two separate occasions—at Braidwood Bible Chapel in Peterborough, Ontario (August 2005 to May 2007), and at Grace Community Church in Glen Rose, Texas (May 2014 to May 2016). In the following pages, it's my pleasure to share with you some of my gleanings. May the Lord bless what is his in these pages, in accordance with his own sovereign purposes, and forgive the rest.

J. Stephen Yuille
Cambridge, Ontario
July 2020

---

[1] John Calvin, *Calvin's Commentaries,* vol. 19, *Commentaries on the Epistle of the Apostle Paul to the Romans* (Grand Rapids: Baker Books, 2003), xxiv.

Introduction (1:1–17)

1
Paul's Greeting (1:1-7)

According to Martin Luther, "This epistle is really the chief part of the New Testament and the very purest gospel, and is worthy not only that every Christian should know it word for word, but occupy himself with it every day, as the daily bread of the soul. It can never be read or pondered too much, and the more it is dealt with the more precious it becomes, and the better it tastes."[1] As F. F. Bruce notes, "There is no saying what may happen when people begin to study the letter to the Romans."[2] That's a delightful thought. As we embark on our study of this letter, I trust God will richly bless us.

We begin with Paul's introduction in 1:1-7. Upon comparing it with those found in his other letters, we find a significant difference—it's long. Why? Paul had never visited the city of Rome; therefore, he feels the need to introduce himself. In so doing, he mentions three important details.

Paul is a servant of Christ Jesus (1:1)
The word "servant" is *doulos*—slave. Clearly, Paul wants his readers to understand that he belongs to Christ and, therefore, lives to do his will. At one time, that wasn't the case. Formerly, Paul was "a blasphemer, persecutor, and insolent opponent" (1 Tim. 1:13). In brief, he was a slave to sin. That's true of all of us, by the way. Christ says, "Truly, truly, I say to you, everyone who practices sin is a slave to sin" (John 8:34). In Paul's case, Christ freed him from his slavery to sin on the road to Damascus. At that moment, Paul became "a servant of Christ Jesus."

There's an important lesson here for us: *We're either slaves of sin or slaves of Christ*. This has three implications.

First, it means that those who are slaves of sin must turn to Christ. "If the Son sets you free, you will be free indeed" (John 8:36). God punished Christ at the cross on behalf of sinners. Those who believe in Christ are united with

---

[1] Martin Luther, *Commentary on Romans* (Grand Rapids: Kregel Publishing, 1976), xiii.
[2] F.F. Bruce, *Tyndale New Testament Commentaries: Romans* (Grand Rapids: Wm. B. Eerdmans, 1988), 58.

him in his death, burial, and resurrection. Christ breaks sin's hold on them and, as a result, he reigns in their lives.

Second, it means that those who are slaves of Christ delight to do his will. As Paul says, "I have been crucified with Christ. It is no longer I who live, but Christ who lives in me. And the life I now live in the flesh I live by faith in the Son of God, who loved me and gave himself for me" (Gal. 2:20). We must continually remind ourselves that we belong to Christ. We've been crucified with him, buried with him, and raised with him. Now, we live to do his will.

Third, it means that those who are slaves of Christ give all the glory to God. In one of his great hymns, Charles Wesley writes,

> Long my imprisoned spirit lay
> fast bound in sin and nature's night.
> Thine eye diffused a quickening ray:
> I woke—the dungeon flamed with light!
> My chains fell off, my heart was free;
> I rose, went forth, and followed Thee.[3]

In a word, we owe our salvation to God. By his sovereign grace and almighty power, he has freed us from slavery to sin. Therefore, we give him all the glory.

Paul is an apostle (1:1)

The term "apostle" is used in three ways in the New Testament (NT). (1) It refers to messengers. (2) It refers to gospel preachers such as Barnabas and Timothy. (3) It refers to Christ's commissioned representatives. In 1:1, Paul uses the term in the third sense. Christ says to his apostles, "As the Father has sent me, even so I am sending you" (John 20:21). This means that Christ appointed his apostles as an extension of his own ministry. He did so in order to lay the foundation of the church. A significant part of that foundation is the NT canon. As B.B. Warfield explains, "The principle of canonicity was not apostolic authorship, but imposition by the apostles as law. ... The authority of the apostles, as by divine appointment founders of the church, was embodied in whatever books they imposed on the churches as law, not merely in those they themselves had written."[4]

---

[3] Charles Wesley, "And Can It Be?" in *The Hymnal for Worship and Celebration* (Waco: Word Music, 1986), 203.

[4] B.B. Warfield, *The Inspiration and Authority of the Bible* (Phillipsburg: P & R Publishing, 1979), 415-416.

Paul's Greeting (1:1-7)

By beginning his letter with this reminder, Paul is emphasizing his apostolic authority. In effect, he's saying, "I'm writing to you as Christ's representative. This letter is from God. By implication, the contents aren't open for debate." I remember conversing years ago with a friend on a particular doctrinal issue. He didn't agree with some of my comments. I quoted Scripture—one of Paul's epistles. My friend responded, "That's Paul's opinion." Regrettably, many people think like that. But such thinking actually demonstrates a complete misunderstanding of apostolic authority. When Paul says he's an apostle, he's reminding his readers that what they're about to hear is from God.

There's an important lesson here for us: *"All Scripture is breathed out by God"* (2 Tim. 3:16). This has three implications.

First, it means the Bible is to be revered. "Whoever despises the word brings destruction on himself, but he who reveres the commandment will be rewarded" (Prov. 13:13). It's to be revered because it's God's Word. Simply put, our attitude toward the Bible is ultimately our attitude toward God. "This, therefore," writes John Bunyan, "teaches us how to judge who fears the Lord. They are those who learn, and who stand in awe of the holy Word of God, the very form of that Word engraved upon the face of their souls."[5]

Second, it means the Bible is to be desired. It's food to satisfy our hunger, water to satisfy our thirst, light to guide our way, and truth to make us wise. It provides the answer to our every need, question, desire, anxiety, doubt, problem, and struggle. The psalmist declares,

> The law of the LORD is perfect, reviving the soul; the testimony of the LORD is sure, making wise the simple; the precepts of the LORD are right, rejoicing the heart; the commandment of the LORD is pure, enlightening the eyes; the fear of the LORD is clean, enduring forever; the rules of the LORD are true, and righteous altogether. More to be desired are they than gold, even much fine gold; sweeter also than honey and drippings of the honeycomb (Ps. 19:7-10).

We'll give an account for the time we idle away in amusements, while this book remains closed. We possess in our hands God's Word. Surely, it is to be desired.

Third, it means the Bible is to be obeyed. As James says, we must seek to

---

[5] John Bunyan, *The Fear of God* (Morgan: Soli Deo Gloria, 1999), 77.

be effectual doers, not forgetful hearers, of God's Word (James 1:22-25). All of us must strive to be like Ezra, who "had set his heart to study the law of the LORD and to do it" (Ezra 7:10). The Bible is to be cherished, studied, and obeyed.

Paul is set apart for the gospel of God (1:1)

Paul makes the same point in Galatians 1:15-16, explaining that God set him apart from his mother's womb and called him through grace so that he might preach among the Gentiles. Here, in 1:1-7, Paul proceeds to describe exactly what he preached: the gospel.

First, he says something about its *origin*: it's "of God" (1:1). Elsewhere, Paul writes, "For I would have you know, brothers, that the gospel that was preached by me is not man's gospel. For I did not receive it from any man, nor was I taught it, but I received it through a revelation of Jesus Christ" (Gal. 1:11-12).

Why is this important? It means the gospel belongs to God. This challenges the relativistic age in which we live. People say, "It doesn't matter what you believe." On the contrary, if God has spoken, it matters.

Second, Paul says something about the gospel's *foundation*: it "was promised beforehand through his prophets in the holy Scriptures" (1:2). In other words, the gospel is rooted in the Old Testament (OT). Paul confirms it in many places. For example, he exhorts Timothy: "But as for you, continue in what you have learned and have firmly believed, knowing from whom you learned it, and how from childhood you have been acquainted with the sacred writings, which are able to make you wise for salvation through faith in Christ Jesus" (2 Tim. 3:14-15). What are the "sacred writings"? They're the OT. Why does Paul commend the OT to Timothy? Because it's "able to make [him] wise for salvation through faith in Christ Jesus."

Why is this important? It stresses the continuity and harmony of Scripture. In Hebrews 3:5-6, we read, "Now Moses was faithful in all God's house as a servant, to testify to the things that were to be spoken later, but Christ is faithful over God's house as a son. And we are his house." Evidently, there's only one house—God's house. Moses was a servant in the house: the old dispensation. Christ is the Son over the house: the new dispensation. The old dispensation doesn't exist for itself, but "to testify to the things that were to be spoken later."

Third, Paul says something about the gospel's *theme:* it's "concerning his

Son, who was descended from David according to the flesh, and was declared to be the Son of God in power according to the Spirit of holiness by the resurrection from the dead, Jesus Christ our Lord" (1:3). Christ himself says, "These are my words that I spoke to you while I was still with you, that everything written about me in the Law of Moses and the Prophets and the Psalms must be fulfilled" (Luke 24:44). Here, Christ refers to the threefold division of the Hebrew Scriptures—Law, Prophets, and Psalms (or, Writings)—thereby stressing that it all points to him.

Why is this important? It places Christ at the centre of God's plan of redemption. All of history hinges upon Christ's humiliation and exaltation. Furthermore, it means Christ's identity is central to the gospel. He humbled himself by becoming a man and he died an agonizing death. His creatures rejected him. Yet, God vindicated him by raising him from the dead. On the judgment day, the only question that will matter is this: "Who do you say that I am?" And the only acceptable answer will be: "You are the Christ, the Son of the living God."

Fourth, Paul says something about the gospel's *purpose*: "to bring about the obedience of faith" (1:5). We're commanded to turn from sin, and to obey God by believing in Christ. In other words, the gospel commands men and women to place their faith in Christ.

Why is this important? It means faith is primarily an act of the will. We must understand the gospel. That's true. Above all else, however, we must embrace the gospel. When I was preaching at a children's camp years ago, I asked, "What does it mean to believe in Christ?" A little boy answered, "It means to make Christ the most important thing in your life." That little boy understood what many adults never grasp.

Fifth, Paul says something about the gospel's *result:* it's "for the sake of his name" (1:5). What is God's name? It has been said that God's name is glorious, "full of majesty," and gracious, "full of mercy."[6]

Why is this important? It means our acceptance of the gospel makes us worshippers. God saves us for his name's sake. Therefore, we should echo the psalmist who declares, "Every day I will bless you and praise your name forever and ever. Great is the LORD, and greatly to be praised, and his greatness is unsearchable" (Ps. 145:2-3).

Sixth, Paul says something about the gospel's *scope*: it's for "the nations"

---

[6] William Gouge, *Domesticall Duties* (London, 1622), 8-13.

(1:5). At the tower of Babel, the nations rejected God. In turn, he abandoned them to their sin while continuing to shower his common grace upon them. Paul explains, "In past generations he allowed all the nations to walk in their own ways. Yet he did not leave himself without witness, for he did good by giving you rains from heaven and fruitful seasons, satisfying your hearts with food and gladness" (Acts 14:16-17). During that time, God restricted his special revelation to Israel. With Christ's advent, however, God again turned to the nations. John declares, "Behold, the Lamb of God, who takes away the sin of the world!" (John 1:29). At the tower of Babel, God confused man's language, dispersing the nations across the face of the earth. On the Day of Pentecost, when he poured out the gift of tongues (languages) upon the church, he united the nations in one house with Christ as its head. Now, in the church, there's neither Jew nor Gentile.

Why is this important? It means the gospel knows no boundaries. It's for the world.

Conclusion

I once had the privilege of visiting John Wesley's chapel in London, England. The guide explained that the church establishment in London had viewed Wesley as dangerous, so they wouldn't permit him to preach in their churches. In response, he went to Epworth, Lincolnshire, where his father had been rector. But even there, they wouldn't permit him to preach. So, what did he do? He stood on his father's tomb in the churchyard and proclaimed the gospel. People came from all over to hear him. Eventually, he returned to London, where he purchased an old foundry to use as a preaching post. They came by the thousands to hear him.[7]

That's the spirit of Paul as conveyed in this introduction (1:1-7). His heart-cry is simply this: "Woe to me if I do not preach the gospel!" (1 Cor. 9:16).

---

[7] For more on John Wesley, see Iain Murray, *Wesley and Men Who Followed* (Carlisle: Banner of Truth, 2003).

2
The Gospel of God: Part 1 (1:1–7)

In this study, we return to Paul's introduction to consider in a little more detail what he says about the gospel. My prayer is that we'll know the gospel as a living truth. An hour of vigorous flossing and brushing (the night before visiting the dentist) won't compensate for twelve months of neglect. The same is true when it comes to applying the gospel. We must apply it consistently, not sporadically; intentionally, not haphazardly; diligently, not carelessly. Here are seven truths concerning the gospel, which we would do well to take to heart.

The gospel originates with God (1:1)
Paul is a "a servant of Christ Jesus." He's a servant in terms of his *position*: he's "called to be an apostle." And he's a servant in terms of his *message*: he's "set apart for the gospel of God." By beginning his letter in this way, Paul affirms the divine authority behind what he writes. In particular, he affirms that God is the author of the gospel.

As we study this letter, I pray we'll see the gospel as the revelation of God whereby we discover him. I pray we'll see the knowledge of God as an end in itself—after all, what could be more practical, beneficial, and wonderful than knowing God? I pray we'll define all things according to God's eternal glory, not our earthly happiness. I pray we'll be amazed by Paul's exaltation of God as the supreme cause and ultimate purpose of all things.

The gospel fulfills a promise (1:2)
Paul says that God promised the gospel "through his prophets in the holy Scriptures." We find the gospel in the days of Adam. God declares to the serpent: "He shall bruise your head, and you shall bruise his heal" (Gen. 3:15). This is a reference to the cross. God promises that Christ will defeat Satan, and that he will deal with the consequences of the fall.

We find the gospel in the days of Noah. He and his family are saved from the waters of God's judgment by entering the ark. This event points to a coming salvation realized in Christ (1 Peter 3:20). We're saved from the waters of God's judgment by virtue of our union with Christ.

We find the gospel in the days of Abraham. God promises to bless all the nations of the earth through Abraham's seed (Gen. 12:1-3). The seed is Christ, of course. He alone is the means by which true blessing is brought to the nations.

We find the gospel in the days of Moses. He leads the children of Israel out of bondage in Egypt. This event points to a coming salvation by which Christ redeems his people from spiritual slavery.

We find the gospel in the days of the judges and kings. The nation of Israel experiences a pattern of rebellion and deliverance. Each of these instances of deliverance points to the coming Saviour—a mighty judge and king who will rescue his people from sin and idolatry.

We find the gospel in the days of the prophets. They speak of a conquering king and a suffering servant. They speak of the Messiah—God's anointed. He will deliver his people from their bondage to sin.

As we study this letter, I pray we'll be devastated by Paul's exposure of our sin and guilt. I pray we'll see that the most dangerous threat to us isn't the sin in the world, but the sin in our hearts. I pray we'll feel our inability to alter our condition before God. I pray we'll realize that true joy escapes us until we come to terms with the sinfulness of our hearts. And I pray we'll see that all our hope rests on God's faithfulness to his promise.

The gospel centres on Christ (1:3-4)
Paul emphasizes two truths in these verses. First, Christ was descended from David; in other words, he's a man. Second, Christ was declared to be the Son of God; in other words, he's God. Both Christ's humanity and deity are essential to the gospel. If he had been God alone, he couldn't have died in our place. If he had been man alone, he couldn't have borne our sin without corruption and he couldn't have borne God's wrath without destruction.

As we study this letter, I pray we'll be overwhelmed by Paul's display of God's grace in Christ. I pray we'll see that God's love goes to unfathomable lengths to save us. Christ paid for all our sin at one moment upon the cross. God cherishes us because he makes us his own by redeeming us. I pray we won't be mere spectators of God's grace—admiring it, singing about it, and talking about it, without ever delighting in it.

The gospel requires the obedience of faith (1:5)
Faith is the means by which we receive God's gift of salvation. We don't contribute anything to the gospel, nor do we make a deal with God. We don't give him faith and obedience so that he will give us salvation and happiness. There's no deal! Even our faith is God's gift to us.

As we study this letter, I pray we'll understand that the gospel isn't about what we can or can't do, but about what God has done in Christ. God changes our hearts by making Christ more and more beautiful. As we put on Christ, we put off sin. I pray we'll understand the relationship between faith and obedience—between resting and striving. We strive to obey because we rest in Christ.

The gospel glorifies God among the nations (1:5)
As explained in the previous study, the nations rejected God at the tower of Babel. In response, God abandoned them to their sin while continuing to shower his common grace upon them. He continued to send the sun and rain upon them and give them harvests (Acts 14:16-17). During that time, God restricted his dealings with humanity to Israel. With Christ's advent, however, God again turned to the nations. John declares, "Behold, the Lamb of God, who takes away the sin of the world" (John 1:29). Now, in the church, there's neither Jew nor Gentile. At the tower of Babel, God confused man's language, dispersing the nations across the face of the earth. At Pentecost, he united the nations in one house with Christ as its head. Why's this important? It means the gospel doesn't know any boundaries.

As we study this letter, I pray we'll be gripped by Paul's fervour for the spread of God's glory among the nations. "For from the rising of the sun to its setting my name will be great among the nations, and in every place incense will be offered to my name, and a pure offering. For my name will be great among the nations, says the LORD of hosts" (Mal. 1:11).

The gospel manifests God's sovereign grace (1:6-7)
Paul mentions three details in these verses about the believers at Rome. (1) They're "called to belong to Jesus Christ." There's a difference between God's general call (heard with the ear) and God's special call (heard with the soul). The first is his invitation, whereas the second is his powerful claim. (2) They're "loved by God." There's a difference between God's general love (for his creation) and God's special love (for his church). He loves his people

in a peculiar way. (3) They're "called to be saints." God sets us apart to himself. He takes us (sinners) as his prized possession.

As we study this letter, I pray we'll be comforted by Paul's assurance that God is the author of salvation from start to finish. I pray we'll enjoy the truth that God holds his people with a mighty arm—even when we feel little joy and sense little assurance. I pray we'll be convinced that God governs every circumstance for our ultimate good.

The gospel imparts grace and peace (1:7)
In Christ, we receive grace and, as a result, experience peace. We receive strengthening grace to endure affliction, sustaining grace to remain faithful, equipping grace to serve God, illuminating grace to understand Scripture, encouraging grace to vanquish fear, enabling grace to obey God, comforting grace to overcome sorrow, and fortifying grace to resist temptation.

As we study this letter, I pray we'll be strengthened by Paul's celebration of what it means to be one with Christ. I pray we'll see that, in Christ, we possess all the perfection we need to please God, all the righteousness we need to stand before God, and all the obedience we need to be accepted by God. I pray we'll see that Christ succeeded in every way we fail. He trusted, obeyed, triumphed, endured, and persevered in our place. Every grace we enjoy first belonged to Christ. He imparts this grace to us by virtue of our union with him. I pray we'll know the kind of peace that flows from knowing Christ.

Conclusion
This is the central theme of Paul's epistle to the Romans: "the gospel of God." Here's truth to make us wise, light to guide our way, hope to calm our fears, and joy to ease our sorrows. My prayer is that we'll know the gospel as a living truth.

3
The Gospel of God: Part 2 (1:8-17)

It's important to stay focused on the gospel. Why? We're easily amused and distracted, and we often fill our lives with things that seem harmless but are detrimental if we don't keep them in their proper place. Consider the following story:

> On Monday, Alice bought a parrot. It didn't talk, so the next day she returned to the pet store. "He needs a ladder," she was told. She bought a ladder, but another day passed, and the parrot still didn't say a word. "How about a swing?" the clerk suggested. So, Alice bought a swing; the next day, a mirror; the next day, a miniature plastic tree; the next day, a shiny parrot toy.
>
> On Sunday morning, Alice was standing outside the pet store when it opened. She had the parrot cage in her hand and tears in her eyes. Her parrot was dead. "Did it ever say a word?" the store owner asked. "Yes," Alice said through her sobs. "Right before he died, he looked at me and asked, 'Don't they sell any food at that pet store?'"[1]

When we try to fill our lives with anything but the main thing (the gospel), we're just like Alice's bird—starving in a cage crowded with pretty toys. When the gospel is no longer at the centre, we soon feel the effects in every facet of our lives—from the home to the church to the workplace and at all points in between. For this reason, we must constantly orient our lives around the gospel: the good news that God saves sinners from his wrath for his glory through Christ's substitutionary death.

We can't save ourselves. It's absurd to think otherwise. For a moment, let's imagine I own a famous painting, displayed proudly in my living room. One day, a dinner guest decides (for some inconceivable reason) to scribble all over it with a black marker. My painting is ruined. Perceiving my displeasure, my

---

[1] C.J. Mahaney, *The Cross Centered Life: Keeping the Gospel the Main Thing* (Sisters, OR: Multnomah, 2002), 18-19.

guest reaches for the magazine stand, tears a picture from a magazine, glues it to the painting, and assures me that the artwork is as good as new. What's my response? For starters, I question my guest's mental health. Then, I ridicule his feeble attempt to restore the painting. He can't fix it. It's ruined.

Likewise, we can't fix ourselves. There are no Band-Aid solutions because the problem runs too deep. Our sin touches every thought, shapes every desire, corrupts every word, and taints every deed. Because of our sin, we're "storing up wrath" for the day when God's righteous judgment will be revealed (2:5). But the good news is that God saves sinners. In Christ, God's wrath is turned away. God punished Christ, so that he might forgive us. God condemned Christ, so that he might justify us. In giving himself, Christ revealed the Father's love for us. In love, he climbed a shameful cross to bear our guilt and shame, pouring out his soul to death.

Christ declares, "Truly, I say to you, unless you turn and become like children, you will never enter the kingdom of heaven" (Matt. 18:3). When our children call for us in the middle of the night or climb into our lap to cuddle; when they cry for us after falling down, take our hand as they stumble over uneven ground, look to us for protection and direction, and call us *daddy* or *mommy*, do we realize what we're witnessing? The way into the kingdom!

Before God's holiness we're humbled for our sinfulness. Recognizing our helplessness to save ourselves, we come to Christ in childlike dependence and look to him alone to save us. Wonder of wonders! God receives us in Christ—his Beloved. He saves us so that we can enjoy the beauty of his glory. He saves us so that we can be satisfied in his incomprehensible greatness and goodness.

This glorious gospel is the *main* thing—our lives must revolve around this centre. That's my overarching aim as we study Paul's epistle to the Romans. I want us to understand and experience the gospel, so that it becomes a living reality.

In the last study, we looked at seven truths concerning the gospel. Here I'm going to add five more.

The gospel causes thanksgiving (1:8)

"First, I thank my God through Jesus Christ for you all, because your faith is proclaimed in all the world." I want to unpack Paul's statement by asking three questions.

Who does Paul thank? "I thank my God." James tells us: "Every good gift and every perfect gift is from above" (James 1:17). God is the source of all blessing; therefore, he's the object of all thanksgiving.

How does Paul thank God? "I thank my God through Jesus Christ." Christ is the means of thanksgiving. Paul explains why in Ephesians 1:3, "Blessed be the God and Father of our Lord Jesus Christ, who has blessed us in Christ with every spiritual blessing in the heavenly places." By virtue of our union with Christ in the heavenly places (Eph. 2:6), we enjoy God's blessings. Just as these blessings descend to us from God through Christ, even so our thanksgiving ascends to God through Christ.

Why does Paul thank God through Jesus Christ? "I thank my God through Jesus Christ for you all, because your faith is proclaimed in all the world." To the Colossians, Paul says, "We always thank God, the Father of our Lord Jesus Christ, when we pray for you, since we heard of your faith in Christ Jesus" (Col. 1:3-4). To the Thessalonians, he says, "We give thanks to God always for all of you, constantly mentioning you in our prayers, remembering before our God and Father your work of faith" (1 Thess. 1:2-3). Why does Paul thank God for their faith? After all, isn't faith an act of our will? Yes, it is. But Paul knows it's God who enables us to believe in Christ; hence, faith is really a gift from God (Eph. 2:8-9). Faith doesn't arise on its own in the human heart. God must bring it into being. Therefore, we should continually thank him for it.

As we study this letter, I pray we'll see that a lack of thanksgiving is a sign that we value and esteem something more than God. It's an indicator that we aren't really God-centred, but self-centred. I pray the mercies of God will overwhelm us. I pray we'll grasp that his forgiveness supersedes our sinfulness, his merit eclipses our guilt, and his righteousness hides our vileness. I pray we'll understand that—no matter what troubles and difficulties we face in life—we never get what we deserve.

The gospel engenders love for God's people (1:9-12)

Having thanked God in 1:8, Paul turns his attention in 1:9-10 to his request: "For God is my witness, whom I serve with my spirit in the gospel of his Son, that without ceasing I mention you always in my prayers, asking that somehow by God's will I may now at last succeed in coming to you." Paul's request raises a couple of obvious questions.

Why hasn't Paul visited Rome? "I have often intended to come to you (but thus far have been prevented)" (1:13). Prevented by what? According to 15:19-23, Paul's ministry had prevented him. However, once his mission in the east is completed, he expects God will send him west. And so, he prays, "asking that somehow by God's will I may now at last succeed in coming to you" (1:10).

Why does Paul want to visit Rome? "For I long to see you, that I may impart to you some spiritual gift to strengthen you—that is, that we may be mutually encouraged by each other's faith, both yours and mine" (1:11-12). To the Philippians, he writes, "For God is my witness, how I yearn for you all with the affection of Christ Jesus" (Phil. 1:8). To the Thessalonians, he writes, "Timothy has come to us from you, and has brought us the good news of your faith and love and reported that you always remember us kindly and long to see us, as we long to see you" (1 Thess. 3:6). In brief, Paul has a deep concern for his fellow believers. The church is a family, and a family longs to spend time together. Specifically, Paul wants to impart "some spiritual gift" to them. According to 16:25, he has in mind his "preaching of Jesus Christ."

As we study this letter, I pray we'll grasp that the church stands at the focal point of God's eternal plan. The Father set his love upon her and predestined her for glory. The Son became a man for her; he endured affliction and rejection for her; he wept, bled, pled, and died for her; he purchased her with his own blood. He married her, thereby becoming one flesh with her. He cherishes and cleanses her; he bestows marvelous gifts and blessings upon her; he guides and protects her. I pray we'll see the church as Christ sees the church, and I pray it will become the arena of our love.

The gospel leads to evangelism (1:13-15)
Paul hasn't been able to visit Rome because his ministry has prevented him (15:19-23). But once his mission in the east is complete, he intends to travel west. He wants to visit Rome so that he can "reap some harvest" among them (1:13). That is to say, he wants to be an instrument by which God saves people. He follows this up with a fascinating declaration: "I am under obligation both to Greeks and to barbarians, both to the wise and to the foolish" (1:14).

As we study this letter, I pray we'll feel Paul's sense of obligation to proclaim the gospel. Mercy experienced is mercy proclaimed. Mercy received is mercy dispensed. Mercy enjoyed is mercy shared. I pray we'll grasp that only those who share the gospel really know the gospel. I pray the mercy of God will stir in us such eagerness and earnestness and fearlessness to proclaim the good news of salvation.

The gospel is the power of God for salvation (1:16)

Paul declares, "I am not ashamed of the gospel." Why would anyone be ashamed of the gospel? It's offensive. It tells people they're terrible sinners. It tells them God is angry with them. It tells them they can't do anything to please God. It tells them they're on their way to hell. It tells them their salvation requires a bloody sacrifice. It tells them that to follow Christ is to suffer with him.

Despite its offensiveness, Paul isn't ashamed of the gospel. It's powerful because it does what nothing else can do. It saves. He knows this firsthand. Elsewhere, he declares, "Christ Jesus came into the world to save sinners, of whom I am the foremost" (1 Tim. 1:15). Interestingly, Paul doesn't use the past tense, but the present tense. He knows the depths of his sin. Christ came into the world to save sinners. We can't save ourselves and we can't change ourselves. We need hyper-plentiful grace to transform our hearts. The gospel (i.e., good news) is that we don't need to earn our way to God because Christ has earned our way for us. Paul's conversion is a pattern of Christ's abounding mercy toward the most sinful, rebellious, and depraved individuals.

As we study this letter, I pray we'll know God's power in the gospel. He has cleansed us from sin's pollution, liberated us from sin's bondage, and redeemed us from sin's penalty. He has broken the chains that bound us. He has destroyed the prison that held us. I pray we'll understand that God doesn't gain anything from us. Salvation is a river flowing one way. It's all mercy.

The gospel reveals the righteousness of God (1:17)

How is the gospel the power of God for salvation? How does it work? If we seek life with God, we first need righteousness. This righteousness is received through faith. When God justifies a sinner, he charges that sinner's sin to Christ and he credits Christ's righteousness to that sinner. Because the sinner's sin is charged to Christ, God forgives the sinner's sin. Because Christ's righteousness is credited to the sinner, God declares the sinner to be righteous.

As we study this letter, I pray we'll see that by virtue of our union with Christ, we're righteous in God's sight. As a result, we have peace with God. We find in him all we could ever want. We find an eternal and spiritual good, suitable to our every need. Our knowledge of him diffuses into our soul a satisfying peace in this life and a tantalizing taste of what awaits us in glory.

Conclusion

Is the gospel the main thing in your life? Centuries ago, Christ said to the Samaritan woman: "If you knew the gift of God, and who it is that is saying to you, 'Give me a drink,' you would have asked him, and he would have given you living water" (John 4:10). Do you know him?

> Take the world, but give me Jesus,
> All its joys are but a name;
> But his love abideth ever,
> Through eternal years the same.
>
> Take the world, but give me Jesus;
> In his cross my trust shall be,
> Till, with clearer, brighter vision,
> Face to face my Lord I see.[2]

---

[2] Fanny J. Crosby, "Give me Jesus" in *The Hymnal for Worship and Celebration*, 443.

4
The Power of the God (1:14-17)

God is "mighty in strength" and "exalted in power" (Job 9:4; 37:23). In the words of Stephen Charnock, God's power is "that ability and strength whereby he can bring to pass whatsoever he please, whatsoever his infinite wisdom can direct, and whatsoever the infinite purity of his will can resolve."[1] Please keep that in mind as we consider Paul's three declarations in 1:14-17.

I am under obligation (1:14)
"I am under obligation both to Greeks and to barbarians, both to the wise and to the foolish." In other words, Paul preaches the gospel to all people without distinction and to all people without exception. As John Wesley declared, "The world is my parish!"[2] It's our duty to call all people in all places to believe in Christ. We're under obligation to do so. The term "obligation" means to owe. If someone loans me money, I'm in debt to that person until I pay it back. If someone gives me money to give to you, I'm in debt to you until I hand it over. Paul is indebted to hand over the gospel.

Paul is indebted because of God's mercy
Paul writes,

> The saying is trustworthy and deserving full acceptance, that Christ Jesus came into the world to save sinners, of whom I am the foremost. But I received mercy for this reason, that in me, as the foremost, Jesus Christ might display his perfect patience as an example to those who were to believe in him for eternal life (1 Tim. 1:15-16).

Clearly, Paul has a deep sense of his own sinfulness and unworthiness. Elsewhere, he writes,

---
[1] Stephen Charnock, *The Existence and Attributes of God* (Grand Rapids: Baker Books, 1990), 2:13.
[2] *Journal*, June 11, 1739. https://www.ccel.org/ccel/wesley/journal.vi.iii.v.html.

I am the least of the apostles, unworthy to be called an apostle, because I persecuted the church of God. But by the grace of God I am what I am, and his grace toward me was not in vain. On the contrary, I worked harder than any of them, though it was not I, but the grace of God that is with me" (1 Cor. 15:9-10).

Given his sinfulness, Paul is keenly aware of the riches of God's mercy toward him. He views himself as a debtor, and thus under obligation to proclaim the gospel.

The lesson is this: *We'll never win souls until we feel our debt to God's mercy.* Our appreciation of God's mercy is directly proportionate to our appreciation of our sin. Only when we see our sin will we see God's mercy. And only when we're overwhelmed by God's mercy will we feel an obligation to proclaim the gospel.

Paul is indebted because of God's call
Paul says that he's "set apart for the gospel of God" (1:1). In Ephesians 3:8, he writes, "To me, though I am the very least of all the saints, this grace was given, to preach to the Gentiles the unsearchable riches of Christ." In Colossians 1:25, he writes, "I became a minister according to the stewardship from God that was given to me for you, to make the word of God fully known." God had given Paul a tremendous privilege, and Paul knows he's under obligation to fulfill it.

The lesson is this: *We'll never win souls until we feel our debt to God's call.* Peter says, "But you are a chosen race, a royal priesthood, a holy nation, a people for his own possession, that you may proclaim the excellencies of him who called you out of darkness into his marvelous light" (1 Peter 2:9). According to this verse, God has saved us for a purpose—so that we might proclaim his excellencies; that is, his glory.

Paul is indebted because of man's need
"For if I preach the gospel, that gives me no ground for boasting. For necessity is laid upon me. Woe to me if I do not preach the gospel!" (1 Cor. 9:16). Paul understands the condition of his fellow man to such an extent that, in Romans 9:3, he actually says, "I could wish that I myself were accursed and cut off from Christ for the sake of my brothers, my kinsmen according to the flesh." That's a striking statement. Martin Luther comments, "It seems incredible that a man would desire to be damned, in order that the damned might be

saved."³ How can Paul say such a thing? We find the answer in 9:2, "I have great sorrow and unceasing anguish in my heart." He knows they're accursed, and he feels hell's horror.

The lesson is this: *We'll never win souls until we feel our debt to man.* Do we see the plight of our fellow man? As Joseph Alleine remarks, "O miserable man, what a deformed monster has sin made you! God made you 'little lower than the angels;' sin has made you 'little better than the devils.'"⁴ Does that stir compassion within us? Years ago, my father and I were going door-to-door, distributing gospel tracts. We didn't even make it to the door of one particular house before the owner started yelling, "What right do you have to push your religion here?" We walked away. I remember my father asking me, "What would you think of a man who kept the cure for cancer to himself?" I would despise such selfishness. What do we think of the person who keeps the gospel to himself? "When a house is on fire," writes Corrie Ten Boom, "and you know that there are people in it, it is a sin to straighten the pictures in that house."⁵

I am eager to preach the gospel (1:15)
"I am eager to preach the gospel to you also who are in Rome." That's an amazing statement. As I heard a preacher comment many years ago, Paul preached in Jerusalem (the religious centre) where he was mistreated; he preached in Athens (the intellectual centre) where he was ridiculed; and he preached in Rome (the political centre) where he was executed.

We too can expect opposition from Jerusalem: the religious centre. They'll tell us we're too narrow-minded. We can expect opposition from Athens: the intellectual centre. They'll tell us we're too ignorant. And we can expect opposition from Rome: the political centre. They'll tell us we're too intolerant. That's difficult to take. It's a real temptation to hide or soften the gospel in order to be accepted by others. It's difficult to preach Christ—"a rock of offense" (9:33)—to a hostile generation. Paul knows all about it, yet he's eager to proclaim the gospel. Why? This brings us to his next declaration.

---

³ Martin Luther, *Lectures on Romans*, in *Luther's Works*, vol. 25 (1515; St. Louis: Concordia, 1972), 380; quoted in John Stott, *The Message of Romans* (Downers Grove: InterVarsity, 1994), 264.
⁴ Quoted in I.D.E. Thomas, *A Puritan Golden Treasury* (Carlisle: Banner of Truth, 2000), 266.
⁵ Quoted in William MacDonald, *My Heart, My Life, My All* (Grand Rapids: Gospel Folio, 1997), 155.

I am not ashamed of the gospel (1:16-17)

"I am not ashamed of the gospel, for it is the power of God for salvation for everyone who believes, to the Jew first and also to the Greek. For in it the righteousness of God is revealed from faith to faith, as it is written, 'The righteous shall live by faith.'" This verse really bothered Martin Luther. He wanted to know how the revelation of God's righteousness could be good news. He thought it was terrible news. Why? God's righteousness condemns us. Eventually, the Holy Spirit opened Luther's eyes to see that the gospel is good news because, in Christ, God gives the righteousness that he demands. Luther realized that salvation is God declaring the sinner to be righteous, because the sinner is clothed in the righteousness of Christ.

That's the essence of the doctrine of justification. (1) Justification is by grace alone. We're unable to help ourselves as we lie languishing in our sin. But God justifies the sinner by grace. It's completely undeserved. (2) Justification is through faith alone. In other words, faith is the means by which God's gift of righteousness is received. (3) Justification is in Christ alone. When God justifies a sinner, he charges that sinner's sin to Christ and he credits Christ's righteousness to that sinner. Because the sinner's sin is charged to Christ, God forgives the sinner. Because Christ's righteousness is credited to the sinner, God declares the sinner to be righteous.

Therefore, in proclaiming the gospel, we announce God's willingness to declare righteous all those who believe in Christ. This gospel is the means by which God manifests his power in the salvation of sinners. That's why Paul is unashamed. That's why Paul is eager to preach the gospel. He's convinced that God rescues sinners through the proclamation of the gospel.

Conclusion

I pray God's mercy will cause us to be zealous for the gospel.

> A zealous man in religion is pre-eminently a man of one thing. It is not enough to say that he is earnest, hearty, uncompromising, thorough-going, whole-hearted, fervent in spirit. He only sees one thing, he cares for one thing; he is swallowed up in one thing; and that one thing is to please God. Whether he lives, or whether he dies—whether he has health or whether he has sickness—whether he is rich, or whether he is poor—whether he pleases men, or whether he gives offence—whether he is thought wise, or whether he is thought foolish—whether he gets blame, or whether he gets praise—whether he gets honour, or

whether he gets shame—for all this the zealous man cares nothing at all. He burns for one thing; and that one thing is to please God, and to advance God's glory.[6]

It's my prayer that our appreciation of God's grace toward us in Christ might cause our hearts to "burn" with zeal for God's glory in the proclamation of his gospel.

---

[6] J.C. Ryle, *Practical Religion* (London: James Clarke & Co., 1959), 130.

Section 1:
Condemnation (1:18–3:20)

5
The Wrath of God (1:18)

If someone were to ask us what the gospel reveals, we'd likely say, God's grace, mercy, or faithfulness. Very few of us would say, God's righteousness. But that's Paul's starting point. "For in [the gospel] the righteousness of God is revealed from faith for faith, as it is written, 'The righteous shall live by faith'" (1:17; Hab. 2:4). God is righteous, and he requires us to be righteous. The problem is we aren't. Mercifully, God counts Christ's righteousness to us when we receive him through faith.

Paul knows this assertion runs contrary to man's opinion of himself. Refusing to recognize his condition before a holy God, man resents the notion that the only way to stand righteous in God's sight is by faith. To counter this mindset, Paul embarks on a detailed description of man's sin. And this brings us to the first major section in the epistle: *Condemnation* (1:18-3:20). Here, Paul takes us inside a courtroom, where he acts as the prosecuting attorney. The judge is God, of course. The accused is humanity, consisting of Gentiles and Jews. The defense attorneys are Mr. Good and Mr. Religious. The witnesses are General Revelation and Special Revelation. Here's an overview of the trial as it unfolds:

> *Paul presents the accusation against humanity*: "For the wrath of God is revealed from heaven against all ungodliness and unrighteousness of men, who by their unrighteousness suppress the truth" (1:18).
>
> *Paul calls his first witness to prove the accusation* (1:19-32). General Revelation (i.e., Creation) testifies against the Gentiles, demonstrating that they suppress the truth by their unrighteousness.
>
> *Paul answers the defense attorney's objection*: But I'm a good person (2:1-16).
>
> *Paul calls his second witness to prove the accusation* (2:17-29). Special Revelation (i.e., Scripture) testifies against the Jews, demonstrating that they suppress the truth by their unrighteousness.

Paul answers the defense attorney's objection: But I'm a religious person (3:1–8).

The judge gives the verdict: All are "under sin" (3:9–18).

The judge passes sentence: The whole world is "held accountable to God" (3:19–20).

In this study, we're going to focus our attention on Paul's accusation: "For the wrath of God is revealed from heaven against all ungodliness and unrighteousness of men, who by their unrighteousness suppress the truth" (1:18). It raises three questions.

What is God's wrath?
This is a potentially confusing subject so we need to proceed carefully. The place to begin is with the *Westminster Confession* of Faith's affirmation that God is "without body, parts, or passions" (Art. 2.1). What does this mean?

First, God is *without body*. When we read in the Bible of the eye of the Lord or the arm of the Lord, we must not think of literal eyes and arms. These are figurative expressions. The eye of the Lord points to his omniscience, while the arm of the Lord points to his omnipotence. God is Spirit. He doesn't have a body.

Second, God is *without parts*. Our being consist of parts: body and soul. Our body consists of parts: bones, blood, eyes, skin, hair, tendons, and organs. All of these parts possess attributes—size, shape, length, colour, etc. But God is without parts, meaning he's a simple being. There's no distinction between his being and his attributes. His attributes can no more be separated from him than he can be separated from himself. This means that he isn't merely wise; he's wisdom. He isn't merely powerful; he's power. He isn't merely good; he's goodness. He isn't merely holy; he's holiness.

Third, God is *without passions*. In other words, he doesn't experience involuntary emotions because he's unchangeable. This confuses us for two reasons. (1) Our emotions are our experiences. But God's emotions aren't his experiences—they don't occur in defined moments of time. (2) Our emotions are caused by external factors. But God's emotions aren't caused by external factors—they aren't his reactions to circumstances.

Perhaps an illustration will help. We often talk about the sun *rising, setting,*

The Wrath of God (1:18)

or *standing*. And we know what we mean by these expressions. The truth is, however, that the sun doesn't do any of these things. It doesn't move because it's fixed. We're moving. We describe the sun in these ways in order to describe our experience of it. Similarly, God doesn't change. He's the uncaused cause of everything. He's a simple being. It's our experience of who he is that changes.

And so when we speak of God's wrath, we aren't talking about an emotional reaction provoked by something external to him. We're simply talking about who he is. According to John Murray, God's wrath is "the holy revulsion of God's being against that which is the contradiction of his holiness."[1] According to William MacDonald, it's "his righteous indignation and fury against sin and unrepentant sinners."[2] Many people struggle with the concept of God's wrath. Why? They make the mistake of defining it according to their own anger. There are four dangers in making such a comparison.[3]

First, our anger is often sinful in its *nature*. That means it's usually an expression of pride, frustration, or impatience. For example, I'm stuck in traffic, so I become angry. I don't understand the instructions for assembling the barbecue, so I become angry. That's sinful. The nature of God's anger is never sinful. It never flows from pride or impatience.

Second, our anger is often sinful in its *occasion*. Often times, it's without just cause, meaning it's based on an error in judgment. Years ago, a friend shared with me his dismay at returning to his campsite in Algonquin Park to find his cooler missing. He was certain that some teenager at the next campsite had stolen it. He was angry. Without stopping to think, he bolted through the woods to the next campsite. Along the way, he heard the sound of someone (or, something) shaking his cooler in the trees. He veered to the right, following the sound. What did he find? A bear! We often err in our judgment. We misunderstand people—their words and actions. Based on these misunderstandings, we become angry. That's sinful. The occasion of God's anger is never sinful. He never errs in his judgment.

Third, our anger is often sinful in its *objective*. It's a loss of control. It isn't governed by reason. It's simply an excuse to vent. We're stuck in traffic on the highway, so we become angry. We start pounding the steering wheel. How does that help? It doesn't. It's irrational. We've assembled a barbecue upside

---

[1] John Murray, *The Epistle to the Romans* (Grand Rapids: Wm. B. Eerdmans, 1980), 35.
[2] William MacDonald, *Alone in Majesty* (Nashville: Thomas Nelson, 1994), 115.
[3] Jonathan Edwards, *Charity and Its Fruits* (Carlisle: Banner of Truth, 2000), 187-196.

down because the instructions are unintelligible. We throw the wrench across the backyard. How does that help? It doesn't. It's irrational. That's sinful. The objective of God's anger is never sinful. He has a reason for his anger.

Fourth, our anger is often sinful in its *measure*. It's often out of proportion to its cause. Simply put, we go overboard. However, the measure of God's anger is never sinful. The psalmist declares, "The LORD is merciful and gracious, slow to anger and abounding in steadfast love" (Ps. 103:8). God's wrath isn't uncontrollable rage; it's his holy disposition toward sinners.

More often than not, then, our anger is sinful. For that reason, we make a huge mistake when we define God's anger according to our own. As J. I. Packer warns, God's wrath "is never the capricious, self-indulgent, irritable, morally ignoble thing that human anger so often is. It is, instead, a right and necessary reaction to objective moral evil."[4] This means that God's wrath is morally right, which, in turn, means that God's wrath is actually an expression of his goodness. We don't think like that, but we should.

We don't call a judge *good* or *just* when he fails to punish a criminal. We call him *bad* or *unjust*. We don't say it was a *good* or *just* punishment when a sentence doesn't meet the crime. We call it a *bad* or *unjust* punishment. So, why do so many people think God's wrath makes him *bad* or *unjust*? On the contrary, if God were indifferent to sin, if he tolerated sin, if he refused to punish sin, that would make him *bad* or *unjust*. But the fact that he punishes sinners actually proves that he's *good* and *just*. In short, God's wrath is an expression of his goodness because it's morally right.

How is God's wrath revealed from heaven?

The verb "revealed" is *apokalupto*. The English equivalent is *apocalypse*. An apocalypse is a revelation—something we see. The verb is in the present tense. That means this revelation of God's wrath isn't restricted to the past or to the future. It's revealed in the present. How?

The wrath of God is revealed from heaven in calamities and disasters. We see it in his destruction of the world with the flood in Noah's day. We see it in his destruction of Sodom and Gomorrah with fire. We see it in the plagues experienced in Egypt. We see it in the calamities and disasters that have plagued this world throughout its history. "Does disaster come to a city, unless the LORD has done it?" (Amos 3:6). The wrath of God is also revealed

---

[4] J.I. Packer, *Knowing God* (Toronto: Holder and Stoughton, 1975), 167.

from heaven in conflicts and wars. We see it in Israel's destruction of the Canaanites. We see it in Assyria's destruction of the northern kingdom of Israel and in Babylon's destruction of the southern kingdom of Judah. We see it throughout human history—conflict after conflict.

Above all else, the wrath of God is revealed from heaven in death. I believe that's Paul's main point, as becomes evident in 1:32, where he affirms that "those who practice such things are worthy of death." God told Adam in the garden, "In the day that you eat of it you shall surely die" (Gen. 2:17). When Adam disobeyed by eating the forbidden fruit, he died—spiritually and physically. Paul confirms it: "Therefore, just as sin came into the world through one man, and death through sin, and so death spread to all men because all sinned" (5:12). From the time of Adam's sin to the present, people have died. Some die at a young age and some at an old age. Some die at the hand of disease, some at the hand of disaster, some at the hand of war, some at the hand of poverty. The point is this: everyone dies. Certainly, this reality confirms that God's wrath is revealed from heaven.

Why is God's wrath revealed from heaven?
Most people think divine wrath is incompatible with divine love, but the opposite is true. Divine love is impossible without divine wrath. God loves goodness. Therefore, anything that corrupts or destroys goodness is the object of his wrath. That's good.

Paul says that God's wrath is revealed from heaven "against all ungodliness and unrighteousness of men who by their unrighteousness suppress the truth" (1:18). In a word, it's revealed against those who are "filled with" unrighteousness, wickedness, covetousness, and malice (1:29). It's revealed against those who are "full" of envy, murder, strife, deceit, and maliciousness (1:29). It's revealed against those who are gossips, slanderers, haters of God, insolent, haughty, boastful, inventors of evil, disobedient to parents, foolish, faithless, heartless, and ruthless (1:29-31). Deep down, man knows that God imposes a death sentence on those who commit sin, but he doesn't care because he has suppressed the truth in his unrighteousness.

Conclusion
Our answers to the above three questions teach us some valuable lessons.

First, *they teach us to praise God*. This may initially seem strange, but we must remember that we praise God because He's good. And, as we've seen,

God's wrath is an expression of his goodness. Therefore, we praise God for his wrath. As C.H. Spurgeon says,

> The terrible Avenger is to be praised, as well as the loving Redeemer. Against this the sympathy of man's evil heart with sin rebels; it cries out for an effeminate God in whom pity has strangled justice. The well-instructed servants of Jehovah praise him in all the aspects of his character, whether terrible or tender.[5]

Second, *they teach us to pursue holiness*. Surely, we should flee from those things that are the object of God's wrath. Paul warns,

> Let no one deceive you with empty words, for because of these things the wrath of God comes upon the sons of disobedience. Therefore do not be partakers with them; for at one time you were darkness, but now you are light in the Lord. Walk as children of light (for the fruit of the light is found in all that is good and right and true), and try to discern what is pleasing to the Lord (Eph. 5:6-10).

---

[5] Quoted in William MacDonald, *Alone in Majesty*, 120-121.

6
A Dreadful Exchange (1:19–32)

By way of reminder, we're approaching these verses as if we were standing inside a courtroom. The judge is God. The accused is humanity (Gentiles and Jews). The prosecuting attorney is Paul. The defense attorneys are Mr. Good and Mr. Religious. The witnesses are General Revelation and Special Revelation. What happens?

Paul presents the accusation against humanity: "For the wrath of God is revealed from heaven against all ungodliness and unrighteousness of men, who by their unrighteousness suppress the truth" (1:18).

Paul calls his first witness to prove the accusation (1:19–32). General Revelation testifies against the Gentiles, demonstrating that they suppress the truth by their unrighteousness.

Paul answers the defense attorney's objection: But I'm a good person (2:1-16).

Paul calls his second witness to prove the accusation (2:17-29). Special Revelation testifies against the Jews, demonstrating that they suppress the truth by their unrighteousness.

Paul answers the defense attorney's objection: But I'm a religious person (3:1-8).

The judge gives the verdict: All are "under sin" (3:9-18).

The judge passes sentence: The whole world is "held accountable to God" (3:19-20).

And so, in this study, the first witness, General Revelation, takes the stand. It confirms Paul's accusation. How? What does it say?

The knowledge of God is plain to man (1:19-20)

"For what can be known about God is plain to them, because God has shown it to them" (1:19). What does God make known? "For his invisible attributes, namely, his eternal power and divine nature, have been clearly perceived, ever since the creation of the world, in the things that have been made" (1:20). In creation, God shows that he exists. That's true, but Paul is actually saying more than that. In creation, God shows what he's like; in particular, he shows his "eternal power." He reveals it in creation's beauty, immensity, complexity, and diversity. "By the word of the LORD the heavens were made, And by the breath of his mouth all their host" (Ps. 33:6).

Because of this revelation of God's "divine nature," man is "without excuse" (1:20). That means we can never plead ignorance in God's sight. Let's imagine you're traveling at 160 km per hour on the highway. An OPP officer pulls you over. When he approaches your car, you say to him: "Officer, I didn't know the speed limit." He replies, "Yeah right. It's posted all along this highway—100 km per hour. You, my friend, are without excuse." That's Paul's point. No one is going to say to God on the judgment day: "If only you had shown yourself to me, I'd have worshipped you." Paul's point is that everyone knows the truth *immediately*. Everyone knows that God exists, and everyone knows something of what he's like. "For what can be known about God is plain to them."

Man suppresses the knowledge of God (1:21)

"For although they knew God, they did not honour him as God or give thanks to him." Everyone knows God exists, and everyone knows something of what he's like. But what does man do? First, he refuses to honour God; that is, he refuses to acknowledge his greatness and goodness. Second, he refuses to thank God; that is, he refuses to acknowledge him as Creator.

Man's problem isn't intellectual. Paul isn't saying that man weighs the evidence, and arrives at the conclusion that God doesn't exist. Paul's point is that people know God exists and they know what God is like, yet they refuse to submit to him. Man's problem is moral, not intellectual. Adam didn't reject God for intellectual reasons. His rebellion was moral in that he refused to honour and thank God. And all of his descendants are guilty of exactly the same sin. The problem isn't that God is hidden, but that people (just like Adam and Eve) want to hide from God.

Man corrupts the knowledge of God (1:21-28)

"For although they knew God, they did not honour him as God or give thanks to him, but they became futile in their thinking, and their foolish hearts were darkened" (1:21). There are two consequences arising from man's suppression of the knowledge of God: his thinking becomes "futile" (empty), and his heart is "darkened" (impervious to the truth). "Claiming to be wise, they became fools" (1:22). What's the result? Man makes three dreadful "exchanges."

Man exchanges the glory of God for an image (1:23)
"And [he] exchanged the glory of the immortal God for images resembling mortal man and birds and animals and creeping things." The term "glory" (*doxa*) refers to the attributes of God which are revealed in creation. Man exchanges that glory for an image in the form of the creature. Man is religious, and he will worship something. Some people think that man's interest in religion proves his interest in God. That isn't so. An interest in religion doesn't prove that man is seeking God; it proves the opposite. It demonstrates that he's running away from the knowledge of God. He doesn't want God as he reveals himself to be, but he's unable to live without him and, therefore, he attempts to fill the void with false gods.

Man exchanges the truth of God for a lie (1:25)
"They exchanged the truth about God for a lie and worshiped and served the creature rather than the Creator, who is blessed forever! Amen." Man rejects God's revelation in creation, ignoring his power, wisdom, and goodness. The truth is there, staring him in the face, yet he rejects it for a lie. Man is determined to rid himself of God. He doesn't want anything to do with truth. He wants the freedom to do as he pleases; thus, he removes God from his world.

Man exchanges the natural function for that which is unnatural (1:26-27)
"Their women exchanged natural relations for those that are contrary to nature; and the men likewise gave up natural relations with women and were consumed with passion for one another, men committing shameless acts with men and receiving in themselves the due penalty for their error." What is Paul saying? He's pointing to the sin of homosexuality as the supreme indication that man willfully suppresses the knowledge of God. Please notice three details.

First, it's an *unnatural* act (1:27). Paul doesn't say that homosexuality is unbiblical, unethical, or unadvisable. He could, but he doesn't. He says it's unnatural. Basic anatomy and biology tell us it's wrong. It's against the created order. In a sense, adultery is a "natural" sin, in that it involves the "natural" use of the body. Homosexuality, on the other hand, is an "unnatural" sin because it uses the body in ways God never intended.

Second, it's a *shameless* act (1:27). For the past several decades, there has been an organized effort to normalize homosexuality within society. We can see how this has unfolded by simply looking at television's progressive portrayal of homosexuality. These programs have desensitized us. Of late, we detect a growing trend to normalize (even celebrate) homosexuality within the church. How's this evident? Some people contend that homosexuality is an acceptable lifestyle provided the partners are consenting adults who are committed to a monogamous, permanent, covenant relationship. According to this view, when the Bible speaks ill of homosexuality, it isn't speaking of monogamous, permanent, covenant relationships between consenting adults of the same sex. It's speaking of casual homosexuality. And so, the Bible only condemns sexual promiscuity—heterosexual and homosexual. This line of argumentation sounds plausible, except for one thing: Paul doesn't merely condemn homosexual promiscuity. Given his travels across the empire, he was undoubtedly familiar with loving and lasting covenant relationships between consenting adults of the same sex. Yet he doesn't make a distinction between casual and covenantal homosexual relationships. He condemns the very "act" as shameless.

Third, it's a *condemned* act (1:27). They "receive the due penalty for their error." The Bible commands us to love others. Some interpret this to mean that we're to accept everyone, including their sexual orientation (whatever that might be). Moreover, they contend that the church needs to recognize that prohibiting covenant homosexuality places unnecessary barriers in the way of unbelievers, whereas granting covenant homosexuals an accepted status within the church makes the church more attractive to society. It sounds *loving*, but it's actually antithetical to true biblical love. We don't love others by allowing them to indulge their "dishonourable passions" (1:26). We love others by upholding God's good and perfect will for their lives.

A Dreadful Exchange (1:19-32)

God reveals his wrath (1:24-28)
Three times in these verses, we read that God abandons man: (1) "God gave them over in the lusts of their hearts to impurity, so that their bodies would be dishonoured among them" (1:24); (2) "God gave them up to dishonourable passions" (1:26); and (3) "God gave them up to a debased mind to do what ought not to be done" (1:28).

What do these verses mean? It will help if we start from the beginning. As we've seen, God reveals himself in creation. That's known as General Revelation. God's attributes are there for all to see, but man willfully rejects that revelation and, therefore, rejects God. Man does so in order to pursue sin. How does God respond? He removes his restraining grace thereby permitting man to enter into even greater rebellion. What's God's restraining grace? It includes such things as law, tradition, government, family, and conscience. These are restraints upon man's sin. Throughout history, God chooses at times to remove these restraints as an act of judgment. That doesn't make God responsible for man's sin. Why? Because he simply permits man to give full vent to what's already in his heart.

Man doesn't care (1:29-32)
In these verses, Paul provides a detailed description of man's sin. He says people are "filled" with four things. (1) They're filled with "unrighteousness." That means they never do what's right in God's sight. (2) They're filled with "evil." That means they willfully choose to do what's wrong in God's sight. (3) They're filled with "covetousness." That means they never do what's right in God's sight and willfully choose to do what's wrong in God's sight, because they want to satisfy their own lusts—their inordinate desires. (4) They're filled with "malice." That means they never do what's right in God's sight and willfully chooses to do what's wrong in God's sight, because they want to satisfy their own lusts at the expense of others.

The extent of man's evil is seen in the fact that people are "full of envy, murder, strife, deceit, [and] maliciousness" (1:29). Paul adds that people are gossips, slanderers, haters of God, insolent, haughty, boastful, inventors of evil, disobedient to parents, foolish, faithless, heartless, and ruthless (1:30-31). To make matters worse, they know they're guilty of ungodliness and unrighteousness, yet choose to do nothing about it. "Though they know God's righteous decree that those who practice such things deserve to die, they not only do them but give approval to those who practice them" (1:32).

Conclusion

This is one of the most alarming texts in all of Scripture, for here we come face to face with our depravity. It's frightening to consider God's decree: "those who practice such things deserve to die." The preacher declares, "Sheol and Abaddon lie open before the LORD; how much more the hearts of the children of man!" (Prov. 15:11). God peers into our hearts, weighing our desires, motives, impulses, and inclinations. He sees our hearts riddled with self-love. This sin is an affront to him—a transgression of his law, rejection of his rule, desecration of his goodness, and violation of his glory. A day is coming when he will deal definitively with sin. "For God will bring every deed into judgment, with every secret thing, whether good or evil" (Eccl. 12:14).

Our only hope is Christ. Three times, we read that God "gave them up." Thankfully, Paul uses this phrase one more time in this epistle: "God gave [Christ] up for us all" (8:32). He did so upon Calvary's cross, where Christ bore the punishment for our sin. This is encouraging news. Where there's brokenness for sin, he promises healing. Where there's conviction for sin, he promises mercy. Where there's weariness for sin, he promises rest. Where there's repentance for sin, he promises forgiveness.

7
A Christian Worldview (1:18-32)

In 1989, I was half-way through my undergraduate degree at the University of Toronto, and I was weathering a storm, generated by cultural marxism, moral relativism, philosophical pluralism, and Christian liberalism. My anchor through it all was Romans 1:18-32. Here are three reasons why this text was (and continues to be) so important to me.

It challenges what man believes
"For what can be known about God is plain to them, because God has shown it to them" (1:19). God makes himself known to all people in all places at all times by means of his creation's diversity, immensity, and complexity. Yet, man has rejected this revelation. And, professing to be wise, he has become a fool (1:22). I realized, at university, that I was surrounded by numerous examples of this foolishness.

Pantheism
Many of the world's religions are pantheistic. Some celebrate nature as the actual embodiment of God. That's known as the *Gaia* hypothesis; i.e., the earth is a living and self-regulating entity.

> Everywhere, all over the earth, human beings have gathered in small groups, laying down their differences and focusing on their common wisdom. They call themselves communities ... coming into unity ... for a new age on earth which shall be the embodiment of every positive thought we hold in our minds, just as the old age embodied our fears. The construction has begun, of a new reality, where the mysteries are revealed in each human being as he or she comes into harmony with the planet as a whole. We celebrate this sunrise ... and the building of the one earth nation.[1]

---

[1] Quoted in Catherine Albenese, *Nature Religion in America: From the Algonkian Indian to the New Age* (University of Chicago, 1990), 153.

But Paul makes it clear in 1:18-32 that the triune God isn't part of creation; rather, he's above creation (Gen. 1:1-2; Job 33:4; Ps. 33:6; 104:30; John 1:3; 1 Cor. 8:6; Col. 1:15-17). The *purpose* of creation is his glory (Ps. 19:1; Isa. 43:7; 60:21; 61:3; Rom. 11:36; Col. 1:16; Rev. 4:11), and the *cause* of creation is his command (Gen. 1:1-3; Ps. 33:6; 148:5). "The universe was created by the word of God, so that what is seen was not made out of things that are visible" (Heb. 11:3). This is the closest biblical statement that God created everything out of nothing (*ex nihilo*), that is, without the use of pre-existent material. In short, God is "over all" (Eph. 4:6).

Materialism

The theory of evolution maintains that, millions of years ago, a one-celled living organism appeared, and that it subsequently evolved into all of the plants and animals in the world. This theory is the epitome of unreasonableness because it attributes marvelous powers of development to nothing. It insists that *nothing* produced *something*. It has resulted in a popular worldview known as materialism (or, naturalism)—the belief that the physical is all that exists. We're born and we die. In between these two poles of nothingness, we seek to define ourselves within the confines of a material (ultimately meaningless) world.

But Paul makes it clear in 1:18-32 that our existence isn't the product of blind chance. We didn't emerge from nothing. On the contrary, we're the product of God's matchless power and wondrous design. "For his invisible attributes, namely, his eternal power and divine nature, have been clearly perceived, ever since the creation of the world, in the things that have been made" (1:20). God exists. God is the Creator. Therefore, the material universe isn't the end. There's meaning beyond it.

Secularism

The word *secular* refers to the restructuring of our worldview to accommodate the irrelevance (or, nonexistence) of God. Secularism believes that man's best interests are found in man.

> For secular humanism, what matters is now and only now. There is no exit from the confines of this present world. The secular is all that we have. We must make our decisions, live our lives, make our plans, all within the closed arena of this time. Man is the measure of all things. He is the ultimate norm by which values are to be determined. He is the

ultimate being and the ultimate authority. All reality and life centre upon man.[2]

But Paul makes it clear in 1:18-32 that God is at the centre of reality. "To think Christianly is to accept all things with the mind as related, directly or indirectly, to man's eternal destiny as the redeemed and chosen child of God."[3]

There are only two options available when it comes to our foundation for knowledge. Either we build the foundation with man as its central component, or we build a foundation with God as its central component.

Any system of thought focused on man will inevitably prove finite and unable to bear the full weight of reality. That's why there are so many conflicting psychological, sociological, and philosophical theories out there. Secularism is a prime example of this. It's unable to address human pain, guilt, and suffering. It's unable to institute social justice, eradicate racial prejudice, overcome chronic poverty, curb civil unrest, or end international conflict. It fails to explain man's condition, make sense of this world, or give any meaning to life. Its only success has been the dehumanization of man. By denying God's existence, it has reduced man to the level of an animal—or even worse, a machine. This philosophical system (which claims to champion man) is really man's worst enemy. It takes from man the only object by which he can understand himself—God. Life only makes sense when it's defined in relation to God. Man receives his meaning from God. He receives his dignity from God. He receives his purpose from God. Without God, man is dehumanized. When this happens, the result is intellectual absurdity.

We must acknowledge that our thinking is dependent, not independent. True knowledge rests on two pillars. (1) "Without faith it is impossible to please him, for whoever would draw near to God must believe that he exists" (Heb. 11:6). (2) "By faith we understand that the universe was created by the word of God, so that what is seen was not made out of things that are visible" (Heb. 11:3).

God exists, and he created the universe. With these two pillars in place, we approach the great philosophical questions. They shape our epistemology, ontology, and morality. Any attempt to formulate these autonomously (with man

---

[2] R.C. Sproul, *Lifeviews: Understanding the Ideas that Shape Society Today* (Old Tappan: Fleming H. Revell, 1986), 35.

[3] Harry Blamires, *The Christian Mind: How Should a Christian Think?* (Ann Arbor: Servant, 1963), 44.

as the starting point) leads to secularism—a skewed view of the nature of reality. As Christians, we deny man's autonomy. Why? Our knowledge isn't perfect, but distorted. Our knowledge isn't original, but derivative. Human reason, therefore, requires something outside of itself to inform it and guide it. This something is God's revelation.

Liberalism
Christian liberalism is an attempt to accommodate Christianity to the prevailing spirit of the age. Its goal is to make Christianity more acceptable to modern culture. Today, it's very active in terms of the homosexual agenda. Here are three examples of what it sounds like. (1) Didn't Jesus accept people? Aren't we supposed to accept people the way they are? Who are we to judge the sincerity and authenticity of those involved in a monogamous, permanent, and covenantal homosexual relationship? Many of them are better Christians than heterosexuals. (2) Didn't Jesus command us to love everyone? We should accept everyone regardless of their sexual orientation. Prohibiting covenant homosexuality places unnecessary barriers in the way of unbelievers. (3) Didn't Jesus welcome sinners? We aren't to focus on unreasonable moral standards. Jesus never spoke against homosexuality. All of the negative comments concerning homosexuality are found in the outdated teaching of the OT or the culturally defined teaching of the apostle Paul. The real Christians are those who get back to Jesus!

But Paul makes it clear in 1:18-32 that man's moral degradation is a manifestation of his willful suppression of the knowledge of God. Christian liberalism refuses to reckon with this. It accepts isolated principles from Christ—not because they're his teachings, but because they agree with the spirit of the age. They pit isolated principles from Christ against the rest of Scripture, thereby repudiating what he actually taught. We can sum up the spirit of Christian liberalism in one simple question: "Did God really say?"

It declares what man lacks
"For his invisible attributes, namely, his eternal power and divine nature, have been clearly perceived, ever since the creation of the world, in the things that have been made. So they are without excuse" (1:20). The creation doesn't merely declare that God exists; it also reveals his nature. In particular, it tells us four things about him.

A Christian Worldview (1:18-32)

God is self-existent

There's nothing prior to God. God doesn't have a beginning, and he isn't dependent upon anything for his existence, meaning his life is uncreated. "The God who made the world and everything in it, being Lord of heaven and earth, does not live in temples made by man, nor is he served by human hands, as though he needed anything, since he himself gives to all mankind life and breath and everything" (Acts 17:24-25).

Because man has placed himself at the centre of the universe, he has lost sight of this self-existent God. We would do well to meditate upon Paul's words: God "is the blessed and only Sovereign, the King of kings and Lord of lords, who alone possesses immortality and dwells in unapproachable light, whom no man has seen or can see" (1 Tim. 6:15-16).

God is self-sufficient

Because God exists in eternity, he's self-sufficient. He doesn't need anything. He didn't need to create the universe. Rather, he chose to create the universe. As A.W. Pink explains,

> God was under no constraint, no obligation, no necessity to create. That he chose to do so was purely a sovereign act on his part, caused by nothing outside himself, determined by nothing but his own mere good pleasure; for he "worketh all things after the counsel of his own good will" (Eph. 1:11). That he did create was simply for his ... glory ... The force of this is [that] it is impossible to bring the Almighty under obligations to the creature; God gains nothing from us.[4]

Because man has placed himself at the centre of the universe, he has lost sight of God's self-sufficiency. We desperately need to recapture this truth. As William MacDonald puts it, "This doctrine reduces us to our proper size."[5] God doesn't need us. He doesn't need us to love him, help him, serve him, or worship him. God has chosen to create for the revelation of his glory. He has chosen to redeem for the revelation of his glory. He has chosen to love for the revelation of his glory.

God is great

Creation declares the greatness of God's power (1:20). What is God's power?

---

[4] A.W. Pink, *Attributes of God* (Grand Rapids: Baker Books), 2-3.
[5] MacDonald, *Alone in Majesty*, 24.

It "is that ability and strength whereby he can bring to pass whatsoever he please, whatsoever his infinite wisdom can direct, and whatsoever the infinite purity of his will can resolve."[6] "God thunders wondrously with his voice; he does great things that we cannot comprehend" (Job 37:5). As Isaac Watts writes,

> I sing the mighty power of God that made the mountains rise,
> that spread the flowing seas abroad and built the lofty skies.
> I sing the wisdom that ordained the sun to rule the day;
> the moon shines full at his command, and all the stars obey.[7]

God is good

"In the beginning God created the heavens and the earth" (Gen. 3:15). Having done so, he declared that it was "very good" (Gen. 1:31). God created a perfect world, entrusting it to man's care. It possessed all that man could ever need and want. It was a world that facilitated man's happiness. Even though the creation has been subjected to futility through man's sin, we still see God's goodness in creation. He continues to uphold creation by the word of his power. He continues to hold the planets in their orbit. He continues to send the sun and the rain to replenish the earth. He continues to sustain the beasts of the field and the birds of the air. He continues to give breath to man. He does so for the benefit of his creatures, thereby demonstrating his goodness toward them.

That's what man lacks. Man lacks a relationship with the One whose "greatness is unsearchable" (Ps. 145:3), the One who's "slow to anger and abounding in steadfast love" (Ps. 145:8), the One whose "mercy is over all that he has made" (Ps. 145:9), the One whose "deeds" are "mighty," whose "splendor" is "glorious," whose "works" are "wonderful," and whose "goodness" is "abundant" (Ps. 145:4-7).

It reveals what man ignores

God is the Creator. This means that man is a mere creature. This, in turn, means that man is accountable to God. God will judge man. He will judge him for failing to worship him. God's greatness in creation points to the fact that he's our Lord. Consequently, we should fear him. God's goodness in creation

---

[6] Charnock, *Attributes of God*, 2:13.
[7] Isaac Watts, "I Sing the Mighty Power of God" in *The Hymnal for Worship and Celebration*, 59.

points to the fact that he's our Father. Consequently, we should trust him.

These two (fear and faith) are the essence of worship. By approaching God in fear, we demonstrate our appreciation of his greatness. By approaching God in faith, we demonstrate our appreciation of his goodness. In so doing, we glorify him. But man fails to do either. Therefore, man fails to worship God. Why? Man has suppressed the truth of God in unrighteousness (1:18). Moreover, he suppresses the truth that God will hold him accountable for doing so (1:32).

Conclusion

As a young (and impressionable) university student, surrounded by the "isms" of the day, it was Romans 1:18-32 that stabilized the ground beneath my feet. It helped me to understand that man is "without excuse" (1:20). This means we don't proclaim the gospel to those who've never heard the truth, but to those who willfully suppress the truth. When Paul preaches to the Gentile audience at the Areopagus in Athens (Acts 17:22-23), he makes two chief points (reminiscent of Romans 1:18-32). (1) Paul appeals to God's *nature*. God made the world and everything in it. He's all-sufficient. He's the source of all life. He's the ruler of all things. (2) Paul appeals to God's *decree*. "He has fixed a day on which he will judge the world in righteousness."

Why does Paul emphasize these two truths? He's simply reminding his audience of what they already know to be true. They've suppressed the knowledge of the truth by their unrighteousness.

By the fall, we've lost the light of reason, but we retain the pride of reason. We can't help ourselves out of this misery. God must remove the veil of ignorance, the veil of blind prejudice, the veil of corrupt affections, and the veil of carnal sense.

8
No Excuse (2:1-5)

We're in the midst of studying the first section in Paul's epistle to the Romans: *Condemnation* (1:18-3:20). And we're in a courtroom—so to speak. The judge is God. The accused is humanity. The accusation is unrighteousness. The first witness is General Revelation. The second witness is Special Revelation. The verdict is guilty. The sentence is condemnation.

We've looked at 1:18-32, where Paul calls his first witness (General Revelation), in order to demonstrate that the Gentiles suppress the truth by their unrighteous. Creation's testimony proves the following. (1) God makes himself known to all people in all places at all times, ensuring that his revelation reaches everyone. (2) Man suppresses the knowledge of God because he hates it. He's born with a heart that's hostile toward God. (3) Man exchanges the glory of God for an idol. He falls into bondage to countless forms of idolatry. (4) He exchanges the truth of God for a lie. He loses sight of reality, and revels in absurdity. (5) The result is behaviour that goes against nature.

At this point, Paul shifts his focus. Why? The defense attorney, Mr. Good, makes an objection.

> Paul, I've been listening to what you've been saying, and I've enjoyed it. I agree with you, wholeheartedly. I don't like what I'm seeing in society. It angers me and frightens me. I'm absolutely shocked at the moral decadence, and I'm completely astounded at the prevalence of all the creepy things you've mentioned. Paul, it wasn't like this back in the good old days. I wish we could turn back the clock, and I wish we could somehow get rid of all those people—especially the unnatural ones you mentioned. Paul, I want to applaud you. I'm glad you spoke out against them. It's about time someone said something. But I have one small objection. You could have said even more about how angry God is with them. You could have told them in no uncertain terms that they're going to burn. I like it when you speak passionately against those things. Paul, I'm so thankful I'm not like them. I'm so thankful I follow a higher code of conduct. I'm not saying I'm perfect, but God knows I'm pretty close—at the very least, I'm better than them. And I'm confident God will overlook my little mistakes and minor indiscretions. After all, isn't

that what grace is all about?

Paul knows some people think just like this, and so he shifts his focus from the *openly immoral* to the *secretly immoral*, from the *outwardly sinful* to the *inwardly sinful*. You see, idolatry runs in one of two directions: *moral debauchery* or *moral hypocrisy*. Paul has addressed the first; now, he's going to take aim at the second. Here's his message: "Therefore you have no excuse, O man, every one of you who judges" (2:1). Please notice two details. (1) Their *guilt*: "everyone who judges." Paul isn't saying we shouldn't distinguish between right and wrong, truth and error, holy and unholy. His point is that we mustn't think that other people deserve God's judgment more than us. (2) Their *condemnation*: "you have no excuse." This is the second time Paul uses this word (1:20). It refers to those who stand before a judge without any rational argument to offer in their defense. And so, Paul's point is that "everyone who judges" is without excuse—that is, they're just as guilty as those mentioned in 1:18-32.

Paul's goal here is to awaken us from our complacency. He wants to shock us. He does so by bringing us before God's tribunal and giving us four reasons why we're without excuse.

God's judgment is fair (2:1)
"In passing judgment on another you condemn yourself, because you, the judge, practice the very same things." On the judgment day, God allows us to set the criteria by which he judges us. How? He uses our own words. Francis Schaeffer spoke of the "invisible tape recorder" around our necks. On the judgment day, God plays it back. He judges us on the basis of our own words. Every time we pass judgment ("that's sin"), we're establishing the criteria by which we'll be judged. And so, we condemn the murderer as deserving God's judgment; God will judge us accordingly—anger. We condemn the immoral as deserving God's judgment; God will judge us accordingly—lust. We condemn the thief as deserving God's judgment; God will judge us accordingly—greed. On the judgment day, God simply confirms our judgment of ourselves.

God's judgment is inescapable (2:2-3)
"But do you suppose this, O man, when you pass judgment on those who practice such things and do the same yourself, that you will escape the judgment of God?" The "you" is emphatic. Paul's point is that we're guilty of the sins he has mentioned in 1:29-30. We often miss the fact that most of those sins are

No Excuse (2:1-5)

related to attitudes, not actions. In effect, Paul is saying, "You may despise the idolatrous and the immoral, but you do the same. You don't worship statues, but you worship wealth. You don't commit adultery, but your mind spends countless hours in the gutter. 'Do you think you will escape the judgment of God?' Don't be so presumptuous!"

God's judgment is certain (2:4)
When it comes to God's kindness, most people make one of two mistakes. First, many *miss* God's kindness. God is before us, behind us, under us, over us—all around us. We can't take one breath apart from God. Every breath of air, every drop of rain, every morsel of food, every second of sleep, every ray of sunshine, every day of health, testify to God's kindness toward us. Many people miss this.

Second, many *misinterpret* God's kindness. They assume it conveys his approval of them. God is the reason I breathe. He's the reason I have food to eat. He's the reason I have a roof over my head. He's the reason I have friends and family. He's the reason I enjoy pretty good health. And so, I presume all is well. But God's kindness isn't designed to convey his approval, but stir our repentance.

Paul asks, "Do you presume on the riches of his kindness and forbearance and patience, not knowing that God's kindness is meant to lead you to repentance?" God's kindness is his activity as Creator and Sustainer. God's forbearance is his endurance of sin against his kindness. God's patience is his endurance of sin against his kindness for a long time. Man's sin deserves immediate judgment; however, God withholds his judgment. According to Paul, these three divine attributes are for our benefit—our repentance. Yet, we "presume on the riches of his kindness and forbearance and patience." The expression "presume" means to think lightly.

God's judgment is accumulative (2:5)
"But because of your hard and impenitent heart you are storing up wrath for yourself on the day of wrath when God's righteous judgment will be revealed." The expression "storing up" means gradual accumulation. The terms "hard" (*sklerotes*) and "impenitent" (*ametanoetos*) are used in the Septuagint in reference to idolatry (Deut. 9:27). Paul's point is that these people are guilty of the same thing as those mentioned in 1:18-32. Man suppresses the knowledge of God by his unrighteousness. The result is always idolatry.

But this idolatry takes two forms. For some, it leads to *moral debauchery*. For others, it leads to *moral hypocrisy*.

Most of us are familiar with the story of the prodigal son (Luke 15). That's a misleading title. It's actually the story of two brothers. The younger brother takes his inheritance, abandons his father, and squanders his money in sin. The older brother stays with his father. He's well behaved. Yet, when his younger brother returns, he resents his father for receiving him. Essentially, the two brothers are the same. Both rebel against their father. The younger brother does so by doing *bad* things, whereas the older brother does so by doing *good* things. Their actions are different, but their motives are the same—selfishness. They're both idolatrous.

We must learn from their example. You see, there are two ways to reject God's mercy in Christ. Some people follow the path of the younger brother, meaning they rebel by doing *bad* things. Some people follow the path of the older brother, meaning they rebel by doing *good* things. But both fall under God's judgment. One day, Christ will inflict "vengeance on those who do not know God and on those who do not obey [his] gospel" (2 Thess. 1:7-8).

Conclusion

Do you minimize the severity of your sin or the certainty of God's judgment? Are you "storing up wrath" for the judgment day? Please understand that hell is an agony that never ends, a pain that never ceases, a sorrow that never subsides, a horror that never lessens, and a torment that never departs. Please understand that there's forgiveness in Christ. In him, we no longer have any reason to fear the sting of death, the terror of judgment, the torment of hell, or the wrath of God. Christ has swallowed it all. He has left nothing for us. Our peace with God is such that he loves us as if we had never been the object of his wrath.

9
Saved by Works (2:6–11)

In Robert Louis Stevenson's *The Strange Case of Dr. Jekyll and Mr. Hyde*, the main character, Dr. Henry Jekyll, is a respectable man who harbors secret inclinations to evil. He would like to act on them, but he's afraid of the consequences. One day, however, he invents a potion that will transform his appearance, enabling him to indulge his evil inclinations in secret. Upon drinking the potion for the first time, he becomes Mr. Edward Hyde: "I knew myself, at the first breath of this new life, to be more wicked, tenfold more wicked, sold a slave to my original evil; and the thought, in that moment, embraced and delighted me like wine."[1] As Mr. Hyde, he indulges all sorts of evil desires. When the potion wears off, he transforms back into Dr. Jekyll. And no one knows the difference.

After a while, however, Dr. Jekyll's sinful indulgence begins to frighten him, and his conscience begins to disturb him. In desperation, he vows never to take the potion again. Moreover, he vows to atone for his misdeeds by committing himself to a life of good works. As time passes, Dr. Jekyll is increasingly impressed with himself: "And then I smiled, comparing myself with other men, comparing my active goodwill with the lazy cruelty of their neglect. And at the very moment of that vain-glorious thought, a qualm came over me, a horrid nausea and the most deadly shuddering. I looked down. I was once more Edward Hyde."[2] Dr. Jekyll hadn't taken the potion, but he had transformed into Mr. Hyde. Why? His good works can't *hide* what he is inside. As a matter of fact, they bring out what he truly is. They aggravate his self-centredness and foster his self-righteousness. They feed his pride. Dr. Jekyll is Mr. Hyde.

Moral debauchery is open. Moral hypocrisy is hidden, but it's just as real, just as powerful, and just as wicked. And Paul addresses it in 2:1–5. "Therefore you have no excuse, O man, every one of you who judges" (2:1). His goal is to demonstrate why the self-righteous are without excuse. He does so by bringing them before God's tribunal, reminding them that God's judgment is

---

[1] Robert Louis Stevenson, *Dr. Jekyll and Mr. Hyde*, in *Robert Louis Stevenson: Four Complete Novels* (New York: Gramercy Books, 1995), 398–399.

[2] Stevenson, *Dr. Jekyll and Mr. Hyde*, 405.

fair, inescapable, certain, and accumulative (2:1-5). In 2:6-11, Paul tells them one more thing about God's judgment: it's impartial. Here he uses a literary device known as *parallelism*.

A. He will render to each one according to his works:
   B. to those who by patience in well-doing seek for glory and honour and immortality,
      C. he will give eternal life;
         D. but for those who are self-seeking and do not obey the truth, but obey unrighteousness,
            E. there will be wrath and fury.
            E. There will be tribulation and distress
         D. for every human being who does evil, the Jew first and also the Greek,
      C. but glory and honour and peace
   B. for everyone who does good, the Jew first and also the Greek.
A. For God shows no partiality.

Paul's point is that there are two groups of people, distinguished by three things.

Different desires: God vs. self
Those who belong to the first group seek to please *God* (B). To be specific, they seek for "glory" (the image of God), "honour" (the favour of God), and "immortality" (the life of God). In a word, they want to become like God in character.

In marked contrast, those who belong to the second group seek to please *self* (D). They suppress the knowledge of God by their unrighteousness. As a result, they exchange the glory of God for idolatry and the truth of God for absurdity. They live for themselves.

Different deeds: good vs. evil
Because the desires of those who belong to the first group are God-centred, their deeds are *good* (B). Because the desires of those who belong to the second group are self-centred, their deeds are *evil* (D).

We must never lose sight of the distinction between *civil* and *moral* goodness. *Civil* goodness describes an action that's good in man's sight. All of us do things that are beneficial to others: paying taxes, obeying laws, supporting charities, assisting neighbors, visiting the sick, protecting the weak, etc. *Moral* goodness, however, describes an action that's good in God's sight. An action is good in God's sight when it's performed for the right motive—its principle is the love of God and its objective is the glory of God. This distinction means that an action might be *civilly* good without being *morally* good. By way of example, a man might give away all he possesses to the poor, yet not do it out of love for God. That would make his action *civilly* (not *morally*) good. Paul makes it clear that unbelievers don't love God. As a matter of fact, they hate God. They suppress the knowledge of God by their unrighteousness. Therefore, their *civilly* good actions are never *morally* good actions in God's sight. Nothing we think is good in God's sight. Nothing we say is good in God's sight. Nothing we do is good in God's sight.

Different destinies: life vs. death
Because the desires of those who belong to the first group are God-centred, their deeds are *good*. Because their deeds are *good*, God gives them *life*: glory, honour, and peace (C). Because the desires of those who belong to the second group are self-centred, their deeds are *evil*. Because their deeds are *evil*, God gives them *death*: wrath, fury, tribulation, and distress (E).

Conclusion
What's Paul's point? "God shows no partiality" (A). It doesn't make any difference if we're openly immoral or secretly immoral—outwardly sinful or inwardly sinful. God will render to each one according to his works (A). What do we learn from this?

Good works are essential to salvation. "The Son of Man is going to come with his angels in the glory of his father, and then he will repay each person according to what he has done" (Matt. 16:27). "I saw the dead, great and small, standing before the throne, and books were opened ... And the dead were judged by what was written in the books, according to what they had done" (Rev. 20:12).

Good works aren't the meritorious cause of salvation. We're saved by grace alone through faith alone in Christ alone. "For by grace you have been saved through faith. And this is not your own doing; it is the gift of God, not a result of works, so that no one may boast" (Eph. 2:8-9).

Good works are the demonstrable evidence of salvation. "He gave himself for us to redeem us from all lawlessness and to purify for himself a people for his own possession who are zealous for good works" (Titus 2:14).

Because works are a necessary result of conversion, we can say that God will save those whose works are good. The flower on the bush, the grape on the vine, the leaf on the tree, the ear on the stalk—none of them give life, but all of them prove life. Such works are only possible as a result of the new birth. Apart from the regenerating work of the Holy Spirit, we can't do anything good in God's sight. For this reason, the moral hypocrite must not sit in judgment upon the moral degenerate. God "will render to each one according to his works."

10
The Secrets of Men (2:12-16)

In these verses, Paul confronts those who assume they're exempt from God's judgment. Why would anyone think that way? There's a mismatch between reality and their *perception* of reality. Paul confronts them by affirming that "God shows no partiality" (2:11). He will judge the openly immoral and secretly immoral—the outwardly sinful and inwardly sinful. God will judge each of us according to our works. In 2:6-11, Paul proves it by describing two kinds of people. (1) They have different destinies (life vs. death). (2) These different destinies are determined by different deeds (good vs. evil). (3) These different deeds are determined by different desires (God vs. self).

Imagine a stream. One mile upstream, there's a herd of cows. They stand in the water, dumping their excrement in the stream. Two miles upstream, there's a factory, dumping its pollutants into the stream. Where we're standing, the water might look clean, smell clean, and taste clean. Guess what? It isn't clean. It isn't safe to drink the water. It's polluted. That's our problem. The fountain is polluted. Even though our actions might look good, they're tainted by our desires (self-love), thereby rendering them unacceptable in God's sight. And that's how God is going to judge us. "Do you suppose you will escape the judgment of God?" (2:3).

God is impartial. All who've sinned "without the law" will perish without the law, and all who've sinned "under the law" will be judged by the law (2:12). What does Paul mean? He's still speaking of two different groups.

Those "under the law" are condemned (2:13). These are the Jews who possess the law written on stones. They'll be judged according to that law. It's the "doers of the law who will be justified." The law written on stones requires perfect obedience. Failure to obey it perfectly results in condemnation.

Those "without the law" are condemned (2:14-15). These are the Gentiles who possess the law written on the heart. This means they possess the knowledge of it. They know something of the difference between vice and virtue (1:32). They establish laws. They commend and condemn one another according to their observance of these laws. The law written on the heart requires perfect obedience. Failure to obey it perfectly results in condemnation.

And so, there's the law given by natural revelation. It's found in man's heart. The Gentiles possess it. There's also the law given by supernatural revelation. It's found in the OT. The Jews possess it. Paul's point is that it doesn't make any difference. Whether we've sinned "without the law" or "under the law," we're condemned. God is impartial.

These verses teach us the following.

God's revelation is clear and constant, yet willfully suppressed (2:12)
"For all who have sinned without the law will also perish without the law, and all who have sinned under the law will be judged by the law." Man is without excuse before God because he willfully suppresses the truth. Everyone knows something of the wrath of God (1:18), the truth of God (1:19), the nature of God (1:20), the decree of God (1:32), and the law of God (2:15). By means of creation, God reveals these things to all people in all places at all times.

God's law is mighty to condemn, but powerless to save (2:13)
"For it is not the hearers of the law who are righteous before God, but the doers of the law who will be justified." We aren't "doers of the law." It can't make us righteous, but it can convince us that we're unrighteous. When it does, we forsake any notion that we can save ourselves.

The conscience testifies to the existence of God (2:14-15)
"For when Gentiles, who do not have the law, by nature do what the law requires, they are a law to themselves, even though they do not have the law. They show that the work of the law is written on their hearts, while their conscience also bears witness, and their conflicting thoughts accuse or even excuse them." When people describe something as evil, they confirm that "the law is written on their hearts." That's known as God's moral law.

The skeptic reasons as follows: "If a good and powerful God exists, there wouldn't be any evil. There wouldn't be any injustice. There wouldn't be any suffering." But the skeptic's reasoning is skewed. If there's no God, how does the skeptic know what's evil? He can speak of pragmatism and utilitarianism, but he can't speak of morality. Evolutionary theory involves natural selection. It depends upon death, destruction, and violence. It includes the survival of the fittest. Therefore, the skeptic can't speak of right and wrong, just and unjust, good and evil, because he has no objective standard by which to define these things. He can't give any reason why humans shouldn't act like animals.

The Secrets of Men (2:12-16)

C.S. Lewis wrote a great deal about this theme in *Mere Christianity* and *The Abolition of Man*. At one time, he was a skeptic. He argued against God's existence because the universe seemed unjust and cruel. One day, the penny dropped. "But how had I got this idea of just or unjust? A man does not call a line crooked unless he has some idea of a straight line. What was I comparing this universe with when I called it unjust?"[1] There's no such thing as evil if there's no such thing as God. To describe something as evil is to declare that the law is written on our heart. To declare that the law is written on our heart is to declare that moral law exists. To declare that moral law exists is to declare that God exists. If God didn't exist, we wouldn't be talking about good and evil.

The law of God is the only foundation for law and order (2:14-15)

> For when Gentiles, who do not have the law, by nature do what the law requires, they are a law to themselves, even though they do not have the law. They show that the work of the law is written on their hearts, while their conscience also bears witness, and their conflicting thoughts accuse or even excuse them.

Historically speaking, there are two kinds of law. (1) Moral (or, natural) law; it's established by God. (2) Civil (or, positive) law; it's established by human governments. The first determines the second. Now we find ourselves in the midst of a shift in our understanding of law. Because of the advent of secularism, many today believe there's no God. Thus, there's no absolute truth. Thus, there's no such thing as moral law. All that's left is civil law. Therefore, civil law isn't found in moral law. It's something the government creates. And so, in college, students learn that laws, values, and ethics are merely the product of individuals and societies.

That view has consequences. (1) It means that law is arbitrary. If there's no moral law, then the government alone determines civil law, leaving no standard by which to judge the government. (2) It means that law is variable. It can vary from country to country. What's illegal in one country may not necessarily be illegal in another country. (3) It means that an act is only illegal if it violates civil law. If there's no violation of civil law, then there's no illegal act. (4) It means that the citizens of one country cannot denounce the actions of

---

[1] C.S. Lewis, *Mere Christianity* (New York: Macmillan, 1943), 45.

the citizens of another country as long as they're obeying their country's civil law.

Nazism was the logical product of Darwinism: the survival of the fittest. "The stronger must dominate and not mate with the weaker."[2] The Nazis only believed in civil law. In committing genocide, they acted consistent with their country's civil law. That was their defense at the Nuremburg trials. On what basis do we call their actions evil? If there's no such thing as moral (natural) law, how can we sit in judgment?

When we describe something as evil, we immediately confirm what Scripture declares: the law is written in man's heart. That's God moral law.

The day of judgment will reveal our deepest secrets (2:16)
"On that day when, according to my gospel, God judges the secrets of men by Christ Jesus." What are these secrets? They're our thoughts, motives, intentions, and desires. All that's hidden within the depths of our hearts will be revealed. Christ "will bring to light the things now hidden in darkness and will disclose the purposes of the heart" (1 Cor. 4:5). That's terrifying.

In the proclamation of the gospel, God's wrath precedes his grace. It must; otherwise, people have no idea why the gospel is good news. When we're convinced that we suffer from a disease, we immediately call for the doctor. When the doctor arrives, we yield ourselves to his counsel, and willingly accept whatever remedy he prescribes. The same is true when it comes to faith in Christ. When we're absolutely convinced of our need, we submit to his cure.

We might be just in our own eyes, and we might be just in the sight of others, but we're unjust in the sight of God. When we compare a candle with the sun, it's nothing. It hides its head in shame. Similarly, when we compare ourselves with God, we ought to hide our heads in shame. "How can a man be in the right before God?" (Job 9:2). How can we be just before God? We can't, apart from Christ. "The righteous shall live by faith" (1:17). We believe that Christ has fulfilled the law's requirement; that Christ has fulfilled the law's penalty; and that God welcomes us in his Beloved Son.

---

[2] A. Hitler, *Mein Kampf*, translated by James Murphy (New York: Fredonia Classics, 2003), 262.

11
Relying on Religious Obedience (2:17-24)

Is it possible you've never really understood the truth you claim to possess? Is it possible you overlook your sin while condemning others? Is it possible you abhor blatant idolatry while secretly worshipping the idols of your own heart? Is it possible you condemn the homosexual while permitting all sorts of unclean thoughts to run through your mind like an open sewer? Is it possible you condemn the liberal while harboring deeply entrenched feelings of envy, anger, bitterness, and resentment? Is it possible you base your relationship with God on who you think you are, what you think you know, or what you think you do? Do you rely on your personal code of conduct? Do you rely on your powerful emotional experiences? Do you rely on your convictions concerning how the family unit should function? Do you rely on your convictions concerning abortion and a host of other social issues? Do you equate any of these things (in themselves) with what it means to be right in the eyes of God?

Are you overly critical? Do people feel uncomfortable around you because they never know what's going to come out of your mouth? Are you overly sensitive? Do you become defensive when people dare to mention your shortcomings? Are you harsh because you must constantly find people who are not as good, not as smart, not as orthodox, or not as godly as you? Are you smug because you think you're pretty good? Are you anxious because you're never sure you've done quite enough?

If so, you're terribly deceived. That's Paul's main message in 2:17-29. By way of review, his thesis is found back in 1:17, "The righteous shall live by faith." How can I be righteous in God's sight? By faith in Jesus Christ! Paul knows people will dismiss his message. Why? "That sounds nice, but I don't need it." And so, Paul knows he must begin by explaining why people do need it. That's what he does in 1:18-3:20.

We're approaching this major section as if we were standing in a court of law. The judge is God. The accused is humanity: Gentiles and Jews. The prosecuting attorney is Paul. The defense attorneys are Mr. Good and Mr. Religious. The witnesses are General Revelation and Special Revelation. What happens?

THE OBEDIENCE OF FAITH

Paul presents the accusation against humanity: "For the wrath of God is revealed from heaven against all ungodliness and unrighteousness of men, who by their unrighteousness suppress the truth" (1:18).

Paul calls his first witness to prove the accusation (1:19-32). General Revelation testifies against the Gentiles, demonstrating that they suppress the truth by their unrighteousness.

Paul answers the defense attorney's objection: But I'm a good person (2:1-16).

Paul calls his second witness to prove the accusation (2:17-29). Special Revelation testifies against the Jews, demonstrating that they suppress the truth by their unrighteousness.

Paul answers the defense attorney's objection: But I'm a religious person (3:1-8).

The judge gives the verdict: All are "under sin" (3:9-18).

The judge passes sentence: The whole world is "held accountable to God" (3:19-20).

We've heard what General Revelation says to the Gentiles. Now, we're going to hear what Special Revelation says to the Jews. In 2:17-29, Paul demonstrates how the Jews misuse Special Revelation. They do so in two closely related ways: they rely on their religious obedience (2:17-24) and they rely on their religious observance (2:25-29). In this study, we're going to consider the first.

How do the Jews view their relationship with God? (2:17-18)
Paul mentions four things. First, they think they're *chosen by God*: "you call yourself a Jew" (2:17). The term *Jew* likely comes from Judah. The Israelites adopted this name for two reasons. It was the last identifiable tribe and the last faithful tribe at the time of the deportations. They reason: "We're Jews. God made a covenant with us. We don't need the gospel because we're a chosen people."

Second, they think they're *blessed by God*: "you rely on the law" (2:17). The term "rely" is a compound word: *epi* (upon) and *anapauo* (to rest or lean). It suggests they view their possession of the law (in itself) as a tremendous privilege. They reason: "God didn't give this revelation to other nations. He gave it to us alone. We don't need the gospel because we're a blessed people."

Third, they think they're *faithful to God*: "you boast in God" (2:17). They claim to worship the true God. They take pride in this. They're monotheists in a sea of polytheism and pantheism. They reason: "We haven't committed idolatry like our forefathers. We don't need the gospel because we're a faithful people."

Fourth, they think they're *devoted to God*: "you know his will and approve what is excellent" (2:18). They have the law. They approve the things that are essential (or, excellent), being instructed out of the law. They're so well instructed in the law that they devote significant time to examining its finer points. They reason: "We don't live like the Gentiles. We observe the Sabbath, refrain from gross immorality, and watch what we eat. We don't need the gospel because we're a devoted people."

How do the Jews view their relationship with others? (2:19-20)

Paul mentions four things. They think they're "a guide to the blind" (2:19). They think they're "a light to those who are in darkness" (2:19). They think they're "a corrector of the foolish" (2:20). They think they're "a teacher of the children" (2:20). These four statements are synonymous. Paul is making the point that the Jews see themselves as superior. This isn't humble orthodoxy, but a feeling of arrogant superiority.

How should the Jews see themselves? (2:21-24)

Paul asks four questions. (1) "You then who teach others, do you not teach yourself?" (2:21). (2) "While you preach against stealing, do you steal?" (2:21). (3) "You who say that one must not commit adultery, do you commit adultery?" (2:22). (4) "You who abhor idols, do you rob temples?" (2:22).

The first three questions correspond to how they view their relationship with others (2:19-20). The fourth question corresponds to how they view their relationship with God (2:17-18). There's a huge disconnect between reality and their perception of reality. As a result, "the name of God is blasphemed among the Gentiles" (2:24). This is a quotation from Isaiah 52:5. The cause of the OT captivity was idolatry (Isa. 50:1-3). Paul's point is that Israel's past sin is their present sin. Nothing has changed. And Israel is still bringing shame upon God's name.

Conclusion

These verses point to a number of truths we dare not miss.

Self-perception is often self-deception

The Jews' view of their relationship with God and others is completely twisted. The problem is that their pride prevents them from properly evaluating themselves before God. They refuse to see themselves as they really are. In Matthew 23:25-28, Christ compares the Pharisees to cups that are clean on the outside, yet filthy on the inside. He also compares them to tombs that are beautiful outside, yet full of bones inside. Their godliness is merely external. The same is true today. People refuse to see themselves as they really are. They fool themselves.

Martyn Lloyd-Jones remarks,

> The trouble with us is that we never look at ourselves in the sight of God: we never remind ourselves of the character and the being and the nature of God. Our religion consists of a certain number of things we have decided to do; and having done them we think all is well. Smugness, glibness, self-satisfaction are surely far too much in evidence among us.[1]

Where are the poor in spirit? Where are those who mourn? Where are the meek? Where are those who hunger and thirst for righteousness? Where are those who are terrified by the fact that God will judge the secrets of men?

Moralism is the world's largest religion

The Jews think they're okay in God's sight. They've never committed blatant idolatry or immorality. The problem is they forget that God will judge their "secrets" (2:16). The same thing happens today. People neglect the fact that God judges according to our desires. "Sin is not merely a matter of actions and of deeds; it is something within the heart that leads to the action ... Sins are nothing but the symptoms of a disease called sin and it is not the symptoms that matter but the disease, for it is the disease that kills and not the symptoms."[2]

In Luke 18:10-13, Christ introduces us to the Publican and Pharisee. The first is conscious of his sin, whereas the second is blind to his sin. John Bunyan

---

[1] Martyn Lloyd-Jones, *Studies in the Sermon on the Mount*, 2 vols. (Grand Rapids: Wm. B. Eerdmans), 1:206.

[2] Lloyd-Jones, *Studies in the Sermon on the Mount*, 1:206.

describes the Publican and Pharisee as "two men in whose condition the whole world is comprehended."[3] In other words, there are only two kinds of people in this world: those who know they're sinners and those who don't.

Hypocrisy is an impediment to the gospel
The Jews think they're okay in God's sight. They know God and his law. They "approve what is excellent, because [they] are instructed from the law" (2:18). They're confident that they're a beacon of light for others (2:19–20). The problem is they don't teach themselves. Their knowledge is speculative (or, notional). It's confined to the head. In other words, their knowledge falls short of their hearts.

The same is true today. Many people "know" the truth. However, it's only head knowledge. It isn't heart knowledge. They're asleep in the light (Eph. 5:14). It's possible to be raised in Christian homes, schooled in Christian doctrine, and immersed in Christian fellowship, yet never feel knowledge in the soul. Saving knowledge is sensible (or, inclinational). It grips, stirs, embraces, and transforms.

The righteous shall live by faith
The Jews think they're okay in God's sight. They rely upon the law. In a word, they're trusting in the flesh—their own effort. The same thing happens today. People trust in their knowledge of God's Word. They trust in their church attendance, clean living, or financial giving. They trust in their perceived experiences. They trust in their prayers or emotions. They trust in their avoidance of heinous sin. They trust in their good reputation or respectable lifestyle. All the while, they fail to trust in Christ.

In all this, Paul is seeking to drive us to Christ. He's trying to remove every ounce of self-confidence so that we trust in Christ. The gospel really is an apparent paradox. On the one hand, it drives us from God, in that it shows us our sin. It shows us our hopelessness and helplessness. It shows us that we're condemned in God's sight. On the other hand, it drives us to God. How? Recognizing our utter inability to do anything to please God, we run to God alone for mercy.

---

[3] John Bunyan, *A Discourse upon the Pharisee and the Publican*, in *The Miscellaneous Works of John Bunyan*, ed. Owen Watkins (Oxford: Clarendon Press, 1988), 10:111.

12
Relying on Religious Observance (2:25-29)

In 2:17-29, Paul speaks to those Jews who think they're okay in God's eyes. He seeks to undermine their false assurance. His approach is like the kids' game Kerplunk. If you've forgotten what that is, let me remind you. It consists of a plastic tube—open at the top and bottom. Around the middle of the tube are holes. You insert sticks through the holes, forming a lattice. Once all the sticks are in place, you dump a couple dozen marbles in the top of the tube. The lattice catches them. Then, each player removes one stick at a time. Invariably, there's always one stick that triggers the release of the marbles, and they crash to the bottom of the tube—Kerplunk. That's what Paul is doing here. He's removing the sticks one by one until the Jews' false assurance comes crashing down.

In 2:17-24, Paul goes after their *religious obedience*. He shows the disconnect between reality and their perception of reality. The Jews are the opposite of what they think they are. They're convinced they're God's people when, in actual fact, they're the very reason the Gentiles blaspheme God's name.

In 2:25-29, Paul goes after their *religious observance*. His main focus is circumcision. The Jews fail to understand that the external sign is useless apart from the internal reality (Jer. 31:33; Ezek. 36:26-27; Col. 2:11-13). Paul says that, for those Jews who break the law, their circumcision becomes uncircumcision (2:25). And he says that, for those Gentiles who keep the law, their uncircumcision is regarded as circumcision (2:26). The mere act of circumcision is meaningless. Paul drives his point home by making three distinctions.

They differ in their object (2:28-29)
Paul distinguishes between one who is circumcised "outwardly" ("in the flesh") and one who is circumcised "inwardly" ("of the heart"). The descendants of Abraham aren't outward Jews, but inward Jews. The members of the Abrahamic covenant aren't outward Jews, but inward Jews. The heirs of the Abrahamic promises aren't outward Jews, but inward Jews.

God gave physical circumcision as a sign of the covenant. However, it was an external sign of an internal reality. Without the internal reality, the external sign was invalid. Ishmael and Esau were physically circumcised yet excluded from the covenant. Why? There was no internal reality. The Jews miss that fact. They boast in the external sign, but Paul makes it clear that the external sign is useless apart from a circumcision of the heart. Those who are circumcised of the heart are the true descendants of Abraham (Phil. 3:3).

They differ in their means (2:29)
Paul distinguishes between one who is circumcised "by the letter" and one who is circumcised "by the Spirit." The former is man's work. The latter is God's work. It's impossible to keep the law by our own efforts. Why? By nature, we're hostile toward God's law. Therefore, we must experience a circumcision of the heart by the Holy Spirit.

They differ in their result (2:29)
Paul distinguishes between circumcision that leads to "praise from men" and circumcision that leads to "praise from God." This is the last stick to be removed, and the marbles come crashing down. Paul is saying that Abraham's true descendants aren't ethnic Jews, but those who've been born again. God is going to judge our secrets—desires and motives. In the flesh, these are always sinful. In the Spirit, these are made acceptable in God's sight. In the words of Augustine,

> The circumcision of the heart is, according to Paul, the cleansed will, that is, the will which has been purified from all illicit desires. This is brought about not by the letter, which demands and threatens, but by the Spirit who helps and heals. For this reason, the praise of such is not of man, but of God, who grants by his grace that for which they are praised.[1]

Conclusion
I know that's a little tricky. But it's so important because the Jews' false assurance (rooted in religious observance) stands as a warning to us.

Why do we rely on our religious observance?
Why do we take a rite or ritual, and turn it into the basis of our confidence before God? Why is this so attractive to us?

---

[1] Quoted in Luther, *Commentary on Romans*, 64.

Relying on Religious Observance (2:25-29)

First, we want identifiable markers with which to reassure ourselves of our standing before God. We want to be able to point to something tangible and say, "That's the reason God's okay with me." I'm baptized. I'm part of that church. I attend worship weekly. I give money regularly. I recite the creed perfectly. I visit the sick faithfully. I read the Bible diligently. We can turn any (or all) of these things into mere religious observance.

Second, we want to control God. We want to make God obligated to us. This is our default position. We think we can control God by means of our performance. That's how most of us operate. If I pray enough, fast enough, and give enough, God will act. If I devote or deprive myself enough, God will act. We desperately want to make God our debtor.

Third, we want to avoid issues related to the heart. God requires a whole heart. "You shall love the Lord your God with all your heart" (Mark 12:30). We like to focus on externals because they draw attention away from things that really enslave us—pride, envy, gossip, greed, covetousness, gluttony, laziness, etc.

What are some examples of how we do this?
There's such a thing as *legal* Christianity. I'm thinking of the man who rests in his behaviour. He gauges his relationship with God on the basis of how well he adheres to a self-imposed code of conduct. He thinks God keeps score. He needs to hear about how bad other people are. He needs to hear the preacher rail against certain sins. He needs to be reassured of the evil that is out there. He's very quick to let people know when they haven't reached his required standard. He lives his life in the accusative case. He appeases his conscious by reassuring himself that he isn't given to riotous excess. He's polite and pleasant. For legal Christianity, behaviour equals righteousness.

There's such a thing as *polemical* Christianity. I'm thinking of the man who rests on controversy. He's always in place on Sunday morning. He reads his Bible to win arguments. He can sniff out a heretic a mile away. Every issue is a hill worth dying on because this is how he defines godliness. He needs to be reminded of how accurate he is in comparison to others. He's only happy when he's disagreeing with someone over something. For him, separation is a mark of spiritual health. He's always on the offensive. Listening to him is like drinking vinegar. For polemical Christianity, controversy equals righteousness.

There's such a thing as *emotional* Christianity. I'm thinking of the man who rests on experience. He believes his inner thoughts, impulses, emotions, and intuitions are the direct work of the Holy Spirit whereby God is communicating with him apart from the Bible. He lives in pursuit of experiences that reassure him of God's closeness. He needs to hear certain music. He needs to hear certain sentiments. He needs to hear of the sensational. He isn't satisfied with solid food but is convinced there's something more. He pursues whatever it takes to stir him—to get him to that place where he can sense God acting immediately upon his soul. For emotional Christianity, experience equals righteousness.

There's such a thing as *doctrinal* Christianity. I'm thinking of the man who rests on knowledge. His religion is all head—no heart (no affection) and no hand (no service). He's detached because he's unable to interact with those who don't know what he knows. For doctrinal Christianity, knowledge equals righteousness.

There's such a thing as *causal* Christianity. I'm thinking of the man who rests on activity. He's unbelievably busy. He's leading studies, visiting people, offering help. He collapses into bed at night. He pickets at abortion clinics, and ministers in the inner city. He's involved in local politics. He's championing civil liberty and confronting racial inequality. He's raising his children God's way. For causal Christianity, activity equals righteousness.

There's such a thing as *traditional* Christianity. I'm thinking of the man who rests on form. He loves rite and ritual. He needs a set ceremony and liturgy to soothe his soul. He needs constancy and uniformity to ease his conscience. He despises change. The form takes precedence over the substance. For traditional Christianity, form equals righteousness.

What does heart religion look like?
"We are the real circumcision, who worship by the Spirit of God and glory in Christ Jesus and put no confidence in the flesh" (Phil. 3:3). Here, Paul gives three marks of someone who has been circumcised in the heart by the Holy Spirit for God's glory.

First, they "worship in the Spirit of God." This means the Holy Spirit is the principle from which their worship flows. That worship includes inward affections such as love, delight, desire, hate, fear, and sorrow. It also includes outward actions. The inward affections are stirred by a deep sense of God's excellence. These, in turn, govern the outward actions. That's worshipping "in the Spirit of God."

Second, they "rejoice in Christ Jesus." According to Thomas Manton,

"Joy is an act of love, begotten in us by the sense of the love of Christ, revealed in the word, and shed abroad in our hearts by the Holy Spirit, whereby the soul is more affected with delight in the grace of the Redeemer than with all other things whatsoever."[2]

Third, they "put no confidence in the flesh." That is to say, they don't trust in their own efforts. They don't trust in externals while remaining void of any internal reality. Paul is saying that those who've been born again put no confidence in the flesh. They're not trusting in anything they've ever done—privileges or performances. They're trusting in Christ alone. They simply cry with the psalmist, "My soul makes its boast in the LORD" (Ps. 34:2).

---

[2] Thomas Manton, *The Complete Works of Thomas Manton* (London: James Nisbet, 1870-1875; repr., Birmingham: Solid Ground Christian Books, 2008), 2:38.

13
The Objections (3:1–8)

What happens when we're losing an argument related to what we think or how we act? The evidence is piled a mile high against us. What do we do? Two options lie before us.

Option 1: We admit our error. We alter our perspective. And we change whatever is wrong with the way we're thinking or acting.

Option 2: We keep fighting by changing tactics. (1) We make excuses in an attempt to justify ourselves. (2) We divert attention away from the real issue. (3) We walk away so that we don't have to face the issue. (4) We go on the offensive by mounting a personal attack. (5) We shift blame by suggesting that responsibility lies elsewhere.

We're far more likely to choose option two over option one. Why? Option one requires humility.

This is precisely what happens in 3:1–8.

Paul has brought an accusation against humanity: "For the wrath of God is revealed from heaven against all ungodliness and unrighteousness of men, who by their unrighteousness suppress the truth" (1:18). He has turned to General Revelation (Creation) to demonstrate that it's true of the Gentiles (1:19-32), and he has turned to Special Revelation to demonstrate that it's true of the Jews (2:17-29). He undermines the Jews' false assurance by showing them that they suppress the truth by relying on their religious obedience and religious observance. His case against the Jews is airtight because the evidence is overwhelming. They're "without excuse," meaning their position is indefensible.

So, what do they do? They choose option two. Paul knows they'll do this. He has confronted it everywhere he has traveled—Corinth, Philippi, Ephesus, Thessalonica, etc. Throughout his journeys, he has experienced opposition from the Jews. He knows how they react to the gospel. He knows how they think. He knows their objections like the back of his hand. Here, he addresses four.

God's purpose (3:1-2)
"Then what advantage has the Jew? Or what is the value of circumcision?" "Paul, you've told us that true Jews are those who are circumcised in the heart by the Spirit. If you're going to redefine what it means to be a Jew, can you please tell us what value there is in being a Jew in the old sense of the word? What was God's purpose in setting us apart from the other nations? Are you telling us there's no advantage in being a part of the nation of Israel?"

"Much in every way. To begin with, the Jews were entrusted with the oracles of God." "My fellow countrymen, we have a tremendous advantage as Jews. But I probably don't have in mind what you have in mind. I'm thinking chiefly of the oracles of God—from Moses to Malachi, God spoke to us. After God called Abraham, he continued to reveal himself to the nations through General Revelation, but he never gave them Special Revelation. They had no Moses. They had no prophets. They had no Scripture. Of all the nations in the world, we're the one nation to which God revealed himself in a special way. What an advantage!"

God's faithfulness (3:3-4)
"What if some were unfaithful? Does their unfaithfulness nullify the faithfulness of God?" "Paul, God made a covenant with us—the nation of Israel. He said that he would be our God, and we would be his people. He made a promise. But you're saying that most of us are unfaithful. You're saying that most of us aren't even real Jews. You're saying that we aren't the heirs of God's covenant with Abraham. If that's true, then God is unfaithful. He has broken his promise."

"By no means! Let God be true though everyone were a liar, as it is written, 'That you may be justified in your words, and prevail when you are judged.'" "My fellow countrymen, that's a horrible insinuation. Do you have any idea what you're saying? Let's place God on one side of the balance and all of humanity on the other side. Guess what? There's no comparison. God alone is faithful. All he says is true—all his precepts, promises, and predictions. He abounds in truth. We don't. What are we in comparison to God? 'In the balances ... [we] are altogether lighter than a breath' (Ps. 62:9). Let's think for a moment in terms of David's experience. He sinned terribly, committing murder and adultery. But he repented. When he repented, he acknowledged that God's punishment was justified. Do you not understand? God is faithful. He's faithful to his promise to bless, if you trust and obey. And he's faithful to his promise to

curse, if you rebel and disobey. God is faithful even in is punishment of sinners. God hasn't reneged on his promise. You've missed the promise because you've refused to believe."

God's righteousness (3:5-6)
"But if our unrighteousness serves to show the righteousness of God, what shall we say? That God is unrighteous to inflict wrath on us?" "Paul, you're saying God is righteous in judging us. That means our unrighteousness shows God's righteousness. In other words, our unrighteousness displays God's character more fully. Well, that seems to benefit him greatly. Isn't it unfair of God to punish us for something that actually benefits him? Isn't it unjust of God to inflict wrath on us?"

"By no means! For then how could God judge the world?" "My fellow countrymen, that's a horrible insinuation. You believe in God. You believe he's the judge. You believe he's the judge of the earth. You believe he will do right when he judges on the last day (Gen. 18:25). How can you believe these things, yet question his judgment at present? God is just. He disposes all things according to the rule of equity. And he renders to all people according to their works. He's the 'Righteous One' (Acts 7:52). His actions are occasionally mysterious, but always righteous. 'The LORD is righteous in all his ways and kind in all his works' (Ps. 145:17). When clouds of darkness surround his providence even then 'righteousness and justice are the foundation of [his] throne' (Ps. 89:14)."

God's grace (3:7-8)
"But if through my lie God's truth abounds to his glory, why am I still being condemned as a sinner?" "Paul, as we understand it, when God forgives sinners, he displays his grace. That's wonderful. But it seems to imply that sinners make God look good. It wouldn't be fair of God to punish someone for doing something that makes him look good. As a matter of fact, your gospel means we ought to sin even more, so that God's glorious grace might abound."

"And why not do evil that good may come?—as some people slanderously charge us with saying. Their condemnation is just." "My fellow countrymen, you're saying we should commit sin because it leads to good—the magnifying of God's grace. But you know the end doesn't justify the means. We're undeserving of the least good, having plunged ourselves into evil. Mercy is an attribute of God whereby he pities us in our misery. He abounds in mercy (Ps. 25:6). How could

you possibly disparage his mercy by suggesting such a thing? If that's what you really think, your condemnation is just."

Conclusion

When people are losing a debate, they keep fighting for their position by diverting the discussion to something else. Have you ever heard of a Red Herring? A herring is a type of fish. When smoked, it turns red, and emits a really strong smell. Centuries ago, hunters used them to train hounds. The herring's smell was used to divert them from the rabbit's scent. A Red Herring is an argument that diverts attention from the real issue. We use them all the time, and this is what the Jews were doing. But Paul won't have any of it. He stays on target, and reiterates his main point: "What then? Are we Jews any better off? No, not at all. For we have already charged that all, both Jews and Greeks, are under sin" (3:9). That has been Paul's point since 1:18. The Gentiles have suppressed the truth by rejecting General Revelation. The Jews have suppressed the truth by misusing Special Revelation. They're all "without excuse."

14
The Verdict (3:9–20)

Since 1:18, Paul has been painting a dark portrait of our sin. It has been discouraging. At the same time, however, it has also been encouraging. Why? The unmasked horror of our sin highlights the matchless beauty of God's grace. We're almost at the end of Paul's description of our sin. We can discern a faint glimmer of light ahead. But (let me warn you) it gets worse before it gets better.

You'll recall we're approaching this major section (1:18–3:20) as if we were standing in a court of law. I trust you're convinced by now of the validity of this approach. See 1:20 ("without excuse"), 2:1 ("no excuse"), 2:5 ("righteous judgment"), 2:11 ("no partiality"), 2:13 ("will be justified"), 3:9 ("under sin"), and 3:19 ("every mouth may be stopped"). These are all legal terms. In this courtroom, the judge is God. The accused is humanity: Gentiles and Jews. The prosecuting attorney is Paul. The defense attorneys are Mr. Good and Mr. Religious. The witnesses are General Revelation and Special Revelation. What happens?

> *Paul presents the accusation against humanity*: "For the wrath of God is revealed from heaven against all ungodliness and unrighteousness of men, who by their unrighteousness suppress the truth" (1:18).
>
> *Paul calls his first witness to prove the accusation* (1:19–32). General Revelation testifies against the Gentiles, demonstrating that they suppress the truth by their unrighteousness.
>
> *Paul answers the defense attorney's objection*: But I'm a good person (2:1–16).
>
> *Paul calls his second witness to prove the accusation* (2:17–29). Special Revelation testifies against the Jews, demonstrating that they suppress the truth by their unrighteousness.
>
> *Paul answers the defense attorney's objection*: But I'm a religious person (3:1–8).

The judge gives the verdict: All are "under sin" (3:9-18).

The judge passes sentence: The whole world is "held accountable to God" (3:19-20).

We've heard what General Revelation says to the Gentiles and what Special Revelation says to the Jews. Now, the judge stands to give his verdict (3:9-18). Paul quotes a series of OT texts. "As it is written ..." These words are in the perfect tense; hence, God's voice comes from the past through the centuries into the present to declare: "None is righteous, no, not one" (3:10).

In the case of the Gentiles, their unrighteousness is obvious. Back in 1:29-31, Paul gives us a vivid description of it. In the case of the Jews, their unrighteousness isn't quite so obvious. Back in 2:6-8, Paul says there are those who "by patience in well-doing seek for glory and honour and immortality," and there are those who "are self-seeking, and do not obey the truth, but obey unrighteousness." The difference between these two groups isn't their external deeds. These may be indistinguishable. The difference is the principle from which their deeds flow. By nature, man is selfishly ambitious. Therefore, all of his actions are marked by unrighteousness. Righteousness doesn't merely refer to deeds that are performed in conformity to a list of rules; rather, it refers to the motives behind those deeds.

And God knows our secrets. He knows man's heart is deceitfully wicked. In the case of the Gentiles, that's evident for all to see. In the case of the Jews, it isn't quite as evident. However, that doesn't change the condition of their heart. On the basis of our actions, we may not appear to be as unrighteous as others. However, God judges our secrets. On that basis, "There is none righteous, no, not one." This is evident in six ways.

In what we think (3:11)
"No one understands." Why? Man is spiritually blind. The cause of his blindness is moral. There's no love for God, and there's no desire to know God.

Back in 1:21-22, Paul says, "For although they knew God, they did not honour him as God or give thanks to him, but they became futile in their thinking, and their foolish hearts were darkened. Claiming to be wise, they became fools." Man's heart is darkened. For that reason, "The natural person does not accept the things of the Spirit of God, for they are folly to him, and he is not able to understand them because they are spiritually discerned" (1 Cor. 2:14).

A.W. Pink provides the following description of this spiritual blindness:

> Fearful indeed are the effects of this darkness. Its subjects are rendered incapable of discerning or receiving spiritual things, so that there is a total inability with respect unto God and the ways of pleasing him. ... As a person who lacks the power of seeing is incapable of being impressed by the strongest rays of light reflected upon him, and cannot form any real ideas of the appearance of things, so the natural man, by reason of this blindness of mind, is unable to discern the nature of heavenly things.[1]

That's a powerful comparison. A blind man is incapable of being impressed by the strongest rays of light reflected upon him. Similarly, a natural man is incapable of being impressed by the strongest rays of the divine glory. In the case of the Gentiles, that's evident in their suppression of General Revelation. In the case of the Jews, it's evident in their suppression of Special Revelation. This spiritual blindness was confirmed at the time of the incarnation. Christ walks among men, performing signs that point to his identity. He asks, "Why do you not understand what I say?" He answers his own question: "It is because you cannot bear to hear my word. You are of your father the devil, and your will is to do your father's desires" (John 8:43-44).

In what we want (3:11)

"No one seeks for God." Sinful self-centredness controls all our seeking because we've elevated something other than God in our hearts. It masters and motivates us. It functions as God. (1) It might be *things*: wealth, recreation, travel, sports, sleep, apparel, food, or sex. (2) It might be *experiences*: marriage, children, security, notoriety, popularity, or success. (3) It might be *feelings*: fear, anger, bitterness, resentment, envy, or disdain.

In what we choose (3:12)

"No one does good." By nature, man is "self-seeking" (2:8). He always seeks what he perceives to be good for himself. The problem is he's lost all perception of good. As a result, "All have turned aside, together they have become worthless" (3:12). The term "worthless" means "spoiled." In what sense is man spoiled? The answer takes us all the way back to creation.

God created the plants, but he doesn't fellowship with them. God created

---

[1] A.W. Pink, *The Doctrine of Human Depravity* (Pensacola: Mt. Zion Publishers), 156.

the animals, but he doesn't fellowship with them. God created man in his image, so that he might fellowship with him. By fellowshipping with God, man delights in God. By delighting in God, man glorifies God. That high calling is summed up in the first question of the *Westminster Shorter Catechism*: "What is the chief end of man? Man's chief end is to glorify God, and to enjoy him forever." Sadly, man was "spoiled" at the fall. Now, his "chief end" isn't to glorify God by enjoying him forever. In his sinful condition, man's chief end is to glorify "self." He has become a "hater of God" (1:30). And he never seeks what he hates.

Admittedly, this is a tricky statement. To explain it, we need to remind ourselves of the meaning of the term *good*. For starters, it doesn't refer to that which is "civilly" (or, "socially") good. People give to the cancer society, volunteer at soup kitchens, and visit the sick in hospitals. These deeds are "civilly" (or, "socially") good. By that, I mean they benefit society. And, in that sense, they're good. No one denies that; however, that isn't what Paul is talking about in 3:12.

By the term *good*, Paul is speaking of that which is "morally" good. Moral goodness is that which is pleasing to God. And that which is pleasing to God is that which is performed for his glory. Look at Paul's definition of goodness back in 2:7, "those who by patience in well-doing seek for glory and honour and immortality." Look at Paul's statement later in 3:23, "for all have sinned and fall short of the glory of God." That which is morally good is that which is done for God's glory. The problem is the natural man never does anything for God's glory. For that reason, his deeds are never "morally" good.

In what we say (3:13-14)

In these verses, Paul references "throats," "tongues," "lips," and "mouths." He's talking about our speech, and his point is that it's corrupt. "I tell you, on the day of judgment people will give account for every careless word they speak, for by your words you will be justified, and by your words you will be condemned" (Matt. 12:37). Christ's point is that words are the best indicator of what's in the heart. "Out of the abundance of the heart the mouth speaks" (Matt. 12:34). In other words, whatever abounds in our heart eventually finds its way out in our speech. James tells us that the tongue (our speech) is "a world of unrighteousness" (James 3:5-6), which quickly descends into malice, deceit, gossip, bitterness, backbiting, and murmuring. It wreaks havoc and creates chaos. It harasses, belittles, and demolishes. It takes no prisoners. It spares no one—no matter how innocent. It destroys reputations, friendships, and families.

In what we do (3:15-17)
"Their feet are swift to shed blood; in their paths are ruin and misery, and the way of peace they have not known." This is how sin affects our relationships. James asks, "What causes quarrels and what causes fights among you?" (James 4:1). He means feuds, disputes, conflicts, and arguments. He answers his question with a question: "Is it not this, that your passions are at war *within you*?" The cause of quarrels doesn't reside outside, but inside. The Greek term for "passions" is the origin of our English word *hedonism*. It refers to the soul's disordered desires. It's what James calls "selfish ambition" (James 3:14, 16)—the desire to be uppermost.

In what we fear (3:18)
"There is no fear of God before their eyes." Paul began this major section (1:18-3:20), stating, "The wrath of God is revealed from heaven against all ungodliness and unrighteousness of men, who by their unrighteousness suppress the truth." He concludes the section with the same thought. In 3:10, he says, "There is none righteous, no, not one." In 3:18, he says, "There is no fear of God before their eyes." Here we have unrighteousness and ungodliness.

What is ungodliness? It's the opposite of godliness—the fear of God. To fear God is to know God's greatness and goodness. It's a sensible knowledge that grips the affections and manifests itself in obedience. By nature, we're ungodly, meaning we don't fear God. Rather than loving God, we love self. Rather than desiring God, we desire sin. Rather than delighting in God, we delight in sin.

Conclusion
In the above six statements, we have God's verdict: guilty. Guilt isn't a feeling. I feel guilty about eating that second piece of pie. I feel guilty about doing that or saying that. We've turned our feelings into the standard by which we determine if we're guilty or not. But guilt isn't a feeling; it's a condition. A convicted felon stands before the judge. The jury submits its decision: guilty. The judge doesn't ask the felon if he feels guilty. No. He pronounces the felon guilty. The felon's "feeling of guilt" is irrelevant. God doesn't ask us if we

feel guilty. He pronounces us guilty: "All are under sin" (3:19).

From this scathing verdict, we derive one of the most foundational doctrines in all of Scripture—the doctrine of total (or, radical) depravity. The term *depravity* means without moral ability. The term *total* means all pervasive. In other words, man lacks moral ability in all he thinks, feels, and does. I want to affirm two reasons why it's so important for us to uphold that doctrine in our day.

The first is *polemical*. I acknowledge that most people don't agree with the doctrine of total depravity. Sadly, I'm talking about people in the professing church. Often times, it's viewed as some sort of aberration of medieval theology. But we must remember that Augustine didn't create it, John Calvin didn't create it, Martin Luther didn't create it, and Jonathan Edwards didn't create it; nor did any other theologian for that matter. If we don't agree with the doctrine of total depravity, then we must understand that our fight is against God's Word. Still, many people don't want to hear it. In Isaiah's day, the people said to the prophets: "Do not prophesy to us what is right; speak to us smooth things, prophesy illusions" (Isa. 30:10). How many people echo that sentiment today? We would do well to heed William Newell's warning: "A preacher who avoids telling men the truth about their sin is the best tool of the devil."[2]

The second is *pastoral*. The doctrine of total depravity is important because it teaches me what I am and, therefore, what I need. (1) It shows me my need of a new heart. David cries, "Create in me a clean heart, O God, and renew a right spirit within me" (Ps. 51:10). I don't need self-help recipes, moral psychology, or how-to seminars. I don't need to get in touch with my inner self. What I need is a new heart. And only God can give it to me. (2) It shows me my need for God's saving grace. Christ says, "No one can come to me unless it is granted him by the Father" (John 6:65). I'm spiritually bankrupt. I'm completely dependent, therefore, upon God's grace for my salvation. (3) It shows me my need for God's sustaining grace. John warns, "If we say we have no sin, we deceive ourselves, and the truth is not in us" (1 John 1:8). Surely, even as Christians, our self-assessment must be that of John Knox: "In youth, in mid-age, and now, after many battles, I find nothing in me but corruption."[3] Only our awareness of that fact will keep us dependent upon God's grace.

---

[2] William Newell, *Romans Verse-by-Verse* (Christian Classics Ethereal Library) chap. 1, www.ccel.org/ccel/newell/romans.ii.html.

[3] Quoted in Taylor Innes, *John Knox* (Edinburgh: Oliphant, Anderson & Ferrier, 1896), 28.

Section 2:
Justification (3:21–5:21)

15
Reformation Day (3:24)

On October 31, 1517, Martin Luther nailed his ninety-five theses to the chapel door in Wittenberg. That event marks the commencement of the Reformation. In actual fact, the seeds of the Reformation were sown many years earlier by the likes of John Wycliffe and John Huss. Nevertheless, the Reformation flourished through Luther's ministry.

He was born on November 10, 1483, in Eisleben, Germany, into a wealthy family. After a typical grammar school education, he studied at the University of Erfurt, earning his B.A. and M.A. His father wanted him to further his studies in law. However, one particular experience changed all that. While traveling home one day, Luther was caught in a thunderstorm. It was so bad that he was literally knocked from his horse to the ground. Overcome with fear, he cried to St. Anne to save him from death. According to the Roman Catholic Church, St. Anne is the patron saint of travelers in distress. Luther promised to become a monk if she would save him. Two weeks later, against his father's expressed command, Luther entered a monastery. As Robert Godfrey explains, "For Luther, the monastic life was the highest form of religious devotion. He had accepted the teaching of the church that those serious about religion and their salvation should become monks."[1]

As a monk, he continued to study, receiving his doctorate in theology at the age of twenty-nine. Yet, he still had no knowledge of Scripture. In those days, theological education involved studying the Patristics and Scholastics rather than the Scriptures. Having served as a professor at the University of Erfurt for several years, he moved to the University of Wittenberg, where he was given the opportunity to lecture on the Bible. And that was the beginning of his laborious study of Scripture.

At this point in his life, Luther was still convinced that salvation was by works, depending upon human effort. Hence, he devoted himself to religious activity in an attempt to earn God's favour. During a visit to Rome, he climbed

---

[1] Robert Godfrey, "Martin Luther" in *Great Leaders of the Christian Church,* ed. J.D. Woodbridge (Chicago: Moody Press, 1988), 189.

the *Scala Santa* (28 stairs) on his knees while saying a *Pater Noster* on each stair. Despite this religious devotion, he was troubled by the Bible's description of God's righteousness. He was convinced that God hates sinners. He knew he was a sinner. And so, he was convinced that God hated him. He knew there was nothing he could do to earn the favour of a righteous God. And so, he feared death, believing it would commence an eternity of unspeakable pain. He was in great despair.

Following a colleague's advice, Luther began to study Paul's epistle to the Romans. He explains what happened:

> I had certainly wanted to understand Paul in his letter to the Romans. But what prevented me from doing so was not so much cold feet as that one phrase in the first chapter: "the righteousness of God is revealed in it." I hated that phrase, "the righteousness of God," which I had been taught to understand as the righteousness by which God is righteous, and punishes unrighteous sinners. Although I lived a blameless life as a monk, I felt that I was a sinner with an uneasy conscience before God. I also could not believe that I had pleased him with my works. Far from loving that righteous God who punished sinners, I actually hated him ... I was in desperation to know what Paul meant in this passage. At last, as I meditated day and night ... I began to understand the "righteousness of God" as that by which the righteous person lives by the gift of God (faith); and this sentence, "the righteousness of God is revealed," to refer to a passive righteousness, by which the merciful God justifies us by faith, as it is written, "the righteous person lives by faith." This immediately made me feel as though I had been born again, and as though I had entered through open gates into paradise itself. From that moment, I saw the whole face of Scripture in a new light. ... And now, where I had once hated the phrase, "the righteousness of God," I began to love and extol it as the sweetest of phrases, so that this passage in Paul became the very gate of paradise to me.[2]

In a word, Luther became convinced of the doctrine of justification by grace alone through faith alone in Christ alone. That wasn't the Roman Catholic understanding of justification. For Roman Catholicism (as confirmed in the Council of Trent), the formal cause of justification is the inherent righteousness that's infused into us. For Luther (and the other Reformers), the

---

[2] Quoted in E.G. Rupp and B. Drewery, eds., *Documents of Modern History* (London: Edward Arnold, 1970), 5-7.

formal cause of justification is the righteousness of Christ that's imputed to us when we believe in him.

Soon after his conversion, Luther realized the error of the Roman Catholic Church. His struggle with Roman Catholicism came to a boiling point in 1517 when the archbishop commissioned Johanne Tetzel to sell indulgences. An indulgence absolves people of their sin, serving to reduce their time in purgatory. Luther found the sale of indulgences to be absolutely repugnant. In nailing his ninety-five theses to the chapel door in Wittenberg, he was inviting the academic community to debate this and other practices. Basically, he argued, "If the pope has the authority to loose souls from purgatory, why does he not just do so?"

That challenge led to a debate with John Eck in 1519. Eck defended the sale of indulgences on the basis of the authority of the pope and the church councils. It was at that time that Luther openly rejected the authority of all human tradition. He argued that all things are to be judged by Scripture alone. The following year, he began writing numerous books that attacked the authority of the Roman Catholic Church.

Unsurprisingly, these writings were not well received. Luther was excommunicated in 1521. At the *Diet of Worms*, Emperor Charles V declared Luther to be an outlaw. However, his teaching spread throughout Germany, receiving widespread support. In 1529, the Emperor re-affirmed Roman Catholicism as the only legal religion in Germany. Luther, and his followers, presented a "protestation" to the Emperor. And, from that point, they were called "Protestants." Luther continued writing and preaching until his death on February 18, 1546. From 1510 to 1546, he preached approximately 3,000 sermons and wrote approximately 60,000 pages. He was tireless in his defense of the faith.

Luther's devotion to the doctrine of justification provides a fitting backdrop for one of the most important texts in Paul's epistle to the Romans; namely, 3:19-27. I'd like to consider briefly what Paul has to say about this doctrine in 3:24-25, "[We] are justified by his grace as a gift, through the redemption that is in Christ Jesus, whom God put forward as a propitiation by his blood, to be received by faith."

Justification is by grace alone

As Paul says, we're justified "by his grace as a gift" (3:24). What does that mean? It must be understood in the context of what Paul has just declared in this epistle. He has demonstrated that the Gentiles have rejected the revelation that's available to them because they're unrighteous. He has also demonstrated that the Jews have rejected the revelation that's available to them because they're unrighteous. In 3:10-18, Paul sums it all up in six statements: "There is none righteous, no, not one;" "No one understands;" "No one seeks for God;" "All have turned aside; together they have become worthless;" "No one does good, not even one;" and "There is no fear of God before their eyes."

That's the doctrine of total depravity. This doctrine teaches me what I am and, therefore, what I need. (1) It shows me my need for a new heart. My thoughts, feelings, and deeds are sinful. Therefore, I don't need therapy. I don't need positive thinking. I don't need moral philosophy. I don't need to try harder. I need to be born again. (2) It also shows me my need for God's grace. I can't save myself. All my thoughts, feelings, and deeds are sinful in his sight. He isn't impressed with anything I do because he knows my every motive. I'm governed by one dominant principle—I'm selfishly ambitious (2:8). I need him to be merciful toward me.

Salvation must, therefore, be by God's grace. And it is. "For by grace you have been saved through faith. And this is not your own doing; it is the gift of God" (Eph. 2:8). This includes the entire order of salvation: election, predestination, calling, justification, and glorification (8:29-30). In 3:24, Paul has justification in view. God imputes Christ's righteousness to me—a sinner. Why? It isn't because of anything in me. It's undeserved, unmerited, and unearned.

Justification is through faith alone
This means that the benefits of Christ's atoning work are only available to those who place their faith in the efficacy of Christ's blood. That sinner confesses with his mouth Jesus as Lord and believes in his heart that God raised him from the dead (10:9). In other words, he doesn't seek to establish his own righteousness by his own effort. Instead, he looks to Christ—namely, to what he has accomplished by his humiliation and exaltation.

Justification is in Christ alone
By faith, we're made one with Christ. As a result, what's ours becomes his, and what's his becomes ours. What does this mean? (1) It means that when God justifies us, he charges our sin to Christ. That's a result of Christ's passive obedience. He died as our substitute, bearing the curse of the law on our

behalf. Because our sin is charged to Christ, God forgives us. (2) It also means that when God justifies us, he credits Christ's righteousness to us. That's a result of Christ's active obedience. He lived as our substitute, fulfilling the law on our behalf. Because Christ's righteousness is credited to us, God declares us to be righteous.

Conclusion

God knows my secrets—my desires (2:16). By nature, I'm selfishly ambitious. By nature, I don't understand him. By nature, I don't seek for him. By nature, I don't do anything that pleases him. I know I'm without excuse. God has revealed himself in creation and in Scripture. Whatever he's revealed, I've rejected. Why? I love my sin more than I love God. I love to worship the creature more than the Creator. I know I deserve God's wrath. "For the wrath of God is revealed from heaven against all ungodliness and unrighteousness of men, who by their unrighteousness suppress the truth" (1:18). That means God's wrath is revealed against me.

Therefore, I need God to be merciful to me. I believe God sent his Son to save sinners like me. I believe Christ is the only Mediator between God and men. I believe his blood is of infinite value in God's sight. And so, I trust in Christ. By believing, my sin is charged to Christ; that means God forgives me. By believing, Christ's righteousness is credited to me; that means God declares me to be righteous in his sight. And that's the doctrine of justification by grace alone through faith alone in Christ alone! And that, says Luther, makes the righteousness of God "the sweetest of phrases."[3]

---

[3] Martin Luther, *Luther's Works*, vol. 34: *Career of the Reformer IV*, ed. Helmut T. Lehmann (Philadelphia: Fortress Press, 1960), 336-337.

16
Righteousness Revealed (3:21-26)

We've completed our study of the first section: *Condemnation* (1:18-3:20). Paul has presented his accusation: we suppress the truth by our unrighteousness (1:18). He has proven his accusation by appealing to two witnesses: Creation and Scripture. The verdict has been read: "All are under sin" (3:9). And the sentence has been declared: condemned. It's a depressing scene. Paul stands in the centre of the courtroom. His witnesses (Creation and Scripture) look on. The defense attorneys (Mr. Good and Mr. Religious) are dazed and confused. The accused (humanity) is overwhelmed. We have no defense. We stand silent before the judge. He has rendered his verdict. Now, he passes sentence (3:19-20).

In the first part of 3:19, Paul affirms, "We know that whatever the law says (*legeo*) it speaks (*laleo*) to those who are under the law." Please notice three details. (1) "The law says"—this refers to the content of the law. (2) "The law speaks"—this refers to the expression of that content. (3) "To those who are under the law"—this refers to the Jews. To sum up, Paul is saying that the law's content is aimed specifically at the Jews.

In the second part of 3:19, Paul affirms, "so that every mouth may be stopped and the whole world may be held accountable to God." Please notice two details. (1) "Every mouth may be stopped"—this means people are unable to offer a defense in the face of overwhelming evidence. (2) "The whole world may be accountable to God"—this means Jews and Gentiles are under God's judgment.

What's the relationship between the two parts? Paul explains how they're related in 3:20, "For by works of the law no human being will be justified in his sight, since through the law comes knowledge of sin." In other words, God gave the law to the Jews. They're under it. Whatever it says, it speaks to them. They can't keep it. And this proves that no one can keep it—Jew or Gentile. Therefore, no one can be justified through the law—Jew or Gentile. As a result, every mouth is closed and the whole world is accountable to God—Jew and Gentile.

That's one of the law's primary functions. It condemns. "Through the law comes knowledge of sin" (3:20). And that's precisely Paul's purpose in 1:18–3:20. He brings the Jews and Gentiles face to face with their sin and, therefore, the fact that "by works of the law no human being will be justified in [God's] sight." Quite simply, we can't do anything to please God. Paul does this to drive us to Christ.

Martin Luther understands Paul's device, stating,

> When a man has learned from the commandments, and perceived his own incapacity, then he will be anxious to know how to keep the commandment, for unless he fulfils the commandment, he will be damned. This will take away all his pride, and he will become as nothing in his own eyes; he will find nothing in himself to make him acceptable to God.[1]

Only when people find themselves in this state of mind are they ready to ask, "What must I do to be saved?"

And so, we come to one of the most precious phrases in all of Scripture: "But now the righteousness of God has been manifested apart from the law" (3:21).

Let's imagine we're still in the courtroom. The sentence has been passed, and we stand in stunned silence. But the judge speaks. In effect, he says, "I'm willing to change the verdict from guilty to innocent. I'm willing to change the sentence from death to life. I'm willing to declare you righteous instead of unrighteous." How? The answer consists of three truths.

This righteous standing comes through faith (3:22-23)

The judge says, "I'm willing to change the verdict from guilty to innocent. I'm willing to change the sentence from death to life. I'm willing to declare you righteous instead of unrighteous. Here's what I want you to do: absolutely nothing. You must simply accept it. You must receive it through faith. It is 'for all who believe' (3:22)."

Why must it be like this? "There is no distinction: all have sinned and fall short of the glory of God" (3:22-23). That's a summary of 1:18-3:20. In particular, it's a summary of 3:10-18. Our sin is evident in what we think, what we want, what we choose, what we say, what we do, and what we fear. This

---

[1] Martin Luther, "The Freedom of a Christian" in *Reformation Writings of Martin Luther*, ed. Bertram Lee-Woolf, vol. 1, *The Basis of the Protestant Reformation* (London: Lutterworth Press, 1952), 361.

means there isn't anything we can do to change God's verdict. We must simply receive this change to our legal status by faith.

The doctrine of justification (i.e., the imputation of Christ's righteousness) shouldn't come as a surprise to anyone because (as Paul says) "the Law and the Prophets bear witness to it" (3:21). In 4:3, Paul quotes from the first division of the Hebrew Scriptures—the law: "Abraham believed God, and it was counted to him as righteousness" (see Gen. 15:6). In 1:17, he quotes from the second division—the Prophets: "The righteous shall live by faith" (see Hab. 2:4). In 4:7-8, he quotes from the third division—the Writings: "Blessed is the one whose lawless deeds are forgiven, and whose sins are covered" (see Ps. 32:1-2). That proves that the doctrine of justification is found in "the Law and the Prophets."

This righteous standing comes by grace (3:24)
The judge says, "I'm willing to change the verdict from guilty to innocent. I'm willing to change the sentence from death to life. I'm willing to declare you righteous instead of unrighteous. There's nothing in you that compels me to do this."

God justifies us "by his grace as a gift." The AV says "freely." The same word is found in John 15:25, "They hated me without a cause." The word refers to something that's totally unwarranted or undeserved. There's nothing in us that induces mercy, compassion, or kindness from God.

This righteous standing comes in Christ (3:24-26)
The judge says, "I'm willing to change the verdict from guilty to innocent. I'm willing to change the sentence from death to life. I'm willing to declare you righteous instead of unrighteous. Here's how this is possible: my Son will take your sin upon himself; my Son will take your guilt upon himself; my Son will take your sentence upon himself; and my Son will take my wrath upon himself."

How can God pardon us when we're guilty? How can he alter our legal standing? He does so "through the redemption that is in Christ Jesus, whom he put forward as a propitiation by his blood, to be received by faith" (3:24).

To redeem means to set free by paying a price. The price is Christ's blood. The OT context for this is the Feast of Passover. Prior to the Exodus, God sent ten plagues upon Egypt. The last plague was the death of the firstborn. To avoid that judgment, the Israelites had to celebrate the Passover. They selected a lamb from the sheep or goats—an unblemished male. They killed it and applied its blood to the doorposts and lintel. Because of that blood, the firstborn of the Israelites was spared. It was not their works that saved them, but the actual sprinkling of blood. They were sinners, as were the Egyptians, and God might justly have punished them by taking away the life of their firstborn. He was pleased, however, to show mercy, accepting the life of the Passover lamb as a substitute.

Just as Israel's exodus from Egypt was realized by the offering of the Passover lamb, our spiritual exodus is based upon the shedding of Christ's blood. Paul says, "Christ our Passover" has been sacrificed (1 Cor. 5:7). In other words, the ransom for our sin has been paid in full. This means that those who believe in Christ have been redeemed "with the precious blood of Christ, like that of a lamb without blemish or spot" (1 Peter 1:18-19). In addition, it means that God "has delivered us from the domain of darkness and transferred us to the kingdom of his beloved Son, in whom we have redemption, the forgiveness of sins" (Col. 1:13-14).

Paul says that redemption is in Christ, "whom God put forward as a propitiation by his blood, to be received by faith" (3:25). The term "propitiation" is *hilastarion*. In the Septuagint, *hilastarion* is the Hebrew *kipporeth*. In the English OT, *kipporeth* is translated "mercy seat." The terms are synonymous. That's confirmed in Hebrews 9:5, where *hilastarion* is actually translated as "mercy seat." It formed the lid of the ark that contained the tables of the law, Aaron's rod, and a pot of manna. At either end of the mercy seat, there was a cherub with its wings outstretched. It was to this mercy seat that the high priest came once a year on the Day of Atonement—one of Israel's seven annual feasts.

On that special day, the high priest bathed himself in water, and put on the holy linen garments. He took a firepan of coals from the brass altar, and two handfuls of sweet incense into the Most Holy Place. He placed the incense on the firepan so that the cloud covered the ark. He also brought a bull as a sin offering for himself and his household. Having killed the bull, he took some of its blood and entered the Most Holy Place, where he sprinkled the blood on top of the mercy seat and in front of the ark—seven times. The reason for the high priest's sin offering was to make atonement for himself and his household. He was a sinner. Consequently, he had to be cleansed from his sin before he could act as a mediator between God and the nation of Israel. Having offered the bull, he then brought two male goats as a sin offering for the nation.

He presented them before God at the door of the tabernacle. He then cast lots for the two goats. The goat upon which God's lot fell was killed. The other goat was set aside as the scapegoat. Blood from the dead goat was taken into the Most Holy Place, where the high priest again sprinkled it on top of the mercy seat and in front of the ark—seven times. Having done so, he laid his hands on the scapegoat and confessed the sins of the nation. Then, he sent it away into the wilderness (i.e., outside the camp) by the hand of a man who stood in readiness.

All of this elaborate ritual points to Christ. He's the high priest. He's the veil. He's the scapegoat. His blood is sprinkled upon the mercy seat. When Christ shed his blood, he paid the penalty for our sin. It was transferred to him. As a result, God's righteousness was fully satisfied by Christ's sacrifice under divine judgment righteously due to sinners. As J.I. Packer explains, "Atonement means making amends, blotting out the offense, and giving satisfaction for wrong done, thus reconciling to oneself the alienated other and restoring the disrupted relationship."[2]

Paul doesn't stop there. He explains why this is so important.

First, it shows God's righteousness in the past. "This was to show God's righteousness, because in his divine forbearance he had passed over former sins" (3:25). What are these "former sins"? They're the sins of his people: Noah, Abraham, Isaac, Jacob, Rahab, Ruth, Moses, David. The OT sacrifices didn't save them (Heb. 10:4), but pointed to Christ who saved them. "On the cross, God was giving a public explanation of what he had been doing throughout the centuries."[3]

Second, it shows God's righteousness in the present. "It was to show his righteousness at the present time, so that he might be just and the justifier of the one who has faith in Jesus" (3:26). God justifies those who believe in Christ. He's just in doing so because Christ has satisfied his wrath by paying the penalty of our sin in full. If God had simply obliterated humanity, he would have been just but not the Justifier. If God had simply received humanity, he would have been the Justifier (in a sense) but not just. Christ, by his substitutionary sacrifice, established a legal basis by which God is both. God has not compromised his righteousness.

---

[2] J.I. Packer, *Concise Theology* (Wheaton: Tyndale House, 1993), 134.
[3] Martyn Lloyd-Jones, *Romans 3:20–4:25* (Grand Rapids: Zondervan, 1971), 103.

Conclusion

According to John Owen, there are four essential components to atonement.[4] (1) There's an offence that must be taken away: sin. (2) There's an offended person who must be pacified: God. (3) There's an offending person who's guilty of the offence: man. (4) There's a sacrifice by which atonement must be made for the offence: Christ. Through Christ's atoning work, God redeems his people. On the basis of Christ's redeeming work, God justifies his people. Quite simply, these three are inseparable, and they're the foundation of the gospel. Justification is by grace alone through faith alone in Christ alone.

When God justifies a sinner, he charges that sinner's sin to Christ. This is a result of Christ's passive obedience. He died as our substitute, bearing the curse of the law on our behalf. Because the sinner's sin is charged to Christ, God forgives the sinner's sin.

When God justifies a sinner, he credits Christ's righteousness to that sinner. This is a result of Christ's active obedience. He lived as our substitute, fulfilling the law on our behalf. Because Christ's righteousness is credited to the sinner, God declares the sinner to be righteous.

Do we grasp this? God knows my secrets and my motives. I'm selfishly ambitious. I don't seek for him. I don't do anything that pleases him. I've never done anything that pleases God in my whole life. I love my sin more than I love God. I love to worship the creature more than the Creator. I deserve God's wrath. I need God to be merciful to me. I believe God sent his Son to save sinners like me. I believe his blood is of infinite value in God's sight. And so, I trust in him. Believing, my sin is charged to Christ. This means God forgives me. Believing, Christ's righteousness is credited to me. This means God declares me to be righteous in his sight.

---

[4] John Owen, *The Death of Death in the Death of Christ* (Carlisle: Banner of Truth, 1999), 154.

17
The Doctrine of Justification (3:23-26)

William Gurnall writes, "Pride loves to climb up, not as Zacchaeus to see Christ, but to be seen."[1] By nature, we're proud—or, as Paul says, "self-seeking" (2:8). Our pride is so pervasive that it keeps us from God. In 3:27, Paul makes the point that the doctrine of justification eradicates such pride, leaving us without any reason to boast.

Justification is by grace alone
In 3:23, Paul says, "All have sinned and fall short of the glory of God." In 3:10-18, he explains what that means. There's none who understands, there's none who seeks for God, and there's none who does good. That's the doctrine of total depravity. It explains what I am, and it explains my need for God's grace.

Until we come face to face with the doctrine of total depravity, we don't know who we are. And we don't see our need of God's grace. John Murray remarks,

> Far too frequently we fail to entertain the gravity of this fact. Hence the reality of our sin and the reality of the wrath of God upon us for our sin do not come into our reckoning. This is the reason why the grand article of justification does not ring the bells in the innermost depths of our spirit. And this is the reason why the gospel of justification is to such an extent a meaningless sound in the world and in the church of the twentieth century. We are not imbued *(filled)* with the profound sense of the reality of God, of his majesty and holiness. And sin, if reckoned with at all, is little more than a misfortune or maladjustment.[2]

Justification is through faith alone
This means that the benefits of Christ's substitutionary sacrifice are only available to the sinner who places his faith in Christ. We aren't saved on account of our faith. It's merely the instrument through which Christ's saving work is applied to us. Do you remember the story in which the Israelites became

---
[1] Quoted in Thomas, *A Puritan Golden Treasury*, 223.
[2] John Murray, *Redemption Accomplished and Applied* (Grand Rapids: Wm. B. Eerdmans, 1955), 117.

impatient because of their journey around the land of Edom? They cry, "Why have you brought us up out of Egypt to die in the wilderness?" God sends snakes among them to punish them for their murmuring. They confess their sin. And so, God tells Moses to make a bronze serpent and place it on a pole. Whoever looks at it is healed. John makes a comparison between that event and Christ's crucifixion, stating, "And as Moses lifted up the serpent in the wilderness, so must the Son of Man be lifted up, that whoever believes in him may have eternal life" (John 3:14-15). There's nothing meritorious about faith. It's simply looking to Christ.

Justification has always been through faith. In 3:25, Paul explains that God put Christ "forward as a propitiation by his blood, to be received by faith. This was to show God's righteousness because in his divine forbearance he had passed over former sins." We see the evidence of that in Scripture. Noah became drunk, yet he "found favour" in God's eyes (Gen. 6:8). Abraham was willing to sacrifice his wife's honour by telling the Egyptians that she was his sister, yet he "was called a friend of God" (James 2:23). Jacob deceived his father and brother, yet God says, "I am … the God of Jacob" (Exod. 3:6). Moses murdered an Egyptian, yet God says, "With him I speak mouth to mouth" (Num. 12:8). David committed adultery and murder, yet God says that David was a "man after his own heart" (1 Sam. 13:14). Here, we have the heroes of the faith, but they're a bunch of sinners. If God is righteous, and all of these men were unrighteous, how could God pass over their blatant sin? He didn't. He justified them on the basis of Christ's propitiatory sacrifice. He justified them through faith.

Justification is in Christ alone

When God justifies a sinner, he charges that sinner's sin to Christ, and he credits Christ's righteousness to that sinner. That's only possible because of Christ's substitutionary life and death. Christ lived as my substitute, fulfilling the law on my behalf. God credits Christ's righteousness to me. Christ died as my substitute, fulfilling the penalty of the law on my behalf. God charges my sin to Christ.

We must remember that justification is the imputation of righteousness, not the infusion of righteousness. By justification, God declares the sinner to be righteous, but he doesn't make the sinner righteous. Martin Luther illustrates this fact by describing the practice of some German farmers, who collected the refuse from their farm animals into piles around their fields. They used this refuse as fertilizer. For much of the year, the fields were dotted with these dunghills. However, when the first snow came, everything was covered with a blanket of snow—even the dunghills. Everything was white and clean and pure. However, what was under the blanket of snow? The dunghills were still there. That's justification. It doesn't change us. God charges our sin to Christ and credits Christ's righteousness to us.

How can he do this? Paul explains, God put Christ "forward as a propitiation by his blood, to be received by faith" (3:25). Christ satisfied God's justice, thereby appeasing his wrath and securing his mercy. Remarkably, many people object to such a notion of atonement. Why?

First, they object to the truth of God's wrath. They argue, "God is love. God is always forgiving. We just need to realize it." And so, they prefer the word *expiation* to *propitiation*. To expiate means to remove the guilt of sin. It's true that Christ removes the guilt of our sin, but that's not what Paul is saying here. The term is *propitiation*. It means to satisfy God's justice, thereby appeasing his wrath and securing his mercy.

Second, they object to the truth of man's sin. They think God hates the sin, but loves the sinner. Such a statement actually reveals a glaring lack of discernment as to the true nature of sin. Sin isn't an entity. It isn't a substance. It doesn't have its own existence. It's a condition of the human heart. We can't divorce sin from the sinner. Sin doesn't exist without the sinner. God doesn't send sin to hell. He sends the sinner to hell. Man, because he's a sinner, is the object of God's wrath. According to the Bible, we are by nature children of wrath (Eph. 2:3).

Because so many people find the truths of God's wrath and man's sin so unpalatable, they change the nature of the atonement. And so, there's what's called the "moral influence theory" of the atonement.[3] Much of evangelicalism adheres to this view of the atonement without even realizing it. It's the idea that the sole purpose of the cross is to make us feel sorry for Christ. Its purpose is to break our hearts as we're moved by Christ's suffering. And I suppose that's part of the problem with so many of the dramas, movies, and sermons depicting Christ's suffering. The emphasis is in the wrong place. Do you remember those women who were following Christ on the way to Golgotha? They were weeping. He turned to them, saying,

---

[3] Lloyd-Jones, *Romans 3:20–4:25*, 106.

> Daughters of Jerusalem, do not weep for me, but weep for yourselves and for your children. For behold, the days are coming when they will say, "Blessed are the barren and the wombs that never bore and the breasts that never nursed!" Then they will begin to say to the mountains, "Fall on us," and to the hills, "Cover us" (Luke 23:28-30).

You see, they should have been weeping for their sin. They should have been weeping for the revelation of God's wrath that was unfolding before their very eyes. If our understanding of the cross only makes us feel sorry for Christ, then we don't get it. What happened at the cross? God displayed Christ publicly "as a propitiation by his blood." God, who is offended by us in more ways than we could ever imagine, must be appeased. His wrath is appeased in Christ's blood—for those who believe. The modern mind finds it so repulsive! So be it! It's the gospel.

Conclusion

Justification is by grace alone through faith alone in Christ alone. That's the reason why boasting is excluded. The doctrine of justification places the entire emphasis upon God—the glory of his power, wisdom, goodness, sovereignty, patience, and (above all else) grace. As the hymn writer Samuel Davies puts it:

> Great God of wonders! All Thy ways
> display Thine attributes divine;
> But the bright glories of Thy grace
> above Thine other wonders shine.[4]

The doctrine of justification magnifies the glory of God's grace because it makes man completely dependent upon him. Grace chose me before the foundation of the world. Grace sent the Son of God into this world to become a man. Grace led the Son of God to the cross to die. Grace united me with Christ. Grace redeemed me from the slave market of sin. Grace reconciled me to God. Grace made me a child of God. Grace made me a joint-heir with Christ. Grace caused me to be born again to a living hope. Grace seated me in the heavenly places in Christ. And, as the old hymn says, "Grace will lead me home." That's sovereign grace! And that accentuates our complete dependence upon him.

---

[4] Samuel Davies, "Great God of Wonders!" in *Hymns of Worship and Remembrance* (Belle Chasse: Truth & Praise, 1950), 15.

The Doctrine of Justification (3:23-26)

Sovereign grace o'er sin abounding,
Ransomed souls, the tidings swell;
'Tis a deep that knows no sounding,
Who its breadth or length can tell?[5]

I want to conclude with two lessons.

The first is *polemical*. The doctrine of justification rises or falls according to our doctrine of sin. As James White wisely notes,

> Change the biblical teaching of man's need, and you will of necessity have to change the nature of the salvation God provides. Every fundamental error regarding the doctrine of justification that man has ever invented flows from a denial of the nature and impact of sin in man's life. Indeed, when one allows man to make any kind of response to God, to cling to any shred of self-righteousness, the result will always be an addition to faith alone as the means of justification.[6]

Modern evangelicalism is very weak when it comes to the doctrine of sin. What are the implications for the gospel? They aren't good. I'm convinced that explains why much gospel preaching today misses the mark. To be blunt, it's lost sight of the target.

The second is *pastoral*. Please listen carefully to this conversion account of C.H. Spurgeon:

> As a boy C.H. Spurgeon attended a service in a Methodist chapel where a layman, not the regular minister, was preaching. The man had little learning. And so, he stuck closely to his text: "Turn to me and be saved, all the ends of the earth!" (Isa. 45:22). As Spurgeon remembered it, the man did not even pronounce the words properly, but that did not matter. The layman launched into his text, and his message went like this: "My dear friends, this is a very simple text indeed. It just says, 'Look.' Now looking don't take a great deal of pain. It ain't lifting your foot or your finger; it is just, 'Look.' Well, a man needn't go to college to learn to look. You may be the biggest fool, and yet you can look. A man needn't be worth a thousand pounds a year to be able to look. Anyone can look; even a child can look. But then the text says, 'Look unto Me.'

---

[5] John Kent, "Sovereign Grace O'er Sin Abounding" in *Hymns of Worship and Remembrance*, 29.

[6] James White, *The God Who Justifies: The Doctrine of Justification* (Minneapolis: Bethany House, 2001), 51.

Many of you are looking to yourselves, but it's no use looking there. You'll never find any comfort in yourselves. Look to Christ. The text says, 'Look unto Me.'" At this point, he noticed Spurgeon and—fixing his eyes on him as if he knew the struggle going on in the boy's heart—continued, "Young man, you look miserable, and you always will be miserable—miserable in life, and miserable in death—if you don't obey my text." Then lifting up his hands as only a good primitive Methodist could do, he shouted, "Young man, look to Jesus Christ." And Spurgeon did.[7]

What an encouragement for the sinner! If you look to Christ, you can be certain he will look to you.

---

[7] Source unknown. For a similar account, see Lewis A. Drummond, *Spurgeon: Prince of Preachers* (Grand Rapids: Kregel Publications, 1992), 21.

18
Deductions (3:27-31)

We're on trial. We hear the charge: all have suppressed the truth by their unrighteousness (1:18). We hear the testimony: all are without excuse (1:19-3:8). We hear the verdict: all are under sin (3:9-18). We hear the sentence: all are the object of God's wrath (1:18). We stand in stunned silence (3:19-20). "But now ..." (3:21). God speaks: "I'm willing to change the verdict from guilty to innocent. I'm willing to change the sentence from death to life. I'm willing to declare you righteous instead of unrighteous." How? (1) This change in our legal status comes through faith (3:21-23) (2) This change in our legal status comes by grace (3:24). (3) This change in our legal status comes in Christ (3:24-25).

Justification is by grace alone through faith alone in Christ alone. In 3:27-31, Paul makes three simple deductions. He directs these primarily at the Jews.

Justification excludes boasting (3:27-28)
"Then what becomes of your boasting? It is excluded" (3:27). The term "boasting" comes from the battlefield. Goliath, for example, boasted before the armies of Israel (1 Sam. 17:8-11.) The Jews boast in the works of the law. But Paul says, "We hold that one is justified by faith apart from works of the law" (3:28). The doctrine of justification excludes boasting because it means we receive everything from God, and we humbly confess our complete dependence upon his mercy.

What is Paul refuting?
Paul knows the Jews think justification is by works. That really comes out later in 10:2, where Paul writes, "For I bear them witness that they have a zeal for God, but not according to knowledge." What don't they understand? According to the context, they don't understand how to get righteousness. They think they can establish their own righteousness. They're wrong. How can they possibly establish their own righteousness? Man is totally depraved. He must get righteousness from somewhere other than himself. Where? He must receive Christ's righteousness by faith.

What is the lesson for us?
It's simply this: the doctrine of justification excludes boasting. If it doesn't, then we've misunderstood it. How could anyone misunderstand it? There are many ways. For example, some people misunderstand the very verses we're considering. In 3:27, Paul says, "Then what becomes of our boasting? It is excluded. By what kind of law? By a law of works? No, but by the law of faith." Here, Paul identifies a "law of works" and a "law of faith." Some people think these refer to two different ways of salvation. Their reasoning goes something like this: In the dispensation of law, God gave the "law of works" to man as a way of salvation. He said, "If you do this, you will be saved." Man failed. And so, in the dispensation of grace, God gave the "law of faith" to man as a way of salvation. In effect, he says, "The law of works is too difficult, so I'm going to make it easier for you. Rather than obeying the law, all you have to do is obey by believing. If you do that, you'll be saved." Such a notion unwittingly turns faith into a work. How? It makes faith a requirement I can fulfill apart from God's grace. God has commanded it; I can do it; therefore, I have every reason to boast.

The above notion has some serious flaws. (1) It contradicts what Paul says in 4:3, "Abraham believed God, and it was counted to him as righteousness." The OT saints were justified through faith. Therefore, the "law of works" and "law of faith" can't refer to two different ways of salvation. Clearly, there's only one way of salvation. (2) It contradicts what Paul says in 3:31, "Do we then overthrow the law by this faith? By no means! On the contrary, we uphold the law." But if there are two ways of salvation (law and faith), then faith doesn't establish law; rather, it nullifies it.

So, what does Paul mean by the "law of works" and the "law of faith"? The word *law* means *principle*. Thus, Paul is saying that we aren't justified by a principle of works but by a principle of faith. Works are meritorious in that they merit payment. Faith isn't meritorious in that it doesn't merit anything. It's simply the instrument by which God justifies the sinner.

Justification abolishes distinctions (3:29-30)
"Or is God the God of Jews only? Is he not the God of Gentiles also? Yes, of Gentiles also" (3:29). Paul makes it clear that God justifies the circumcised (Jews) and uncircumcised (Gentiles) through faith. Therefore, he's the God of both Jews and Gentiles. As we know, the distinction between Jews and Gentiles began back in Genesis 12 with the call of Abraham after the tower of

Babel. Subsequently, God called Isaac, and then Jacob. From Jacob, the nation of Israel arose. Until Christ's advent, God focused almost exclusively upon Israel. With Christ's advent, however, that changed forever. Now, "there is not Greek and Jew, circumcised and uncircumcised ... but Christ is all, and in all" (Col. 3:11).

What is Paul refuting?
Paul knows the Jews think they're God's chosen people, and he knows they despise the Gentiles. He addresses their error throughout this epistle (1:5, 16; 2:9-11, 28-29; 3:9, 20, 23; 9:1-6). What's the advantage in being a Jew? Paul tells us: "They were entrusted with the oracles of God" (3:1). What a privilege! The calling of the Jews served a specific purpose in the unfolding of God's plan of redemption. However, they shouldn't mistake that for some sort of superiority. They aren't better than the Gentiles just because they're Jews. With Christ's advent, the distinction is gone.

John the Baptist declares, "Behold, the Lamb of God, who takes away the sin of the world" (John 1:29). Christ declares, "For God so loved the world, that he gave his only Son" (John 3:16). Again, Christ declares,

> I am the good shepherd. I know my own and my own know me, just as the Father knows me and I know the Father; and I lay down my life for the sheep. And I have other sheep that are not of this fold. I must bring them also, and they will listen to my voice. So there will be one flock, one shepherd. For this reason the Father loves me, because I lay down my life that I may take it up again (John 10:14-17).

At Pentecost, the exalted Christ gave gifts to men. In particular, he gave the gift of tongues. At the tower of Babel, God confused man's language, dispersing man across the face of the earth. At Pentecost, the different tongues (i.e., languages) symbolize that God has united the world in one house with Christ as its head.

Paul explains all of that in Ephesians 2. As Gentiles, we were "separated from Christ," "excluded from the commonwealth of Israel," "strangers to the covenants of promise," "without God in the world," and "without hope." "But now," says Paul, "in Christ Jesus you who once were far off have been brought near by the blood of Christ" (Eph. 2:13). He became our peace. He made both groups into one. He broke down the barrier of the dividing wall. He made the two into one new man. He established peace. He reconciled them both in one body to God. He preached peace to those who were far away and those who were near. He gave us access in one Spirit to the Father. Now, we're no longer "strangers and aliens," but we're "fellow citizens with the saints" and "members of the household of God" (Eph. 2:19).

What is the lesson for us?
It's true that the calling of the Jews served a specific purpose in the unfolding of God's plan of redemption. But God is one. He justifies the circumcised and uncircumcised through faith. He's the God of Jews and Gentiles. The doctrine of justification abolishes distinctions. Despite that fact, some people still believe in "anthropological dualism." What do I mean by that? I mean some believe there are actually two separate people of God—his earthly people (Israel) and his heavenly people (the church). Yet, the Bible says there's only one household of God. According to Hebrews 3:1-6, Moses was a faithful servant in God's house—that's the old dispensation. Christ is a faithful Son over God's house—that's the new dispensation. There's only one house because there's only one God.

Justification establishes the law (3:31)
"Do we then overthrow the law by this faith? By no means! On the contrary, we uphold the law." The doctrine of justification by grace alone through faith alone in Christ alone doesn't nullify the law. On the contrary, it establishes the law. It does so in two ways.

First, the law demands obedience. It says, "You must be righteous like God." The doctrine of justification doesn't nullify that. It establishes it. How? Christ obeyed the law. Christ fulfilled all righteousness. Paul says, "But when the fullness of time had come, God sent forth his Son, born of woman, born under the law, to redeem those who were under the law, so that we might receive adoption as sons" (Gal. 4:4-5). That's Christ's active obedience. By coming into this world as a man, he put himself under the law. He obeyed it perfectly by loving God with all his heart, soul, mind, and strength. He established the law.

Second, the law demands a penalty from those who disobey it. It says, "You've disobeyed me. You must pay the penalty: death." The doctrine of justification doesn't nullify that. It establishes it. How? Christ paid the law's penalty. Paul says, "Christ redeemed us from the curse of the law by becoming a curse for us—for it is written, 'Cursed is everyone who is hanged on a tree'—so that in Christ Jesus the blessing of Abraham might come to the Gentiles, so that we might receive the promised Spirit through faith" (Gal. 3:13-14). That's Christ's passive obedience. At the cross, he became a curse for us. He established the law.

When we're united with Christ, our sin becomes his. He has paid its penalty at the cross. The law's penalty, therefore, is satisfied. When we're united with Christ, his righteousness becomes ours. God imputes it to us. The law's requirement, therefore, is fulfilled. How does the doctrine of justification nullify the law? It doesn't. On the contrary, it establishes the law in every way.

What is Paul refuting?
In this, Paul is refuting a common misunderstanding of justification, which goes like this: "The law requires that we do something, yet Paul says we don't do anything. So, isn't his doctrine of justification undermining the law's requirements?" The answer is "no." Nothing that the law requires has been compromised, because Christ has done it all.

What is the lesson for us?
Paul makes it clear that the formal cause of justification is Christ's righteousness imputed to us when we're united with him. We struggle with balancing that with the doctrine of sanctification—the impartation of Christ's righteousness to us. At times, we're tempted to look inward to find the grounds of justification. You can search all you want, but you'll never find it there.

Christ has fulfilled the law, in that he has paid its penalty and he has fulfilled its requirement. Therefore, God doesn't justify us on the basis of anything we do. He justifies us on the basis of what Christ has done. May we never lose sight of that! In the words of Jerry Bridges, may we "continually face up to our own sinfulness and then flee to Jesus through faith in his shed blood and righteous life!"[1]

---

[1] Jerry Bridges, *The Discipline of Grace* (Colorado Springs: NavPress, 1994), 58.

19
Father Abraham (4:1-8)

In 3:21-26, Paul declares the doctrine of justification. We're under sin and, therefore, condemned in God's sight. When God justifies us, he alters our legal standing. He changes the verdict from guilty to innocent, and the sentence from death to life. He declares us to be righteous instead of unrighteous. He does this by grace through faith in Christ. In 3:27-31, Paul explains three implications of justification: it excludes boasting, it abolishes distinctions, and it establishes the law. Now, in 4:1-25, Paul defends the doctrine of justification. He knows the Jews in particular will stumble over it. Why? It runs contrary to what they've believed for generations.

And so, let's imagine everyone is exiting the courthouse. As Paul descends the steps outside the courthouse, he notices a group of Jews waiting for him. "Oh boy, here we go!" They sat through the trial. They heard the accusation (all suppress the truth), the testimony (all are without excuse), the verdict (all are under sin), and the sentence (all are objects of God's wrath). They also heard the judge declare that he's willing to change the verdict by grace through faith in Christ. Now, they're waiting for Paul. They confront him. "Paul, this isn't what our Scriptures teach. This isn't what our forefathers believed. This can't be right." Paul responds. "You're mistaken. This isn't new. This is exactly what our Scriptures teach. This is exactly what our forefathers believed. You doubt it? Well, let's consult two men. First, let's consult our greatest father: Abraham. Second, let's consult our greatest king: David. And let's see what they have to say about the subject. Let's see what they think about the doctrine of justification."

Do you understand what he's doing? If he can demonstrate that both Abraham and David believed exactly what he believes, then the Jews must re-evaluate their position. They'll be left with no other alternative.

So, Paul takes them back to Abraham. Essentially, he tells them that their understanding of justification is far removed from Abraham's experience. He shows them that God justified Abraham by grace alone through faith alone in Christ alone. He does so by presenting four arguments: (1) Abraham was justified apart from works (4:1-8); (2) Abraham was justified apart from circumcision (4:9-12); (3) Abraham was justified apart from the law (4:13-17); and (4) Abraham was justified through faith (4:18-25).

For now, we're going to consider his first point: Abraham was justified apart from works (4:1-8). Paul begins with a question: "What then shall we say was gained by Abraham, our forefather according to the flesh?" (4:1). I'm reading from the ESV. This translation gives the impression that the phrase, *according to the flesh*, refers to Abraham. In other words, Paul is saying that Abraham is the father of the Jews. That's a possible translation. The AV, however, states, "What shall we say then that Abraham our father, as pertaining to the flesh, hath found?" This translation gives the impression that the phrase, *pertaining to the flesh*, refers to the verb *found*. In other words, Paul is asking what Abraham found according to the flesh.

I'm inclined toward the second translation because I think it makes much more sense in the context. In 2:23, Paul rebukes the Jews for boasting in the law. In 3:27, he argues that the doctrine of justification excludes "boasting." Now, he wants to prove that Abraham had no reason to boast before God because he never "gained" (or, achieved) anything according to the flesh. Abraham didn't gain anything by his own effort. So, how could he boast before God?

On the contrary, "Abraham believed God, and it was counted to him as righteousness" (4:3). Here, Paul quotes Genesis 15:6, where God promises Abraham that he will have a son, and that his descendants will be as numerous as the stars. Paul's argument is this: "Don't stumble over this doctrine of justification. It isn't new. How do you think Abraham was justified? He didn't achieve anything by his own effort. He was justified through faith." Genesis 15:6 is the first declaration in Scripture of the doctrine of justification. Abel, Seth, Noah, Shem were all justified through faith. But it's here that the doctrine is stated clearly for the first time. This verse contains the three key elements of justification: faith, imputation, and righteousness. In 4:4-8, Paul explains what he means by each.

What is faith? (4:4-5)

Here, Paul contrasts two men. The first is "the one who works" (4:4). The second is "the one who does not work" (4:5). The man who works receives his wage. That wage isn't given as a gift, but as "his due." After all, he's earned it. If you put in a week's work at the school, factory, hospital, shop, or wherever, you receive your wage at the end of the week. You don't thank your employer for your wage as a favour. He owes it to you. It's his debt to you.

Now, the man who doesn't work doesn't receive a wage. If he receives anything, it's a gift. That's faith. Believing, therefore, is the opposite of working. It doesn't earn us anything. It doesn't entitle us to anything. Many preachers compare it to open hands reaching out to receive a gift. By believing we simply accept God's gift.

What is imputation? (4:4-5)
"Now to the one who works, his wages are not counted as a gift but as his due. And to the one who does not work but believes in him who justifies the ungodly, his faith is counted as righteousness." In these verses, the Greek verb is translated *to count, impute, reckon, or credit*. It's a word associated with accounting. A banker takes money from one account and credits it to another. That's what God does. He takes Christ's righteousness and credits it to us—to our account. Why's that important? James White tells us:

> The righteousness that is imputed by faith is Christ's perfect righteousness, and the resulting relationship, secured by the work of the Divine Substitute himself, produces the very peace Paul promised (Rom. 5:1), and all the praise and glory can go solely to God for his work in Christ (*Soli Deo Gloria*). "Impute" is a small word, but the sin-wearied soul who realizes what it really means finds it to be a true source of hope and constant encouragement.[1]

What is righteousness? (4:6-8)
In 4:6, Paul says, "David also speaks of the blessing of the one to whom God counts righteousness apart from works." That righteousness isn't ours. It's Christ's. That's seen in Paul's quotation of Psalm 32:1-2, where David gives a three-fold description of those who are "blessed." (1) God forgives their lawless deeds (4:7). The term *forgiveness* is *aphiemi*. It's a compound word: *apo* (from) and *hiemi* (to send away). So, the idea behind forgiveness is "sending away." When God forgives, the penalty of the offense is removed. When God forgives, the cause of the offense is removed. (2) God covers their sins (4:7). This is the only place the term *covered* is used in the NT. It conveys the idea of "hiding from view." (3) God doesn't take their sin into account (4:8). In other words, he doesn't impute their sin to them. He doesn't count it against them.

---

[1] White, *God Who Justifies*, 112.

That's what it means to be blessed. God forgives our lawless deeds; God covers our sins; and God doesn't impute sin to us. Rather, he credits righteousness to us. That's Christ's righteousness. We're accepted before God in Christ. And that's blessedness.

Conclusion

That's Paul's first argument—Abraham wasn't justified through works. From it, I want to take six doctrines.

First, *justification through faith is the covenant of grace*. Paul makes it clear that Abraham was justified by grace alone through faith alone in Christ alone. In this regard, Christ says, "Your father Abraham rejoiced that he would see my day. He saw it and was glad" (John 8:56). Abraham didn't know everything about Christ. Nevertheless, he looked beyond God's immediate promise concerning his seed to something of far greater significance. He knew something of God's plan of redemption in Christ. He believed God. And God justified him. The same is true of David. He didn't know everything about Christ. Nevertheless, he looked beyond God's immediate promise concerning his seed to something of far greater significance. He knew something of God's plan of redemption in Christ. He believed God. And God justified him.

It's extremely significant that Matthew begins his gospel account, stating: "The record of the genealogy of Jesus Christ, the son of David, the son of Abraham" (Matt. 1:1). God's promise to send a Saviour began in Genesis 3:15 with the seed of the woman. It was repeated in the covenant with Abraham and in the covenant with David. It was fulfilled in Christ. That's the covenant of grace, encompassing all those whom God justifies by grace alone through faith alone in Christ alone. For those of us who are Christians, that should be a tremendous encouragement. God will be faithful to his covenant. Therefore, we can sing,

> A debtor to mercy alone,
> of Covenant mercy I sing;
> Nor fear, with Thy righteousness on,
> my person and off'rings to bring.
> The terrors of law and of God
> with me can have nothing to do;
> My Saviour's obedience and blood
> hide all my transgressions from view.[2]

---

[2] Augustus Toplady, "A Debtor to Mercy Alone" in *Hymns of Worship and Remembrance*, 326.

Second, *justification is through faith, not by works*. Paul makes it clear that Abraham didn't achieve anything according to the flesh. He wasn't justified because of his works. He was justified through faith. The Jews had made a God of their works. In John 8, they cry, "Our father is Abraham." That was their confidence. And they were adamant. But Christ says to them, "No. You're of your father the devil. And you want to do the desires of your father." Today, many people make the same mistake. They make a God of their "supposed" goodness. They put their confidence in the flesh—their effort. But man's state is such that he can't bring anything to God. Yet, he insists upon bringing something—his goodness, his work, his effort, his suffering, his sacrifice, his service. He will lay these at the feet of God, refusing to admit that the natural man can't please God. His confidence is in the flesh (his own effort) rather than Christ.

Third, *believing is the opposite of working*. When a life preserver is thrown to a drowning man, he takes hold. Is there anything meritorious about his taking hold? Many people err in this regard. They think their faith is the reason God justifies them. They think God made Abraham righteous *because of* his faith. They think God was looking for someone with something that he could accept in place of righteousness. He found Abraham, who had a little faith. On that basis, God reckoned Abraham's faith to him as righteousness. And so, they conclude all they need is a little faith. God will reckon it to them as righteousness. Recently, I debated this very issue with someone. We weren't discussing Abraham, but Noah. Moses says, "Noah found favour in the eyes of the Lord ... Noah was a righteous man, blameless in his generation. Noah walked with God" (Gen. 6:8-9). This man's argument went like this: "God found something in Noah. Noah was a sinner, but Noah had faith by nature. And God took that little faith and reckoned it as righteousness." That's false. The fact that Noah found favour in God's eyes doesn't point to Noah's goodness, but to God's grace. Noah's righteousness isn't his righteousness. It's an imputed righteousness. The Bible never says that people are saved *because of* their faith. I've been very careful to use the preposition *through* rather than the preposition *by*. There's nothing wrong with saying *by faith* as long as we understand what we mean by it. In English, the preposition *by* can mean *because of* or *through*. By using it, some people think we're justified *because of* faith. We aren't. We're justified *through* faith. There's a huge difference. Our faith isn't the efficient cause of our justification. God's grace is the efficient cause of our justification. Faith is the instrumental cause of justification.

Fourth, *God justifies the ungodly*. That's what Paul says in 4:5. The Scriptures are full of examples of this truth: Noah, Abraham, Jacob, Moses, Ruth, etc. David is a prime example. In 4:7-8, Paul quotes David's words in Psalm 32. What's the context of this psalm? David has committed adultery and murder. What does he say? Blessed is the man whose lawless deeds are forgiven, whose sins are covered, whose sin isn't imputed to him. He's talking about himself. That shows us God justifies the ungodly. As a matter of fact, we can't be justified unless we're ungodly. Christ says, "I came not to call the righteous, but sinners" (Matt. 9:13). What does he mean? He means everyone is unrighteous, but not everyone knows it. Christ didn't come to call those who won't acknowledge their need. He didn't come to call those who still trust in their own goodness. He didn't come to call those who still hold on to their own efforts. He didn't come to call those who think justification is a debt paid in response to something they've done. No! He came to call the ungodly and the unrighteous—those who put no confidence in the flesh. So many people stumble over this. They think they must fulfill certain conditions necessary for justification. They think they must be sad enough, earnest enough, holy enough, good enough. No! Christ alone has fulfilled the conditions necessary for justification.

Fifth, *justification is external*. Blessed is "the one to whom God counts righteousness" (4:6). That righteousness isn't internal, but external. So many people are convinced that there must be something in them that's the basis of God's justification. They fail to comprehend that when God justifies a sinner, he doesn't make him inherently righteous. We must never put sanctification ahead of justification.

Sixth, *justification through faith is the key to happiness*. The happy man is the justified man. Paul declares, "We rejoice in hope of the glory of God" (5:2). If you lack joy, I can tell you why. You've lost sight of this truth. Have you stopped trusting in your own effort? Are you looking to Christ? That's true joy. Blessed is the man to whom God credits righteousness apart from works.

20
Timing Is Everything (4:9-12)

In 3:1-26, Paul declares the doctrine of justification. In 3:27-31, he explains three implications of this doctrine. In 4:1-25, he defends this doctrine. He does so by appealing to Abraham: (1) Abraham was justified apart from works (4:1-8); (2) Abraham was justified apart from circumcision (4:9-12); (3) Abraham was justified apart from the law (4:13-17); and (4) Abraham was justified through faith (4:18-25). We've considered the first. Now, we turn to the second.

Before doing so, I want to return for a moment to 4:3, where Paul quotes Genesis 15:6. This verse is found in two other places in the NT: Galatians 3:6 and James 2:23. James' quote appears somewhat problematic. Why? He seems to contradict Paul by affirming that justification is by works. "The Scripture was fulfilled that says, 'Abraham believed God, and it was counted to him as righteousness'—and he was called a friend of God. You see that a person is justified by works and not by faith alone." To resolve this apparent contradiction between Paul and James, we need to understand three facts.

First, Paul uses the term *faith* strictly in the sense of heart belief. It's a faith that grips the soul. Her sisters are called *love* and *hope*. James doesn't use the term *faith* strictly in the sense of heart belief. He also uses it for head belief. He says, "You believe that God is one; you do well. Even the demons believe—and shudder!" (James 2:19). There's a difference between heart belief and head belief. The difference between the two is seen in their works. When James says that Abraham wasn't justified by faith alone, he's speaking of head belief. Abraham believed with his heart. And that was evident in his works.

Second, Paul uses the term *works* to describe the means by which some people seek salvation. He has in mind the "works of the law." He has in mind the "flesh." James doesn't use the term *works* in that sense. He uses it to describe that which accompanies salvation. Therefore, there's no contradiction with Paul's teaching. As a matter of fact, Paul says exactly the same thing in Ephesians 2:8-10. He doesn't say it in Romans 4 because that isn't his point. He isn't dealing with the fruit of justification. He's dealing with its cause.

Third, Paul uses the term *justification* to describe the imputation of

Christ's righteousness to the sinner. God justified Abraham through faith. When? It's recorded in Genesis 15. God made certain promises concerning Abraham's seed. Abraham believed. God imputed righteousness to him. James uses the term *justification* in a different sense. He writes, "Was not Abraham our father justified by works when he offered up his son Isaac on the altar?" (James 2:21)? But Abraham wasn't justified when he offered Isaac on the altar (Gen. 22). He was justified when he believed God's promise concerning his seed (Gen. 15). So, what's James' point? Simply this: he isn't referring to the imputation of righteousness to Abraham, but to the perfecting of his faith. He says, "You see that faith was active along with his works, and faith was completed by his works; and the Scripture was fulfilled that says, 'Abraham believed God, and it was counted to him as righteousness'" (James 2:22-23). Abraham was already justified in the sense of the imputation of Christ's righteousness. When he offered Isaac on the altar, he confirmed the reality of his faith.

There's an important lesson here for us. We affirm that justification is by grace alone through faith alone in Christ alone. That's Paul's emphasis in Romans 4. Christ has fulfilled all the conditions necessary for justification. However, we also affirm that justifying faith isn't dead. A person can give intellectual assent to the teaching of the Bible yet go straight to hell. Many people agree with the gospel. However, James in effect says, "That doesn't make you any better than the devils!"

With that said, we return to Paul's argument in 4:9-12.

The question (4:9)

"Is this blessing then only for the circumcised, or also for the uncircumcised?" What "blessing"? Paul describes it in the preceding verses, where he mentions three things about the blessed man. (1) God forgives his lawless deeds (4:7). When God forgives, he removes the penalty of our sin. "The Lord has laid on him the iniquity of us all" (Isa. 53:6). (2) God covers his sins (4:7). This is the only place the term *covered* is used in the NT. It's the idea of hiding from view. "I am he who blots out your transgressions for my own sake, and I will not remember your sins" (Isa. 43:25). (3) God doesn't take his sin into account (4:8). In other words, he doesn't impute his sins to him. He doesn't count it against him. "I have blotted out your transgressions like a cloud and your sins like mist" (Isa. 44:22).

In brief, the blessed man is the justified man. In *The Pilgrim's Progress*, as

Christian arrives at the Place of Deliverance, he sings:

> Thus far did I come laden with my sin;
> Nor could ought ease the grief that I was in,
> Till I came hither: What a place is this!
> Must here be the beginning of my bliss?
> Must here the burden fall from off my back?
> Must here the strings that bound it to me crack?
> Blest cross! Blest sepulcher! Blest rather be,
> The man that there was put to shame for me![1]

Is this blessed man circumcised or uncircumcised? In other words, is circumcision necessary for justification? That's Paul's question.

The answer (4:10-11)
Paul appeals to Abraham, drawing our attention to two facts. The first fact concerns the *timing* of Abraham's circumcision (4:10). God justified Abraham while he was uncircumcised. As a matter of fact, according to Jewish reckoning, twenty-nine years passed between Abraham's justification (Gen. 15) and circumcision (Gen. 17).

The second fact concerns the *function* of Abraham's circumcision (4:11). He received the sign of circumcision as a seal of the righteousness he had by faith. (1) It was a *sign*. A sign doesn't give you what you need. It simply confirms that you need it. Signs don't have any magical power. Let's say I want to drive to Ottawa. I see a sign on the highway: Ottawa is 100 km ahead. I don't pull over to wait for that sign to get me where I want to go. It can't do anything for me other than point. Circumcision was a sign of what was really needed—a new birth. (2) It was a *seal*. A seal doesn't give you what you have. It simply confirms that you have it. Seals don't have any magical power. Let's say I receive my diploma for graduating from school. It bears several signatures and a seal. The seal doesn't cause me to graduate. It can't do anything for me other than confirm. Circumcision confirmed the fact that Abraham had already believed God, and that God had already justified Abraham.

The implication (4:11-12)
So, Abraham wasn't justified because of circumcision. Paul draws out the implications of this. (1) It means Abraham is the father of all who aren't

---

[1] John Bunyan, *The Pilgrim's Progress* (Uhrichsville: Barbour Books, 1985), 36.

circumcised yet believe (4:11). (2) It means Abraham is the father of all who are circumcised yet believe (4:12). The common denominator is faith. As Paul makes clear elsewhere: "In Christ Jesus neither circumcision nor uncircumcision counts for anything but only faith working through love" (Gal. 5:6).

Conclusion

Why do we need to hear this? Just like the Jews of Paul's days, we like to turn "marks" into the object of our faith—a decision, ordinance, experience, lifestyle, distinctive, etc. Why do we like to turn "marks" into the object of our faith? There are a number of reasons, but the most common is this: We like to think there's something we can do to please God. But we can't. God won't accept anything from us. He justifies us without a cause. Christ is the object of our faith because he lived the life we were required to live, and he died the death we were condemned to die. God is satisfied with those who look to Christ because he's satisfied with Christ.

21
Guaranteed (4:13-17)

Our trial has ended. We've heard the accusation (all suppress the truth), the testimony (all are without excuse), the verdict (all are under sin), and the sentence (all are the object of God's wrath). But, thankfully, God is willing to change the verdict from guilty to innocent, and to change the sentence from death to life. He's willing to justify us. How? (1) "By" grace alone (3:24). (2) "Through" faith alone (3:22). (3) "In" Christ alone (3:24).

As Paul leaves the courthouse, he notices that some of his countrymen are waiting for him. They have a rather grim look on their faces. "Paul, this isn't what our Scriptures teach. This isn't what our fathers believed. Therefore, it can't be right." Paul responds. "You're mistaken. This is exactly what our Scriptures teach, and this is exactly what our forefathers believed. You doubt it? Let's ask our greatest father (Abraham) what he thinks (Gen. 15:6). And let's ask our greatest king (David) what he thinks (Ps. 32:1-2). Both were justified by grace alone through faith alone in Christ alone. It looks to me like you need to re-evaluate your position."

Paul doesn't let up. He has played defense; now, he goes on the offense. He has defended what he believes; now, he attacks what they believe. They think justification is by grace through circumcision. Paul appeals to Abraham to demonstrate it isn't (4:9-12). They think justification is by grace through law. Paul appeals to Abraham to demonstrate it isn't (4:13-17).

What is the promise? (4:13)
"For the promise to Abraham and his offspring that he would be heir of the world did not come through the law but through the righteousness of faith." The promise is that Abraham would be "heir of the world." That poses a slight problem because we never read of such a promise in the OT. Or do we? "I will give to you and to your offspring after you the land of your sojourning, all the land of Canaan, for an everlasting possession" (Gen. 17:8). "Evildoers shall be cut off, but those who wait for the LORD shall inherit the land" (Ps. 37:9). "The meek shall inherit the land and delight themselves in abundant peace" (Ps. 37:11). "Those blessed by the LORD shall inherit the land, but those

cursed by him shall be cut off" (Ps. 37:22). "The righteous shall inherit the land and dwell upon it forever" (Ps. 37:29). "Wait for the LORD and keep his way, and he will exalt you to inherit the land" (Ps. 37:34). "Blessed are the meek, for they shall inherit the earth" (Matt. 5:5).

God's covenant with Abraham includes three things: offspring, blessing, and land. There's a material fulfillment of these promises in the history of the nation of Israel (1 Kings 4:21). However, the promises point beyond the material to the spiritual. The offspring is Christ, and all who believe in him. The blessing is the gospel. The land is the renewed heaven and earth. In Adam, we lost the inheritance. In Christ, we regain the inheritance.

When was the promise given? (4:13)
Paul states two facts, so that we're absolutely clear on this. First, the promise didn't come "through the law." As a matter of fact, God gave the law 430 years after the promise. Obviously, therefore, the law has nothing to do with it. Second, the promise did come "through the righteousness of faith." In other words, the promise belongs to those who are justified by grace through faith in Christ.

How is the promise fulfilled? (4:14-17)
If it depends on man's effort, the promise is void (4:14-15). The promise can't depend on our obedience of the law. Why not? God gave it to show us our sin. In so doing, it doubles our guilt. Let's suppose I drive down the highway, stop the truck, climb a fence, and hunt on someone's property. I've broken the law. Now, let's imagine the same scenario, except this time there are signs posted all along the fence: "Private Property. Keep Out. Trespassers will be prosecuted." I've deliberately shaken my fist at the law. That's what the law does. It makes us transgressors. It makes our sin blatantly obvious. In doing so, it's a vehicle of wrath. If the promise depends on the law, then it depends on us. If it depends on us, then it's void.

If, however, it depends on God's grace, the promise is guaranteed (4:16). God justifies us "by his grace as a gift" (3:24). The fulfillment of God's promise rests on his grace. Therefore, it's guaranteed. In 4:17, Paul quotes God's promise to Abraham: "I have made you the father of many nations" (Gen. 17:5). This promise is remarkable because it demonstrates God's power. When God made this promise, Abraham and Sarah could no longer conceive. But God called into existence that which did not exist—Isaac and his physical descendants. "Therefore from one man, and him as good as dead, were born descendants as many as the stars of heaven and as many as the innumerable grains of sand by the seashore" (Heb. 11:12). But Paul makes it clear that the offspring in view isn't Abraham's physical descendants, but his spiritual descendants—i.e., those who share his faith. God has made Abraham the father of a multitude of nations. God has called into existence that which did not exist.

Conclusion

Paul's main point in 4:1-17 is simply this: justification is apart from works, apart from circumcision, and apart from the law. In a word, Abraham didn't achieve anything according to the flesh (4:1). Justification, therefore, doesn't depend upon us. It depends upon God—"who gives life to the dead and calls into existence the things that do not exist" (4:17). What impact should this have upon us?

First, *it should increase our humility.* God "gives life to the dead and calls into existence the things that do not exist." That means we don't contribute anything to our justification.

Second, *it should increase our joy.* God "gives life to the dead and calls into existence the things that do not exist." Can you think of a greater cause for joy? Paul says in 5:2, "We rejoice in hope of the glory of God." Our meditation upon these great truths should stir our hearts to rejoice in God our Saviour.

Third, *it should increase our faith.* God "gives life to the dead and calls into existence the things that do not exist." That means it doesn't depend on us. The object of faith isn't our works, duties, efforts, victories, experiences, feelings, or anything like that. The object of faith is God.

22
In Hope against Hope (4:18-22)

In 4:1-25, Paul defends the doctrine of justification by grace alone through faith along in Christ alone. He knows the Jews will struggle with it. Why? They're committed to a law of works, meaning they trust in their own effort. And so, Paul defends the doctrine of justification by appealing to Abraham. He makes four arguments: (1) Abraham was justified apart from works; (2) Abraham was justified apart from circumcision; (3) Abraham was justified apart from the law; and (4) Abraham was justified through faith. We've considered the first three. Now, we turn to the last. To appreciate fully what Paul says in 4:18-22, we must set the context by looking at Genesis 15:1-6.

The reward

In Genesis 15:1, we read that the "word of the LORD" comes to Abraham. It includes a commandment: "Do not fear!" This commandment is followed by two declarations: "I am a shield to you;" and "Your reward shall be very great." What's God saying? Well, what's the context? The verse begins with these words: "After these things." What things? The answer is found in the preceding chapter, where we learn that four kings defeat the five kings of Canaan. They take captives, including Lot. But Abraham chases after them with his 318 men. And he's victorious. When he returns from the battle, he meets Melchizedek, king of Salem. Melchizedek blesses Abraham, saying, "Blessed be Abram by God Most High, Possessor of heaven and earth; and blessed be God Most High, who has delivered your enemies into your hand!" (Gen. 14:19-20). The name *God Most High* is *El Elyon*—the strongest of the strong or the mightiest of the mighty.

We find a similar title for God in Daniel 4. Nebuchadnezzar has an awful dream in which he sees a magnificent tree that's cut down. He also sees a man whose mind is changed into that of an animal. Daniel interprets the dream, explaining that God is going to humble Nebuchadnezzar. This humbling will continue until he recognizes that "the Most High rules the kingdom of men and gives it to whom he will" (Dan. 4:25). About a year later, the prophecy is fulfilled. For seven years, Nebuchadnezzar roams the fields like an animal.

This continues until he lifts up his eyes to heaven and recognizes that God is Most High. Nebuchadnezzar declares,

> His dominion is an everlasting dominion, and his kingdom endures from generation to generation; all the inhabitants of the earth are accounted as nothing, and he does according to his will among the host of heaven and among the inhabitants of the earth; and none can stay his hand or say to him, "What have you done?" (Dan. 4:34-35).

He's God Most High, Possessor of heaven and earth. This means "he does according to his will among the host of heaven and among the inhabitants of the earth." Abraham knows it, for God Most High had given him the victory over the four kings.

So, that's the context for what we read in Genesis 15:1, "After these things the word of the Lord came to Abram." First, God says, "I am a shield to you." Abraham has just interfered in a war. Perhaps he expects the four kings to return one day with four more kings to exact vengeance. Is Abraham afraid? God's words seem to suggest so: "I am a shield to you." In other words, "God Most High will protect you." Second, God says, "Your reward shall be very great." The king of Sodom offers Abraham all the spoils of war, but Abraham rejects his offer (Gen. 14:23). And so, God says, "Do not fear, Abram, your reward shall be very great." In other words, "God Most High will reward you."

The question
The mention of a reward leads Abraham to ask an obvious question. God has called him from his homeland, shown him the land of Canaan, and promised that his descendants will be like the dust of the earth. A significant amount of time has passed since then. Now, God says, "Your reward shall be very great." When Abraham hears the word "reward," he immediately thinks in terms of a son. He doesn't have one, despite the fact that God has promised that his descendants will be like the dust of the earth. Perhaps Abraham is curious, so he asks, "O Lord God, what will you give me, for I continue childless, and the heir of my house is Eliezer of Damascus?" (Gen. 15:2).

The promise
God answers Abraham's question with two related promises. (1) "This man shall not be your heir; your very own son shall be your heir" (Gen. 15:4). This

means Abraham's heir would be his natural child. (2) "Look toward heaven, and number the stars, if you are able to number them. ... So shall your offspring be" (Gen. 15:5).

The response
God Most High, Possessor of heaven and earth, has spoken. Abraham believes him, and God reckons it to him as righteousness (Gen. 15:6).

The hope
This exposition of Genesis 15:1-6 sets the context for Romans 4:18-22. Paul begins by saying, "In hope he *[Abraham]* believed against hope, that he should become the father of many nations, as he had been told" (4:18). What does this mean?

First, what does it mean that Abraham believed "against hope"? It means Abraham looks at his circumstances and contemplates two undeniable facts. (1) He considers "his own body, which was as good as dead" (4:19). (2) He considers "the barrenness of Sarah's womb" (4:19). Abraham is painfully aware that they're well beyond the age of childbearing. Yet, God has promised him a son, and God has promised him that his descendants will be as numerous as the stars. Humanly speaking, God's promise is hopeless. However, Abraham believes "against hope."

Second, what does it mean that Abraham believed "in hope"? It means that Abraham, in addition to contemplating his circumstances, contemplates his God. And he's "fully convinced that was able to do what he had promised" (4:21). How can Abraham be so sure? The answer: he knows his God. In Genesis 15:2, Abraham refers to God as *Adonai Yahweh*. (1) The name *Adonai* means supreme Lord. It means God is the King of kings and Lord of lords. There's no doubt in Abraham's mind—his God "does according to his will among the host of heaven and among the inhabitants of the earth." His God has made a promise, and there's nothing that will prevent his God from keeping his promise. (2) The name *Yahweh* is God's personal name. He's the great I AM. He's eternal, immortal, immutable, and faithful. Abraham contemplates his God. He deduces certain facts from his contemplation. Again, his God has made a promise, and there's nothing that will prevent his God from keeping his promise.

Therefore, "in hope he *[Abraham]* believed against hope." On the one hand, Abraham ponders his circumstances. On the other hand, he ponders his

God—*Adonai Yahweh*. What conclusion does he arrive at? He's "fully convinced that God was able to do what he had promised." And so, Abraham doesn't "waver" (4:19); rather, he grows "strong in his faith." And, in so doing, he glorifies God (4:20).

As Martyn Lloyd-Jones explains,

> The one thing that mattered with Abraham was that God had spoken, that God had made a promise; and because it was God who had spoken, and because it was God who had made the promise, Abraham says, "Nothing else need be considered at all." ... What a wonderful way this is of looking at faith and defining faith. Faith is that which always glorifies God. Faith is to believe God simply and solely because he is God. Nothing glorifies God more than this; nothing is so insulting to God as not to believe his word.[1]

Conclusion

From the above, I want to affirm four foundational doctrines concerning faith.

First, *the object of faith is God*. Abraham looks at his circumstances—overwhelming! Yet, he doesn't "waver." Why? He also looks at his God. We must learn from that. Regularly, we focus upon our circumstances instead of focusing upon our God. We're staggered by our circumstances. We despair at the state of the world or the state of the church. We despair at temptation and tribulation. We despair at the loss of health or the prospect of death. As a result, we grow weak in faith. We're like Peter, walking upon the water. We fix our gaze upon our circumstances, losing sight of God. We shake our heads in bewilderment. And we begin to sink. Has that ever happened to you? We need to be like Abraham—a realist. "Faith is the assurance of things hoped for, the conviction of things not seen" (Heb. 11:1). There really isn't any such thing as blind faith. On the contrary, faith is looking at our circumstances, looking at our God, and concluding, I will trust in God who's most certainly able to do all that he has promised.

Second, *the rule of faith is the Word of God*. We read twice in Genesis 15:1-6 that the "word of the LORD" came to Abraham. That's the rule of his faith. Abraham gets himself into trouble when he deviates from that. In Genesis 16:2, we read that he "listened to the voice of Sarai." She suggests that he help God fulfill his promise by fathering a child with Hagar. We all know the

---

[1] Lloyd-Jones, *Romans 3:20–4:25*, 225.

In Hope against Hope (4:18-22)

result. We must learn from that. The rule of faith is the Word of God. We cause ourselves all sorts of problems when we deviate from what God has promised. He hasn't promised us immunity from illness, civil strife, personal loss, suffering, or death. God hasn't promised us a perfect family, a perfect career, or a perfect life. God hasn't promised us a life free of disorder, discomfort, discouragement, or danger. Often times, we "waver" in faith because we're focused upon these things. We've lost sight of the rule of faith—God's Word. What has God promised us? He's promised that nothing will separate us from his love (8:39). That's our hope. We may pass through many unpleasant experiences in life, but that doesn't alter God's promise.

Third, *the strength of faith is the knowledge of God.* Abraham knows God; therefore, he believes God. There's a direct relationship between his knowledge of God and his faith in God. We must learn from that. If I'm weak in faith, I know why. It's because I've lost sight of God. For that reason, I must make it my chief business in life to pursue a deep knowledge of God in his Word. Related to that, we must make certain that our knowledge of God isn't merely theoretical. We must apply what we know to life. I must apply what I know when I'm struggling with illness, persecution, temptation, or tribulation. I must apply what I know when I'm struggling with personal loss. I must apply what I know when I'm facing death. This doesn't mean I'm not afraid. It means I'm a realist. I contemplate my circumstances, yet I don't waver. Why? I believe in hope against hope, because I know my God.

Fourth, *the result of faith is the glory of God.* Abraham looks at his circumstances and his God. Despite his circumstances, he believes God. And he grows "strong" in faith, thereby "giving glory to God." We must learn from that. When we hold to God's promises despite our circumstances, we glorify him, in that we declare our confidence in his unsearchable greatness. But when we permit our circumstances to get the better of us, we rob God of his glory, in that we cast doubt upon his unsearchable greatness. Have you ever wondered why God put Abraham through all that? God promised him a son. Why did he wait so long in fulfilling his promise? The answer is simple: God glorified himself in Abraham. Abraham believed God. His circumstances couldn't shake him. And that declared God's greatness, God's goodness, God's sufficiency, God's excellence, and God's majesty. That's a very profitable way in which to view our circumstances. We may not know why we pass through certain experiences. The reason may simply be this: God is glorifying himself through the simple fact that his goodness and greatness compel us to believe in hope against hope.

23
Believing God (4:23-25)

Abraham believed "in hope against hope." He was a realist, looking at his circumstances and his God. Knowing both, he was "fully assured that God was able to do what he had promised" (4:21). In the last study, we derived four doctrines from Abraham's example: (1) the object of our faith is God; (2) the rule of our faith is the Word of God; (3) the strength of our faith is the knowledge of God; and (4) the result of our faith is the glory of God.

In this study, we're going to develop the first doctrine: the object of faith is God. Why? Because that's what Paul does in 4:23-25. He begins, "But the words 'it was counted to him' were not written for his sake alone, but for ours also." Paul wants us to learn from Abraham's example. Primarily, he wants us to learn that we must be "fully assured that God [is] able to do what he [has] promised." Such assurance flows from contemplating the object of our faith. In 4:24-25, Paul describes the object of our faith, stating, "It will be counted to us who believe in him who raised from the dead Jesus our Lord, who was delivered up for our trespasses and raised for our justification." There are four key thoughts in this statement concerning the object of our faith.

Christ's resurrection is a historical fact
We believe "in him *who raised from the dead* Jesus our Lord" (4:24). Josephus (the Jewish historian) wrote,

> Now, there was about this time, Jesus, a wise man, if it be lawful to call him a man, for he was a doer of wonderful works, a teacher of such men as receive the truth with pleasure. He drew over to him both many of the Jews, and many of the Gentiles. He was (the) Christ; and when Pilate, at the suggestion of the principal men amongst us, had condemned him to the cross, those that loved him at the first did not forsake him, for he appeared to them alive again the third day, as the divine prophets had foretold these and ten thousand other wonderful things concerning him; and the tribe of Christians, so named from him are not extinct at

this day.[1]

My purpose isn't to offer an apologetic for Christ's resurrection. Others have done an admirable job of that. My purpose is to affirm the link that exists between Christ's resurrection and our faith. As Paul says, "If Christ has not been raised, then our preaching is vain, your faith also is vain" (1 Cor. 15:14). Again, "If Christ has not been raised, your faith is worthless; you are still in your sins" (1 Cor. 15:17).

Christ's resurrection declares his person
We believe "in him who raised from the dead Jesus *our Lord*" (4:24). When asked by the Jewish religious leaders for a sign, proving his claim to be the Son of God, Christ responds, "Just as Jonah was three days and three nights in the belly of the sea monster, so shall the Son of Man be three days and three nights in the heart of the earth" (Matt. 12:40). He's referring of course to his resurrection, which confirms his identity.

That's made perfectly clear in Matthew 22:41-45, where Christ asks the Pharisees a simple question: Whose son is the Christ? They answer correctly: "The son of David." Christ asks another question based on Psalm 110:1, "If Christ is the son of David, then why does David say, The LORD *[Yahweh]* says to my Lord *[Adon]*: 'Sit at my right hand, until I make your enemies your footstool'"? To paraphrase: "If Christ is the son of David, then why does David call the Christ his *Adon*? How can Christ be the son of David and the Lord of David?" The answer of course is the incarnation. Christ is the God-man.

Now, the question for us is this: When did "the LORD *[Yahweh]* say to my Lord *[Adon]*: 'Sit at my right hand, until I make your enemies a footstool'"? He did so at Christ's resurrection. Peter makes that clear in his sermon in Acts 2. At the end of that sermon, he quotes Psalm 110:1, and then declares, "Let all the house of Israel know for certain that God has made him both Lord and Christ, this Jesus whom you crucified" (Acts 2:36). Christ is "our Lord."

Christ's resurrection declares his work
We believe "in him who raised from the dead Jesus our Lord, who was delivered up for our trespasses and raised for our justification" (4:24-25). Here, Paul describes two aspects of Christ's work.

---

[1] Flavius Josephus, *The Antiquities of the Jews* in *Josephus: The Complete Works*, ed. J.I. Packer and Merrill C. Tenney, trans. William Whiston (Nashville: Thomas Nelson, 1998), 576.

First, he says, Christ "was delivered up for our trespasses." That means there was a precise design to Christ's death; namely, to atone for our sin. That's called "propitiation." Back in 3:25, Paul says that God "displayed [Christ] publicly as a propitiation by his blood." In other words, Christ shed his blood in order to satisfy God's justice, thereby appeasing God's wrath and securing God's mercy.

Second, Paul says, Christ "was raised for our justification." There are two components to justification: God forgives us our sin, and God credits Christ's righteousness to us. Christ fulfilled the law, and he paid its penalty at the cross. On that basis, God forgives us and credits Christ's righteousness to us. Now, Paul actually says that Christ "was raised for our justification." That means God declared his satisfaction with Christ's atoning work (the basis for our justification) by raising him from the dead.

Christ's resurrection reveals God's power

We believe "in him who raised from the dead Jesus our Lord, who was delivered up for our trespasses and raised for our justification" (4:24-25). In other words, we believe in God who manifested his power in raising Christ from the dead. That's precisely what Abraham believed. Back in 4:17, Paul says, Abraham believed God "who gives life to the dead and calls into existence the things that do not exist." What does he mean? We must understand that statement on four levels in order to arrive at its full significance.

First, God gives life to the dead in that he enabled Abraham and Sarah to conceive. In 4:19, Paul says that Abraham "considered his own body, which was as good as dead (since he was about a hundred years old)," and, "he considered the barrenness of Sarah's womb." When it comes to bearing children, Abraham and Sarah are as good as dead. However, God gives life to the dead. He caused Isaac's birth. It was supernatural. "Therefore from one man, and him as good as dead, were born descendants as many as the stars of heaven and as many as the innumerable grains of sand by the seashore" (Heb. 11:12).

Second, God gives life to the dead in that he spared Isaac while upon the altar (Gen. 22). Abraham had bound Isaac to the altar. But God intervened. In reference to that event, we read that Abraham "considered that God is able to raise people even from the dead, from which he also received him back as a type" (Heb. 11:19). There was no doubt in Abraham's mind that God knew what he was doing. He was certain that "God is able to raise people even from the dead." And so, he had every confidence that God would still fulfill his promise even if Isaac died upon the altar. But God intervened. And Abraham received Isaac back "from the dead."

Third, God gives life to the dead in that he raised Christ from the dead. Isaac was a type of Christ. Abraham received Isaac back from the dead, figuratively speaking. Well, Christ died upon the altar—the cross. Yet, God raised him from the dead. In Ephesians 1:19-20, Paul prays that we may know "what is the immeasurable greatness of his power toward us who believe, according to the working of his great might that he worked in Christ when he raised him from the dead."

Fourth, God gives life to the dead in that he raises us from spiritual death. Paul says, "But God, being rich in mercy, because of the great love with which he loved us, even when we were dead in our trespasses, made us alive together with Christ—by grace you have been saved" (Eph. 2:4-5). We're united with Christ. Therefore, we partake of is resurrection life. As such, we're the seed of Abraham. God literally "calls into existence the things that do not exist" (4:17).

Conclusion

God has promised to forgive us our iniquity and to remember our sin no more. That's justification. God has promised to put his law within us and to write it upon our hearts. That's sanctification. God has promised to be our God. That's adoption. All of that is found in Jeremiah 31:33-34. Given my circumstances, it's hopeless. I'm corrupt to the core. But I believe "in hope against hope." I believe in the One who "gives life to the dead and calls into existence the things that do not exist." It doesn't depend upon me. Paul begins this chapter, asking what Abraham achieved according to the flesh? The answer is nothing. He believed God. Similarly, what can we achieve according to the flesh? The answer is nothing. We simply look to God "who raised from the dead Jesus our Lord, who was delivered up for our trespasses and raised for our justification." What a glorious thought!

24
The Benefits of Justification (5:1-5)

Paul's epistle to the Romans consists of five major sections. We're in the second (3:21-5:21), where Paul focuses our attention on the doctrine of justification. He explains it (3:21-31), defends it (4:1-25), and celebrates it (5:1-11).

In the second book of *The Pilgrim's Progress*, John Bunyan tells the story of Christiana (Christian's wife). At some point in her journey, she enters the house of Interpreter. He leads her into a room, where she sees two men. The first is holding a muck-rake in his hand. He's raking the dust for anything he can use—straw and sticks. The second man is above the man with the muck-rake. He's offering to trade the crown for the muck-rake. But the man with the muck-rake won't look in any direction but down. He's absorbed with raking the muck.

Interpreter says, "It is to let you know that earthly things, when they occupy people's minds, carry their hearts away from God." Most people live as though the things of this earth are all that matter. God offers them membership in his family. He offers them heavenly treasures and eternal pleasures (Ps. 16:11; Luke 12:33). He offers them the crown of glory that will never fade away (1 Peter 5:4). He offers them a renewed universe in which righteousness dwells (2 Peter 3:13). He offers them eternity without pain, sorrow, or death (Rev. 21:4). He offers them the beatific vision, whereby they behold his glory in Christ Jesus (Matt. 5:8). But most people never look up. They're absorbed with their muck-rake. They're so busy collecting straw and sticks that they never consider what God offers them.

Christiana begins to weep: "Oh, deliver me from this muck-rake."[1] Do we grasp what God offers us?

Unshakeable peace (5:1)

"Therefore, since we have been justified by faith, we have peace with God through our Lord Jesus Christ." The term *peace* means binding together what has been separated. In 1:18, Paul says, "The wrath of God is revealed from

---

[1] John Bunyan, *The Pilgrim's Progress: The Second Part* (Uhrichsville: Barbour Books, 1985), 233.

heaven against all ungodliness and unrighteousness of men, who by their unrighteousness suppress the truth." In 2:5, he adds, "Because of your hard and impenitent heart you are storing up wrath for yourself on the day of wrath when God's righteous judgment will be revealed." These verses imply that God's wrath is revealed in the present and the future. In Ephesians 2:3, Paul says we're "children of wrath" by nature. We don't understand, we don't seek after God, and we don't do any good. We're sinful. Therefore, we're God's enemies. Having been justified by faith, that's no longer the case. Now, we're bound together with God.

Paul identifies the *source* of this peace as Christ: "We have peace with God through our Lord Jesus Christ" (5:1). Six times in 5:1-11, Paul uses the preposition *through* (*dia*), thereby making it perfectly clear that Christ is the only reason we have peace with God. He says the same thing in Colossians 1:20, Christ made "peace through the blood of his cross." This peace was achieved by Christ's atoning work on the cross whereby he satisfied God's justice, appeased God's wrath, and secured God's mercy. Now, we're bound together with God.

Paul identifies the *foundation* of this peace as grace: "Through him we have also obtained access by faith into this grace" (5:2). Christ is the veil that was torn in two, opening the way to God. Now, we stand before God in grace. God is our Friend and Father, in Christ. God's throne isn't a judgment seat but a mercy seat, in Christ. God isn't a terrifying Judge but a loving Father, in Christ. He isn't a condemning God but a pardoning God, in Christ. He isn't a threatening God but an accepting God, in Christ. In Christ, we no longer have any reason to fear the sting of death, the terror of judgment, the torment of hell, or the wrath of God. Christ has swallowed it all. He has left nothing for us. Our peace with God is such that he loves us as if we had never been the object of his wrath.

Unfettered access (5:2)
"Through him we have also obtained access by faith into this grace in which we stand." We didn't have access into God's presence before he justified us (3:23). But now, we do. The expressions "we have" and "we stand" are in the perfect tense, meaning they're a continuous state. In other words, we aren't standing on thin ice that might suddenly give way.

Some time ago, there was a man who wanted to cross the frozen St. Lawrence River. He had his doubts about whether the ice could hold him, so he decided to test it by placing his hand firmly upon it. Afterwards, having mustered up a modicum of faith, he got down on his knees and began to shuffle—albeit gingerly—across the ice. When he got to the middle of the frozen river, where he was trembling with fear, he heard a noise behind him. When he turned around, he saw a team of horses pulling a carriage and making their way down to the river. Upon reaching the river, the horses, with carriage in tow, didn't stop, but bolted right onto the ice, and past him, while he remained there on all fours, turning a deep shade of red.[2]

We stand on a firm foundation: God's grace to us in Christ. We approach God as our reconciled Father. In Christ, the sinful failings of our best actions aren't scrutinized by a severe Judge but accepted by a loving Father. In Christ, we draw near to God with comfort and confidence. In Christ, we pray to God with boldness. In Christ, we cry out to God as children cry out to their father. We enjoy the liberties and privileges of the children of God.

Unalterable hope (5:2)
"We rejoice in hope of the glory of God." The expression "glory of God" refers to our inheritance in Christ. In 8:16-17, Paul says, "The Spirit himself bears witness with our spirit that we are children of God, and if children, then heirs—heirs of God and fellow heirs with Christ, provided we suffer with him in order that we may also be glorified with him." In Philippians 3:20-21, he writes, "But our citizenship is in heaven, and from it we await a Saviour, the Lord Jesus Christ, who will transform our lowly body to be like his glorious body, by the power that enables him even to subject all things to himself." In Colossians 3:4, he writes, "When Christ who is your life appears, then you also will appear with him in glory."

What does all that mean? (1) It means we'll be free from the evil of sin. At present, God is sanctifying us by his Spirit. That process will be completed when we see him. We'll be free from the commission of sin. All our thoughts, emotions, and actions will be governed by his perfect will. We'll also be free from the temptation to sin. At present, we're enticed by the flesh and the world. But that will end. (2) It means we'll be free from the evil of suffering. "He will wipe away every tear from their eyes, and death shall be no more,

---

[2] R. Kent Hughes, *1001 Great Stories and Quotes* (Wheaton: Tyndale, 1988), 155.

neither shall there be mourning, nor crying, nor pain anymore, for the former things have passed away" (Rev. 21:4). (3) It means we'll enjoy perfect communion with God. Christ says, "Blessed are the pure in heart, for they shall see God" (Matt. 5:8). I'm not so sure that's a sight of the eye. I don't doubt for one moment that we'll behold God's glory in Christ. I don't doubt for one moment that we'll behold manifestations of God's majesty. My point is simply this: we can never see God with the eye. He's infinite Spirit. I'm more inclined to think that Christ's promise in Matthew 5:8 is a sight of the soul. God will impart himself to us according to the fullest capacity of our souls. In so doing, he will become to us "fullness of joy" (Ps. 16:11).

By virtue of our union with Christ, we draw near to God. We find in him all we could ever want. Our knowledge of God diffuses into our soul a satisfying peace in this life and a tantalizing taste of what awaits us in glory. We live in anticipation of the day we'll see God (Matt. 5:8). In one sense, we see him now through the eyes of faith, but that's nothing in comparison to what's coming. At present, we see God's perfections in their effects, namely his works of creation, providence, and redemption; but in the future, we will see him perfectly. We will be like Christ and, therefore, able to commune with God to the fullest capacities of our souls. There will be nothing to obscure, confound, or hinder our enjoyment of him. Our knowledge of God will be full and perfect, constant and complete, resulting in hitherto unknown delight as we rest fully and finally in him.

Unparalleled joy (5:3-5)

As we might expect, this hope can't be contained. Three times, Paul says, "we rejoice" (5:2, 3, 11). The verb is *kauchaomai*. It really means to *exult* or *glory*. In the words of Thomas Manton, exultation is "a ravishment as cannot be compressed."[3]

In the immediate context, "we rejoice in our sufferings" (5:3). We don't rejoice for our suffering. We rejoice because we know suffering starts a chain reaction. First, it "produces endurance" (5:3). Endurance is single-mindedness. Suffering causes us to narrow our focus. Second, "endurance produces character" (5:4). Character is the confidence that comes through testing. Another word for this is maturity. Third, "character produces hope" (5:4). Those who are battle tested have experienced God's faithfulness firsthand,

---

[3] Thomas Manton, *An Exposition on the Epistle of James* (London: Banner of Truth, 1968), 23.

which nurtures hope. Fourth, "hope does not put us to shame" (5:5). It doesn't let us down. Why not? As our hope grows, so too does our experience of God's love. The Holy Spirit doesn't pour warm, fuzzy feelings into our heart. He pours God's love into our hearts. How? He points us to God's promises in Christ. In so doing, he makes us aware that God loves us.

This is perspective. Years ago, I lectured at a Bible School in the city of Kathmandu in Nepal. From the hotel restaurant, I had a wonderful view of the Himalayas. As I gazed upon them day after day, their enormity had an awe-inspiring effect. They made me feel awfully small. One evening, I sat outside, watching the sun descend behind the snow-capped mountains. As the sky darkened, the stars gradually appeared. From where I sat, the stars were mere specks in the sky—insignificant in comparison to the Himalayas. But here's a fascinating question: If I had been able to travel to the stars, how would the Himalayas have appeared from that vantage point? Do you see where I'm going with this? We easily and quickly lose perspective in the midst of suffering. When we look at it from the vantage point of the doctrine of justification, we find a reason to rejoice. Rejoicing in suffering proclaims the wondrous truth that Christ is more valuable to us than all that life can give and all that death can take.

Paul's point in these verses is this: we exult in our tribulations because they're the means by which we know Christ's love experientially. As Thomas Manton explains,

> In *tribulations* we may have much experience of grace, of the love of God, and our own sincerity and patience; and that is ground of rejoicing. ... The rule holds good in all kinds of tribulations or sufferings; they occasion sweet discoveries of. ... They are happy occasions to discover more of God to us, to give us a greater sense and feeling of the power of grace; and so we may take pleasure in them.[4]

Conclusion

"For those who believe unto the saving of the soul," writes John Owen, "Christ is precious—the sun, the rock, the life, the bread of their souls—everything that is good, useful, amiable, desirable, here or unto eternity."[5] When Adam and Eve disobeyed in the garden, they—along with all their posterity—

---

[4] Manton, *Epistle of James*, 25–26.
[5] John Owen, *The Works of John Owen*, ed. W. H. Gould (London: Johnstone & Hunter, 1850; repr., Edinburgh: Banner of Truth, 1977), 1:3.

fell into bondage to sin and death. Upon the cross, however, Christ bore God's judgment in our place. We enter into the blessings of his substitutionary sacrifice when we believe in him. He unites us to himself by the Holy Spirit, whereby we enjoy all that he purchased for us. This makes Christ precious beyond compare.

25
Much More (5:6–11)

We're condemned in God's sight, but he's prepared to justify us—to change the verdict from guilty to innocent, and the sentence from death to life. (1) God justifies condemned sinners *by grace*. He justifies us without a cause. There's nothing in us that merits it. (2) God justifies condemned sinners *through faith*. This means justification is a gift we receive. We don't contribute anything to it, and we don't add anything to it. (3) God justifies condemned sinners *in Christ*. He charges our sin to Christ who died as our substitute, bearing the curse of the law on our behalf. He credits Christ's righteousness to us. He lived as our substitute, fulfilling the law on our behalf.

What are the benefits of justification? Last study, we considered four: (1) unshakeable peace; (2) unfettered access; (3) unalterable hope; and (4) unparalleled joy. Here are three more.

Unconditional love (5:6-8)
Paul clearly has God triune in view in these verses. He speaks of the Father and the Spirit in 5:5. He speaks of the Father and the Son in 5:8. The Father is God, the Son is God, and the Spirit is God. Yet the Father isn't the Son, the Son isn't the Spirit, and the Spirit isn't the Father. That is to say, God is three distinct persons in one substance. It's a mystery—a cause for wonder. We behold God triune at the dawn of the old creation: he creates through his Word by his Spirit. We behold God triune at the dawn of the new creation: Christ emerges from the water, the Spirit descends like a dove, and the Father declares, "This is my beloved Son in whom I am well pleased" (Matt. 3:17).

God's triunity is crucial for understanding his love. In a word, God is the object of his love. That means he's satisfied in himself. He doesn't need to love us, nor does he need us to love him. And that's precisely the kind of love we need. We need someone to love us who doesn't need us. It means we don't need to earn God's love. We don't need to merit God's love. We don't need to worry that God's love for us will change. We don't need to worry that God's love for us depends upon our performance.

Paul's point is that God shows this love. How? Christ died for us when we were "weak" (5:6), "ungodly" (5:6), "sinners" (5:8), and "enemies" (5:10). A few people might die for a good man. We see examples of this throughout human history. But who will die for an evil man? Christ reveals God's love for us in that he died for us even when we hated him.

George Swinnock writes,

> His name is love, his nature is love, all his expressions were love, all his actions were love. He preached love, his lips dropped love, he practiced love, he lived in love, he was sick with love; nay, he died for love. It was love that took upon him our nature; it was love that walked in our flesh; it was love that went up and down doing good; it was love that took our infirmities; it was love that gave sight to the blind, speech to the dumb, ears to the deaf, life to the dead; it was love that was hungry, thirsty, and weary; it was love that was in a bloody agony; it was love that was sorrowful unto his own death; it was love that was betrayed, apprehended, derided, scourged, condemned, crucified; it was love that had his head pierced with thorns, his back with cords, his hands and feet with nails, and his side with a spear. Love left a glorious crown, and love climbed a shameful cross.[1]

Untouchable confidence (5:9-10)

"Since, therefore, we have now been justified by his blood, much more shall we be saved by him from the wrath of God. For if while we were enemies we were reconciled to God by the death of his Son, much more, now that we are reconciled, shall we be saved by his life." How can I be certain that God won't give up on me? I'm a failure. How can I be certain that God won't change his mind? Paul presents two arguments to make a single point. Both arguments hinge on the expression "much more." This expression is the key because it tells us that Paul is reasoning from the greater to the lesser. We reason like this all the time. He ran a marathon last month so he won't have any trouble walking around the block. He completed his college degree in mathematics so he won't have any trouble counting the eggs in the carton. Here are the two arguments.

First, Christ saved us while we were sinners (5:10). How "much more" will he keep us saved now that we're his friends!

Second, Christ saved us by his death (5:9). How "much more" will he keep us saved by his life!

---

[1] George Swinnock, *The Works of George Swinnock* (Edinburgh: Banner of Truth, 1992), 1:199.

"Prone to wander, Lord I feel it. Prone to leave the God I love."[2] But here's a precious truth. Our justification before God doesn't depend on our performance, but Christ's performance. Our preservation in the way doesn't depend on our effort, but Christ's effort. Our arrival home doesn't depend on our ability, but Christ's ability. He guides us all the way. He feeds us with heavenly manna. He protects us in ways we aren't even aware. He heals us when we're wounded. He carries us when we're ill. He bears patiently with our weaknesses. Why? He loves us.

Unmatched blessedness (5:11)
"More than that, we also rejoice in God through our Lord Jesus Christ, through whom we have now received reconciliation." This marks the third time Paul uses the expression "we rejoice." Here it reaches a crescendo. Formerly, God was a cause of dread. But now, he's a cause of exultation. We exult in his glorious grace in saving us. We exult in his glorious faithfulness in keeping us. We exult in his glorious power in enlivening us. We exult in his glorious wisdom in changing us. We exult in his glorious love.

Conclusion
God alone is blessedness, and this is what Christ has purchased for us. "For Christ also suffered once for sins, the righteous for the unrighteous, that he might bring us to God" (1 Peter 3:18). When we come to him through Christ, he becomes ours. His power is ours to protect us; his wisdom is ours to direct us; his mercy is ours to pity us; his grace is ours to pardon us; his love is ours to refresh us; his joy is ours to satisfy us. On top of all this, He's "our God forever and ever" (Ps. 48:14). He isn't our God for a day, week, month, or year, but "forever and ever." He isn't our God for a thousand years, but "forever and ever." He isn't our God for a million years, but "forever and ever." Truly we can say, "Blessed are the people to whom such blessings fall! Blessed are the people whose God is the LORD" (Ps. 144:15).[3]

---

[2] Robert Robinson, "Come Thou Fount of Every Blessing" in *Hymns of Grace* (Los Angeles: The Master's Seminary Press, 2015), 104.

[3] I am indebted to George Swinnock for his insights in *The Works of George Swinnock*, 4:508.

26
The Tale of Two Adams (5:12-19)

In this study, we arrive at 5:12-19. Admittedly, these are difficult verses. Nevertheless, I want to encourage you to strive to understand them. Why? If we don't understand these verses, we'll never understand the doctrine of original sin, the doctrine of justification, or the doctrine of sanctification. In other words, we'll never truly understand the gospel. And if we don't grow in our understanding of the gospel, we'll never grow in maturity as Christians. To help us, I want to look at three things.

The context
To set the context for these verses, we need to return to 1:17, where Paul quotes Habakkuk 2:4, "But the righteous shall live by faith." What does he mean by that? His explanation begins in the first section, *Condemnation* (1:18-3:20), with a description of man's condition. The Gentiles suppress God's General Revelation. The Jews suppress God's Special Revelation. To sum up, there's none righteous, none who understands, none who seeks for God, none who does any good, and none who fear God. Paul proceeds to explain the good news in the second section, *Justification* (3:21-5:21). By dying, Christ satisfied God's justice, thereby appeasing God's wrath and securing God's mercy. On that basis, God justifies those who believe in Christ. He forgives them their sin, and he imputes Christ's righteousness to them.

Near the end of this second section (5:12-21), Paul summarizes everything he has said thus far in this epistle by affirming that, when it comes to humanity, there are two federal heads (or, representatives). At the head of the old humanity stands Adam. All of Adam's descendants are condemned in him. At the head of the new humanity stands Christ. All of Christ's descendants are justified in him. In other words, union with Christ is the basis of justification. We're justified by grace alone through faith alone in Christ alone.

In 5:12-21, Paul also summarizes everything he's about to say in this epistle. In the third section, *Sanctification* (6:1-8:39), he unfolds the relationship between these two blessings of the covenant. By justification, God declares his people righteous. By sanctification, he makes his people righteous. This work of sanctification is twofold. First, it involves the mortification of the old man—what we were in Adam. Second, it involves the vivification of the new man—what we are in Christ.

Therefore, just as union with Christ is the key to justification, it's also the key to sanctification. Arguably, that makes 5:12-21 the most important passage in the entire epistle. Almost everything must be understood in relation to it. So, that's the context.

The structure

The structure of these verses is tricky. At this point, the AV is the most helpful translation in determining the flow of Paul's argument. In 5:12, Paul initiates a comparison with the words *just as*. Obviously, the words *even so* complete the comparison. The problem is we don't find those words in 5:13-17. They don't appear until 5:18. That means 5:13-17 are an interruption in Paul's main argument. The AV makes this perfectly clear by placing 5:13-17 in brackets.

How do we account for this interruption? At the end of 5:12, Paul makes a statement that requires some clarification—"because all sinned." He proceeds to explain it in 5:13-14. At the end of 5:14, Paul makes another statement that requires some clarification—"a type of him who was to come." He proceeds to explain it in 5:15-17. So, in 5:13-17, we have two parentheses. Paul includes them to clarify some of his comments. Having done so, he returns in 5:18-19 to complete the comparison he introduced in 5:12. Then, in 5:20-21, Paul builds on a statement he made in 5:13 concerning the law. So, that's the structure.

The content

For the moment, we're going to limit our study to 5:12, 18-19. Please notice four phrases in 5:12. (1) "Just as sin came into the world through one man." The term "came" means invaded. The term "world" refers to humanity (3:6, 19). So, what's Paul's point? Simply this: sin invaded humanity through Adam. (2) "And death through sin." The term "death" refers to separation from God. It was the punishment for Adam's sin. (3) "And so death spread to all men." In other words, the punishment for Adam's sin passed to all humanity. (4) "Because all sinned." The words "all sinned" refer to a single act, in which all participated; that is, Adam's sin. This explains why death spread to all men—we're all guilty of original sin.

In this verse, therefore, Paul establishes the fact that Adam's sin impacted his descendants. Paul begins with the words "just as." That's significant, because it initiates a comparison. Paul is saying that just as Adam's sin impacted his descendants, even so ... what exactly? Paul doesn't complete the comparison until 5:18-19, where he states, "Therefore, as one trespass led to condemnation for all men, so one act of righteousness leads to justification and life for all men. For as by the one man's disobedience the many were made sinners, so by the one man's obedience the many will be made *[constituted]* righteous."

So, what's Paul's point? Simply this: there are two federal heads (or, representatives). (1) There's the *first* Adam: Adam. He's the federal head of all his descendants: the old humanity. Through his one transgression, there resulted condemnation to all men. That means God reckons (or, imputes) Adam's disobedience (or, unrighteousness) to his descendants. His sin is their sin, his guilt is their guilt, and his condemnation is their condemnation. (2) There's the *last* Adam: Christ. He's the federal head of all his descendants: the new humanity. Through his one act of righteousness, there resulted justification of life to all men. That means God reckons (or, imputes) Christ's obedience (or, righteousness) to his descendants. His righteousness is their righteousness.

This paradigm is known as "federal (or, covenant) theology." How does God reckon Adam's sin to his descendants? How does God reckon Christ's righteousness to his descendants? He does so by way of covenant. To begin with, God established a covenant with Adam as the head of the old humanity. It's called the "covenant of works" or "covenant of creation." In it, God promised life to Adam if he obeyed. In failing to keep that covenant, Adam brought condemnation upon himself and his descendants. Everyone has broken that covenant in him. Therefore, everyone is under the curse: death. But praise God! Why? There's another covenant: the covenant of grace. According to it, God graciously accepts Christ's perfect obedience on behalf of those who believe in Christ. Christ has fulfilled the covenant of works on behalf of his people: the new humanity. That means Christians are no longer in Adam (under the covenant of works) because they have been united with Christ (under the covenant of grace), who has fulfilled the covenant of works on their behalf.

Conclusion
That's the substance of the comparison in 5:12, 18-19. What do we learn from it?

First, *it teaches us the evil nature of sin*. Paul says, "Just as sin came into the world through one man" (5:12). By one man's sin, sin invaded humanity. We saw that back in 3:10–18. There's none who understands. There's none who seeks for God. There's none who does any good. Now, we know the reason why. Adam passed his corrupt human nature to us. If you aren't saved, that's the starting point. You must see your sinful state before God. You must see your absolute dependence upon God's grace. You must see that your only hope is Christ. If you're saved, that's still your reference point. We must never lose sight of what we were before God saved us. That alone will cause us to depend upon his sustaining grace.

Second, *it teaches us the mortal nature of sin*. Paul says, "Death spread to all men because all sinned" (5:12). By one man's sin, all of humanity was condemned to death. Hypothetically speaking, if you were born yet never sinned, you would still die. Why? "As by one man's disobedience the many were made *[constituted]* sinners" (5:18). God reckoned Adam's sin to you. Adam committed one sin, and yet that one sin resulted in the death of every human being. That means sin is serious. To that one sin, add your lifetime of sin. If one sin merited death for the entire human race, what does my lifetime of sin merit?

Third, *it teaches us the absolute necessity of union with Christ*. By nature, I'm under the covenant of works. I owe God perfect obedience. But I can't do what God requires. I need someone to do it for me. I need Christ, who has fulfilled the covenant of works. Therefore, I need to be united to him, so that his righteousness is reckoned to me. Are you in Christ? Have you been united with him? "And there is salvation in no one else, for there is no other name under heaven given among men by which we must be saved" (Acts 4:12).

27
The Reign of Death (5:13-17)

We've considered 5:12, 18-19. We've seen that, in his dealings with humanity, God has appointed two federal heads (or, representatives). Adam stands at the head of his seed: the old humanity. Christ stands at the head of his seed: the new humanity. Adam's "one trespass led to condemnation for all men"; but Christ's "one act of righteousness leads to justification and life for all men." By Adam's "disobedience the many were made sinners"; but by Christ's "obedience the many will be made righteous." That's federal (or, covenant) theology. (1) There's the covenant of works (or, creation). God made it with Adam as the head of the old humanity. In it, God promised life to Adam if he obeyed. By disobeying, Adam brought condemnation upon himself and his descendants. (2) There's the covenant of grace. In it, God graciously accepts Christ's perfect obedience on behalf of those who believe in Christ. That means Christians are no longer in Adam (under the covenant of works) because they have been united with Christ (under the covenant of grace), who has fulfilled the covenant of works on their behalf.

Now let's return to 5:12-19 in order to fill in the gap—the two parentheses in 5:13-17.

The first parenthesis (5:13-14)
In the first, Paul explains what he means by the last statement in 5:12, "because all sinned." In short, God gave a commandment to Adam in the garden. He gave the law to Moses at Sinai. All those who lived between these two events died. Here's the question: If "sin is not counted where there is no law," then why did all those people die? When Paul says, "sin is not counted," he doesn't mean God turned a blind eye to their sin. He means God didn't reckon their sin as transgression. Why not? Simply because they didn't have any expressed commandments to transgress, since the law didn't come until Sinai. Therefore, their "sinning was not like the transgression of Adam." Nevertheless, they died. Why? They were guilty of transgressing God's commandment to Adam. Why? God reckoned Adam's disobedience to all his posterity. That, therefore, is the meaning of the phrase "because all sinned" at the end of 5:12.

Let me sum it up as follows:

Fact #1: "Sin indeed was in the world before the law was given." That's obvious. We see it in Cain's murder of Abel. We see it in God's assessment of humanity at the time of the flood. We see it in the destruction of Sodom and Gomorrah. We see it in the lives of the patriarchs. We see it in Jacob's sons.

Fact #2: "But sin is not counted where there is no law." If there's no law, there's no punishment. You can't be charged, arrested, and imprisoned for something that isn't forbidden by law.

Fact #3: "Yet death reigned from Adam to Moses, even over those whose sinning was not like the transgression of Adam." God gave a commandment to Adam and the law to Moses. Death reigned between the two, meaning there must have been a law. People hadn't sinned "like the transgression of Adam," but they had transgressed God's commandment to Adam.

Therefore, everyone sinned in Adam. Universal death demonstrates universal guilt, which demonstrates universal sin.

The second parenthesis (5:15-17)

In the second parenthesis, Paul explains what he means by the last statement in 5:14, "a type of the one who was to come." The term "type" implies that Adam prefigured another: Christ. That's confirmed in 1 Corinthians 15:45, where Paul writes, "Thus it is written, 'The first man Adam became a living being'; the last Adam became a life-giving spirit." In the context of 5:12-19, Adam is a type of Christ, in that he stands at the head of all those who are one with him, whereas Christ stands at the head of all those who are one with him. God reckons the "act" of each respective head to all who are united with that head. And so, God reckons Adam's disobedience to all his descendants. Similarly, he reckons Christ's obedience to all his descendants. That's the similarity.

However, Paul wants to convey to his readers that Adam and Christ aren't exactly the same. He says, "The free gift is not like the trespass" (5:15). Why not? He gives at least four reasons. (1) They differ in their *essence* (5:15). Adam's trespass resulted in "death"—the natural result of his disobedience. In other words, it was deserved. However, Christ's free gift resulted in "grace"—the supernatural result of his obedience. In other words, it was undeserved. (2) They differ in their *end* (5:16). Adam's trespass resulted in "condemnation." However, Christ's free gift resulted in "justification." (3) They differ in their *extent* (5:16). It was Adam's "one trespass" that led to condemnation. In other words, we don't need to commit any additional sin in our lifetime in order to deserve God's condemnation. We're condemned because of Adam's sin. However, Christ's free gift, "following many trespasses," led to justification That means Christ had to die for all violations of God's law committed throughout human history—not just Adam's sin. (4) They differ in their *effect* (5:17). Adam's transgression resulted in the reign of "death." However, Christ's free gift resulted in the reign of "life."

Conclusion
That completes our exposition of 5:12-19. Before making a couple of remarks by way of application, I want to acknowledge the fact that many people object to my interpretation of these verses.

One objection is as follows: "You say everyone is condemned because of Adam's disobedience. Well, if you're consistent, that must mean everyone is saved by Christ's obedience. After all, isn't that what Paul says in 5:18? Doesn't Paul believe in universalism?"

No, Paul most certainly doesn't believe in universalism. That's obvious from a simple reading of 2:5-10. So, how do we explain what Paul says in 5:18? The answer hinges upon a proper understanding of the term *all*. How do the NT writers use the term *all*? They use it in three ways. (1) At times, it means "all without distinction"—that is, some of all sorts (e.g., Matt. 9:35; Mark 1:5; Luke 3:15; John 3:26; 8:2; 12:32; Acts 2:17; 10:12; 22:15; Rom. 14:2; 1 Cor. 9:22; 2 Cor. 3:2; Eph. 6:21; Phil. 4:13; 1 Tim. 2:1; Heb. 8:11). That's the most common use in the NT. (2) At times, it means "all without exception" (e.g., Col. 1:16-17). (3) At times, it means "all without exception within a defined group." In 5:18, Paul uses the term *all* in this third sense. He declares, "so one act of righteousness leads to justification and life for all men." Who are the "all men?" They're all those who are in Christ. In 1 Corinthians 15:22, Paul writes, "For as in Adam all die, so also in Christ shall all be made alive."

Another objection is this: "You say everyone is condemned because of Adam's disobedience. That seems to suggest I'm accountable for someone else's sin. That isn't fair."

My response is this: Who are we to judge what's fair? Whether it seems fair to you or me is irrelevant. Furthermore, we need to recognize the implications of rejecting the doctrine of original sin. If we reject the fact that "by the one man's disobedience the many were made *[constituted]* sinners," we must also reject the fact that "by the one man's obedience the many will be made righteous." If we don't believe in the imputation of Adam's sin, then we can't believe in the imputation of Christ's righteousness. In other words, we can't have a biblical doctrine of justification without a biblical doctrine of original sin. It's impossible.

In conclusion, I'd like to mention an important lesson we can take from these verses. It's this: *they show us that the essence of salvation is union with Christ*. At the incarnation, God the Son united himself with his people in their humanity. He fulfilled all righteousness on their behalf. He was crucified, buried, raised, and exalted on their behalf; now, he intercedes on their behalf. From the right hand of the Majesty on High, he has sent forth the Holy Spirit by whom we're made one with him. Through that union, we enter into the privileges and blessings of the covenant of grace. Above all else, Christ's righteousness becomes ours. That should encourage us. We're saved for one reason and one reason alone—we're one with Christ.

Christ died for my sins—he bore each of my sins in his body on the cross. God treats Christ as if he had committed all my sins. It was not my general sin that was charged to Christ, but my particular sins. He died for Noah's drunkenness. He died for Abraham's deceit. He died for Lot's debauchery. He died for Jacob's stubbornness. He died for Moses' anger. He died for Rahab's harlotry. He died for Samson's unfaithfulness. He died for Gideon's foolishness. He died for David's adultery. He died for Hezekiah's pride. He died for Thomas' doubt. He died for Peter's denial. He died for Paul's violence.

We must strive to see the completeness of justification in Christ. All of our sins were placed on him. No sin was exempt. No sin was forgotten. No sin escaped notice. Not the least of our sins was left off the long list which Christ had with him upon the cross. This truth should bring us to a deep sense of the wonder of Christ's redeeming love.

28
Super Abounding Grace (5:20-21)

In 5:12-19, Paul makes a comparison. There are two men: Adam and Christ. There are two humanities: those in Adam (physical descendants) and those in Christ (spiritual descendants). There are two actions: Adam's disobedience and Christ's obedience. There are two results: condemnation for those in Adam and justification for those in Christ. There are two covenants: the covenant of works and the covenant of grace.

Just as Adam is the head of his people, so Christ is the head of his people. Just as Adam's disobedience is counted to his people, so Christ's obedience is counted to his people. Just as Adam's people are condemned in him, so Christ's people are justified in him. Just as Adam's people incur death through him, so Christ's people incur life through him.

Now, this comparison begs a question. If the entire plan of redemption rests on these two men, two humanities, two actions, two results, and two covenants, then why did God give the law? What purpose does it serve? Paul answers this question in 5:20-21.

The law came in to increase the trespass (5:20)
"Now the law came in to increase the trespass." Paul is referring here to a particular moment in human history: Sinai. Was there no law before Sinai? There was. God has written the law upon our hearts (2:15). Everyone knows murder is wrong, adultery is wrong, lying is wrong. We might suppress our knowledge of God's law, but when we do we're acting contrary to what we know is true. When Paul says the law entered, he's referring to the time when God actually wrote it down (Deut. 9:10). Until then, people sinned. They knew they were sinners. They were accountable for their sin. However, their sin wasn't reckoned to them as transgression because there was no law to transgress. That changed at Sinai. There, God gave detailed commandments. He did so in order to "increase the trespass." How does the law do that?

The law increases our knowledge of sin

In 3:20, Paul says, "Through the law comes knowledge of sin." In 7:7, he says, "If it has not been for the law, I would not have known sin." The law reveals what it means to sin. That's true; however, Paul seems to be saying more than that. He isn't merely saying that we know what it means to sin, but that we know sin. How?

First, the law shows us the nature of sin. In the first commandment, God says, "You shall have no other gods before me" (Exod. 20:3). That summarizes the first table of the law. In the tenth commandment, God says, "You shall not covet" (Exod. 3:17). That summarizes the second table of the law. So, these two commandments summarize the entire Decalogue. Christ confirms that fact in Matthew 22:36–40, stating, "You shall love the Lord your God with all your heart and with all your soul and with all your mind." That's another way of saying, "You shall have no other gods before me." Christ also says, "You shall love your neighbor as yourself." That's another way of saying, "You shall not covet." That means the essence of the law is love. To obey God is to love God. To disobey God is to hate God. The law proves it. You see, sin isn't primarily what I do, but what I am. There's none who understands (3:11). There's none who seeks after God (3:11). There's none who does good (3:12). As C.H. Spurgeon says, "Man is fallen: every part and passion of his nature is perverted: he has gone astray altogether, is sick from the crown of his head to the soles of his feet; yea, is dead in trespasses and sins and corrupt before God."[1]

Second, the law shows us the power of sin. God commands, "You shall have no other gods before me." I can't do that. I have all sorts of gods in my life. God commands, "You shall not covet." I can't do that. I covet all sorts of things. Why? I'm in the power of sin's grip. In 8:7, Paul writes, "The mind that is set on the flesh is hostile to God, for it does not submit to God's law; indeed, it cannot." As Christ makes clear, "Everyone who practices sin is a slave to sin" (John 8:34).

The law increases our desire for sin

By nature, we're attracted to what we know is wrong. If you prohibit a child from doing something, you create a greater desire in that child to do it than if you'd remained silent. How do you get teenagers to do what you want? You

---

[1] C.H. Spurgeon, *The Metropolitan Tabernacle Pulpit*, vol. 21 (London: Passmore & Alabaster, 1876); quoted in A.W. Pink, *The Doctrine of Human Depravity*, 138.

tell them to do the opposite of what you want. I have done things in my life simply because I knew they were wrong. I still remember the first time I was warned against touching my tongue against anything metal when it's cold outside. What did I do later that same day? I licked the posts of my hockey net while playing street hockey. I never would have done that if I hadn't been told not to.

Our depraved nature inclines us toward what we know is wrong. God gave the law "to increase the trespass" (5:20). The law reveals God's will. The law tells us what's expected of us. In so doing, it challenges the one thing that's so precious to us—our autonomy. That was a large part of the fall. God told Adam and Eve to refrain from eating the fruit of the tree of the knowledge of good and evil. Satan approaches Eve. What does he promise? He promises self-autonomy. "You shall be like God." That's all she had to hear.

We secretly resent being told what to do. Therefore, we secretly delight in transgressing God's law. That's exactly what Paul says back in 1:32, "Though they know God's righteous decree that those who practice such things deserve to die, they not only do them but give approval to those who practice them."

A burden
All told, the purpose of the law is to increase our awareness of sin. This is powerfully illustrated in John Bunyan's *Pilgrim's Progress*.

> As I walked through the wilderness of this world, I lighted on a certain place, where was a Den, and I laid me down in that place to sleep: And as I slept, I dreamed a dream. I dreamed, and behold I saw a Man clothed with rags, standing in a certain place, with his face from his own house, a Book in his hand, and a great Burden upon his back. I looked, and saw him open the Book, and read therein; and as he read, he wept and trembled; and not being able longer to contain, he broke out with a lamentable cry, saying, What shall I do?[2]

Pilgrim reads from a book. In response to what he reads, he trembles. Why? What has he read? The law. He knows he has broken God's law. He knows he has disobeyed God. He knows he has offended God. And so, he feels the weight of his sin. That's the burden upon his back. How does he react? He cries, "What shall I do?" At that moment, all else pales in comparison to his desire to be free from the burden of his sin. Again, what brought him to that

---

[2] Bunyan, *Pilgrim's Progress*, 1.

place? The answer is the law. And that's what Paul describes in 5:20, "The law came in to increase the trespass."

Where sin increased, grace abounded all the more (5:20)

The more sin is known the more grace is known. Are you familiar with *The Hunchback of Notre Dame* by Victor Hugo? Quasimodo lives in the cathedral tower. He falls in love with a gypsy girl, Esmeralda. When she's wrongly accused of murder, he rescues her from the gallows, and hides her in the cathedral tower. At one point, he begins to cry in front of Esmeralda. She asks him why he's crying. He replies, "I never knew how ugly I was until I saw how beautiful you are." Unrest makes us appreciate peace. Sickness makes us appreciate health. Drought makes us appreciate rain. Noise makes us appreciate quiet. Isolation makes us appreciate friends. Thirst makes us appreciate water. So too, God's law makes us appreciate God's grace.

Again, this is illustrated in John Bunyan's *The Pilgrim's Progress*:

> Now I saw in my dream, that the highway up which Christian was to go, was fenced on either side with a wall, and that wall was called *Salvation*. Up this way therefore did burdened Christian run, but not without great difficulty, because of the load on his back. He ran thus till he came at a place somewhat ascending, and upon that place stood a cross, and a little below, in the bottom, a sepulcher. So I saw in my dream, that just as Christian came up with the cross, his burden loosed from off his shoulders, and fell from off his back, and began to tumble, and so continued to do, till it came to the mouth of the sepulcher, where it fell in, and I saw it no more.[3]

Again, what's the burden upon Pilgrim's back? It's the weight of his sin. He feels guilty. Why? He has read the book—God's law. He knows God's will. He knows he has disobeyed God. He knows he has offended God. So, he runs to the cross. What happens? "His burden is loosed from off his shoulders." The sepulcher (or, grave) swallows it up. Later, three shining ones appear to Christian. The first says, "Thy sins be forgiven." How? His sin is reckoned to Christ at the cross, where he paid its penalty. The second strips him of his rags and clothes him with new garments. How? Christ's righteousness is reckoned to him. The third sets a seal upon his forehead. How? This is the sealing with "the promised Holy Spirit" (Eph. 1:13). These three constitute the doctrine

---

[3] Bunyan, *Pilgrim's Progress*, 35-36.

of justification.

And that's what Paul has in mind in 5:20. The law increases the trespass. As a result, sin increases. However, that isn't the end of the story. Paul says, "Where sin increased, grace abounded all the more." What does he mean? He explains exactly what he has in mind in Galatians 3:24, "So then, the law was our guardian until Christ came, in order that we might be justified by faith." It works as follows. I read God's law. As a result, I see my sin and my sinfulness. I see the nature of my sin; it permeates me. I see the power of my sin; it controls me. That's why God gave the law. As Martin Luther says, "These precepts are given that proud and blind man might, by them, learn the disease of his own *spiritual* impotency."[4] I'm humbled by my inadequacy and my inability. I'm conscious of my sin, mindful of my need, and ready for help. I find that help in Christ, who "died for the ungodly" (5:6). When I believe in Christ, God reckons Christ's righteousness to me. In that way, the law leads me to Christ "in order that [I] might be justified by faith."

Three times, Paul says that death reigned in Adam (5:14, 17, 21). Paul uses kingdom terminology because he wants us to think in terms of a tyrannical dictator with absolute control. That's life in Adam. Death reigns because sin reigns. It strikes anyone anytime anywhere. There's no escape. But Paul gives us the good news. (1) Grace reigns. God breaks death's tyrannical control. (2) Grace reigns through righteousness. This is *how* God breaks death's tyrannical control. He does so in Christ. By faith, we become the righteousness of God. (3) Grace reigns through righteousness leading to eternal life. This is *why* God breaks death's tyrannical control. So that we might enjoy the glory of God's grace forever. What will it mean for finite creatures to experience the infinite glory of God?

Conclusion

What do we learn from this verse?

First, *we learn the true function of the law*. The covenant of works condemns. The covenant of grace justifies. Where does the law fit? It came "to increase the trespass" (5:20). In one sense, the law is part of the covenant of works, in that it shows us our sin. In another sense, the law is part of the covenant of grace, in that it drives us to Christ. As Augustine explains, "The law ... was not given to make sinners alive—it is divine grace alone which by faith makes

---

[4] Martin Luther, *The Bondage of the Will*, in *Martin Luther's Works*, ed. H. T. Lehmann (Philadelphia: Fortress Press, 1960).

alive—but to show with what strong chains of sin those are bound and held captive by their own power."⁵ That's the role of the law.

Second, *we learn that true conversion is impossible without the law*. People must see their need before they'll turn to Christ. They only see their need in the law. One of the reasons the church is so superficial today is this: many professing believers have never come face-to-face with their sin as exposed by the law.

Third, *we learn that true evangelism is impossible without the law*. Many people regard sin light-heartedly because the law is rarely preached. Regarding this, R.C. Sproul writes,

> One of the leaders of the recent emerging church movement boasts that he has not mentioned the word "sin" in the last ten years of his preaching. He wants to make sure that his people will not feel crushed by guilt or by a loss of their self-esteem. When the acute awareness of guilt is removed from the conscience, there is no sense of the burden of sin. There is no sense of being under the crushing weight of the law of God that bears down upon our souls relentlessly.⁶

Fourth, *we learn that true worship is impossible without the law*. In Luke 7, we read about Christ's visit to the home of a Pharisee. There's a particular woman present—a "sinner." She weeps over Christ's feet, drying them with her hair. The Pharisee is offended that Christ doesn't shun her. How does Christ respond to the Pharisee? "I tell you, her sins, which are many, are forgiven—for she loved much. But he who is forgiven little, loves little." Christ's point is obvious. We only appreciate the heights of God's love in forgiving us when we appreciate the depths of our sin. That, in turn, causes us to worship.

In Mark 10, we find the story of the rich young ruler. He visits Christ, asking, "What must I do to inherit eternal life?" Christ responds by quoting six commandments—the law. The young man says, "Teacher, all these I have kept from my youth." Really? Christ says, "You lack one thing: go, sell all that you have and give to the poor, and you will have treasure in heaven; and come, follow me." Christ wasn't giving that young man something to do in order to inherit eternal life! Christ was correcting his misunderstanding of the law. When Christ says, "Sell all that you have and give to the poor," he's simply

---

⁵ Quoted in Luther, *Commentary on Romans*, 98.
⁶ R.C. Sproul, "Christian Loses His Burden" Ligonier Ministries, January 1, 2006. https://www.ligonier.org/learn/articles/christian-loses-his-burden.

reminding that young man of the foremost commandment. What is it? "You shall have no other gods before me." Or, "You shall love God with all your heart, soul, mind, and strength." Christ is telling that young man in no uncertain terms, "You haven't kept the law. You're an idolater. You love your money more than God. The law doesn't exist to tell you what you can do. The law exists to tell you what you can't do. The law exists to tell you what you are. You think you can keep the law. You think you've kept the law. You're mistaken. If you want eternal life, here's the starting point—you must understand who and what you are!" How does the young man respond? He goes away.

How many people are like that? Have you ever been humbled by God's law? Have you ever seen the true nature of your sin? Have you ever seen the absolute power of sin over you? Have you ever felt your helplessness before God? Have you ever believed in Christ?

> Marvelous Grace of our loving Lord,
> Grace that exceeds our sin and our guilt,
> Yonder on Calvary's mount outpoured,
> There where the blood of the lamb was spilt.[7]

---

[7] Julia Johnston, "Marvelous Grace of our Loving Lord" in *The Hymnal for Worship and Celebration*, 201.

29
The Struggle of Two Kingdoms (5:21)

What's a citizen? According to the Oxford Dictionary, a citizen is "a person who is legally recognized as a member of a country or city."

We're legally recognized as members of the country of Canada; therefore, we're citizens of Canada. That makes us different from citizens of other countries. We may differ politically; our form of government is very different from what's practiced in Saudi Arabia. We may differ culturally; our culture is very different from what's found in Mozambique. We may differ linguistically; our language is very different from what's spoken in Pakistan. Clearly, there are numerous factors that distinguish citizens of one country from another.

We're also legally recognized as members of a city—in my case, Cambridge. That makes us different from citizens of other cities. We're different from the citizens of London (England) or Harare (Zimbabwe) or Moscow (Russia). Again, there are numerous factors that distinguish citizens of one city from another.

In the early fifth century, there was a man named Augustine. He was the bishop of Hippo in North Africa. He wrote numerous books, including *The City of God*. In it, he describes the history of two cities: the city of man and the city of God. The difference between the citizens of these two cities isn't found in their language, culture, or anything like that. The difference is found in their love. They love different things. According to Augustine, the citizens of the city of man possess an "earthly love of self" and "contempt of God" whereas the citizens of the city of God possess a "heavenly love of God" and "contempt of self." In other words, the citizens of the city of man love self and hate God whereas the citizens of the city of God love God and hate self.

What is "self?" We find it in Satan's words to Eve: "God knows that when you eat of it your eyes will be opened, and you will be like God, knowing good and evil" (Gen. 3:5). God tells Adam and Eve not to eat from the tree of the knowledge of good and evil. He doesn't give a reason. Satan lies to Adam and Eve, telling them that the reason God doesn't want them to eat from this tree is because he doesn't want them to become like him. Satan had fallen as a result of his desire to be like God. Now, he encourages Adam and Eve to desire the same thing: "You will be like God." In effect, he says, "Just think about it. You will be completely autonomous. You will be free from God. You will be happy without God. You will be God of your own life." That's *self*!

And so, there's the city of man, consisting of those who love self and hate God. And there's the city of God, consisting of those who love God and hate self. The existence of these two cities is prophesied in Genesis 3:15, where God declares, "I will put enmity between you and the woman, and between your offspring and her offspring." The seed of the serpent is the city of man. The seed of the woman is the city of God. God says that he will put enmity between the seed of the serpent (city of man) and the seed of the woman (city of God). The city of man is man-centred. The city of God is God-centred. Therefore, they have competing values and goals. The city of man seeks to exalt and glorify man, whereas the city of God seeks to exalt and glorify God. As a result, there's conflict between the two.

That conflict erupts in Genesis 4, where we read that Cain murders Abel. Cain gives rise to the city of man. That city is traceable throughout human history. In the Bible, it's typified in the cities of Babylon and Rome. It's the world—ungodly society, seeking to live without God. Abel is replaced with Seth, who gives rise to the city of God. That city is also traceable throughout human history. It's all those in Christ. We have Seth's godly line to Noah. Then, we have the patriarchs. Then, we have the believing remnant within the nation of Israel. Then, we have the New Testament church. That's God's household—the city of God. Since the time of Cain and Abel, these two cities have been at enmity.

That brings us to 5:21, where Paul writes, "So that, as sin reigned in death, grace also might reign through righteousness leading to eternal life through Jesus Christ our Lord." Here, we have two kingdoms.

The reign of sin in death

On the one hand, we have the reign of sin in death. In 5:14 Paul says, "Death reigned from Adam to Moses." In 5:17, he says, "Death reigned through that one man." Three times, therefore, Paul uses "kingdom" terminology to stress the fact that sin and death reign over those in Adam. That means sin is their king, Lord, or master. As Christ says, "Everyone who practices sin is a slave of sin" (John 8:34). That kingdom began at the time of man's fall in the garden. It's epitomized in four things we read about Cain in Genesis 4.

First, Cain offers an unacceptable sacrifice to God (Gen. 4:1-7). Abel

The Struggle of Two Kingdoms (5:21)

offers his sacrifice by faith (Heb. 11:4). That means he trusts in God and his promise to send a Saviour. He obeys God by bringing a blood sacrifice. Cain, however, doesn't offer his sacrifice by faith. He doesn't trust in God. He disobeys God by refusing to bring a blood sacrifice. As a result, God rebukes Cain. Cain responds by becoming angry. Who's the object of his anger? God.

Second, Cain murders his own brother (Gen. 4:8-9). What drives him to do that? John tells us: "Because his deeds were evil and his brother's righteous" (1 John 3:11-12). Cain is angry with God. Cain's anger extends to Abel because he's a living reminder to Cain of God. When the opportunity arises, he murders his brother.

Third, Cain refuses to repent (Gen. 4:10-15). God calls Cain to account for murdering Abel. Cain's response is callous: "Am I my brother's keeper?" In other words, "What do I care?" Cain doesn't feel any remorse whatsoever. God judges Cain. How does Cain respond? He complains, "My punishment is too great to bear!" Cain thinks he's the victim. He disobeys God by offering an unacceptable sacrifice. He murders his brother. Through all that, God shows tremendous patience. Yet, Cain refuses to acknowledge any wrongdoing. He refuses to repent.

Fourth, Cain goes out from God's presence (Gen. 4:16-24). In other words, he's totally removed from fellowship with God. He settles in the land of Nod. The term *Nod* signifies "wandering." How fitting! Cain loses contact with God—the One who's great in lovingkindness, whose greatness is unsearchable, whose mercies are over all his works, whose acts are mighty, whose splendor is glorious, whose works are wonderful, and whose goodness is abundant (Ps. 145:3-9).

That's the reign of sin in death. And that's the city of man.

The reign of grace through righteousness to eternal life
On the other hand, we have the reign of grace through righteousness to eternal life (5:21). Paul uses a similar expression in 5:17, "Those who receive the abundance of grace and the free gift of righteousness [will] reign in life through the one man Jesus Christ." The reign of grace consists of those who are in Christ. Please notice that it's through righteousness. That means God's righteousness has been satisfied in Christ, and God has graciously reckoned Christ's perfect righteousness to all those who believe in him. What do these citizens of the city of God look like? Turning again to the opening chapters of Genesis, we find three marks.

THE OBEDIENCE OF FAITH

They're aware of God's greatness
Adam and Eve have another child after Cain kills Abel. They name him "Seth." Why? "God has appointed me another offspring in place of Abel" (Gen. 4:25). That statement reveals God's greatness in three ways. (1) God's greatness is seen in the fact that he gives life: "God has appointed me another offspring." Paul declares, "God himself gives to all mankind life and breath and everything" (Acts 17:25). He's the Creator. He's the source of all life, because he "has life in himself" (John 5:26). That means he's self-existent. What a great God! (2) God's greatness is seen in the fact that he remains faithful: "God has appointed me another offspring in place of Abel." Cain killed Abel. Here's the seed of the serpent waging war against the seed of the woman. But it isn't the end. God made a promise. And so, he gives Seth in place of Abel, thereby demonstrating his faithfulness. He always does what he promises. Why? "I the LORD do not change" (Mal. 3:6). That means he's immutable. What a great God! (3) God's greatness is seen in the fact that he controls events: "God has appointed me another offspring in place of Abel, for Cain killed him." God permitted Cain to kill Abel. God gave Seth to Adam and Eve. Was God in control of the situation? Most certainly. God works all things according to the counsel of his will. He declares, "I will accomplish all my pleasure" (Isa. 46:10). What a great God!

In short, God is a great God who performs great works. Elihu declares, "God thunders wondrously with his voice; he does great things that we cannot comprehend" (Job 37:5). The citizens of the city of God grasp that.

They're aware of man's smallness
Seth has a son. He calls him "Enosh," meaning "frail" or "mortal" (Gen. 4:26). Why? He knows man is dust. After the fall, God declares to Adam: "You are dust, and to dust you shall return" (Gen. 3:19). In Genesis 5, we have a genealogy from Seth to Noah. Eight times, we find this statement: "he died." I think God is trying to tell us something: "You're dust!" Seth understands. And he calls his son "mortal." We're all mortal. That has three implications. (1) For starters, death is unavoidable. We will die. It may be a disease like cancer. It may be a car accident. It may be a heart attack. We don't know. It may strike us when we're eight or eighty. We don't know. We know this: it will happen. Some people act like it's never going to happen. Satan tries to convince people that life is long. "You have plenty of time," says he. It's a lie. "You are a mist that appears for a little while and then vanishes" (James 4:14).

The Struggle of Two Kingdoms (5:21)

(2) Next, death is uncontrollable. The preacher declares, "No man has power to retain the spirit, or power over the day of death" (Eccl. 8:8). God alone determines when we die: "Since his days are determined, and the number of his months is with you, and you have appointed his limits that he cannot pass" (Job 14:5). There's nothing we can do to avoid, delay, or escape it. (3) Lastly, death is unnatural. God didn't make us to die. Paul says, "The wages of sin is death" (Rom. 6:23). Death entered the world, because of Adam's sin.

Most people act like they'll live forever. Don Whitney shows the folly of this:

> In his dying words, the famous French infidel Voltaire said to his doctor, "I will give you half of what I am worth if you will give me six-months' life." So desperate were his cries when his time was gone that the nurse who attended him said, "For all the wealth in Europe I would not see another infidel die." Similarly, the last words of the English skeptic Thomas Hobbes were "If I had the whole world, I would give it to live one day."[1]

Too late! The citizens of the city of God don't make this mistake. They're aware of their mortality, stemming from their sinfulness. And they're aware of their smallness.

They call upon the name of the LORD

When people see God's greatness and their own smallness, they feel their need. As a result, they call upon God (Gen. 4:26). What a contrast to the city of man! Lamech proclaims, "If Cain is avenged sevenfold, then Lamech seventy-sevenfold." In other words, "I don't need God, and I don't want God." That's the cry of someone, who wants to be God of his own life. That's the cry of someone, who loves self and hates God. In sharp contrast, the citizens of the city of God call upon the name of the LORD. (1) This call is marked by humility. They know they're worthless. They know they deserve God's punishment. (2) This call is marked by sincerity. They know they're helpless. They know they can't do anything to impress God. (3) This call is marked by intensity. They know they're hopeless. They know their situation is desperate. They're not looking to try God on for size. They're not looking for a crutch or a charm. They're not looking for a therapist. They want God. Hence, they call

---

[1] Don Whitney, *Spiritual Disciplines for the Christian Life* (Colorado Springs: NavPress, 1991), 138.

upon the name of the LORD with intensity.

Conclusion

The history of God's people appears to be full of ups and downs. The reign of sin appears to triumph with Cain's murder of Abel, but God calls Seth. The reign of sin appears to triumph with man's apostasy, but God calls Noah. The reign of sin appears to triumph with the nations' rebellion at Babel, but God calls Abraham. The reign of sin appears to triumph with Israel's enslavement in Egypt, but God delivers Israel. The reign of sin appears to triumph with Israel's idolatry, but God preserves a remnant. The reign of sin appears to triumph with the Assyrian and Babylonian invasions, but God restores his people from captivity. The reign of sin appears to triumph with the crucifixion of Christ, but God raises him from the dead. The reign of sin appears to triumph at various junctures in the history of the church, but God preserves his people. And so it continues to this day.

We should be greatly encouraged because we know the final outcome of this struggle. As for the reign of sin and death (the city of man): "'Rejoice over her, O heaven, and you saints and apostles and prophets, for God has given judgment for you against her!' Then a mighty angel took up a stone like a great millstone and threw it into the sea, saying, 'So will Babylon the great city be thrown down with violence, and will be found no more'" (Rev. 18:20-21). As for the reign of grace through righteousness (the city of God), its destiny is quite different. Christ declares,

> The one who conquers, I will make him a pillar in the temple of my God. Never shall he go out of it, and I will write on him the name of my God, and the name of the city of my God, the new Jerusalem, which comes down from my God out of heaven, and my own new name. He who has an ear, let him hear what the Spirit says to the churches (Rev. 3:12-13).

Section 3:
Sanctification (6:1–8:39)

30
Union with Christ (6:1-23)

As we study Scripture in detail, we must never lose sight of the big picture. That's another way of saying that the individual parts must be interpreted in the context of the whole. That's particularly true in the case of Paul's epistle to the Romans. We must keep the overall context of the book in view as we interpret its individual parts. That makes review important. And that's where we're going to begin in this study. As you know, Paul states his main theme in 1:17, "But the righteous shall live by faith." From there, he explains what that means.

In his first major section, *Condemnation* (1:18-3:20), Paul takes us into God's courtroom to show us our need. He accuses us of suppressing the truth by our unrighteousness (1:18). The judge is God. The accused is humanity: Jew and Gentile. The witnesses are General and Special Revelation. The verdict is guilty: there's none righteous, none who understands, none who seeks after God, and none who does good (3:10-18). We're condemned.

In his second major section, *Justification* (3:21-5:21), Paul declares that God justifies sinners by grace alone through faith alone in Christ alone. He proves it by appealing to Abraham, who was justified apart from works, circumcision, and the law. In brief, "Abraham believed God, and it was counted to him as righteousness" (4:3). Then, Paul explains the result of justification. We have peace with God. Plus, we exult in hope of the glory of God, we exult in our tribulations, and we exult in God.

Still in this second section (5:12-21), Paul summarizes all that he has said thus far by affirming that there are two federal heads. (1) Adam is the head of the condemned. That's the old humanity. God established a covenant with Adam as the head of his descendants. God promised life to Adam if he obeyed. In failing to obey, Adam brought condemnation upon himself and his descendants. By his one transgression, there resulted condemnation to all men. By his disobedience, the many were made sinners. That's known as the covenant of works. (2) Christ is the head of the justified. That's the new humanity. God graciously accepts Christ's obedience on behalf of those who believe in him. By his one act of righteousness, there resulted justification and life to all men.

By his obedience, the many will be made righteous. That's known as the covenant of grace.

Now, the covenant of grace actually contains two blessings. The first is justification: the removal of the penalty of sin. That means God forgives us, imputing righteousness to us. The second is sanctification: the removal of the power of sin. That means God cleanses us, imparting righteousness to us. Both of these blessings belong to those who are in Christ.

In his third major section, *Sanctification* (6:1–8:39), Paul explains the second blessing in light of the first. He does so by way of three metaphors. In chapter 6, he describes two masters: sin and righteousness (6:18). The Christian is no longer enslaved to sin, but to righteousness. In chapter 7, he describes two marriages: law and grace (7:4). The Christian is no longer married to law, but to grace. In chapter 8, he describes two minds: flesh and Spirit (8:6). The Christian no longer walks according to the flesh, but according to the Spirit.

And that's more or less Paul's thought-flow in 1:17–8:39. With that general overview in place, we're in a good position to study chapters 6–8 in detail. Before we do, however, we need to make sure we grasp a central theme in these chapters. I'm referring to the doctrine of union with Christ.

The nature of union with Christ

We're in Christ. What does that mean? In the words of John Flavel, "It is an intimate conjunction of believers to Christ, by the imparting of his Spirit to them."[1] That's what Paul describes in 1 Corinthians 12:13, "For in one Spirit we were all baptized into one body." The Holy Spirit unites us to Christ, thereby making us one with him. There are three metaphors in the Bible that describe that union.

The first is in Ephesians 5:30-31, where Paul quotes Genesis 2:23-24, "Then the man said, 'This at last is bone of my bones and flesh of my flesh; she shall be called Woman, because she was taken out of Man.' Therefore a man shall leave his father and his mother and hold fast to his wife, and they shall become one flesh."

In these verses, we see three important features of the relationship between Adam and Eve. (1) Eve is taken out of Adam—out of his side. She is, therefore, flesh of his flesh and bone of his bones. Adam calls her "woman," which

---

[1] John Flavel, *The Works of John Flavel* (London: Banner of Truth, 1968), 2:37.

means: "taken out of man." That's important, because it shows that God didn't form Eve independent of Adam. On the contrary, her existence is contingent upon Adam. (2) Eve is brought to Adam. They're jointed together. And they become one flesh. In other words, God views the two as one. (3) Eve completes Adam. Prior to God's creation of Eve, "there was not found a helper fit for him" (Gen. 2:20). That means Adam lacked something: Eve. Once God created Eve, Adam was complete.

There are invaluable lessons here concerning the marriage relationship. That, however, is beyond the scope of our study. In Ephesians 5:32, Paul says, "This mystery is profound, and I am saying that it refers to Christ and the church." In other words, the conjugal union between husband and wife is a great mystery, however, Paul is speaking primarily of the relationship between Christ and his church. That means the union between Adam and Eve typifies the union between Christ and his church. How? (1) As Eve is taken out of Adam, so too the church is taken out of Christ—out of his side. The church is, therefore, flesh of his flesh and bone of his bones. In what sense is the church taken out of Christ's side? When Christ died, the soldier pierced his side with a spear. Water and blood flowed from that wound in his side. And that was the purchasing price for the church. In Ephesians 5:25, Paul says, Christ "loved the church and gave himself up for her." (2) As Eve is brought to Adam, so too the church is brought to Christ. They're joined together, becoming one flesh—one body. Christ is the head (Eph. 5:23). And we're the members (Eph. 5:30). How are we joined together? Paul provides the answer in 1 Corinthians 12:13, "For in one Spirit we were all baptized into one body." The Holy Spirit dwells in us, thereby uniting us to Christ and to every other member of Christ's mystical body. (3) As Eve completes Adam, so too the church completes Christ. In Ephesians 1:23, Paul says, we're "his body, the fullness of him who fills all in all." The church is the "fullness" of Christ. That doesn't mean Christ lacks something as the eternal Son of God. He's perfect and complete. It does mean that, as mediator, he's incomplete without his body.

The second metaphor is that of the head and its members (Eph. 5:25-32). Christ is the head of the body. And we're members of the body. This metaphor means that believers stand to Christ in the same relation as the members of a physical body stand to their head, and Christ stands to believers in the same relation as the head of a physical body stands to its members. What's this relationship? Body parts only have life because of their relationship to the head. If you remove a body part from that relationship, it ceases to live. It can't do anything on its own. I know someone who lost part of his finger a few years ago. The moment that piece of finger was disconnected from the body, it ceased to live. And that's the relationship that exists between Christ and the church. He's our head. He's our life.

The third metaphor is that of the vine and its branches (John 15:1-5). It conveys pretty much the same idea as that of the head and its members. Christ says, "I am the vine; you are the branches. Whoever abides in me and I in him, he it is that bears much fruit, for apart from me you can do nothing" (John 15:5). The idea is that of absolute dependence. We don't know very much about vines, but we all have trees in our yards. At times, we trim those trees. When we cut off a branch, what happens to it? It dies. Why? Its life is completely dependent upon its relationship to the trunk. The roots are nourished from the soil. That nourishment is transferred to the trunk. From there, it travels to the branches. Without that sap, the branches die. They don't possess life in and of themselves. Similarly, Christ is the vine, and we're the branches. There's a vital, organic union between him and us. We draw on his life through the Holy Spirit, who dwells in us.

Paul sums it all up like this: "I have been crucified with Christ. It is no longer I who live, but Christ who lives in me. And the life I now live in the flesh I live by faith in the Son of God, who loved me and gave himself for me" (Gal. 2:20). It's no longer I who live, but Christ lives in me! Christ has taken hold of me through his Spirit. And I have taken hold of Christ through faith. I'm in Christ. And he's my life.

The purpose of union with Christ
According to Ephesians 5:26-27, the purpose of this union is "that he might sanctify her, having cleansed her by the washing of water with the word, so that he might present the church to himself in splendor, without spot or wrinkle or any such thing, that she might be holy and without blemish." There are three important details in these verses.

First, Christ unites himself to his bride so that he might "sanctify" and "cleanse" her. The act of sanctifying is positive. It means he sets his bride apart for himself—for his service. The act of cleansing is negative. We cleanse whatever is dirty. Likewise, Christ cleanses his bride from the pollution of her sin.

Second, Christ accomplishes this cleansing "by the washing of water with the word." What's the word? Christ prays, "Sanctify them in the truth; your word is truth" (John 17:17). It's the Word of God. Christ says, "You are clean because of the word that I have spoken to you" (John 15:3). James says, "Of his own will he brought us forth by the word of truth, that we should be a kind of first fruits of his creatures" (James 1:18). Peter says, "Since you have been born again, not of perishable seed but of imperishable, through the living and abiding word of God" (1 Peter 1:23). There is, therefore, an inseparable link between cleansing and the Word.

Third, Christ's goal is to present his bride to himself, "without spot or wrinkle or any such thing, that she might be holy and without blemish." He cherishes us because we're members of his body (Eph. 5:29). For that reason, he sanctifies and cleanses us. His aim is simple: that we would be holy and blameless before him.

Conclusion

I want to conclude with the words of Martyn Lloyd-Jones: "If you have got hold of this idea you will have discovered the most glorious truth you will ever know in your life."[2] He's referring to the doctrine of union with Christ.

When we have a hold of it, it will stir our *faith*. Salvation is much more than forgiveness from sin and assurance of heaven. It's union with Christ. I was in Adam, under the covenant of works. I was enslaved to sin and death. I was part of the seed of the serpent (the city of man). Now, I'm in Christ, under the covenant of grace. That increases my faith.

When we have a hold of it, it will stir our *hope*. "In one Spirit we were all baptized into one body." That union has a purpose: so that Christ might sanctify us. That's something Christ does in order to present us before himself. "Now may the God of peace himself sanctify you completely, and may your whole spirit and soul and body be kept blameless at the coming of our Lord Jesus Christ. He who calls you is faithful; he will surely do it" (1 Thess. 5:23-24). That increases my hope.

When we have a hold of it, it will stir our *love*. Christ "loved the church and gave himself up for her." He loves his church in spite of her unworthiness, pollution, and rebellion. She's filthy, and needs cleansing. She's repugnant, and needs washing. He still loves her. He cherishes her as his own body. He wants the best for her. He won't be satisfied until she's perfect. He desires to put her on display for every creature to stare in wonder. He says, "You are

---

[2] Martyn Lloyd-Jones, *Romans 7:1-8:4* (Grand Rapids: Zondervan, 1973), 277.

altogether beautiful, my love; there is no flaw in you" (Cant. 4:7). If anything should increase our love for Christ, it's his love for us. With faith, hope, and love, we can truly sing,

> The church's one foundation is Jesus Christ her Lord.
> She is his new creation by water and the Word.
> From heaven he came and sought her to be his holy bride.
> With his own blood he bought her, and for her life he died.[3]

---

[3] Samuel Stone, "The Church's One Foundation" in *The Hymnal for Worship and Celebration*, 277.

31
A Death Certificate (6:1-10)

In 5:12-21, we arrive at the pinnacle of the letter, in which Paul makes a comparison. There are two men: Adam and Christ. There are two humanities: those in Adam (physical descendants) and those in Christ (spiritual descendants). There are two actions: Adam's disobedience and Christ's obedience. There are two results: condemnation for those in Adam and justification for those in Christ. Just as Adam is the head of his people, so Christ is the head of his people. Just as Adam's disobedience is counted to his people, so Christ's obedience is counted to his people. Just as Adam's people are condemned in him, so Christ's people are justified in him.

Let's imagine Paul has shared these truths with his audience, leaving them in stunned silence. As he makes his way down the street, he notices a man walking straight at him. He has his eyes fixed on Paul. "I want a word with you." Paul stops dead in his tracks. "I understand your teaching on justification, but I'm very concerned. This notion that our works don't contribute to our justification will result in moral laxity. It'll make people think they can live however they like." Paul opens his mouth to reply but stops when he hears someone else calling his name. He turns to see a man approaching him from across the street. This man has a woman (who isn't his wife) hanging on his arm. His nose is bright red and his eyes are glazed because he has been drinking all night at the local pub. "Paul, I just love your teaching on justification. It doesn't depend on my works. It doesn't matter how I live. I'm justified." Paul catches sight of the first man out of the corner of his eye. His eyebrows are raised as if to say: "This is precisely what I'm talking about."

How does Paul respond to these two men? We have his answer in 6:1-23. In 6:1-14, he says that those who are justified can't continue in sin, because they're free from sin. In 6:15-23, he says that those who are justified can't continue in sin because they're enslaved to righteousness. John Stott notes that these two answers parallel each other in five ways.[1] (1) In both, Paul begins by exalting God's grace (6:1,15). (2) In both, Paul asks the same question

---

[1] Stott, *Message of Romans*, 167-68.

concerning the relationship between sin and grace (6:1, 15). (3) In both, Paul gives the same response: "By no means!" (6:2, 15). In so doing, he distances himself from any suggestion that his doctrine of justification leads to antinomianism. (4) In both, Paul makes the same diagnosis: "Do you not know?" (6:3, 16). In other words, he appeals to knowledge. (5) In both, Paul stresses the discontinuity between union with Adam and union with Christ.

Baptism into Christ (6:1-5)
Paul begins in 6:1 by asking a question: "Are we to continue in sin that grace may abound?" To understand his question, we need to define his terms. (1) The term "continue" means "to stay with someone" or "to stay in one place." We see that in 1 Corinthians 16:7-8, where Paul writes, "For I do not want to see you now just in passing. I hope to spend some time with you, if the Lord permits. But I will stay *[continue]* in Ephesus until Pentecost." Evidently, the word conveys the idea of permanence. (2) The term "sin" is connected to the last verse of the preceding chapter—"sin reigned in death" (5:21). The reign of sin in death consists of all those who are in Adam. They're slaves to sin. In 6:1, therefore, "sin" isn't *actual* sin, but *inherent* sin—corrupt human nature.

Our definition of these terms is important because it demonstrates that in 6:1 Paul isn't talking about committing a sin; rather, he's talking about continuing in sin. His question is this: "Is it possible for a Christian to continue in sin?" Paul's answer is blunt: "By no means!" He tells us why in 6:2, "How can we who died to sin still live in it?" What does he mean by that?

According to one theory, Paul is suggesting that we're dead to sin, in that we're unresponsive to it. We're like a corpse that doesn't respond to any stimuli. There are a couple of problems with that theory. (1) It doesn't make any sense given Paul's exhortation in 6:11-13, "Consider yourselves dead to sin." If we're already dead (unresponsive) to sin, then why does Paul tell us to consider ourselves dead (unresponsive) to sin? That's difficult to grasp. (2) It doesn't make any sense in light of Christian experience. We know we aren't unresponsive (or, insensitive) to sin. On the contrary, it takes very little to tempt us to sin. I think it's worth inserting a pastoral note here. Perhaps you've struggled with the contents of this verse. Your struggle might go something like this: "If I'm dead (unresponsive) to sin, then why does it feel like sin is alive and well in me?" That can create a dilemma for many of us. I believe, however, that the dilemma stems from a faulty interpretation of what it means to be dead to sin.

So, what does Paul mean in 6:2 when he says we're "dead to sin?" I believe we find the answer in 6:10, where he says, "For the death he died he died to sin, once for all, but the life he lives he lives to God." That's Christ's death. How did Christ die to sin? Did Christ die to sin by becoming unresponsive to sin? No, that wouldn't make any sense. Christ died to sin by bearing its penalty. In other words, Christ's death to sin wasn't *moral*, but *legal*. And that's what Paul means in 6:2. We're "dead to sin," because we're united with Christ, who bore its penalty. We're dead to sin—legally.

Paul expands on all that in 6:3-5 by explaining that we've been "baptized into Christ Jesus." In Galatians 3:27, Paul comments, "For as many of you as were baptized into Christ have put on Christ." That means we're one with him. Because we're one with him, what's his is ours. That means his death is ours: "we have been united with him in a death like his" (6:5). And it means his life is ours: "we shall certainly be united with him in a resurrection like his" (6:5). In 6:6-7, Paul explains the first. In 6:8-10, he explains the second.

The significance of Christ's death (6:6-7)
In 6:6-7, Paul explains the significance of Christ's death for those who are in union with him. First, we know "that our old self was crucified with him" (6:6). What's the old self? It's all that we were in Adam. Our life in Adam is now dead. It's a "legal" death—something that happens by virtue of our union with Christ. We're baptized into Christ's death. That means the merit of his death is ours. That means the penalty of our sin is paid in full. That means our "old self" is dead—legally.

Second, we know "that our old self was crucified with him in order that the body of sin might be brought to nothing" (6:6). What's our "body of sin?" It's our sinful human nature. Sin reigns in us, swaying every faculty. By union with Christ, we die—legally. That legal death means we now live in Christ. That also means the Holy Spirit dwells within us, renewing us in Christ's likeness. The purpose of that indwelling is that "the body of sin might be brought to nothing." One day, it will be eradicated.

Third, we know "that our old self was crucified with him in order that the body of sin might be brought to nothing, so that we would no longer be enslaved to sin" (6:6). The result of our "old self" being crucified with Christ is that our "body of sin" is done away with. That means the Holy Spirit dwells within. The result is we're no longer "slaves to sin." Paul says, "One who has died has been set free *[justified]* from sin" (6:7). That means sin is no longer the dominant governing principle within.

The significance of Christ's life (6:8-10)

In 6:8-10, Paul explains the significance of Christ's life for those who are in union with him. First, we know "that Christ, being raised from the dead, will never die again (6:9).

Second, we know that "death no longer has dominion over him" (6:9). Christ was born under the law. He bore the penalty of the law, in that he died. But that death couldn't hold him, because he was perfect. Having died, he passed beyond death's jurisdiction forever. As Christ declares, "I am the first and the last, and the living one. I died, and behold I am alive forevermore, and I have the keys of Death and Hades" (Rev. 1:17-18).

Third, we know that "the death he died he died to sin, once for all, but the life that he lives he lives to God" (6:10). As already mentioned, he didn't die to sin in the sense that he became insensitive to it or ceased from it (he had nothing to cease from). He died to sin in a legal sense. He bore its penalty. Having done so, he was raised from the dead. Now, he lives to God. Paul's point is that we live with him. Our old self is crucified—that's a judicial death. Our body of sin is "done away with." We're no longer slaves to sin. Instead, we live to God, seeking to glorify him.

Conclusion

Several important lessons can be drawn from these verses.

First, *we see the danger of legalism*. We fall into legalism when we stress sanctification at the expense of justification. According to Roman Catholicism, God justifies on the basis of sanctification. That's why they don't believe in assurance. Many evangelicals struggle with assurance for the same reason. They're looking within for some reason why God should justify them. But they'll never find it. God doesn't justify the sanctified. He sanctifies the justified. That's because he justifies the ungodly (4:5). Paul makes that clear in these verses. He exhorts us to consider ourselves "dead to sin." That moral death (i.e., sanctification) flows from a legal death (i.e., justification). We're to consider ourselves dead (morally) to sin, because we're dead (legally) to sin. We must never lose sight of that order. When we do, we fall prey to legalism. We begin to think that something in us accounts for God's justifying us. We must guard against that.

Second, *we see the danger of antinomianism.* We fall into antinomianism when we stress justification at the expense of sanctification. There's an antinomian spirit in all of us in that we tend to make light of our sin. That's seen in the notion that it's possible to be justified, not sanctified. Another way of stating it is this: it's possible to have Christ as priest, but not king. That false notion is so persistent today. We hear it everywhere: "Jesus may be your Saviour, but is he your Lord?" Such a notion is nonsense. If he isn't your Lord, neither is he your Saviour. There's no such thing as a Christian who's justified but isn't being sanctified. Paul makes that clear in these verses: "We know that our old self was crucified with him in order that the body of sin might be brought to nothing, so that we would no longer be enslaved to sin" (6:6). It's all, or it's nothing.

Third, *we see the importance of knowledge.* Twice, Paul appeals to his readers' knowledge (6:6, 9). Why is that significant? We can't take to heart what we don't understand. We can't live what we don't know. For that reason, let us strive to "grow in the grace and knowledge of our Lord and Saviour Jesus Christ" (2 Peter 3:18). Our identity in Christ is everything. It's the difference between feast and famine; fullness and emptiness; a refreshing oasis and a crippling desert; heaven and hell; an eternity of joy and pleasure and an eternity of pain and sorrow.

32
A Moral Imperative (6:11-14)

There's something particularly noteworthy about these verses. It's this—Paul has penned 149 verses without issuing a command. Here, he issues three. His method is significant because it indicates how we grow in holiness. In short, the imperative flows from the indicative. What's the indicative? "Jack is sitting. Jill is standing." What's the imperative? "Jack, stand up! Jill, sit down!" When we say the imperative flows from the indicative, we mean that our obedience flows from our appreciation of our identity in Christ. Having explained what it means to be "baptized into Christ Jesus" (6:1-10), Paul draws out the implications by way of three commands.

Know who you are! (6:11)
"So you also must consider yourselves dead to sin and alive to God in Christ Jesus." What does Paul mean?

Clearly, he doesn't mean we're unresponsive to sin. The term *dead* is *nekros*, not *thanatos*. The latter refers to the penalty for sin. The former refers to lifelessness. It's used, for example, to describe the condition of the unsaved (John 5:25; Eph. 2:1) The Christian, therefore, must consider himself "lifeless" when it comes to sin. He isn't lifeless. He's still very much alive to sin. However, the Holy Spirit unites him to Christ. Therefore, "our old self was crucified with him in order that the body of sin might be brought to nothing, so that we would no longer be enslaved to sin" (6:6). Now, we are to act like it.

Please notice the term "so" or "therefore" at the start of the verse. Paul is referring to what he has said in 6:1-10. There, he makes the point that we've been baptized in Christ. That means we're united with him in his death and in his life. This is tricky. I want you to notice two statements. The first is in 6:13, "as those who have been brought from death to life." The second is in 6:12, "let not sin reign in your mortal bodies." According to 6:13, I'm alive. According to 6:12, I'm dead. So, which is it? It's both. These two phrases summarize the Christian's present existence. We're alive in the new creation life of the age to come, while continuing to live in the present age.

And so, as Christians, we can't continue in sin. Why? We've died (legally) to it in Christ. Now, we must consider ourselves "dead" (lifeless) to it.

Be who you are! (6:12)
"Let not sin therefore reign in your mortal body, to make you obey its passions." Please notice a couple of things in this verse. First, the term "passions" refers to the realm of our desires. Second, the term "body" refers to the conduit for our desires—the vehicle by which our desires find expression. God calls me to align my desires with who I am in Christ. DeYoung notes,

> In effect God says to us, "Because you believe in Christ, by the Holy Spirit I have joined you to Christ. When he died, you died. When he rose, you rose. He's in heaven, so you're in heaven. He's holy, so you're holy. Your position right now, objectively and factually, is as a holy, beloved child of God, dead to sin, alive to righteousness, and seated in my holy heaven—now live like it."[1]

Guard who you are! (6:13)
"Do not present your members to sin as instruments for unrighteousness, but present yourselves to God as those who have been brought from death to life, and your members to God as instruments for righteousness." The *members* of the mortal body include all that constitutes our being—every faculty (physical and spiritual). The term *instruments* literally means *armaments*. The image is that of a soldier who must render his armaments to his military commander for service. The unbeliever presents the members of his mortal body to sin. Why? Sin is his military commander. But sin is no longer our commander.

Conclusion
There are many erroneous concepts of mortification. (1) It isn't the absolute annihilation of sin in believers. John says, "If we say we have no sin, we deceive ourselves, and the truth is not in us" (1 John 1:8). Sin won't be eradicated until glorification. (2) It isn't the suppression of, or cessation from, sinful acts. People do that for all sorts of reasons. The old and infirm, for example, may cease from certain sinful acts simply because they have no choice. That shouldn't be confused with mortification. (3) It isn't the castigation of the body. Paul says, "These have indeed an appearance of wisdom in promoting

---

[1] Kevin DeYoung, *The Hole in our Holiness: Filling the Gap between Gospel Passion and the Pursuit of Godliness* (Wheaton: Crossway, 2012), 105.

self-made religion and asceticism and severity to the body, but they are of no value in stopping the indulgence of the flesh" (Col. 2:23).

So, what's mortification? It's simply the overthrowing of sin's dominion. How do we mortify sin? We find the answer in many different verses. Let me give you a few examples. (1) "By the fear of the LORD one turns away from evil" (Prov. 16:6). We mortify sin by cultivating the fear of God. That's a godly fear whereby we stand in awe of his greatness and goodness. That causes us to hate sin. (2) "If your right eye causes you to sin, tear it out and throw it away" (Matt. 5:29). We mortify sin by denying self. The world and the devil are great enemies, but not our greatest enemy. Sin is our greatest enemy. It's deeply entrenched within us. We must deny it. (3) "Abstain from every form of evil" (1 Thess. 5:22). We mortify sin by avoiding all occasions to sin. We must avoid whatever causes us to stumble. (4) "Be strong in the Lord and in the strength of his might" (Eph. 6:10). We mortify sin by depending upon God. When I am weak, I am strong. That makes pride one of my greatest enemies. (5) "Count it all joy, my brothers, when you meet trials of various kinds, for you know that the testing of your faith produces steadfastness" (James 1:2-3). We mortify sin by recognizing God's purpose in affliction. "In this you rejoice, though now for a little while, if necessary, you have been grieved by various trials" (1 Peter 1:6). Through affliction, God deals with our sin. (6) "Run that you may obtain it" (1 Cor. 9:24). We mortify sin by appreciating the prize: Christ. We discipline ourselves for the purpose of godliness (1 Tim. 4:7). Why? godliness is great gain. It holds promise for this life and the life to come. (7) "But what fruit were you getting at that time from the things of which you are now ashamed? For the end of those things is death" (Rom. 6:21). We mortify sin by meditating upon the evil of sin. It causes us shame and sorrow. It troubles our conscience. It hurts our loved ones. It grieves our God. What benefit do we derive from it?

This is a daily battle. Joel Beeke explains,

> I once read of a missionary, who had in his garden a shrub that bore poisonous leaves. He also had a child who was prone to put anything within reach into his mouth. Naturally, the father dug the shrub out and threw it away. The shrub's roots, however, went very deep. Soon the shrub sprouted again. Repeatedly, the missionary had to dig it out. There was no solution but to inspect the ground every day and to dig up the shrub every time it surfaced. Indwelling sin is like that shrub. It needs constant

uprooting. Our hearts need continual mortification."[2]

---

[2] Joel Beeke, *Overcoming the World: Grace to Win the Daily Battle* (Phillipsburg: P&R Publishing, 2005), 109–110.

33
Two Masters: Part 1 (6:15-18)

To understand what Paul is saying in 6:15-23 requires some mental effort on our part. I hope you're convinced of the need for that. Joel Beeke warns, "An anti-intellectualist gospel will spawn an irrelevant gospel that does not get beyond 'felt needs.'"[1] That's the weakness of much gospel preaching today. It isn't an exposition of Scripture. Rather, it's a discourse on moral philosophy aimed at "felt needs." For that reason, it's often irrelevant. In this letter, Paul proclaims the gospel. We must seek, therefore, to understand what he's saying in order to grasp that gospel.

In 6:1, Paul asks, "What shall we say then? Are we to continue in sin that grace may abound?" Similarly, in 6:15, he asks, "What then? Are we to sin because we are not under law but under grace?" It's essentially the same question. Why does Paul ask it? In the first five chapters, he explains the doctrine of justification. (1) He demonstrates that we're sinful. We're selfish and self-centred. We don't know God, love God, or obey God. In that state, we can't please God. (2) He demonstrates that Christ pleases God. He lived a perfect life. He satisfied God's justice when he died on the cross. He appeased God's wrath and secured God's mercy. (3) He demonstrates that salvation comes through believing in Christ. Why? Christ has done everything. We don't do anything. We simply believe in him. "If you confess with your mouth Jesus is Lord and believe in your heart that God raised him from the dead, you will be saved" (10:9).

Paul knows that some people will think his doctrine of justification leads to antinomianism. They'll reason as follows: "If I'm justified by grace through faith in Christ, then I can sin without worrying about it. I believe in Christ; therefore, I'm saved. It doesn't make any difference how I live." Paul responds in this chapter. The first part of his answer is found in 6:1-14, those who are justified can't continue in sin because they're free from sin. The second part of his answer is found in 6:15-23, those who are justified can't

---

[1] Joel Beeke, *Puritan Evangelism: A Biblical Approach* (Grand Rapids: Reformation Heritage Books, 1999), 39.

continue in sin because they're enslaved to righteousness.

We're slaves either to sin or obedience (6:16)

"Do you not know that if you present yourselves to anyone as obedient slaves, you are slaves of the one whom you obey, either of sin, which leads to death, or of obedience, which leads to righteousness?"

Slavery is synonymous with power. And that's what Paul wants to convey by using this analogy. He wants us to see that we're under the power of something. There are two possibilities: sin or obedience. Paul has already made this point in 5:21, "So that, as sin reigned in death, grace also might reign through righteousness leading to eternal life through Jesus Christ our Lord." There are two reigns: the reign of sin, which includes all in Adam; and the reign of grace, which includes all in Christ. There are two humanities: Adam and Christ. Those in Adam are under the covenant of works. Through his transgression, there resulted condemnation to all men in him. Those in Christ are under the covenant of grace. Through his one act of righteousness, there resulted justification of life to all men in him. Those in Adam are slaves to sin. Those in Christ are slaves to obedience. Paul's point is: we can't be both. If we obey sin, then we're slaves to sin. If we obey obedience, then we're slaves to obedience.

We were slaves to sin (6:17)

"But thanks be to God, that you who were once slaves of sin." Before God saved us, we were enslaved to sin. One of the clearest statements of that fact is associated with the flood. According to Moses, God saw that "every intention of the thoughts of [man's] heart was only evil continually" (Gen. 6:5). That statement teaches us three facts about sin. (1) It teaches us that sin's control is inherent: "Every intention of *the thoughts of his heart* was only evil continually." In other words, sin grips the heart. "The heart is deceitful above all things, and desperately sick" (Jer. 17:9). (2) It teaches us that sin's control is total: "*Every intention* of the thoughts of his heart was only evil continually." Because man's heart is evil, his thoughts are evil. His mind is "darkened" (Eph. 4:18) and "defiled" (Titus 1:15). Because man's thoughts are evil, his intentions are evil. Because man's intentions are evil, his actions are evil. (3) It teaches us that sin's control is continual: "Every intention of the thoughts of his heart was only evil *continually.*" As David confesses, "Behold, I was brought forth in iniquity, and in sin did my mother conceive me" (Ps. 51:5). From day one, we're enslaved to sin.

Two Masters: Part 1 (6:15-18)

We were committed to God's Word (6:17-18)
"But thanks be to God, that you who were once slaves of sin have become obedient from the heart to the standard of teaching to which you were committed." I have two questions.

First, what does Paul mean when he says we became "obedient from the heart?" Back in 2:6, he says, God "will render to each one according to his works." There are those whose deeds are evil. God will give them wrath, indignation, tribulation, and distress (2:8-9). There are those whose deeds are good. God will give them life, glory, honour, and peace (2:7, 10). The difference between these two groups is their heart. Those whose deeds are evil are selfishly ambitious (2:8). Those whose deeds are good seek for glory, honour, and immortality (2:7). Their heart is good, because God has circumcised it (2:29). That's the new birth. And that's what Paul is describing in 6:17.

Second, what does Paul mean when he says we became "obedient from the heart to the standard of teaching to which we were committed." The AV is a little weak here. It says, "Ye have obeyed from the heart that form of doctrine which was delivered you." That gives the impression that God's Word was delivered to us. But that isn't what Paul says. We're the subjects in the sentence. And the verb *committed* is in the passive voice. Therefore, Paul doesn't say, "You became obedient from the heart to the standard of teaching which was committed to you." But he says, "You became obedient from the heart to the standard of teaching to which you were committed." That's a huge difference. We were committed to God's Word. Who committed us to God's Word? God.

That's why Paul declares, "Thanks be to God!" (6:17). We were slaves of sin. Suddenly, we became obedient from the heart to God's Word. How? It certainly wasn't our doing. We were helplessly and hopelessly enslaved. It was God who committed us to his Word. That's the new birth. That's the new creation. That's what Paul says in 1 Corinthians 1:30, "*Because of him* you are in Christ Jesus, who became to us wisdom from God, righteousness and sanctification and redemption."

Conclusion
By way of conclusion, I want to affirm six lessons.

First, *slavery to sin is the natural condition of everyone born into this world.* That's the doctrine of total depravity. Very few people believe that. But I want to be clear—we will never look solely to God's grace to save us until we see

The Obedience of Faith

our utter inability to do anything good. We will never rest solely in Christ as our Saviour until we see our utter inability to please him. Paul repeatedly stresses the seriousness of sin in these chapters. (1) In chapter one, he describes the *fruit* of sin. God has revealed himself in his creation and in his Word. But we've suppressed that revelation. And we've rejected God. And so, we're filled with all unrighteousness, wickedness, greed, and evil. We're full of envy, murder, strife, deceit, and malice. We're gossips, slanderers, and haters of God. We're insolent, arrogant, boastful, inventors of evil, disobedient to our parents, without understanding, untrustworthy, unloving, and unmerciful. (2) In chapter two, Paul describes the *deceitfulness* of sin. Very few people think they're sinners. They think they're better than most other people. But Paul tells us that God will judge our secrets. (3) In chapter three, Paul describes the *nature* of sin. It's something that grips us. There's none who understands; sin darkens the mind. There's none who seeks after God; sin hardens the heart. There's none who does any good; sin enslaves the will. Sin is all pervading. It leaves man totally bankrupt. (4) In chapter five, Paul describes the *origin* of sin. It began with Adam. We're guilty of Adam's sin because he acted as our representative. Furthermore, we've inherited Adam's fallen human nature.

Why does Paul keep emphasizing our sin? For one simple reason: he knows we can't be saved until we get it! People won't trust in Christ alone until they see their absolute need for Christ alone.

Second, *Christian freedom isn't the ability to do what I want, but the ability to do what God wants*. We must be careful not to confuse free will and freedom. Free will is the ability to do what I want. Freedom is the ability to do what God wants. Our free will is enslaved to sin. Therefore, we have no desire to do what God wants. When God saves us, we become obedient from the heart. He implants in us a desire to do his will.

Third, *conversion is a radical transformation of the heart*. We were enslaved to sin. Now, we're enslaved to obedience. The Bible describes that transformation in many different ways. Paul says, "At one time you were darkness, but now you are light in the Lord" (Eph. 5:8). Again, "Therefore, if anyone is in Christ, he is a new creation. The old has passed away; behold, the new has come" (2 Cor. 5:17). John says, "We know that we have passed out of death into life" (1 John 3:14). Simply put, something changes. Jonathan Edwards explains what:

They who are truly converted are new men, new creatures; new, not only within, but without; they are sanctified throughout, in spirit, soul and body; old things are passed away, all things are become new; they have new hearts, new eyes, new ears, new tongues, new hands, new feet; i.e., a new conversation and practice; they walk in newness of life, and continue to do so to the end of life.[2]

Does that describe us?

Fourth, *thanksgiving is the soul's expression of freedom*. When we understand our former bondage to sin and the fact that it is by God's doing that we're now in Christ, we overflow with gratitude.

Long my imprisoned spirit lay
fast bound in sin and nature's night.
Thine eye diffused a quickening ray:
I woke—the dungeon flamed with light!
My chains fell off, my heart was free,
I rose, went forth, and followed Thee.[3]

Fifth, *conversion creates an insatiable appetite for God's Word*. When we were in bondage to sin, we had no appetite for God's Word. In John 8, Christ tells us that man is enslaved to sin. As a result, man rejects God's Word, fails to understand God's Word, can't bear to hear God's Word, and fails to believe God's Word. That changes radically when a person is born again. God's Word becomes central. They love it above all else. That fact is troubling given the state of today's church. Do we love the word or the world? It's a difference in one letter, but it's also a difference between heaven and hell.

Sixth, *justification is antithetical to antinomianism*. The doctrine of justification by grace alone through faith alone in Christ alone doesn't lead to antinomianism. That's Paul's main point in this chapter. He clearly demonstrates that justification leads to sanctification. These are the two inseparable blessings of the covenant of grace. God justifies the sinner by removing the penalty of sin, and imputing righteousness to him. God sanctifies the sinner by breaking the power of sin, and imparting righteousness to him. Both of these blessings flow from our union with Christ. You can't have one without the other. You can't say, "I have Christ as my Saviour, but not my Lord!" That

---

[2] Jonathan Edwards, *On Religious Affections*, in *The Works of Jonathan Edwards* (Peabody: Hendrickson Publishers, 1998), 1:316.

[3] Charles Wesley, "And Can It Be?" in *The Hymnal for Worship and Celebration*, 203.

challenges the thinking of many today. They say, "I like justification, but I'm not so keen on sanctification. I'm happy to take God's forgiveness, but I'm going to coast until I get to heaven." That's impossible. And that's Paul's point: "What then? Are we to sin because we are not under law but under grace? By no means!"

34
Two Masters: Part 2 (6:19-23)

In 5:12-21, Paul explains that there are two federal heads. (1) There's Adam. God promised life to Adam if he obeyed. In failing to obey, Adam brought condemnation upon his descendants. By his one transgression, there resulted "condemnation for all men." That's known as the covenant of works. (2) There's Christ. God graciously accepts Christ's obedience on behalf of those who believe in him. By his one act of righteousness, there resulted "justification and life for all men." That's known as the covenant of grace.

As I've said many times, the covenant of grace contains two blessings. The first is justification: the removal of the penalty of sin. God forgives us, imputing righteousness to us. The second is sanctification: the removal of the power of sin. God cleanses us, imparting righteousness to us. These two blessings belong to those who are in Christ.

In chapters 6-8, Paul focuses upon the relationship between justification and sanctification. In chapter 6, he describes two masters: sin and righteousness. The Christian is no longer enslaved to sin, but to righteousness. In chapter 7, he describes two marriages: law and grace. The Christian is no longer married to law, but to grace. In chapter 8, he describes two minds: flesh and Spirit. The Christian no longer sets his mind upon the flesh, but upon the Spirit.

At present, we're considering 6:15-23. In 6:15, Paul asks, "What then? Are we to sin because we are not under law but under grace?" Does justification lead to antinomianism? Paul proves it doesn't by way of six statements. Last study, we looked at three. (1) We're slaves either to sin or obedience. (2) We were slaves to sin. (3) We were committed to God's Word. Now, we turn our attention to the remaining three.

We're free from sin (6:18)
"Having been set free from sin, [you] have become slaves of righteousness." The result of God committing us to his Word is that we're free from sin. Its power is broken. When a slave is set free, he isn't required to obey his master. That's what Paul says about our relationship to sin. It controlled us. Now,

we're free. Paul explained how in 6:6, "We know that our old self was crucified with him in order that the body of sin might be brought to nothing, so that we would no longer be enslaved to sin." The old self is all that we were in Adam. But God punished Christ for what we were in Adam. When we're united with Christ, we share in the merit of his death. Therefore, our old self has been condemned, judged, and crucified. We're dead to sin, because Christ died to sin. Union with Christ means the Holy Spirit dwells within us. Therefore, the dominion of sin is broken. Sin is no longer the governing principle in us.

We're slaves of righteousness (6:18)

"Having been set free from sin, [you] have become slaves of righteousness." In other words, having moved from the reign of sin to the reign of grace, we've become slaves of obedience (6:16), righteousness (6:18), and God (6:21). These expressions are synonymous. They mean we've become "obedient from the heart to the standard of teaching to which we were committed" (6:17). We're new creatures. The new creation (or, new birth) means we love God. From this love flows a desire to obey God.

Christ explains all of this in John 15, where he tells us he's the vine, and we're the branches. There's a vital union between him and us, meaning we derive our life from him. That's why Christ says, "I am the vine; you are the branches. Whoever abides in me and I in him, he it is that bears much fruit, for apart from me you can do nothing" (John 15:5). What's this fruit? It's obedience. Christ says, "You did not choose me, but I chose you and appointed you that you should go and bear fruit and that your fruit should abide, so that whatever you ask the Father in my name, he may give it to you. These things I command you, so that you will love one another" (John 15:15-16). Again, the emphasis is upon union with Christ. Christ took hold of me by the Holy Spirit. That means I live in Christ. That also means I take on the character of Christ. The branches are merely an extension of the vine. The quality of the branches is determined by the quality of the vine. The fruit of the branches is determined by the health of the vine. The branches can't do anything apart from the vine. They simply produce what the vine gives them. And so, I bear fruit—obedience from the heart.

We present our members as slaves to righteousness (6:19-23)

In 6:19, Paul admits his analogy is imperfect: "I am speaking in human terms, because of your natural limitations." You see, slavery suggests tyrannical control. But that isn't how we're to envision our slavery to righteousness. Paul simply uses the analogy of slavery because he wants us to grasp the significance of the alteration in our status. When I was enslaved to sin, I presented myself to sin to obey it. And I had no obligation to obey righteousness. Now, however, I'm a slave to righteousness. And so, I present myself to righteousness to obey it. And I'm under no obligation to obey sin (6:19-20). In 6:21-23, Paul builds on that, encouraging his readers to weigh the benefit of slavery to sin against the benefit of slavery to God.

Slavery to sin leads to death (6:21). Paul asks, "But what fruit were you getting at that time from the things of which you are now ashamed?" We didn't derive any benefit. On the contrary, "the end of those things is death." (1) We lost physical life. After Adam's sin, God declares, "You are dust, and to dust you shall return." (2) We lost spiritual life. After Adam's sin, his mind was darkened, his heart was hardened, and his will was enslaved. He no longer possessed the ability to fellowship with God. (3) We lost eternal life. After Adam's sin, God banished him from the garden so that he had no access to the tree of life.

Slavery to God leads to life (6:22). Paul says, "But now that you have been set free from sin and have become slaves of God, the fruit you get leads to sanctification and its end, eternal life." (1) We gain physical life. At the promised resurrection, we will put on immortality. (2) We gain spiritual life. That means the image of God is being renewed in us. And we have fellowship with God. (3) We gain eternal life. That means we will attain to an intimacy with God that Adam would have experienced had he passed the test.

Upon comparing the two, what do we discover? We discover that, truly, "the wages of sin is death, but the free gift of God is eternal life in Christ Jesus our Lord" (6:23). Our awareness of this should motivate us to present ourselves as slaves to righteousness.

Conclusion

By virtue of our union with Christ, he has become to us righteousness and sanctification. The two are distinct, yet inseparable. Christ has taken his bride to himself. He's determined to cleanse her from her pollution. He will present her to himself in all her glory. It's a certainty because he has set his love upon her (Eph. 5:26-27).

35
Two Marriages (7:1-6)

Paul's theme in chapters 6-8 is sanctification. In 6:1-7:6, his objective is clear. He proves that God's grace doesn't encourage sin but holiness. Why does Paul deal with this subject here? The answer is found back in 5:20-21, "Now the law came in to increase the trespass, but where sin increased, grace abounded all the more, so that, as sin reigned in death, grace also might reign through righteousness leading to eternal life through Jesus Christ our Lord." This statement raises two issues. (1) It raises the issue of the relationship between sin and grace. Paul says, "Where sin increased, grace abounded all the more." Doesn't such a statement encourage sin? Paul shows it doesn't in chapter 6. (2) It also raises the issue of the relationship between law and grace. Paul says, "The law came in to increase the trespass." Doesn't such a statement belittle the law? Paul shows it doesn't in chapter seven.

In sum, Paul proves his point by employing three illustrations. Each begins with the question: "Do you not know?" (1) The first is baptism (6:1-14). There are two men. Do you not know you're united to Christ? Act like it! God's grace doesn't encourage sin but holiness. (2) The second is slavery (6:15-23). There are two masters. Do you not know you're enslaved to Christ? Act like it! God's grace doesn't encourage sin but holiness. (3) The third is marriage (7:1-6). There are two marriages. Do you not know that you're married to Christ? Act like it! God's grace doesn't encourage sin but holiness.

We've considered the first two. Here we turn our attention to the third.

The question (7:1)
"Or do you not know, brothers—for I am speaking to those who know the law—that the law is binding on a person only as long as he lives?" What does Paul mean by "law" in this verse? For starters, he isn't referring to the Mosaic law. That comes later. Here, he's referring to law in general. He's simply acknowledging the fact that we're subject to law. That's a fact of life. As long as we live, law (in its various forms) has jurisdiction (dominion or authority) over us. However, that jurisdiction ends when we die. Why? Simply put, law can't do anything to a dead man. While we live, for example, we're under obligation

to the law of Canada. It has jurisdiction over us. If we break it, we pay the penalty. When we die, however, it loses jurisdiction. It can't exact any penalty. It can't do anything to us. Paul wants us to grasp two basic principles from that: (1) law has jurisdiction over us; and (2) death frees us from law's jurisdiction.

The illustration (7:2-3)

Paul uses marriage to illustrate the two principles that he established in 7:1.

What's the first principle? Law has jurisdiction over us. According to Paul, that's seen in marriage. He says that a woman is under the jurisdiction (dominion or authority) of her husband (7:2). And she's bound to him by law as long as he lives.

What's the second principle? Death frees us from law's jurisdiction. That too is seen in marriage. According to Paul, if a married woman is joined to another while her husband is still alive, she's an "adulteress" (7:3). Why? By law, she's under the jurisdiction of her husband. If, however, her husband dies, she's "free from the law" (7:3). In other words, the law that bound her to her husband loses its jurisdiction. And she's free to enter into a new relationship.

The application (7:4)

In 7:1, Paul establishes two principles. In 7:2-3, he illustrates these two principles in the context of marriage. In 7:4, he arrives at his main point.

What's the first principle? It's this: law has jurisdiction over us. We see that in the case of marriage. A woman is under the jurisdiction of her husband. So, what's Paul's point? Simply this: the law has jurisdiction over us. Here, Paul is talking about the Mosaic law. We're joined to it. We're married to it. How? We're in Adam. God established a covenant with Adam: the covenant of works. That covenant required perfect obedience. That covenant is still active. In one sense, the Mosaic law is a reiteration of the covenant of works, in that it requires perfect obedience from us. And it condemns us to death for failing to render that obedience.

What's the second principle? It's this: death frees us from law's jurisdiction. We see that in the case of marriage. If a woman's husband dies, she's free from her husband's jurisdiction and she's free to be joined to another. So, what's Paul's point? Simply this: just as death ends the jurisdiction of a husband over his wife, even so death ends the law's jurisdiction over us. Who died? Christ died. And he satisfied the law's penalty in his death. We're united with Christ. Thus, we "have died to the law." That verb is in the aorist passive. It means God reckoned us dead to the law because we're one with Christ. We're no longer joined to it.

Having been released from the law's jurisdiction through Christ's death, we're free to "belong to another, to him who has been raised from the dead, in order that we may bear fruit for God" (7:4). As we were joined to the law, now we're joined to Christ. We're married to him. Do you remember Paul's metaphor in Ephesians 5? As Eve was taken from the side of Adam, even so the church is taken from Christ's side. As Eve was brought to Adam so that they were joined together, even so the church is brought to Christ so that they're joined together. As Eve completes Adam, even so the church completes Christ. He loves her, cherishes her, sanctifies her, cleanses her, and presents her to himself in all her glory.

The implication (7:4-6)
What's the result of this new marriage (or, new covenant)? We find the answer in the last phrase in 7:4, "in order that we may bear fruit for God." Paul expands on this in 7:5-6, making a comparison between our old marriage and our new marriage.

Our old marriage was unable to produce fruit (7:5). Why? When we were married to the law (under the covenant of works), we were "in the flesh" — unregenerate. Plus, our "sinful passions ... were at work in our members to bear fruit for death." There's nothing wrong with the affections as created by God. However, we were selfishly ambitious (2:8). Hence, our affections were inordinate. Simply put, we were corrupt. And so, our old husband didn't have anything to work with. He was unable to impregnate us because we were spiritually barren. He only served to arouse "our sinful passions."

However, our new marriage is able to produce fruit (7:6). Paul says, "We serve in the new way of the Spirit and not in the old way of the written code." Paul uses a similar expression back in 2:28-29, where he distinguishes between spiritual and physical circumcision. Do you remember? There are three differences. (1) They have a different object. Physical circumcision is outward, but spiritual circumcision is inward. (2) They have a different cause. Physical circumcision is by the letter (man's doing), but spiritual circumcision is by the Spirit (God's doing). (3) They have a different result. Physical circumcision leads to praise from men, but spiritual circumcision leads to praise from God.

Returning to 7:6, we see what Paul means. The "old way of the written code" is life with the old husband under the old covenant. It's the unregenerate man. That marriage produced "fruit for death." The "new way of the Spirit" is life with the new husband under the new covenant. It's the regenerate. That marriage produces "fruit for God."

Conclusion

So, here we have the story of two marriages. (1) There's marriage to the law. In this state, man's unregenerate. He serves in the "old way of the written code." It's about man's doing. This marriage produces "fruit for death." (2) There's marriage to Christ under the covenant of grace. In this state, man's regenerate. He serves in the "new way of the Spirit." It's all about God's doing. And this marriage produces "fruit for God."

How do we move from the old to the new marriage? We die "to the law through the body of Christ" (7:4). I believe we can affirm four doctrines from these verses.

First, *the law can't save us.* The legalist may be concerned with Paul's comments in 5:20, where he seems to belittle the law. The legalist wants to know how a person can be righteous and holy without the law. Paul's answer is that the law was never intended to make us righteous. The law was designed to reveal our bondage to sin. (1) This doctrine shows us the error of confusing responsibility with ability. Much of the confusion concerning the function of the law arises from the idea that if God commands it, I must be able to obey it. That isn't true. God didn't give the law to show us what we can do, but what we can't do. Someone objects, "That isn't fair!" Yes, it is, because God's commands are given to man as he stood in innocence. Man's fall into sin doesn't alter God's law. (2) This doctrine also shows us our need to trust in Christ. We must forsake any notion that we can save ourselves. We can't. The law shows us that we must be absolutely perfect in order to be saved. The law also shows us that we can't be absolutely perfect. That means we can't save ourselves. We must look beyond ourselves for a Saviour.

Second, *union with Christ is the only cause of salvation.* In simple terms, we need someone to act on our behalf. We need Christ. He was born under the law. He obeyed it. He died, thereby paying the penalty for our sin. His death ends the law's jurisdiction over all who are one with him. Peter declares, "And there is salvation in no one else, for there is no other name under heaven given among men by which we must be saved" (Acts 4:12). (1) This doctrine shows us the error of thinking there are many ways to God. Most people think all religions possess some truth, but none possesses all the truth. Others say that

Two Marriages (7:1-6)

knowledge isn't important as long as we're sincere. What a fallacy! In 10:2, Paul says that the Jews "have a zeal for God, but not according to knowledge." That zeal won't do them any good. Union with Christ is the only cause of salvation. (2) This doctrine also shows us the need to trust in Christ. Do you trust in Christ alone for your salvation? Do you trust in his perfect obedience and in his substitutionary death?

Third, *union with Christ is the only cause of fruit.* Our marriage to the law produced "fruit for death." Our marriage to Christ under the covenant of grace produces "fruit for life." (1) This doctrine shows us the error of thinking it's possible to be united with Christ without bearing fruit. That's impossible! "For we are his workmanship, created in Christ Jesus for good works, which God prepared beforehand, that we should walk in them" (Eph. 2:10). (2) This doctrine also shows us the need to trust in Christ. He takes hold of us by his Spirit. We take hold of him by faith. That union is what it means to abide in him. As we abide in him, he works in us. "You did not choose me, but I chose you and appointed you that you should go and bear fruit and that your fruit should abide" (John 15:16).

Fourth, *union with Christ is the only cause of assurance.* Paul says, "There is therefore now no condemnation for those who are in Christ Jesus" (8:1). We're joined to Christ by covenant. And he will never break his covenant. (1) This doctrine shows us the error of feeling condemned in God's sight. As Christians, we often err in our understanding of sorrow and repentance. The cause of our sorrow and repentance as Christians isn't an awful foreboding of having broken God's law—our old husband. The cause of our sorrow and repentance as Christians is the realization that we've sinned against our spouse—Christ. (2) This doctrine also shows us our need to trust in Christ.

> "Let us rejoice and exult and give him the glory, for the marriage of the Lamb has come, and his Bride has made herself ready; it was granted her to clothe herself with fine linen, bright and pure"—for the fine linen is the righteous deeds of the saints. And the angel said to me, "Write this: Blessed are those who are invited to the marriage supper of the Lamb." And he said to me, "These are the true words of God" (Rev. 19:7-9).

36
Holy & Righteous & Good (7:7–12)

I'd like to begin with a brief reading from John Bunyan's *Pilgrim's Progress*.

> Then he took him by the hand, and led him into a very large parlor that was full of dust, because never swept; the which after he had reviewed a little while, the Interpreter called for a man to sweep. Now when he began to sweep, the dust began so abundantly to fly about, that Christian had almost therewith been choked. Then said the Interpreter to a Damsel that stood by, bring hither water, and sprinkle the room; the which when she had done, it was swept and cleansed with pleasure. Then said Christian, What means this? The Interpreter answered, This parlor is the heart of a man that was never sanctified by the sweet Grace of the Gospel: The dust is his Original Sin, and inward corruptions that have defiled the whole man. He that began to sweep at first, is the Law; but she that brought Water, and did sprinkle it, is the Gospel. Now, whereas thou sawest that so soon as the first began to sweep, the dust did so fly about, that the room by him could not be cleansed, but that thou wast almost choked therewith; this is to shew thee, that the Law, instead of cleansing the heart (by its working) from sin, doth revive, put strength into, and increase it in the soul, even as it doth discover and forbid it, for it doth not give power to subdue.[1]

To summarize: The room is man's heart. The man, who sweeps the dust, is the law. The woman, who pours the water, is the gospel. Bunyan's point is simply this: the law stirs sin, yet never subdues sin. And that's Paul's point in Romans 7. John Flavel explains this very well:

> The scope of the apostle ... in this chapter, is to state the due use and excellence of the law ... First, by denying to it a power to justify us. ... Second, by ascribing to it a power to convince us ... It cannot make us righteous, but it can convince us that we are unrighteous. It cannot heal, but it can open and discover the wounds that sin has given us.[2]

---

[1] Bunyan, *Pilgrim's Progress*, 26–27.
[2] Flavel, *Works*, 2:287–288.

That's a very helpful summary of the chapter. There are three sections: the jurisdiction of the law (7:1-6), the function of the law (7:7-12), and the limitation of the law (7:13-25). We've covered the first. In it, Paul begins with a question, in which he establishes two principles: law has jurisdiction over us; and death frees us from that jurisdiction. Paul then illustrates these two principles in the context of marriage: the husband has jurisdiction over his wife; and the husband's death frees his wife from that jurisdiction. Paul then applies these two principles to us: we were under the law's jurisdiction; and Christ's death freed us from that jurisdiction. Paul concludes this section by explaining the purpose of this new marriage: "that we may bear fruit for God."

Now, we turn our attention to the second section: the function of the law (7:7-12). Paul knows his comments in the first section will raise some eyebrows. And so, he anticipates a question: "What shall we say then? That the law is sin?" (7:7). In other words, "The law can't save us. Instead, it arouses the sinful passions that are at work in the members of our body to bear fruit to death. That must mean the law is sinful." Paul responds, "By no means!" The law isn't our problem. We don't need to be released from the law because of the law, but because of our sin. The law isn't sinful. On the contrary, it's holy and righteous and good. Why?

The law reveals sin (7:7)
"If it had not been for the law, I would not have known sin." What does Paul mean? He doesn't mean that he wouldn't have been aware of sin without the law. Back in 2:15, he makes it clear that the law is written upon man's heart. That means man possesses an inherent knowledge of God's law. And man's conscience bears witness according to his conduct. So, what does Paul mean? He's simply saying that he wouldn't have been aware of the real nature of sin without the law. Paul gives an example of what he means: "For I would not have known what it is to covet if the law had not said, 'You shall not covet'" (7:7). Paul is talking about an experiential knowledge as opposed to a theoretical knowledge. Through the law, Paul realized sin isn't primarily concerned with man's deeds, but desires.

That's Christ's message in Matthew 5. The Pharisees were satisfied with their own righteousness. They didn't murder or commit adultery. To paraphrase, Christ says, "If you rage, you're guilty of murder. If you lust, you're guilty of adultery." In other words, the desire is as damnable as the deed. As a Pharisee, Paul didn't realize this until the law was brought home with power.

Holy & Righteous & Good (7:7–12)

He knew the law—theoretically. But he didn't know it—experientially. However, through the Holy Spirit's work, he came to know the law, and he came to know his sin.

We can interpret the law externally and superficially until we reach the tenth commandment. This commandment specifically forces us into the realm of the heart. We've separated the gift from the Giver. Consequently, we attach our happiness to a person, possession, or experience. We make it our ultimate end. "You shall not covet." Many of us assure ourselves that we don't covet. But we only have to answer a few questions to see how prevalent it is in our hearts. What do we dream about it? What stirs envy in us? What stirs bitterness in us? What circumstances do we think need to change in order for us to be content? This shows us that God is not on the throne of our hearts. The law breaks sin down into its most basic element: we're idolatrous.

The law provokes sin (7:8)

"But sin, seizing an opportunity through the commandment, produced in me all kinds of covetousness. For apart from the law, sin lies dead." When Paul says, "apart from the law, sin lies dead," he doesn't mean sin is completely inactive apart from the law. He's speaking in relative terms. Apart from the law, man certainly sins. With the law, man sins even more. Why? The law provokes sin. How?

First, it arouses hostility. Paul writes, "For the mind that is set on the flesh is hostile to God, for it does not submit to God's law; indeed, it cannot" (8:7). We resent being told what to do. That's why many people claim to be atheists. They don't want God because they don't want to be accountable to God. That's why many people dislike law and order in society. They don't want to be accountable for their actions. By nature, man resents authority. What does the law do? It lays out rules and regulations. In so doing, it stirs something that lurks deep within man. It challenges his self-autonomy. It challenges "self," thereby arousing hostility.

Second, it arouses obstinacy. Paul says, "Though they know God's righteous decree that those who practice such things deserve to die, they not only do them but give approval to those who practice them" (1:32). Man hates the idea that he's accountable to God. His stubbornness is so pervasive that he will actually disobey what he knows to be God's ordinance. Moreover, he will encourage others to do the same.

The law condemns sin (7:9-11)

"I was once alive apart from the law, but when the commandment came, sin came alive and I died" (7:9). Here, Paul describes life and death in relative terms. Basically, there was a time when he was alive apart the law. He had studied the law since his childhood, yet he lacked any experiential knowledge of it. Without this, he was alive. He thought all was well with his soul. And he was self-satisfied. As he says elsewhere: "And I was advancing in Judaism beyond many of my own age among my people, so extremely zealous was I for the traditions of my fathers" (Gal. 1:14). Again, "as to righteousness under the law, blameless" (Phil. 3:6). However, the time came when he died. Why? The law struck home, and sin became alive. Paul means the law revealed and provoked his sin. He saw the depths of his depravity. That killed him, making him utterly weak.

The law is holy, righteous, and good (7:12)

"So the law is holy, and the commandment is holy and righteous and good." Given the function of the law in revealing, provoking, and condemning sin, people might think that the law is evil. Paul disagrees. It's holy, in that it reveals the character of God. It's righteous, in that it's fair in all that it demands. It's good, in that it's for our benefit. Its function is to humble us before God so that we might trust in Christ.

The law isn't the problem, but points to the problem. Let's imagine a glass of water. It contains deadly germs. They're difficult to see because they've sunk to the bottom. Let's imagine I stir the water with a spoon. The deadly germs begin to rise. We can see them. Is that the spoon's fault? Is the spoon responsible for the deadly germs in the water? No. It has simply enabled us to see what was always there.

Conclusion

Paul has clearly answered his question back in 7:7, Is the law sin? No! How can it be? It does exactly what it was given to do. J.I. Packer sums up Paul's teaching in these verses in three points.

> (1) The effect of the law is to give men knowledge of sin—not merely of the abstract notion of sin, but of sin as a concrete reality within themselves, a spirit of rebellion against God, and of disobedience to his commandments. (2) The way in which the law gives this knowledge is by declaring God's prohibitions and commands; for these first goad sin

into active rebellion and then make men aware of the specific transgressions and shortcomings of motive and deed into which sin had led them. (3) The law gives no ability to anyone to perform the good, which it prescribes, nor can it deliver from the power of sin.[3]

What do we learn from this description of the law? I want to mention two important lessons.

First, *one of the greatest obstacles to salvation is ignorance of sin.* Unbelievers never really "know" their sin through the law. Prior to his conversion, for example, Paul didn't really know his sin. And so, he had a high opinion of himself. He thought he was alive. He thought all was well. That's the condition of all unbelievers. They don't know their true condition. Christ says, "For you say, I am rich, I have prospered, and I need nothing, not realizing that you are wretched, pitiable, poor, blind, and naked" (Rev. 3:17). How many people go through life like that? (1) This shows us how persistent we must be in preaching the law. We must seek to stir the dust in people's hearts so that they choke on it. Many people regard sin light-heartedly because the law is rarely preached. (2) This shows us how dependent we must be upon the Holy Spirit. Only the Holy Spirit can open the eyes of man's heart so that he truly sees his sin. (3) This shows us how prepared we must be for man's enmity. Man will despise anyone who stirs the dust in his heart. Archibald Alexander observes, "When God raised up preachers, animated with a burning zeal, who labored faithfully to convince their hearers of their ruined condition, and of the necessity of a thorough conversion from sin, the opposition to them was violent."[4] (4) This shows us how intolerant we must be of those who downplay man's sin. God declares, "They have healed the wound of my people lightly, saying, 'Peace, peace,' when there is no peace" (Jer. 6:14). (5) This shows us how thankful we must be that God has awakened us from our blind state. "But thanks be to God, that you who were once slaves of sin have become obedient from the heart to the standard of teaching to which you were committed" (6:17).

Second, *one of the greatest signs of life is feeling you're dead.* We see the truth of that in Paul's example. At one time, he was alive apart from the law. However, when the law came in power, he died. His self-satisfaction vanished. How

---

[3] J.I. Packer, *Keep in Step with the Spirit: Finding Fullness in Our Walk with God* (Grand Rapids: Baker Books, 1984), 221.
[4] Archibald Alexander, *Biographical Sketches of the Founder and Principal Alumni of the Log College* (Philadelphia: Presbyterian Board of Education, 1851), 17.

important is that? God declares, "But this is the one to whom I will look: he who is humble and contrite in spirit and trembles at my word" (Isa. 66:2). Christ says, "Blessed are the poor in spirit; for theirs is the kingdom of heaven" (Matt. 5:3). Who are these people? They are those who recognize that they're without moral virtues adequate to commend themselves to God. In this state, they're utterly dependent upon God's grace. What do they do? William Perkins answers, "Finding no goodness in their hearts, they despair in themselves, and fly wholly to the mercy of God in Christ, for grace and comfort."[5]

---

[5] William Perkins, *The Works of William Perkins* (London: John Legate, 1631), 3:4.

37
Sold Under Sin (7:13-25)

J.I. Packer writes,

> Some will assure us that it is a waste of time preaching to modern hearers about the law and sin, for (it is said) such things mean nothing to them. Instead (it is suggested) we should just appeal to the needs which they feel already, and present Christ to them simply as One who gives peace, power, and purpose to the neurotic and frustrated—a super-psychiatrist, in fact.[1]

We must not allow our appetite to dictate our handling of the Bible. We must remember that our perceived needs aren't necessarily our real needs. We think we know what we need; however, our assessment of our needs is usually determined by our circumstances—the temporal, not the eternal.

With that said, we come to a passage of Scripture that has perplexed countless believers. There are three main views.

According to the first, Paul is describing the unbeliever's conversion experience. Those who hold to this view maintain that Paul can't be describing a Christian in these verses, because his statement in 7:14 ("I am of the flesh, sold under sin") is irreconcilable with what he says in 6:6, 17, 22, namely, that the Christian is free from sin. I will speak to that in just a moment. For now, following their argument through, we find that they believe that Paul is describing the internal struggle that occurs in a person prior to conversion. That struggle culminates in conversion as heard in the cry of 7:24, "Wretched man that I am! Who will deliver me from this body of death?" I don't agree with that view. Why? For the following reason: if 7:24 depicts conversion, then 7:25 must necessarily be a post-conversion experience. What does Paul say in 7:25? "So then, I myself serve the law of God with my mind, but with my flesh I serve the law of sin." Isn't that the same state Paul describes in 7:14-23? If so, it means the unbeliever's pre-conversion struggle and the believer's post-

---

[1] J.I. Packer, *A Quest for Godliness: The Puritan Vision of the Christian Life* (Wheaton: Crossway Books, 1990), 169.

conversion struggle are precisely the same. That's rather anti-climactic.

According to the second view, Paul is portraying the Christian's normal experience—a state that can only be described as spiritual despondency. I don't believe that's what Paul is doing. Why? (1) If Paul is describing the Christian's normal experience, then we must conclude that the main result of the gospel is to make us miserable. That contradicts what Paul states in 5:1-2 and 8:1-2. (2) If Paul is describing the Christian's normal experience, then we must conclude that the doctrine of sanctification is meaningless. That contradicts what Paul states in 6:6, 17, 22, namely, that we're free from sin and enslaved to righteousness.

That leaves us with the third view, according to which Paul is speaking as a regenerate man who describes himself as he is in himself, not in Christ. The key to this view is found in 7:13, where Paul asks, "Did that which is good, then, bring death to me?" The term "then" indicates that the question arises from something said in the preceding verses. In 7:11, Paul says that sin killed him through the commandment. Yet, in 7:12, he says, "The law is holy, and the commandment is holy and righteous and good." If that's true, then here's the question: "Did that which is good become the cause of death for me?" In other words, how can something so good do something so bad? Paul responds in 7:13 by stating four facts. (1) "By no means!" In other words, the law isn't the cause of my death. (2) "It was sin." In other words, my sin is the cause of my death. (3) "Producing death in me through what is good." The law is good, yet it condemns me. My sin is the cause of that condemnation. Therefore, my sin actually effects my death through that which is good. (4) "In order that sin might be shown to be sin, and through the commandment might become sinful beyond measure." In other words, the fact that sin effects my death through the law (something good) shows me just how utterly sinful I am.

The first word in 7:14 is "for." This indicates that what follows in 7:14-25 builds upon what Paul says in 7:13. In other words, Paul's purpose in 7:14-25 is to demonstrate what he says in 7:13, namely, the fact that sin effects my death through the law (something good) thereby showing me just how utterly sinful I am. And so, in 7:14-25, Paul speaks as a regenerate man, who knows the law is holy, righteous, and good, but still doesn't find anything good in himself. He does so in order to demonstrate how utterly sinful sin is.

Returning for a moment to the first view, we're now in a position to respond to the notion that Paul can't be describing a Christian in 7:14-25, because his statement in 7:14 ("I am of the flesh, sold under sin") is irreconcilable with what he says in 6:6,17,22, namely, that the Christian is free from sin. My response is this: there's no contradiction if we keep in mind what Paul is doing in 7:14. He isn't describing the full picture. He's simply explaining that even a regenerate man, who knows the law is good, still won't find anything in him that's inclined to the law. Why? He's sinful. Therefore, the law actually proves that sin is utterly sinful.

The question (7:11-13)
Paul is wrestling with a question that emerges from two seemingly contradictory facts.

Fact #1: sin kills through the law (7:11). The law says that God (not us) is the measure of what's right and wrong, good and bad, true and false. When we evaluate ourselves by the standard of God's law, we discover that we're condemned.

Fact #2: the law is holy and righteous and good (7:12).

Here's the question that emerges from these two seemingly contradictory facts: "Did that which is good, then, bring death to me" (7:13)? That is to say, how can something so good do something so bad?

The answer (7:13)
How does Paul respond? "By no means!" He makes two key points.

Point #1: "It was sin, producing death in me through what is good ..." That is to say, sin is the killer, while the law is merely the weapon.

Point #2: "... in order that sin might be shown to be sin, and through the commandment might become sinful beyond measure." The fact that sin causes my death through the law (something that is holy and righteous and good) proves that sin is "sinful beyond measure"—utterly sinful.

The proof (7:14-25)
Paul proves it from his own experience. Is he describing a pre-conversion or post-conversion experience? The answer is found in three observations.

First, this man knows he's a sinner. He cries, "I am of the flesh, sold under sin" (7:14). Again, "I know that nothing good dwells in me, that is, in my flesh" (7:18). The unregenerate man never talks like that. Paul says, "I was once alive apart from the law" (7:9). Prior to his conversion, he didn't know his sin. He thought he was okay. That's how the unregenerate man thinks. He doesn't see his sin. He never cries, "I am of the flesh, sold under sin."

Second, this man knows the law is good. He states, "We know that the law is spiritual" (7:14). Again, "I agree with the law" (7:16). Again, "I delight with the law of God" (7:22). The unregenerate man never talks like that. Why? "For the mind that is set on the flesh is hostile to God, for it does not submit to God's law; indeed, it cannot" (8:7). This man knows the law is holy, righteous, and good. He joyfully concurs with it. That's a work of the Holy Spirit.

Third, this man knows he needs Christ. He cries, "Who will deliver me from this body of death? Thanks be to God through Jesus Christ our Lord!" (7:24-25). The unregenerate man never talks like that. "For, being ignorant of the righteousness of God, and seeking to establish their own, they did not submit to God's righteousness" (10:3). The unregenerate man never feels his need for Christ, because he never feels his sin.

Paul knows the law is spiritual, but he can't obey it (7:14-21)
Paul shows us that although the regenerate man knows the law is spiritual, he (in and of himself) can't obey it. We can get our minds around the contents of these verses by asking three questions.

First, what do we know? According to 7:14, we know: "I am of the flesh, sold under sin." According to 7:18, we know: "Nothing good dwells in me, that is, in my flesh." Paul uses the term *flesh* in four different ways in his epistles—in reference to humanity, the body, meat, and human nature. When he uses it in reference to human nature, he usually means sinful human nature. And that's what he means here. He's of flesh. He's sold into bondage to sin. In other words, nothing good dwells in him. How can he say that after what he says in chapter 6 about being free from sin? The answer: he isn't describing who he is in Christ, but who he is in himself. We must remember his purpose— to prove that the law reveals that my sin is utterly sinful by showing me my inability to obey it.

Second, how do we know we're of flesh, sold into bondage to sin? We know it because of our internal struggle. In 7:15, Paul says, "For I do not do what I want, but I do the very thing I hate." In 7:19, he says more or less the same thing: "For I do not do the good I want, but the evil I do not want is what I keep on doing." In a word, even though I agree with the law, I can't obey it. And even though I love the law, I can't obey it. Why? Sin is too strong. That proves nothing good dwells in me.

Third, what are the implications? According to 7:16-17 and 7:20, if I'm doing what I don't want to do, then I'm no longer the one doing it. It's sin, which dwells in me. Here, Paul personifies sin in order to stress the grip it has on him. Even though he loves the law, he can't obey it. Why? He's of flesh, sold into bondage to sin. Conclusion: "I find it to be a law *[principle]* that when I want to do right, evil lies close at hand" (7:21).

Paul has proved his point. What point? He wants to prove that the law (something good) shows me just how utterly sinful I am. He has proved it by demonstrating that even the regenerate man, who knows the law is spiritual, finds nothing "in himself" that's inclined to that law.

Paul joyfully concurs with the law, but he can't obey it (7:22-25)
In 7:22-25, Paul shows us that although the regenerate man joyfully concurs with the law, he (in and of himself) can't obey it. He proves that by explaining that there are two laws. On the one hand, there's the law of God (7:22, 23, 25). The regenerate man joyfully concurs with it in the inner man (7:22). It reigns in his mind (7:23). And he serves it with his mind (7:25). On the other hand, there's the law of sin (7:23, 24, 25). It reigns in the members of his body (7:23). It wages war against the law of God (7:23). It makes him a prisoner (7:23). And he's powerless to do anything about it. He cries in 7:24-25, "Wretched man that I am! Who will deliver me from this body of death? Thanks be to God through Jesus Christ our Lord!"

Again, Paul has proved his point: the law (something good) reveals that my sin is utterly sinful by showing me my utter inability to obey it. He has done so by explaining that even the regenerate man (who "joyfully concurs" with the law) doesn't find anything "in himself" that's inclined to that law.

Conclusion
And so, what do we learn from these verses? We learn exactly what Paul wants us to learn—the law shows us that our sin is utterly sinful by showing us our inability to obey it. Even the regenerate (who know the law is good and who joyfully concur with the law) don't find anything "in them" that's inclined to that law.

Thankfully, that isn't the whole story. We don't despair. Why? Simply because we don't trust in our flesh: our effort, our obedience, our goodness, or anything else in us. Like Abraham, we know we haven't achieved anything "according to the flesh" (4:1). Our hope is in Christ! That was Paul's main point back in 7:1-6. There, he establishes two principles: law has jurisdiction over us; and death frees us from law's jurisdiction. He then illustrates these two principles in the context of marriage; the husband has jurisdiction over his wife; and the husband's death frees his wife from that jurisdiction. Paul then explains how that applies to us: we were under the law's jurisdiction; and Christ has freed us from that jurisdiction by his death. Finally, Paul explains the purpose of this new marriage—to bear "fruit for God."

In 7:14–25, we have a confirmation of all that. The old marriage is powerless to produce fruit for God. It can't, because we're of flesh. That means we're spiritually barren. All the law does is show us how utterly sinful we are. Even the regenerate man (who knows the law is good) will never find anything "in himself" that wants to obey it. But Paul's point is this: we don't look for anything in ourselves. We look to Christ. We're married to Christ "in order that we may bear fruit for God."

38
No Condemnation (8:1-4)

We arrive at what one author calls "the best chapter in the Bible."[1] I ask you to pay close attention to three things.

First, pay close attention to the glory of the triune God. We can distill the doctrine of the Trinity into three statements. (1) The Father isn't the Son, the Son isn't the Spirit, and the Spirit isn't the Father. They're distinct persons. (2) The Father is God, the Son is God, and the Spirit is God. They're one in being. (3) God is triune: three persons in one being. These three persons know each other, love each other, and rejoice in each other, in eternity. This means that God is perfectly and infinitely happy. This knowing each other, loving each other, and rejoicing in each other in eternity is God's glory. God extends his glory to us, so that we participate in his knowing, loving, and rejoicing. By the end of chapter 8, I want us to be convinced that a personal and relational God wants us to fellowship with him in his knowledge, love, and joy.

Second, pay close attention to the ministry of the Holy Spirit. There are twenty-one references to the Holy Spirit in this chapter. That means this chapter has more references to the Holy Spirit than any other chapter in the Bible. Do you think this is significant? I think so. It teaches us what it means to walk by the Spirit (8:1-4), live by the Spirit (8:5-11), kill by the Spirit (8:12-14), cry by the Spirit (8:15-17), groan by the Spirit (8:18-26), pray by the Spirit (8:27-30), and triumph by the Spirit (8:31-39) By the end of chapter 8, I want us to be convinced of what it means to walk "in the new way of the Spirit" (7:6).

Third, pay close attention to the efficacy of the gospel. This chapter begins with "no condemnation" (8:1) and ends with "no separation" (8:39). It's a description of our journey from conversion to glorification. It's the chapter we want when collapsing under the burden of sin, when melting in the fire of affliction, when bearing the weight of sorrow, when expiring upon our death bed. It's magnificent. By the end of chapter 8, I want us to be convinced that we

---

[1] Derek W.H. Thomas, *How the Gospel Brings Us All the Way Home* (Orlando: Reformation Trust, 2011).

would be immeasurably poorer without this chapter.

With that said, we begin by considering 8:1-4. How can we be certain that God won't condemn us? The answer is threefold.

A glorious condition (8:1-2)

"There is therefore now no condemnation for those who are in Christ Jesus." Paul introduced this theme back in 5:1, "Since we have been justified by faith, we have peace with God." The term "peace" means binding together what was separated. We were separated from God, because of our sin. But Christ has satisfied God's justice, thereby appeasing God's wrath and securing God's mercy. Now, we're bound together with God. Paul now states negatively in 8:1 what he states positively in 5:1.

Why is there no condemnation for those in Christ? Paul explains, "For the law of the Spirit of life has set you free in Christ Jesus from the law of sin and death" (8:2). There are two very different interpretations of these verses. (1) There are those who believe "the law of sin and of death" is the power (or, principle) of the flesh in us whereas "the law of the Spirit of life" is the power (or, principle) of the Spirit in us. They believe the latter has set us free from the former. That's sanctification. They interpret this verse in that way, because that's how the term *law* is often used in the preceding chapter (7:21, 22, 23, 25). (2) There are those who believe "the law of sin and of death" is the Mosaic law. In chapter 7, Paul demonstrates that the law is holy, righteous, and good. It was intended for life. However, it has resulted in sin and death. That isn't the law's fault. Our sin is to blame. As for the "law of the Spirit of life," it's simply an expression for faith (3:27).

I'm inclined to the second interpretation for two reasons. (1) Clearly, what Paul says in 8:2 flows from what he says in 8:1. After all, the verse begins with the conjunction *for* or *because*. This means that the reason there's no condemnation for those in Christ is this: they're free from the law. If, by "law," Paul means the "principle of sin," then he's making sanctification the basis of justification. If that's so, then he would seem to contradict what he has said to this point in his letter. He has already made it clear that God justifies the ungodly or the unholy (4:5). (2) Clearly, what Paul says in 8:3 flows from what he says in 8:2. It too begins with the conjunction *for* or *because*. In 8:3, Paul speaks about what the law couldn't do, because it was weak through the flesh. If the law is the "principle of sin," then Paul's describing what the principle of sin couldn't do, because it was weak through the principle of sin. That

No Condemnation (8:1-4)

doesn't make any sense. Surely, he's talking about the law. And so, he must also be talking about the law in 8:2. Otherwise, it's difficult to determine the relationship between the two verses.

Therefore, the reason there's no condemnation for those who are in Christ is because Christ has set them free from the law. In a word, they're justified.

A glorious salvation (8:3)

How did our condition change? The answer lies outside our performance. We couldn't do anything. The law reveals God's righteousness, and it requires righteousness from us. The problem is it can't help us produce that righteousness. Why? It's "weakened by the flesh." The flesh is human nature. What's wrong with human nature? It's enslaved to sin (7:5, 14, 18). That means we're morally incapable of obeying God (3:12). The law is powerless to do anything about that. But God did what the law couldn't do. He did something "in order that the righteous requirement of the law might be fulfilled in us" (8:4). What did he do?

God sent his own Son

I have three questions. First, when did the Father send his Son? He sent him when Christ was born into this world. In John's Gospel, Christ makes that claim at least forty times. On one particular occasion, he says that the Father has set his seal upon him (John 6:27). A seal indicates authenticity. When universities confer degrees or governments issue documents, their seal is affixed. Why? These indicate authenticity. When the Father sealed Christ, he confirmed his authenticity. He confirmed he had sent him. At the time of Christ's baptism, the Father declared, "This is my beloved Son, with whom I am well pleased" (Matt. 3:17). And the Holy Spirit descended upon him.

Second, what did the Father send his Son to do? (1) The Father sent his Son to be a prophet—a greater prophet than Moses (Deut. 18:18; Isa. 42:6-7; Luke 4:18-19). Prophets reveal. They declare God's truth. (2) The Father sent his Son to be a priest—a greater priest than Aaron (Ps. 110:4; John 10:11; Heb. 7:21-25). Priests reconcile. They mediate between God and man. (3) The Father sent his Son to be a king—a greater king than David (Ps. 2:6-7; Matt. 28:18). Kings rule. They ensure that people follow God's will.

Third, why did the Father send his Son to do that? First, we need a prophet to reveal God to us. (1) We need a prophet to tell us about God. God is a spirit, infinite, eternal, and unchangeable. How can we know anything about such a

God? We need Christ. Why? "No one has ever seen God; the only God, who is at the Father's side, he has made him known" (John 1:18). Christ declares "All that I have heard from my Father I have made known to you" (John 15:15). (2) We need a prophet to dispel the darkness that pervades our mind. We're insensible to spiritual truth. We need Christ to enable us to understand what he tells us about God. After the resurrection, he said to his disciples: "Then he said to them, 'These are my words that I spoke to you while I was still with you, that everything written about me in the Law of Moses and the Prophets and the Psalms must be fulfilled.' Then he opened their minds to understand the Scriptures" (Luke 24:44-45).

Second, we need a priest to reconcile us to God. (1) We need a priest to mediate between God and us by removing our sin and shame. We're sinners. We're under the sentence of death. We need Christ to pay that penalty. Paul says, "Christ redeemed us from the curse of the law by becoming a curse for us" (Gal. 3:13). That means Christ has satisfied God's justice. On that basis, God forgives us. (2) We need a priest to mediate between God and us by giving us what we lack. We need righteousness. We need Christ's righteousness. As Paul says back in 5:18, "One act of righteousness leads to justification and life for all men." God imputes Christ's righteousness to us.

Third, we need a king to rule over us. (1) We need a king to break the power of sin. We're in bondage to it. We need Christ, who's stronger than the "strong man" that binds us. Christ "attacks him" and "overpowers him" (Luke 11:21-22). He subdues our will, bringing it into line with God's will. That's what we read of in 6:22, "But now that you have been set free from sin and have become slaves of God, the fruit you get leads to sanctification and its end, eternal life." (2) We need a king to protect us. We're vulnerable to the flesh, the world, and the devil. We need someone to guard us from these enemies. We need someone to fight on our behalf. We need Christ, who breaks our enemies with a rod of iron. We need Christ, who's invested with all power and authority in heaven above and in hell below.

God sent his own Son in the likeness of sinful flesh
I have two questions. First, what's the flesh? As I've mentioned before, it's human nature. Christ became flesh in that he became a man. John says, "The Word became flesh and dwelt among us" (John 1:14). That means the Holy Spirit united Christ's human nature (body and soul) to Christ's divine nature. They're united while remaining distinct. That means he's fully God and fully

No Condemnation (8:1-4)

man in one person. As the *Creed of Chalcedon* states, Christ is,

> To be acknowledged in two natures, inconfusedly, unchangeably, indivisibly, inseparably; the distinction of natures being by no means taken away by the union, but rather the property of each nature being preserved, and concurring in one Person and one Subsistence, not parted or divided into two persons, but one and the same Son, and only begotten, God the Word, the Lord Jesus Christ.

Second, what's the likeness of sinful flesh? For starters, Paul isn't saying that Christ's human nature is sinful. According to Paul, Christ "knew no sin" (2 Cor. 5:21). According to Peter, Christ "committed no sin" (1 Peter 2:22). So, what does Paul mean when he says that God sent Christ in the likeness of sinful flesh? He means that Christ has the same human nature as us. That's true. However, Christ doesn't have the same fallen human nature as us. By the expression, "likeness of sinful flesh," Paul means that Christ's human nature had all the negative effects of sin upon it—hunger, thirst, pain, weariness, etc. Why's that so important? It's important, because,

> He had to be made like his brethren in all things, so that he might become a merciful and faithful high priest in things pertaining to God, to make propitiation for the sins of the people. For since he himself was tempted in that which he has suffered, he is able to come to the aid of those who are tempted (Heb. 2:17).

God sent his own Son as an offering for sin
The AV and ESV simply state, "for sin." The NASB, on the other hand, states, "as an offering for sin"—although the expression "as an offering" is in italics. Why do the translators of the NASB insert that phrase? They want to indicate what's clearly meant by the phrase "for sin." In the Septuagint, the expression "for sin" is often used to translate "sin offering" (Lev. 4:3; Num. 8:8; Ps. 39:6; Heb. 10:6). It's used in the same sense here. That means God sent his Son for sin—that is, as an offering for sin. Christ's sacrifice satisfies God's justice, thereby appeasing God's wrath and securing God's mercy.

In 8:3, Paul says, God "condemned sin in the flesh." The word "condemned" means the same thing it does in 8:1—punishment. God punished sin in the flesh. Whose flesh? God imputed sin to Christ, and punished him accordingly. He did that "so that the righteous requirement of the law might be fulfilled in us." It's like this: the law requires righteousness from us, but we can't give it. As a result, we're condemned. However, Christ has taken that condemnation upon himself. Christ has fulfilled the righteousness of the law. When we're united to him by faith, the penalty is removed and his righteousness is imputed to us. Therefore, the requirement of the law is fulfilled.

A glorious renovation (8:4)

When Adam disobeyed, we lost two things: the favour of God and the image of God. Christ died to restore both. He secures our pardon (justification) and our renewal (sanctification). In so doing, he deals with the penalty of sin and the power of our sin. Paul emphasizes the second in this verse. Christ died so that the righteous requirement of the law might be fulfilled in us—that is, that he might sanctify us. Can we fulfill the law as a covenant of works? No, certainly not. As a rule of obedience? Yes. Not perfectly, but sincerely. This is the fruit of the Holy Spirit working in us.

Conclusion

"There is therefore now no condemnation for those who are in Christ Jesus." How can I be sure? (1) God has condemned my sin in Christ's flesh. I'm united to Christ. His death is my death. Therefore, the penalty for my sin is gone. God can't require it twice. It would be a miscarriage of justice if he did. (2) God has fulfilled the law in me. Christ's righteousness has been imputed to me. God doesn't require anything more from me. That's how I know there's no condemnation for those who are in Christ Jesus.

> Blessed assurance, Jesus is mine!
> O what a foretaste of glory divine!
> Heir of salvation, purchase of God,
> Born of his Spirit, washed in his blood.[2]

---

[2] Fanny J. Crosby, "Blessed Assurance" in *The Hymnal for Worship and Celebration*, 345.

39
Walking by the Spirit (8:5-13)

God has done something glorious. He has sent his Son "in the likeness of sinful flesh" and "for sin" (8:1-4). Because of the fall, we lost the favour of God (resulting in condemnation) and the image of God (resulting in corruption). Christ died to restore both. Please notice the last statement in 8:4, "who walk not according to the flesh but according to the Spirit." There are two kinds of people. Some walk according to the flesh, and some walk according to the Spirit. How do we tell them apart?

Different appetites (8:5)
"For those who live according to the flesh set their minds on the things of the flesh, but those who live according to the Spirit set their minds on the things of the Spirit." The term "mind" refers to our intentions and purposes. We give our full attention to whatever we set our minds on. We say of the athlete, "He has set his mind on winning gold at the Olympics." We mean that he has devoted himself to his goal. In 8:5, Paul makes the point that we've set our minds on either the "flesh" or the "Spirit." That simply means we're devoted to one or the other.

What are the things of the flesh?
For starters, what's the flesh? It's fallen human nature (7:5, 14, 18). Because human nature is fallen, it's captive to its sensitive appetite—what it sees, tastes, smells, hears, and feels. For that reason, it abuses the creature. We have an example of that in Esau. As Isaac's firstborn, he was entitled to the birthright. One day, he returns from hunting. He's famished and fatigued. Jacob has prepared some food and he offers it to Esau in exchange for his birthright. Esau agrees. What was he thinking? Esau was a godless man, "who sold his birthright for a single meal. For you know that afterward, when he desired to inherit the blessing, he was rejected, for he found no chance to repent, though he sought it with tears" (Heb. 12:16). That's what it means to set the mind on the things of the flesh. It's human nature, enslaved to sin. In that state, man has lost all perspective. Thomas Shepard explains, "Because it never found

that infinite sweetness in God himself, the soul lusts after and delights in the creature for itself, loves pleasure for pleasure, delights in the creature for the creature, not for God ... And here the soul of man cleaves night and day, committing spiritual whoredom before the face of God."[1]

What are the things of the Spirit?
They're the opposite of the things of the flesh. This means that those whose mind is set upon the things of the Spirit aren't captive to the sensitive appetite. They value things according to their true worth. Therefore, they value God's truth. (1) They appreciate the seriousness of man's sin. They say with Paul, "I am of flesh, sold under sin ... I know that nothing good dwells in me, that is, in my flesh" (7:14, 18). They're under no illusion as to what they are in God's sight. (2) They appreciate the two blessings of the covenant of grace. In justification, God removes the penalty of sin. In sanctification, God breaks the power of sin. (3) They appreciate union with Christ. He's our Prophet, who reveals God to us. He's our Priest, who reconciles us to God. He's our King, who rules over us. Appreciating these truths, they exult in hope of the glory of God. Yes, they still struggle with sin. Yes, they still lament their coldness and unfaithfulness. But, in it all, they know what they want—God.

Different ends (8:6)

"For to set the mind on the flesh is death, but to set the mind on the Spirit is life and peace." Paul says the same thing in chapter 6, describing two masters: sin and righteousness. You're enslaved to one or the other. If you're enslaved to sin, you're dead. If you're enslaved to righteousness, you're alive. Paul says the same thing in chapter 7, describing two marriages: law and grace. You're married to one or the other. If you're married to the law, you're dead. If you're married to grace, you're alive. Paul says the same thing in chapter 8, describing two minds: flesh and Spirit. You're set on one or the other. If your mind is set on the flesh, you're dead. If your mind is set on the Spirit, you're alive.

These three comparisons build on the chief comparison that Paul makes in 5:12-19, where he describes two men: Adam and Christ. You're united to one or the other. (1) By birth, you're united to Adam. That union has two implications. First, you share in his sin by imputation. God made a covenant with you in Adam. When Adam sinned, you sinned. God imputes his sin to you. His

---

[1] Thomas Shepard, *The Parable of Ten Virgins*, in *The Works of Thomas Shepard* (Ligonier: Soli Deo Gloria, 1990), 2:28.

guilt and condemnation are yours. You're under the sentence of death. Second, you share in his sin by propagation. When Adam sinned, he lost the image of God. Human nature became corrupt—the flesh. He passed that corrupt nature to you. You're dead. (2) By the new birth, you're united to Christ. That union has two implications. First, you share in his righteousness by imputation. God made a covenant with you in Christ. God imputes his righteousness to you. You're justified in God's sight. The death sentence is gone. Second, you share in his righteousness by propagation. When you're united to Christ, he implants his seed in you thereby producing fruit for God. You're alive.

Paul sums it up like this: "The first man Adam became a living being; the last Adam became a life-giving spirit" (1 Cor. 15:45).

Different conditions (8:7-11)

"For the mind that is set on the flesh is hostile to God, for it does not submit to God's law; indeed, it cannot. Those who are in the flesh cannot please God" (8:7-8). Paul proceeds to explain the two minds in greater detail. Specifically, he demonstrates that these two appetites arise from two conditions. These conditions are distinguished by four marks.

A Carnal Mind	*A Spiritual Mind*
It's death (8:6)	It's life (8:6)
It's at war with God (8:7)	It's at peace with God (8:6)
It's unable to obey God (8:7)	It's able to obey God (8:7)
It's unable to please God (8:8)	It's able to please God (8:8)

Why is the mind set on the flesh hostile toward God? The flesh (fallen human nature) has substituted "self" for God. In 8:7, Paul says, "It does not subject itself to the law of God." Why? "It cannot." For that reason, "Those who are in the flesh cannot please God" (8:8). Why doesn't the leopard eat cabbage? It's against its nature. Why doesn't the sparrow eat beef? It's against its nature. Why doesn't the carnal mind believe in God? It's against its nature. Our sin (self-love) alienates us from God. It enslaves us, darkening our minds, hardening our hearts, and binding our wills. This condition is the flesh. It's death. It's at war with God. It's unable to obey God. It's unable to please God.

"You, however, are not in the flesh but in the Spirit, if in fact the Spirit of God dwells in you. Anyone who does not have the Spirit of Christ does not belong to him" (8:11). The verb *dwell* (*oikeo*) comes from the term *house* (*oikos*). This means that the Holy Spirit dwells in us as if we were his house. And his presence means we belong to Christ. Paul draws out the implications.

Our body is dead because of sin (8:10)
Interestingly, Paul doesn't say we're going to die. He says, "the body is dead." Have you ever heard the expression, "He's a dead man"? It means the person's death is so certain that it's viewed as having happened. That's Paul's point. The sentence was passed in the Garden (Gen. 2:17). We're born under the sentence of death. We're born with the seeds of disease, decay, and death already in us.

Our spirit is alive because of righteousness (8:10)
I know what you're thinking: "That isn't what Paul says." The verse reads: "The Spirit is life because of righteousness." That's the ESV. "The spirit is alive because of righteousness." That's the NASB. So, which is it? Should it read "Spirit" or "spirit"? Paul is making a contrast similar to what he makes in 2 Corinthians 4:16. There, he talks about the "outer nature" (body) wasting away, and the "inner nature" (soul or spirit) being renewed. He seems to be making the same point here. Although my body is dead, my soul is alive. Please notice it's in the present tense. Why's it alive? The ground of this life is Christ's righteousness (8:1). In Christ, we no longer have any reason to fear the sting of death, the terror of judgment, the torment of hell, or the wrath of God. Christ has swallowed it all. He has left nothing for us. Our peace with God is such that he loves us as if we had never been the object of his wrath.

Our body will rise from the dead (8:11)
Paul affirms that God raised Christ from the dead and that the Holy Spirit dwells in us. Because that's true, we can be absolutely certain that God will raise us from the dead. He will give life to our "mortal bodies."

Different obligations (8:12-13)
"So then, brothers, we are debtors, not to the flesh, to live according to the flesh." At one time, we were under obligation to the flesh. We were enslaved to it. But now, we're under obligation to Christ. Therefore, we consider

ourselves to be "dead to sin and alive to God in Christ Jesus" (6:11). "For if you live according to the flesh you will die, but if by the Spirit you put to death the deeds of the body, you will live." It's important to notice two details here.

First, the verb "putting to death" is in the present tense. It's a continuous action. That's significant. Why? It tells us that sanctification isn't a dramatic or climactic experience. It's often depicted as such. Some people describe it as a second blessing. Some people describe it as an altar experience. That's misleading. The present tense of the verb tells us that sanctification is a continuous battle with sin.

Second, the expression "deeds of the body" points to the object of mortification. Paul says the same thing in 6:12-13,

> Let not sin therefore reign in your mortal body, to make you obey its passions. Do not present your members to sin as instruments for unrighteousness, but present yourselves to God as those who have been brought from death to life, and your members to God as instruments for righteousness.

There's nothing wrong with the body as created by God. There's nothing wrong with the senses as created by God. There's nothing wrong with the affections as created by God. The problem is sin. When the soul turns from God to "self," it no longer seeks satisfaction in God. On the contrary, it views satisfaction as gratifying its sensitive appetite. Therefore, the senses become inordinate (Mark 7:20-23).

How do we put to death the deeds of the body? Here's where many err. They think the problem is the senses in themselves. And so, they turn to monasticism, legalism, or asceticism. But those aren't the answer. We must attack the source. The problem is the heart. (1) We must avoid sin. "But put on the Lord Jesus Christ, and make no provision for the flesh, to gratify its desires" (Rom. 13:14). (2) We must avoid anything that lessens our resolve against sin. "I discipline my body and keep it under control" (1 Cor. 9:27). (3) We must be vigilant. "Be watchful, stand firm in the faith, act like men, be strong" (1 Cor. 16:13). (4) We must feed the soul. "But I say, walk by the Spirit, and you will not gratify the desires of the flesh" (Gal. 5:16). (5) We must remember our calling. "Beloved, I urge you as sojourners and exiles to abstain from the passions of the flesh, which wage war against your soul" (1 Peter 2:11).

Conclusion

Regrettably, many think it's possible to be a Christian while walking "according to the flesh." They refer to such a person as a "carnal" Christian. This is a mistake. Paul does use the term *carnal* in reference to the Corinthian Christians (1 Cor. 3:1). He does so because of their jealousy and hostility (1 Cor. 3:3). However, Paul isn't describing two kinds of Christians: carnal and spiritual. Strictly speaking, a carnal man walks according to the flesh. He's an unbeliever. A spiritual man walks according to the Spirit. He's a believer.

Are you a Christian? How do you know? Well, how do you walk? What's your mind set on? That's the answer. Jonathan Edwards hits the mark when he says,

> Such a difference is there between true saints and natural men: natural men have no sense of the ... excellency of holy things ... But the saints, by the mighty power of God, have it discovered to them; they have that supernatural, most noble and divine sense given them, by which they perceive it; and it is this that captivates their hearts, and delights them above all things.[2]

What do you want? What is the habitual frame of your heart? "Where you treasure is, there your heart will be also" (Matt. 6:21). Can you say that God is your happiness, that God's Son is your Saviour, that God's Spirit is your guide, that God's Word is your rule, that God's holiness is your desire, and that God's promises are your hope? Do you seek first the kingdom of God?

---

[2] Jonathan Edwards, *Religious Affections* (Minneapolis: Bethany House Publishers, 1996), 103.

40
The Climax of the Bible (8:14-17)

Each of us is familiar with the term *adoption*. Sadly, it's used very casually today—we talk about adopting a pet, book, highway, or whatever. The term actually has a far more noble significance than these trivial matters. Simply put, adoption is the permanent placement of a child in a family, with all the rights and privileges associated with that family. Paul tells us that God has adopted us. That means God has placed us in his family, with all the rights and privileges of that family. "In love he predestined us for adoption to himself as sons through Jesus Christ, according to the purpose of his will, to the praise of his glorious grace, with which he has blessed us in the Beloved" (Eph. 1:5-6).

Why does Paul use the term *predestined* and not *destined*? The answer: he wants to stress the fact that God determined before creation that he would adopt us. That's important, because it means adoption is God's first choice. It isn't an afterthought. God didn't create the world in hope that he would have natural children—only to discover he had a bunch of little rebels on his hands. No. God predestined us to adoption as sons. He did so before the foundation of the world.

The term *adoption* comes from two words: *huios* (son) and *tithemi* (to place). God literally places us as sons in his family. He says, "I will be a father to you, and you shall be sons and daughters to me" (2 Cor. 6:18; Isa. 43:6). I know that's a difficult relationship for some of us to appreciate. For some, the word *father* actually stirs painful memories. Please don't make the mistake of permitting a negative childhood experience to rob you of the wonder of this relationship. (1) God cares for us. "Are not two sparrows sold for a penny? And not one of them will fall to the ground apart from your Father. But even the hairs of your head are all numbered. Fear not, therefore; you are of more value than many sparrows" (Matt. 10:29-31). (2) God listens to us. "If you then, who are evil, know how to give good gifts to your children, how much more will your Father who is in heaven give good things to those who ask him!" (Matt. 7:11). (3) God plans for us. "For it was fitting that he, for whom and by whom all things exist, in bringing many sons to glory, should make the founder of their salvation perfect through suffering" (Heb. 2:10). (4) God disciplines us. "For the Lord disciplines the one he loves, and chastises every son whom he receives" (Heb. 12:6).

God lavishes the tremendous blessing of adoption upon us "according to the purpose of his will" (Eph. 1:5). He doesn't need us because we're special. He doesn't love us because we're cute. He doesn't adopt us because we're precious. We aren't any of those things. That shouldn't offend us. On the contrary, it should encourage us. If it did depend on us, then God wouldn't have adopted any of us. Before creation, God selected out of the human race, foreseen as fallen, those whom he would adopt. "This divine choice," writes J.I. Packer, "is an expression of free grace, for it is unconstrained and unconditional, not merited by anything in those who are its subjects."[1] You see, human history is simply a record of how God has done that. As Jonathan Edwards explains,

> God had a design of glorifying himself from eternity; yea, to glorify each person in the Godhead. The end must be considered as first in order of nature, and then the means; and therefore we must conceive, that God having professed this end, had then as it were the means to choose; and the principal means that he selected was this great work of redemption.[2]

He redeemed us, justified us, and adopted us—all to the praise of the glory of his grace! Paul celebrates this wonderful truth in 8:14-17.

We reflect our Father's likeness (8:14)

"For all who are led by the Spirit of God are sons of God." We usually use the expression, "led by the Spirit," in reference to divine guidance. We say, for example, "The Spirit is leading me to take that job or to marry that person." But that isn't what Paul means here. It's important to notice that the verse begins with the conjunction *for*, which ties it to the preceding verse, where we read that those who live according to the Spirit "put to death the deeds of the body" (8:13). Those who are "led by the Spirit," therefore, are those who mortify their sin.

We're familiar with the expression, "like father like son." That's Paul's point here. We're to be "imitators of God, as beloved children" (Eph. 5:1). The term "imitate" literally means to mimic. Children mimic their parents—

---

[1] Packer, *Concise Theology*, 149.
[2] Edwards, *A History of the Work of Redemption*, in *Works*, 1:534-535.

THE CLIMAX OF THE BIBLE (8:14-17)

for good or bad. Well, we're to mimic our heavenly Father. We do so in two ways. First, we reflect our Father's *goodness*. "Be merciful even as your Father is merciful" (Luke 6:36). "Love your enemies and pray for those who persecute you, so that you may be sons of your Father who is in heaven" (Matt. 5:44-45). Second, we reflect our Father's *holiness*. "You shall be holy, for I am holy" (1 Peter 1:16). "Be blameless and innocent, children of God without blemish in the midst of a crooked and twisted generation, among whom you shine as lights in the world" (Phil. 2:15).

Our chief act of worship isn't exaltation or admiration or adoration. Our chief act of worship is imitation. We're the children of God. As such, we reflect our Father's likeness.

We enjoy our Father's favour (8:15)
"For you did not receive the spirit of slavery to fall back into fear, but you have received the Spirit of adoption as sons." The expression, "spirit of slavery," has been at the centre of some discussion over the years. There are two major schools of thought as to its significance. (1) On the one hand, some believe the spirit of bondage is bondage to sin. It's the unregenerate state. If that's true, then Paul is saying that we're no longer unregenerate but regenerate. While that's a fact, is it what Paul means here? I don't believe so. (2) On the other hand, some believe the spirit of bondage is conviction for sin. They believe that both instances of the word *spirit* in this verse refer to the Holy Spirit. Therefore, the Spirit of bondage is an activity performed by the Holy Spirit, whereby he convicts us of sin. I agree.

The sons of God have experienced the Spirit of bondage in that the Spirit has performed in them what Paul describes back in 7:9, "I was once alive apart from the law, but when the commandment came, sin came alive and I died." Paul was alive apart from the law. That means he thought everything was okay. One day, however, the Holy Spirit shook him to the core. How? He showed him the true meaning of the law. And Paul suddenly understood he was damned. Sin became alive, and Paul died. That's the Spirit of bondage.

The "Spirit of adoption" eases terror by leading us to Christ where we find forgiveness. He bore the punishment due to our sin. "There is therefore now no condemnation for those who are in Christ Jesus" (8:1). This is a radical change in our status. We approach God as our reconciled Father. He isn't a terrifying God but a loving God. He isn't a condemning God but a pardoning God. He isn't a threatening God but an accepting God.

We perceive our Father's delight (8:15-16)

"But you have received the Spirit of adoption as sons, by whom we cry, 'Abba! Father!' The Spirit himself bears witness with our spirit that we are children of God." The Holy Spirit testifies by means of our renewed affections. (1) We love God by obeying his Word. "Whoever keeps his commandments abides in God, and God in him. And by this we know that he abides in us, by the Spirit whom he has given us" (1 John 3:24). To "keep" God's commandments doesn't mean that we fulfill them perfectly, but that we seek to obey them sincerely. (2) We love holiness by mortifying sin, "Beloved, we are God's children now, and what we will be has not yet appeared; but we know that when he appears, we shall be like him, because we shall see him as he is. And everyone who thus hopes in him purifies himself as he is pure" (1 John 3:2-3). A desire to mortify sin is a mark of adoption. (3) We love others by showing compassion. "No one has ever seen God; if we love one another, God abides in us and his love is perfected in us" (1 John 4:12). Our love for others is the fruit of God adopting us into his family.

If we have any experience of this love (even to a small degree), then we can be certain that the Holy Spirit is sanctifying us. This is how the Holy Spirit witnesses to our adoption. By the Holy Spirit's assistance, our conscience is able to discern the marks (according to Scripture) of those who are the children of God.

We obtain our Father's inheritance (8:17)

Paul says that we're "heirs of God and fellow heirs with Christ." There are at least three components to this inheritance.

First, we inherit the world (4:13). God's covenant with Abraham included three things: offspring, blessing, and land. There's a material fulfillment of these promises in the history of the nation of Israel (1 Kings 4:21). However, the promises point beyond the material to the spiritual. The offspring is Christ, and all who believe in him. The blessing is the gospel. The land is the renewed world.

Second, we inherit God (5:2). At present, we see God's perfections in their effects, namely his works of creation, providence, and redemption; but in the future, we'll see him perfectly. Our knowledge of God will be full and perfect, constant and complete, resulting in hitherto unknown delight as we rest fully and finally in him.

Third, we inherit a glorified soul and body (8:22-23). All the negative effects of sin will be removed.

Conclusion
If you aren't a Christian, then you aren't a child of God. I know that runs contrary to what most people say today. They talk about the fatherhood of God; "We're all God's children." That's a fallacy. By nature, we're all "children of wrath" (Eph. 2:3). We need to be adopted. But praise God! Why? "But to all who did receive him, who believed in his name, he gave the right to become children of God" (John 1:12). As Christians, how should we respond to this wonderful truth?

First, *it should make us imitate him*. Paul exhorts, "Therefore be imitators of God, as beloved children" (Eph. 5:1). A father and son have many similarities. In this context, Paul is talking about character. "You are light in the Lord. Walk as children of light" (Eph. 5:8).

Second, *it should make us revere him*. The Bible says, "Besides this, we have had earthly fathers who disciplined us and we respected them. Shall we not much more be subject to the Father of spirits and live?" (Heb. 12:9). There's a wonderful measure of intimacy and familiarity between father and son. However, that never gives way to disrespect. We don't dread God, but we fear him.

Third, *it should make us trust him*. Christ says, "For the Gentiles seek after all these things, and your heavenly Father knows that you need them all. But seek first the kingdom of God and his righteousness, and all these things will be added to you" (Matt. 6:32-33). I know what my daughters need. I also know what they want. Often times, they're miles apart. How true is that when it comes to our needs? There's what we need, and there's what we want. We can be certain that God will give us what we really need.

Fourth, *it should make us bless him*. Paul says, "Blessed be the God and Father of our Lord Jesus Christ, who has blessed us in Christ with every spiritual blessing in the heavenly places" (1:3). Here's a precious syllogism that we would do well to keep in mind. Major premise: adoption is the permanent placement of a child in a family with all the rights and privileges associated with that family. Minor premise: God has adopted us as his sons. Conclusion: we're part of God's family.

> Behold, what love, what boundless love,
> The Father has bestowed
> On sinners lost, that we should be

Now called the sons of God![3]

---

[3] Robert Boswell, "Boundless Love" in *Hymns of Worship and Remembrance*, 5.

41
Future Glory (8:18)

"You're too heavenly-minded to be of any earthly good!" Have you ever heard someone say that? I know who coined the phrase but I don't really know what he meant by it. Taken at face value, it's simply untrue. As a matter of fact, the opposite is true—you're of no earthly good unless you're heavenly-minded. You'll never persevere in the midst of tribulation unless you're heavenly-minded. You'll never accept the loss of material possessions unless you're heavenly-minded. You'll never be zealous for the salvation of souls unless you're heavenly-minded. You'll never devote yourself to the means of grace unless you're heavenly-minded. You'll never discipline yourself for the purpose of godliness unless you're heavenly-minded. You'll never strive to mortify sin unless you're heavenly-minded.

Generally speaking, the problem is we aren't heavenly-minded. That's at the root of many of our problems. And so, in this study, we're going to consider 8:18, "For I consider that the sufferings of this present time are not worth comparing with the glory that is to be revealed to us." My prayer is that this verse will help us to become more heavenly-minded. I want to proceed by asking three questions.

What does it mean to consider?
In this context, the verb *consider* refers to a process of reasoning that leads to a conclusion. We engage in such "consideration" all the time. (1) The mother considers. She compares the discomfort of bearing a child with the reward of having a child. She doesn't consider the discomfort worthy to be compared to the reward. Therefore, she's prepared to bear the discomfort. (2) The athlete considers. He compares the pain of mastering his sport with the reward of winning a championship. He doesn't consider the pain worthy to be compared to the reward. Therefore, he's prepared to bear the pain. (3) The worker considers. He compares the difficulty of performing his job with the reward of completing his job. He doesn't consider the difficulty worthy to be compared to the reward. Therefore, he's prepared to bear the difficulty.

Do you get the idea? Paul says, "For I consider that the sufferings of this present time are not worth comparing with the glory that is to be revealed to us." There's his present suffering on the one hand, and there's his future glory on the other. He considers. He uses his power of reasoning to compare the two. What's his conclusion? He doesn't conclude that future glory is slightly greater than present suffering. He doesn't conclude that future glory is twice as great as present suffering. He doesn't conclude that future glory is one hundred times or one thousand times greater than present suffering. He concludes, "The sufferings of this present time are not worth comparing with the glory that is to be revealed to us."

What are the sufferings of this present time?
When we hear the term *suffering*, we think of ailments, calamities, deaths, etc. But Paul isn't talking about any of these. He's describing something that's unique to Christians—namely, "the sufferings of Christ" (1 Peter 4:12-16). Paul knew that kind of suffering. He says to Timothy: "You, however, have followed my teaching, my conduct, my aim in life, my faith, my patience, my love, my steadfastness" (2 Tim. 3:10). In Antioch, they forced him out of the city; in Iconium, they attempted to stone him; and, in Lystra, they stoned him and left him for dead (Acts 13-14).

That kind of suffering has continued since Paul's day. We see it in Christians who suffered at the hands of the Jews in the first century. We see it in Christians who suffered in the Roman amphitheatre in the second and third centuries. We see it in Christians who suffered at the hands of the Roman Catholic Church in the Middle Ages. We see it in Christians who suffered at the time of the Reformation. We see it in Christians who suffered while spreading the gospel in Africa and Asia in the eighteenth and nineteenth centuries. We see it in Christians who suffer today in places like China, North Africa, and the Middle East. What's the cause of this suffering? Christ tells us: "If the world hates you, know that it has hated me before it hated you. ... A servant is not greater than his master. If they persecuted me, they will also persecute you" (John 15:18-20).

What is the glory that is to be revealed to us?
We look "for our blessed hope, the appearing of the glory of our great God and Saviour Jesus Christ" (Titus 2:13). That means we will see Christ in all his glory. It will be a sight of the eye, and it will be a sight of the soul. How will

that sight impact us? John Flavel captures the impact in five words.[1]

First, it will be a "liberating" sight. "But our citizenship is in heaven, and from it we await a Saviour, the Lord Jesus Christ, who will transform our lowly body to be like his glorious body, by the power that enables him even to subject all things to himself" (Phil. 3:20-21). We will be free from sin. We will be free from the devil's temptations, the world's opposition, the church's tribulations, and the body's afflictions.

Second, it will be an "affecting" sight. "And after my skin has been thus destroyed, yet in my flesh I shall see God, whom I shall see for myself, and my eyes shall behold, and not another" (Job 19:26-27). On the judgment day, all will stand before God. For the unbeliever, it will be a cause of dread. For the believer, it will be a cause of joy.

Third, it will be "satisfying" sight. "As for me, I shall behold your face in righteousness; when I awake, I shall be satisfied with your likeness" (Ps. 17:15). My mind will be satisfied, in that it won't be able to know more. My affections will be satisfied, in that they won't be able to love more. In short, my soul will find its perfect rest in God. "God will be all in all" (1 Cor. 15:28).

Fourth, it will be a "transforming" sight. "When he appears we shall be like him, because we shall see him as he is" (1 John 3:2). We will be like a mirror, reflecting the character of God.

Fifth, it will be an "everlasting" sight. Paul says, "Then we who are alive, who are left, will be caught up together with them in the clouds to meet the Lord in the air, and so we will always be with the Lord" (1 Thess. 4:17).

That's what Paul considered. Over here, he looks at his present suffering. Over here, he looks at his future glory. What does he conclude? He concludes that the present suffering isn't worthy to be compared with the future glory. "For this light momentary affliction is preparing for us an eternal weight of glory beyond all comparison, as we look not to the things that are seen but to the things that are unseen. For the things that are seen are transient, but the things that are unseen are eternal" (2 Cor. 4:17-18).

Conclusion

We learn a great deal from the above. (1) We need to compare the passing pleasure of sin with the eternal pleasure of knowing God. "For what will it profit a man if he gains the whole world and forfeits his soul? Or what shall a

---

[1] Flavel, *Works*, 1:194-195.

man give in return for his soul?" (Matt. 16:26). (2) We need to compare the cost of following Christ with the reward of following Christ. "And whoever does not take his cross and follow me is not worthy of me. Whoever finds his life will lose it, and whoever loses his life for my sake will find it" (Matt. 10:38-39).

Consideration opens the door between the head and heart, presenting to the affections that which is most important. In so doing, it heals what ails us. (1) *Vanity*. Many Christians are in the grip of entertainment. A sight of future glory will cure you. (2) *Melancholy*. Many Christians are in the grip of despair. A sight of future glory will cure you. (3) *Apathy*. Many Christians are in the grip of indifference. Their interest is waning. Their devotional life is stagnant. A sight of future glory will cure you. (4) *Sensuality*. Many Christians are in the grip of lust. It's like a drug. A sight of future glory will cure you. (5) *Gluttony*. Many Christians are in the grip of greed. They value the creature far more than the Creator. A sight of future glory will cure you. "If we did but walk closely with God one hour in a day in this duty, O what influence would it have upon the whole day besides, and, duly performed, upon the whole life!"[2]

---

[2] John Janeway, *Preface* in Richard Baxter, *The Saints' Everlasting Rest* (New York: American Tract Society), 5.

42
The Creation's Groaning (8:19-25)

"For the creation waits with eager longing for the revealing of the sons of God" (8:19). The expression anxious longing is *apokaradokia*—watching with head outstretched. If you've ever lined up for a parade, you've certainly found yourself stretching your neck to see what's coming from further down the road. That's the idea here. As translated by J.B. Philips, "The whole creation is on tiptoes to see the wonderful sight of the sons of God coming into their own." By way of explanation, Paul states three facts concerning creation—one past, one present, and one future.

The creation was subjected to futility (8:20)
"For the creation was subjected to futility, not willingly, but because of him who subjected it, in hope." When did that happen? In Genesis 1:31, God sees that his creation is very good. With that assessment, we arrive at the end of the creation account. In Genesis 2:1, Moses declares, "Thus the heavens and the earth were finished, and all the host of them." God created the heavens and the earth. He created the sky, sea, land, sun, moon, and stars. He created the plants and animals. He created man in his image, appointing him to rule over creation. There's beauty, harmony, and symmetry. All things serve the function for which they were created, in that they glorify God. It's wonderful, until Adam's sin ruins it all. "Because you have listened to the voice of your wife and have eaten of the tree of which I commanded you, 'You shall not eat of it,' cursed is the ground because of you" (Gen. 3:17).

The creation will be set free (8:21)
"In hope that the creation itself will be set free from its bondage to corruption and obtain the freedom of the glory of the children of God." When God subjected the creation to futility, he did so "in hope." That's likely a reference to Genesis 3:15, where God tied creation's destiny to the seed of the woman. That means God will set creation free from the curse when he glorifies his sons in Christ—the seed of the woman. Christ refers to that as the "regeneration" (Matt. 19:28). Paul refers to it as "the summing up of all things in Christ"

(Eph. 1:10) and "the reconciliation of all things" (Col. 1:20). Peter refers to it as the "new heavens and new earth, in which righteousness dwells" (2 Peter 3:13). John refers to it as "a new heaven and a new earth" (Rev. 21:1). We have a beautiful description of it in Isaiah 11:6-9, culminating in this statement: "for the earth shall be full of the knowledge of the LORD as the waters cover the sea."

God created Adam and Eve to be fruitful and multiply, and to fill, subdue, and rule over the earth. They sinned. They failed. But Christ is the last Adam. He has taken a bride to himself—the church. Together, they fulfill the creation mandate that Adam and Eve failed to fulfill. Christ and his bride are fruitful. They fill the earth. They subdue it. They rule over it. However, this reality is "now" and "not yet." Right now, Christ rules over the new creation. But we don't yet experience the full reality of that. When we're glorified, we will.

Soon after the four children enter the land of Narnia, they meet Mr. Beaver. He shares with them several of the prophecies concerning Aslan and Narnia: "When Adam's flesh and Adam's bone sits at Cair Paravel in throne, the evil time will be over and done."[1] Narnia is in winter's grip. When the four children are enthroned, that grip will end. Similarly, all creation is affected by the fall. It's subjected to futility. However, it will be released from its bondage when the sons of God are enthroned with Christ.

The creation groans and suffers (8:22)

"For we know that the whole creation groans and suffers the pains of childbirth together until now." It was subjected to futility—that's past. It awaits the revelation of the sons of God—that's future. In the meantime, it groans. We see that in numerous ways.

The sky groans. Recently, I was sitting at my office desk. There's a window directly above it. The night sky was bright red—beautiful. That's undeniable. Yet, the sky groans. That's evident in hurricanes, tsunamis, and tornados.

The earth groans. The snow-capped mountains, the rugged coastlines, the mighty canyons, the wind-swept deserts, the fertile valleys, the gentle hills, the dew-soaked fields, the majestic forests, the rushing rivers, the placid lakes, and we could go on. It's beautiful. Yet, it groans. The earth's plates push and pull, resulting in earthquakes and volcanoes. We've had numerous reminders of that in the past couple of years. The earth groans.

---

[1] C.S. Lewis, *The Lion, the Witch, and the Wardrobe* (New York: HarperCollins, 1994), 81.

The animals groan. I enjoy watching nature shows on TV. Recently, we watched the *March of the Penguins*—a documentary tracing their annual migration to Antarctica. It was fascinating. At the same time, it was brutal. Animal life is so fragile. Add to that the predatory instinct. The animals groan.

These are but a few examples, but they serve to illustrate that creation yearns for something else. Its groans are anticipatory. In the case of a mother, the groans associated with childbirth express present pain and (at the same time) an expectation. That's the same for creation. Paul uses the imagery of childbirth because creation's groans are anticipatory. They actually give birth to a new order—a new heaven and a new earth in which righteousness dwell.

Conclusion

There's so much we can take from these verses. (1) They show us the severity of sin. God subjected the entire created order (the world and everything in it) to futility on account of Adam's sin—one sin. What does that tell us about sin? Surely, this should lead to repentance. (2) They show us the futility of creation. At the time of creation, God declared all things to be good. Therefore, we should enjoy creation. However, we should remember that there's a new order coming. That should lead to prudence. We must be very careful how we use God's creatures, guarding against abuse and misuse. (3) They show us the sovereignty of God. God subjected creation to futility. He did so in hope. Hope isn't a vague sentiment, but a confident expectation. God's eternal plan included the subjection of creation to futility, and it includes the restoration of creation to glory. That should lead to reverence. "What God is there in heaven or on earth who can do such works and mighty acts as yours?" (Deut. 3:24).

Those are important lessons. However, I'd like us to focus on one phrase in these verses: "the freedom of the glory of the children of God." John Flavel affirms that the Christian will be free from seven chains.[2]

First, we will be free from "defiling corruptions." The guilt of sin is pardoned by justification. The power of sin is broken by sanctification. And the presence of sin is removed by glorification. Our salvation, therefore, has two realities: "now" and "not yet." We're seated in the heavenly places in Christ, yet we haven't entered into the full experience of that. When we do, the lusts of the flesh and of the mind will be gone. All those struggles will be over. All those nagging sins will be over.

---

[2] Flavel, *Works*, 3:113-117.

Second, we will be free from "sinking sorrows." There are losses that seem crippling at times. Wayward children, debilitating illness, and unrelenting depression—these are all "sinking sorrows." They cause us to cry out with Naomi, "Do not call me Naomi (*pleasant*); call me Mara (*bitter*)" (Ruth 1:20). But the day is coming when we will be free from all that.

Third, we will be free from "entangling temptations." All standards of modesty and decency are quickly disappearing from our society. Materialism has a death grip on our society, promising happiness. Satan is so clever. He uses adversity to make us bitter. He uses prosperity to make us complacent. He attacks from every angle—often without any perception on our part. One day, we will be free from it all.

Fourth, we will be free from "distressing persecutions." We're overwhelmed by present suffering (8:18). But, in that day, we'll be free from slander, ridicule, or worse.

Fifth, we will be free from "pinching wants." We have material wants. We have emotional wants. More importantly, we have spiritual wants—we lack faith, joy, peace, love, etc. We struggle in prayer. We lack understanding when it comes to interpreting God's Word. We lack zeal. These deficiencies plague us. What will it be like when every encumbrance is removed? We will be completely focused on God. The mind won't be able to think of anything greater. The heart won't love anything greater.

Sixth, we will be free from "distracting fears." We're afraid of so many things—some legitimate and some illegitimate. We fear sin and temptation and tribulation. That will be gone. We fear men—what people think about us, what people say about us. We fear the future. What's going to happen tomorrow? What will happen if that happens? I'm not condoning all these fears. I'm simply acknowledging they exist. One day, we'll be free from their grip.

Seventh, we will be free from "deluding shadows." These are the deceitful vanities of the world. "'Vanity of vanities,' says the preacher, 'All is vanity!'" (Eccl. 12:8). Here, the preacher declares the absurdity of life without any reference point to God. Even as Christians, we can succumb at times to these deluding shadows. One day, they'll be but a shadow of a memory.

43
The Believer's Groaning (8:26-27)

Is future glory worth present suffering? Is future joy worth present sorrow? Is the future reward worth the present sacrifice? Is future pleasure worth present pain? Is the future crown worth the present cross? Paul's answer is an emphatic *yes*. "For I consider that the sufferings of this present time are not worth comparing with the glory that is to be revealed to us" (8:17). What's our response? We groan inwardly, wait eagerly, and hope patiently (8:23-25).

Now, I want you to notice the very first word in 8:26, "Likewise." It means that Paul is going to give us additional pastoral counsel for dealing with suffering. He has fixed our attention on the hope of glory. Now, he turns our attention to the power of prayer.

The believer struggles (8:26)
"Likewise the Spirit helps us in our weakness. For we do not know what to pray for as we ought." In what sense are we weak? We're saved, awaiting salvation; we're adopted, awaiting adoption; and we're redeemed, awaiting redemption. This means we live with the tension of the "now" and "not yet" realities of salvation. We groan inwardly, wait eagerly, and hope patiently. As we do, there are many things that don't make sense.

A father's unconverted daughter is making an absolute mess of her life. She refuses to listen to him (or anyone else for that matter). She's convinced she knows everything. She makes bad choice after bad choice. He watches helplessly as she plunges herself into an ever-deepening and ever-widening pit of self-destructive behaviour. This father is *weak*. He doesn't know how to pray.

A wife's dream of a happy marriage evaporates in an instant as she discovers her husband's infidelity. They've been married fourteen years. How's she going to cope with the betrayal? How's she going to handle the rejection? How's she going to deal with the uncertainty? What kind of an impact will this have on their children? This wife is *weak*. She doesn't know how to pray.

A husband sits quietly beside his wife's hospital bed as she breathes her last. Their dreams of growing old together left in a crushed and trampled heap on the ground. What now? There are two small children at home. He's gripped with crushing fear and overwhelming grief. What's he going to do? How's he going to cope? This husband is *weak*. He doesn't know how to pray.

A man loses his job and faces an uncertain future. How's he going to provide for his family? How's he going to cover his son's medical expenses? How's he going to cover his daughter's college tuition? How's he going to start over at 53 years of age? What was the point of his 30 years of loyalty? This man is *weak*. He doesn't know how to pray.

A woman realizes she's about to lose everything for Christ's sake. She lives in an environment increasingly hostile to Christianity. She has no advocate. She has no way of defending herself. She fears for her life. She fears for her loved ones. She's surrounded by injustice. This woman is *weak*. She doesn't know how to pray.

Do you get the idea? We possess God's revealed will in Scripture. We know we're to pray for wisdom, patience, fortitude, etc. We know we're to pray, "Your will be done!" But we don't know what God is doing in most circumstances. We simply don't know what his will is in many instances. We struggle to pray as we navigate the "now" and "not yet" realities of salvation.

The Spirit intercedes (8:26)

"Likewise the Spirit helps us in our weakness. For we do not know what to pray for as we ought, but the Spirit himself intercedes for us with groanings too deep for words." Paul assures us that the Holy Spirit "helps us in our weakness." The verb translated "help" conveys the idea of a man who's carrying a heavy load. He soon realizes it's beyond his strength. He's unable to carry it on his own. It's weighing him down. Thankfully, another man comes alongside to help bear the load. Similarly, the Holy Spirit helps us by bearing the load. He "intercedes for us with groanings too deep for words." He doesn't remove our weakness, but makes our prayers intelligible.

Before moving on, I'm concerned that we avoid three potential errors here.

First, this isn't an excuse for neglecting to pray. Some may be tempted to think like this: "I don't know how to pray. The Holy Spirit intercedes for me. So, I don't need to bother." That isn't what Paul says, and it certainly isn't what Paul does. He prays without ceasing—and so should we. The fact that the Holy Spirit intercedes for us isn't an excuse not to pray. On the contrary, it's an incentive to pray.

Second, this isn't the gift of tongues. Some of our Pentecostal friends appeal to this verse to support the contention that the gift of tongues is "ecstatic" speech (i.e., groaning) as opposed to articulate language. But what does Paul say? He says that the Holy Spirit intercedes with "groanings too deep for words." There's nothing in this verse that indicates that this groaning is expressed as ecstatic speech in our experience.

Third, this isn't a second blessing. This isn't something to be sought by the laying on of hands or by anything like that. This is normal Christian experience that results from simply doing what Paul says in 8:18. If we "consider" the temporal versus the eternal and the material versus the spiritual, we'll groan in anticipation of the coming glory.

The Father knows (8:27)
"And he who searches hearts knows what is the mind of the Spirit, because the Spirit intercedes for the saints according to the will of God." Paul affirms that God "knows what is the mind of the Spirit," meaning he hears the voice of the Holy Spirit interceding for us in tune with his own will. Here's the question: What does the Holy Spirit request on our behalf? I believe Paul gives the answer in the next two verses, where he affirms that we're "called according to [God's] purpose" (8:28). What's God's purpose? He has predestined us "to be conformed to the image of his Son, in order that he might be the firstborn among many brothers" (8:29). Therefore, the Holy Spirit's intercession is in accordance with God's ultimate purpose for us—glorification.

The Holy Spirit "intercedes for us with groaning too deep for words." The Father searches our hearts. He hears this groaning. And he hears the Holy Spirit's clear intention that certain decisions and circumstances come about in the exact way that will bring the most glory to God. F.F. Bruce explains,

> The aspirations after holiness and glory which he creates in the lives of believers are too deep to be adequately articulated in words ... when the human spirit is in closest harmony with the Spirit of God, words may not only prove inadequate; they may even hinder prayer. But God, before whom the thoughts of all are like an open book, recognizes in those unspoken "sighs" deep in his people's hearts the voice of the Spirit interceding for them in tune with his own will, and answers them accordingly.[1]

---

[1] Bruce, *Romans*, 162.

Conclusion

Why should this encourage us? First, we should be encouraged that God doesn't expect us to know his will in each and every circumstance of life. His revealed will is that we obey him, honour him, and glorify him. But we don't know his secret will. We don't need to know everything.

Second, we should be encouraged that the Holy Spirit intercedes for us in the midst of our weakness. This doesn't mean we don't pray. It means he makes our prayers intelligible.

Third, we should be encouraged that, as God searches our hearts, he hears perfect prayer requests. Why? The Holy Spirit intercedes according to the will of God. He knows God's will in every circumstance.

Fourth, we should be encouraged that God answers these prayers, accomplishing far more than we ask or think (Eph. 3:20). And this imparts peace that surpasses all understanding (Phil. 4:7).

44
Glorified (8:28-30)

Paul introduces a subject in 8:17 that holds his attention until the end of the chapter—suffering. What do we say to those who are suffering? What do we say to the Christian who has surrendered multiple internal organs to the surgeon's knife in an attempt to stem the cancer slowly eating away at his body? What do we say to the Christian who feeds and dresses and bathes her once vibrant husband who no longer even remembers her name? What do we say to the Christian who has suffered irreparable physical or mental trauma in an accident? What do we say to the Christian who has limited skills and qualifications, and therefore very limited opportunities? What do we say to the Christian who raises her two children by herself while paying support to her deadbeat husband because she happens to make more than him? What do we say to the Christian who lives in Syria and is afraid to send his kids to school, afraid to open his shop, and afraid to worship at the church because a significant segment of the population actually believes they would be serving God by killing him?

If we're suffering, Paul has something to say to us. (1) He offers us the hope of glory (8:18-25). We're heirs. We inherit a great God, a renewed universe, and a renewed body and soul. (2) He offers us the power of prayer (8:26-27). We don't understand what God is doing. Hence, we don't know what to pray. But the Holy Spirit intercedes for us. (3) He offers us the sovereignty of God (8:28-30). Working backwards through these verses, we discover that God has glorified us, justified us, called us, predestined us, and foreknown us. Therefore, "we know that for those who love God all things work together for good, for those who are called according to his purpose" (8:28).

I want you to notice three details about the five verbs in 8:29-30.

First, they're in the *active voice*. The active voice: "I eat the apple." The passive voice: "The apple was eaten by me." These verbs are in the active voice, meaning each verb describes what God does. God foreknew. God predestined. God called. God justified. God glorified. What did we do? Nothing.

Second, they're in the *past tense*. The present tense: "I eat the apple." The future tense: "I will eat the apple." The past tense: "I ate the apple." These verbs are in the past tense, meaning each verb describes what God has done. That raises a problem because God hasn't done all of these things for all of his people. Has he already glorified us? He has from the vantage point of his decree. He has decreed these things for his people; thus, they're an absolute certainty.

Third, they're *transitive*. A transitive verb has an object. In other words, the object receives the verb's action. Each verb describes what God has done to a specific group of people. Those whom God foreknew, he predestined, called, justified, and glorified. It's the same group of people from start to finish.

This unbreakable chain demonstrates the absolute sovereignty of God in the salvation of his people. As a Christian, my security rests in God's sovereignty. This unbreakable chain is the reason why we *know* all things work together for good for those who "love God" and "are called according to his purpose." These five links are his unalterable plan for his children. This unbreakable chain firmly grounds our salvation in his sovereign plan for us. And everything (including suffering) is subservient to his plan. That's Paul's point.

We're going to work backwards through these verses. In this study, we begin with the truth that God has glorified us. What's Paul talking about? He has already told us (8:11, 17-19, 23). Let me sum it up in three statements.

We will see God

"Blessed are the pure in heart, for they shall see God" (Matt. 5:8). The Bible makes it clear that no one can see God. Why? He dwells in unapproachable light (1 Tim. 6:16). There can be no sight of God's essence because there's no "proportion" between a human eye and that which is infinite and invisible. When we read in the Bible of someone "seeing" God (like Jacob, Moses, Gideon, Manoah), we must understand that they saw a *theophany*—the divine glory veiled in a physical form.

What will it be like to see Christ in glory? Some people see him *carnally* with the eye of flesh. That's true of all those who saw him during his incarnation—while he was on earth. Some people see him *fiducially* with the eye of faith. That's true of all who believe in him (John 6:40). And some see him *beatifically* with the eye of glory: "Blessed are the pure in heart, for they shall see God" (Matt. 5:8). To see Christ beatifically is to be like him—conformed to his image. To be conformed to his image is to love him fully. To love him fully is to enjoy him completely.

God will make us spiritually glorious

"For now we see in a mirror dimly, but then face to face. Now I know in part; then I shall know fully, even as I have been fully known" (1 Cor. 13:12). On that day, we'll be renewed in Christ's image. In Ephesians 4:23, Paul says we're "to put on the new self, created after the likeness of God in true righteousness and holiness." In Colossians 3:10, he says we have put on "the new self, which is being renewed in knowledge after the image of its creator."

Every thought, impulse, and desire will terminate in Christ. Our love for him will burn so intensely that it will bring our hearts into perfect alignment with God's will.

God will make us physically glorious

"So is it with the resurrection of the dead. What is sown is perishable; what is raised is imperishable. It is sown in dishonour; it is raised in glory. It is sown in weakness; it is raised in power" (1 Cor. 15:42-43). (1) Our bodies will be "imperishable." At present, our bodies are subject to decay because they're susceptible to change. (2) Our bodies will be "glorious." At present, our bodies are marred by imperfections and abnormalities. (3) Our bodies will be "strong." At present, our bodies are susceptible to disease, weariness, forgetfulness, and a host of weaknesses. (4) Our bodies will be "spiritual." This doesn't mean that our bodies will be immaterial, but that they will be fully conformed to the life given by the Holy Spirit. Our bodies will be more disposed to spiritual uses.

Conclusion

It's important that we pray regularly for the Holy Spirit to open our spiritual eyes, in order to know this hope to which God has called us (Eph. 1:18). "For I know that my Redeemer lives, and at last he will stand upon the earth. And after my skin has been thus destroyed, yet in my flesh I shall see God, whom I shall see for myself, and my eyes shall behold, and not another. My heart faints within me!" (Job 19:25-27). There are four articles of faith in these few verses. (1) There's a promised redeemer: "my Redeemer lives." (2) There's a promised reckoning: "and at last he will stand upon the earth." (3) There's a promised resurrection: "after my skin has been thus destroyed, yet in my flesh I shall see God." (4) There's a promised reward: "whom I shall see for myself, and my eyes shall behold, and not another."

What's our response? "My heart faints within me!" This is an expression of longing. A sight of glory makes our love more fervent, our hope more stable, our faith more active, our comfort more constant, our obedience more uniform, and our resolve more steadfast.

It purges the heart of sin. "And everyone who thus hopes in him purifies himself as he is pure" (1 John 3:3). This explains why sin has so much power over us. We fail to consider the blessedness to come. We fail to set our minds on things above.

It severs the heart from the world. "But our citizenship is in heaven, and from it we await a Saviour, the Lord Jesus Christ, who will transform our lowly body to be like his glorious body" (Phil. 3:20-21). Can we compare the light of a candle with the light of the sun? No. We should hold earthly things very loosely.

It encourages diligence. "Forgetting what lies behind and straining forward to what lies ahead, I press on toward the goal for the prize of the upward call of God in Christ Jesus" (Phil. 3:13-14). Do we view glory as a prize? If so, it will sweeten our labor.

It encourages obedience. "We exhorted each one of you and encouraged you and charged you to walk in a manner worthy of God, who calls you into his own kingdom and glory" (1 Thess. 2:12). What does it mean to walk worthy of God? It means to live in a way suitable to God's character, reflecting his likeness.

It encourages sincerity. "Whatever you do, work heartily, as for the Lord and not for men, knowing that from the Lord you will receive the inheritance as your reward" (Col. 3:24). Future glory infuses the most mundane of tasks with meaning.

It supports in times of trouble. "For I consider that the sufferings of this present time are not worth comparing with the glory that is to be revealed to us" (Rom. 8:18).

45
Justified (8:28–30)

Peter tells us that "salvation" is a subject "into which angels long to look" (1 Peter 1:12). The term "long" expresses earnest desire. We long for things we desperately want. The angels desperately want to "look into" salvation—to understand the fullness of the gospel. We find this phrase "look into" elsewhere in the Bible. Upon arriving at the empty tomb, Peter is described as "stooping and looking in" (Luke 24:12). He had to bend down in order to get the view he wanted. That's what the angels are doing. They're investigating salvation.

Now, here's an interesting question. Why do the angels long to look into salvation? They want to see the glory of their Creator. They delight in their God; therefore, they long to look into that which reveals their God. "Through the church the manifold wisdom of God is made known to the rulers and authorities in the heavenly places" (Eph. 3:10).

Personally, I find this challenging. The angels don't have any personal interest in salvation. They're "elect" angels (1 Tim. 5:21)—not in terms of salvation but preservation. God kept them from falling when Lucifer (and some of the angels) rebelled. If the elect angels long to look into a salvation that means nothing to them, then how should we long to look into a salvation that means everything to us?

That's precisely what we're doing in 8:28–30. In these verses, Paul points us to God's work in our salvation. We began, in the last study, with glorification. We can summarize it in three statements. (1) We will see God. (2) God will make us spiritually glorious. (3) God will make us physically glorious. "Father, I desire that they also, whom you have given me, may be with me where I am, to see my glory" (John 17:24).

Who does God glorify? He doesn't glorify everyone. He glorifies a select group of people—those whom he justifies. Now, this is a major theme in Paul's epistle to the Romans. I'm going to condense just about everything he says about it into seven statements.

Justification is a change in our legal status (8:1)
"There is therefore now no condemnation for those who are in Christ Jesus." We enter this world condemned. We have three strikes against us: (1) imputed sin (5:18-19); (2) original sin (3:10-18); and (3) actual sin (1:29-30). We're condemned in God's sight. But he graciously changes the verdict from condemned to justified, and he changes the sentence from death to life.

God justifies us as a free gift (3:24)
"[We] are justified by his grace as a gift, through the redemption that is in Christ Jesus," The AV says "freely." The same word is found in John 15:25, "They hated me without a cause." The word refers to something that's totally unwarranted or undeserved. There's nothing in us that evokes God's mercy, compassion, or kindness.

When Christ shed his blood, he paid the penalty for our sin, which God had reckoned to him. God's offended justice was fully satisfied by Christ's sacrifice under divine judgment righteously due to us. As we sing:

> My sin, not in part but the whole,
> is nailed to the cross, and I bear it no more,
> praise the Lord, praise the Lord, O my soul![1]

God justifies us by treating us as if we did what Christ did (5:18-19)
"Therefore, as one trespass led to condemnation for all men, so one act of righteousness leads to justification and life for all men. For as by the one man's disobedience the many were made sinners, so by the one man's obedience the many will be made righteous." God imputes our sin to Christ and imputes Christ's righteousness to us. In other words, God treats Christ as if he had lived our lives. On the cross, he's scourged so that we might be healed, and cursed so that we might be blessed. He dies so that we might live. Now, God treats us as if we had lived Christ's life, meaning he reckons Christ's perfect righteousness to us.

Faith is the hand of the soul by which we receive Christ (3:25)
"God put forward [Christ] as a propitiation by his blood, to be received by faith." We receive all the benefits of Christ's work through putting our trust in him alone. Faith is only the instrument by which we embrace Christ. It's the

---

[1] Horatio Spafford, "It is Well with My Soul" *Hymns of Grace*, 407.

object of our faith that matters. If you venture out on to a frozen pond, it isn't your faith that keeps you from crashing into the water. True, it takes faith to step on to the pond, but it's the object of your faith, the twelve inches of ice, that keeps you safe. Believe in Christ with all your heart, but don't put your faith in your faith.

We are sinning saints (4:5)
"And to the one who does not work but believes in him who justifies the ungodly, his faith is counted as righteousness," It's important to understand that the imputation of Christ's righteousness to us doesn't change us. It alters our standing in God's sight. Our acceptance in God's sight, therefore, isn't determined by what we've done, but by what Christ has done. On this side of glorification, we will always be sinning saints.

Good works follow justification (2:6-7)
"He will render to each one according to his works: to those who by patience in well-doing seek for glory and honour and immortality, he will give eternal life." Because works are a necessary result of conversion, we can say that God will save those whose works are good. The flower on the bush, the grape on the vine, the leaf on the tree, the ear on the stalk—none of them give life, but all of them prove life. There's nothing we contribute to our salvation but our sin, no merit we bring but Christ's, and nothing necessary for justification except for faith alone.

Justification is the greatest source of joy and peace (5:1)
"Therefore, since we have been justified by faith, we have peace with God through our Lord Jesus Christ." The term peace means binding together what has been separated. We're no longer God's enemies. This peace is achieved by Christ's atoning work on the cross. In Christ, we no longer have any reason to fear the wrath of God. Christ has swallowed it all, and he has left nothing for us.

Conclusion
The doctrine of justification should break the back of hopelessness. We must hear it over and over again. And we must believe it over and over again. Rather than filling our minds with fear, worry, regret, and shame, we need to fill them with Christ. We must live continually in the sight of Christ's infinite merit.

We immerse ourselves in the blessings of union of Christ. We contemplate our standing in Christ. When we think of our sin, we remember his forgiveness. When we think of our guilt, we remember his merit. When we think of our weakness, we remember his strength. When we think of our pride, we remember his humility. When we think of our failures, we remember his sufferings. When we think of our need, we remember his fullness. When we think of our temptation, we remember his tenderness. When we think of our vileness, we remember his righteousness.

46
Called (8:28–30)

What does it mean to be called? To answer that, we need to distinguish between two calls in Scripture.

First, there's the *general* call. That's Christ's voice in the proclamation of his Word by the preacher. It's heard with the ear. It's indiscriminate. Simply put: God invites all people without exception to salvation. The terms are simple: Christ died for sinners; you're a sinner; you must repent; and you must believe in Christ for salvation. Christ declares, "Come to me, all who labor and are heavy laden, and I will give you rest" (Matt. 11:28).

That can't be what Paul is talking about in our text. Why not? He makes it clear that those whom God calls are justified and glorified. But not everyone is justified and glorified. Therefore, not everyone is called—at least not in the sense Paul means it here.

Second, there's the *effectual* call. That's Christ's voice in the application of his Word by the Spirit. It's heard with the heart. The *Westminster Shorter Catechism* explains it like this: "Effectual calling is the work of God's Spirit, whereby convincing us of our sin and misery, enlightening our minds in the knowledge of Christ, and renewing our wills, he persuades and enables us to embrace Jesus Christ, freely offered to us in the gospel."

We see these two calls in the case of Lydia: "The Lord opened her heart (*the special call*) to pay attention to what was said by Paul (*the general call*)" (Acts 16:14). This special call bears two marks.

This call is essential

We can't come to God: "No one can come to me unless the Father who sent me draws him" (John 6:44). We can't obey God: "For the mind that is set on the flesh is hostile to God, for it does not submit to God's law; indeed it cannot" (Rom. 8:7). We can't please God: "Those who are in the flesh cannot please God" (Rom. 8:8). We can't know God: "The natural person does not accept the things of the Spirit of God, for they are folly to him, and he is not able to understand them because they are spiritually discerned" (1 Cor. 2:14).

Why is this the case? When Adam sinned, he plunged all of humanity into spiritual darkness (3:10-18). The will always chooses what the mind thinks best and the heart wants most. No one thinks God is best, and no one wants God most. Man is dead in his sin. Why doesn't the unbeliever come to God, obey God, please God, or know God? It's against his nature. Sin enslaves us, darkening our minds, hardening our hearts, and binding our wills. This condition is called "the flesh." It's at war with God. We need divine intervention. God must call us.

Thomas Watson explains,

> If you consider what power sin has in a man, it is a miracle that he should forsake it. Sin is a man's self, like a member of the body which is not easily parted with. Sin is woven and incorporated into the nature of a man. It is as natural to sin as for fire to burn. Sin has bewitched and stolen away the heart. Now, that sin which has gotten such power over a man should be beaten out of all its forts and castles, what a wonder this is! How is it but from invincible grace? The Spirit draws sweetly but irresistibly. It allures yet conquers. Grace sits paramount in the soul. It is that strong water which eats asunder the iron chain of sin. Grace repels and beats back corruption.[1]

This call is effectual
We have a dog at home. I often let her loose to play in the backyard. When it's time for her to come in, I call her. My voice goes up a couple of octaves. I make silly noises. I shake her box of dog biscuits. Why? I'm coaxing her to do something she might not necessarily want to do. That *isn't* how God calls. He doesn't invite us. He doesn't encourage us. He doesn't coax us. He doesn't beg us. He calls us effectually whereby we respond willingly.

When God calls, it's like Christ standing in the ship—the wind howling above him, the rain pouring down upon him, and the waves crashing all around him. He calls out: "Be quiet!" The storm stops.

When God calls, it's like Christ standing before a groveling demoniac who mutilates himself, breaks the chains that bind him, and lives among the tombs. He calls out: "Be gone!" The demon departs.

When God calls, it's like Christ standing beside a tomb containing the body of a friend who had died a few days earlier. He calls out: "Come forth!" The dead man emerges.

When God calls, it's like "in the beginning" when he declared, "Let there

---

[1] Thomas Watson, *The Mischief of Sin* (London: Thomas Parkhurst, 1671), 147.

be light!" There was light.

Christ declares, "Everyone who has heard and learned from the Father comes to me" (John 6:45). Again, "My sheep hear my voice, and I know them, and they follow me" (John 10:27). George Swinnock writes,

> Men and angels may call long enough to the blind to see, and the dead to live, and all in vain. But if God say to a sinner that lies rotting in the grave, almost eaten up of the vermin of lusts, unsavory, and stinking in the eyes of all men, sinner, come forth from you cursed carnal condition; the man that was bound hand and foot, fettered by the devil, his jailer, comes forth, is loosed of his bonds, and lives forever.[2]

Conclusion

By calling us God changes our hearts thereby producing faith (2 Thess. 2:13-14). By believing in Christ we become one with him (Gal. 2:20). Because we're one with Christ, God looks upon us as if we did what Christ did (1 Cor. 1:30). Because God looks upon us as if we did what Christ did, he pronounces the sentence of justification (2 Cor. 5:21). Because God justifies us, he glorifies us. What use may we make of this glorious truth?

It corrects us. "For many are called, but few are chosen" (Matt. 22:14). God's special call is the breaking out in time of his eternal purpose to save his people. When I was younger, I insisted that we must accommodate divine sovereignty to human capability. I've since learned that the opposite is true. We must accommodate human capability to divine sovereignty. There was a time when I had to surrender my philosophical presuppositions—namely, the notion that I possess the power of ultimate self-determination. I don't.

It challenges us. "Therefore, brothers, be all the more diligent to make your calling and election sure" (2 Peter 1:10). Many years ago, I bought into a form of "free grace" theology, according to which saving faith is viewed as a singular act through which one experiences the grace of God. Once the grace of God is received, an individual no longer needs to believe. That's why there are countless people who live however they please yet think they're saved simply because they said a prayer—they believed. By the special call, God doesn't produce an *act* of faith but an *attitude* of faith.

It motivates us. "I therefore, a prisoner for the Lord, urge you to walk in a manner worthy of the calling to which you have been called" (Eph. 4:1). God

---

[2] Swinnock, *Works*, 4:448.

has called us to be like his Son in goodness and holiness. We need to be reasonable and act accordingly.

It encourages us. "This is the will of him who sent me, that I should lose nothing of all that he has given me, but raise it up on the last day" (John 6:39). Salvation doesn't depend on me. It depends on God. From election to glorification, I'm dependent upon God's saving and sustaining grace. I believe that God chose me from all eternity, that he predestined me to share the glory of his Son, and that he called me out of death into life enabling me to believe in Christ. That said, I'm convinced that he'll complete what he has started.

It humbles us. "What do you have that you did not receive?" (1 Cor. 4:7). The answer is nothing. The only thing that distinguishes me from the unbeliever is God's good pleasure. Where would I be without God's sovereign grace? It completely rules out boasting because it implies a reliance on God not only for the provision of salvation on the cross but also for the application of salvation to my heart.

It compels us. "I endure everything for the sake of the elect, that they also may obtain the salvation which in Christ Jesus goes with eternal glory" (2 Tim. 2:10). The fact that God has the right and power to call whomever he will from every people group on the face of the earth is the only reason I still preach. This is the dynamite of God in the hard places of world evangelization.

It overwhelms us. "For from him and through him and to him are all things. To him be the glory forever. Amen" (Rom. 11:33). I never felt the full wonder of grace until I surrendered my claim to have the final say in salvation. I never gave God all the glory for my salvation until I saw myself so utterly helpless that he had to do it all, or else I'd still be dead in my trespasses and sins.

47
Predestined (8:28-30)

This is a subject that elicits a plethora of reactions—from horror to jubilation, from anger to thanksgiving, from cynicism to wonder.

We can't avoid it. I've met people who attempt to sidestep it. How? (1) "I don't believe in predestination." You have to. It's part of the Bible. (2) "I don't care about predestination." You have to. It's part of the gospel.

We should be excited about the doctrine of predestination. God intends for it to comfort us. These two (security and adversity) are the greatest causes of perplexity in a believer's life. The doctrine of predestination resolves them. When rightly understood, it exalts God, inspires awe, breeds humility, enlarges faith, strengthens hope, and cultivates patience.

But we need to be careful how we approach it, taking our lead from Scripture. First, it never argues about predestination. It makes assertions. That's it. Second, it reproves those who want to argue about predestination (9:20). Before we ask our questions, submit our arguments, or present our objections, we must acknowledge that we're assuming that our puny minds are capable of understanding the works of an infinite being. Third, it never answers our questions about predestination. It doesn't provide a philosophical explanation. It doesn't attempt to resolve inherent tensions. It proceeds on the premise that God is boundless whereas our minds are small, sinful, and skewed.

So, what can we affirm?

God is unsearchable

"I am the first and the last; besides me there is no god. Who is like me? ... Let them declare what is to come, and what will happen" (Isa. 44:6-7). God is from himself—his own first cause; for himself—his own last end; and by himself—completely independent. We have a greater chance of holding the stars in the palm of our hand, measuring the mountains on a scale, gathering the oceans in a thimble, and balancing the world's skyscrapers on a needle, than we do of finding out God. Sooner or later, in our study of God, we run into mystery—not confusion and not contradiction, but mystery (more than our minds can grasp). When we refuse to embrace mystery, we usually embrace heresy.

God decrees all things

"I am God, and there is none like me, declaring the end from the beginning and from ancient times things not yet done, saying, 'My counsel shall stand, and I will accomplish all my purpose'" (Isa. 46:9-10). God is self-existent and all-sufficient. God is eternal, immortal, and unchangeable. God is simple, meaning he can't be divided into parts. This necessarily means that God's sovereign will is inseparable from God. This means that his decrees are as eternal as himself.

God decrees all things in two ways

"This Jesus, delivered up according to the definite plan and foreknowledge of God, you crucified and killed by the hands of lawless men" (Acts 2:23). By an act of his will, God decrees all things that come to pass. But he does so in two ways. (1) He wills that which is good; and he produces the good that he decrees. (2) He wills that which is evil; and he permits the evil he decrees. As Thomas Manton explains, "God foresees nothing as certainly future but what he has before determined shall be, nothing good but what he has decreed to perform, nothing bad but what he has decreed to permit."[1]

All of God's decrees come to pass

"But he is unchangeable, and who can turn him back? What he desires, that he does" (Job 23:13). God is unchangeable. All conditions are included in his plan. If that's true, then why does the Bible indicate that God repented? For example, we read that God repented he had made man on the earth. This means he disapproved of man's sin. It doesn't mean he changed his mind. "I am the LORD. I do not change" (Mal. 3:16). If God changes, there is no God.

One of God's decrees is predestination

"For those whom he foreknew he also predestined." The verb means to determine a horizon and set out for it. God has decreed that his people will be conformed to the image of Christ in holiness and happiness. The object of God's foreknowledge isn't what we do or say, but us personally. It might help to set this in the context of Christ's declaration: "I know my own" (John

---

[1] Manton, *Works*, 7:393.

10:14). Doesn't Christ know everyone? No, not in the sense he means here. Christ is saying that he's intimately acquainted with his "own." "I never knew you; depart from me" (Matt. 7:23).

The effects of predestination cannot be its cause
"God chose you as the first fruits to be saved, through sanctification by the Spirit and belief in the truth" (2 Thess. 2:13). Paul doesn't say God chose us because of these things: "sanctification" and "belief." He says that chose us "to be saved." "Sanctification by the Spirit" and "belief in the truth" are the means by which he applies that salvation. In other words, God didn't predestine us so that we might believe. We believe because God predestined us. All good is the fruit of predestination. If it were the cause, then predestination would be post-destination.

Predestination doesn't prevent anyone from being saved
"God desires all people to be saved and to come to the knowledge of the truth" (1 Tim. 2:4). God isn't the case of anyone's destruction. We're free because our choices are our own, but our choices aren't free from our darkened mind and hardened heart. In a word, we possess a free will that's in bondage to sin.

We shouldn't obsess over questions concerning predestination. Here's the only question that should concern us: What must I do to be saved? This is the question of the broken-hearted, the troubled conscience, the convicted sinner. Sinners are in danger of hell. The only thing that matters is how to escape it. God takes no pleasure in the destruction of the wicked (Ezek. 18:23). God has made provision for sinners. God calls sinners. God receives sinners who repent. "The LORD is near to the broken-hearted and saves the crushed in spirit" (Ps. 34:18). If sinners fail to respond, they alone are to blame.

Predestination doesn't make God unjust
"Every mouth may be stopped, and the whole world may be held accountable to God" (Rom. 3:19). What does it mean to be fair? It means to give someone what he deserves. When the angels rebelled, God condemned them (1 Tim. 5:21). He didn't make any provision for their salvation. Was that unfair? No. He gave them what they deserved. We're sinners. Does God owe us anything? No. God is at liberty to do whatever he wants with us. We deserve to be punished. God is at liberty to inflict that punishment now. Or, God is at liberty to delay that punishment until the future. Or, God is at liberty to save whomever

he pleases from that punishment. God is at liberty to have mercy on whomever he will have mercy.

Most people who struggle with predestination are really struggling with something else: total depravity and divine wrath.

Predestination is a special cause of peace and comfort
In Christ, we're the object of God's eternal love. We aren't in the grip of blind forces such as fortune, luck, chance, or fate. All that happens to us is divinely planned. We always have his *attention*: "through [Christ] we have access in one Spirit to the Father" (Eph. 2:18). And we always have his *affection*: he cares for us (1 Peter 5:7). If we wander, he guides us; if we stumble, he holds us; if we fall, he lifts us; if we err, he corrects us; if we grieve, he comforts us.

48
Foreknown (8:28-30)

God is unsearchable. "I am the first and the last; besides me there is no God. Who is like me? ... Let them declare what is to come, and what will happen" (Isa. 44:6-7). This unsearchable God is a sovereign being. He's the first cause of every action, impulse, thought, and breath. The motions of all his creatures depend upon his concurrence. The power that made everything maintains everything: he "upholds the universe by the word of his power" (Heb. 1:3). If he were to withhold his influence, the fire wouldn't burn, the eye wouldn't see, the sun wouldn't shine, the wind wouldn't blow, the hand wouldn't move, the bird wouldn't fly, and the grass wouldn't grow. He's the principle of cohesion that holds the entire cosmos in place. It's impossible for any part of creation to exist for a moment apart from him. He rules the universe fully and completely.

There's no proportion between this boundless God and our bound intellect, between this limitless God and our limited mind, between this infinite God and our finite understanding. God does "marvelous things without number" (Job 5:9). Can we "find out" God? We're but small children, standing on the beach, trying in vain to hold the ocean in a bucket. Sooner or later, we run into mystery.

Here's a case in point: God "foreknew" us.

What does it mean to foreknow?
Many people assume Paul is saying that God foreknew those who would choose to believe in him. There are four reasons why that interpretation is problematic.

First, if God's foreknowing is his knowing in advance those who would choose to believe in him, then no one is saved. Why do I say that? Paul has made it clear that no one seeks for God (3:11). He has also made it clear that no one pleases God (8:8).

Second, if God's foreknowing is his knowing in advance those who would choose to believe in him, then there's no security. If God's role in our salvation depends on us, we don't have any reason to feel secure.

Third, if God's foreknowing is his knowing in advance those who would choose to believe in him, then predestination is contingent on us. But that contradicts what Paul says in 9:16, "So then it depends not on human will or exertion, but on God who has mercy."

Fourth, if God's foreknowing is his knowing in advance those who would choose to believe in him, then salvation is based on works. But that contradicts what Paul says in 11:5-6, where he equates God's foreknowing with his "gracious choice."

When Paul says, "God foreknew us," he means God knew us in advance. He foreknew us, just as he predestined us, called us, justified us, and glorified us. The object of God's foreknowing isn't what we do or say. It's *us*. Christ proclaims, "I know my own" (John 10:14). Who are his "own"? "You have given me authority to give eternal life to all whom *you have given me*" (John 17:2). "I am not praying for the world but for those whom *you have given me*" (John 17:9). "I desire that they also, whom *you have given me*, may be with me where I am, to see my glory" (John 17:24).

Prior to creation, God chose out of humanity, foreseen as fallen, those whom he would give to Christ. (1) This gracious choice is unchangeable: "God's firm foundation stands, bearing this seal: 'The Lord knows those who are his'" (2 Tim. 2:19). (2) This gracious choice is unto salvation: "God has not destined us for wrath, but to obtain salvation through our Lord Jesus Christ" (1 Thess. 5:9). (3) This gracious choice is according to God's will: "It depends not on human will or exertion, but on God, who has mercy" (Rom. 9:16). (4) This gracious choice is designed to accentuate God's glory: "He chose us ... to the praise of his glorious grace" (Eph. 1:6).

All branches of the church have a doctrine of election. They differ in terms of the condition upon which God elects. (1) Sacerdotalists: He elects those whom he foresees receiving grace through the church (2) Lutherans: He elects those whom he foresees not resisting his grace (3) Remonstrant Arminians: He elects those whom he foresees cooperating with him (4) Wesleyan Arminians: He elects those whom he foresees believing and persevering (5) Evangelical Arminians: He elects those whom he foresees believing in a singular act. (6) Calvinists: "I will have mercy on whom I have mercy" (Rom. 9:15).

What about the balance between divine sovereignty and human responsibility?

We maintain this balance by proclaiming six truths. (1) We must believe in order to please God. "Without faith it is impossible to please him" (Heb. 11:6). (2) Everyone who believes in Christ will be saved. "I am the bread of life; whoever comes to me shall not hunger, and whoever believes in me shall never thirst" (John 6:35). (3) We're unwilling to believe. "No one can come to me unless the Father who sent me draws him" (John 6:44). (4) God must enable us to believe: "For by grace you have been saved through faith. And this is not your own doing; it is the gift of God" (Eph. 2:8). "For to you it has been granted for Christ's sake, not only to believe in him, but also to suffer for his sake" (Phil. 1:29). (5) Faith is a fruit of election: "But we ought always to give thanks to God for you, brothers beloved by the Lord, because God chose you as the first-fruits to be saved, through sanctification by the Spirit and belief in the truth" (2 Thess. 2:13).

We see this balance in Acts 13:38-39, where Paul declares, "Let it be known to you, therefore, brothers, that through this man forgiveness of sins is proclaimed to you, and by him everyone who believes is freed from everything." It's clear that we must believe in order to be saved. God will forgive everyone who believes. However, no one will believe apart from God's sovereign grace. And so, Paul goes on to say, "As many as were appointed to eternal life believed" (Acts 13:48).

What is the benefit of this doctrine?
First, it shapes our understanding of the gospel. If we don't understand the doctrine of election, then we will not fully understand the doctrines of justification, sanctification, and glorification. The entire order of salvation rests upon this doctrine. A less than biblical understanding of election will skew our understanding of other doctrines.

Second, it reveals God's love in a special way. God set his love upon us before the foundation of the world (Eph. 1:3). He saw us dead in our trespasses and sins, and yet he set his love upon us in Christ. We don't need to earn God's love. We don't need to merit God's love. We don't need to worry that God's love for us will change.

Third, it changes us. "What do you have that you did not receive?" (1 Cor. 4:7). The only thing that distinguishes the believer from the unbeliever is the doctrine of election. This realization elicits gratitude, cultivates humility, compels service, encourages forgiveness, and promotes holiness.

Fourth, it comforts us. "The sheep hear his voice; and he calls his own sheep by name and leads them out" (John 10:3). He knows us by name. He knows everything about us. He loves us anyway. He embraces us with a special love. He delights in us. He approves of us. He's aware of our needs, our tears, our fears, our struggles, our worries. We're his children.

Conclusion

God foreknew us, predestined us, called us, justified us, and glorified us. In stating these five facts, Paul's main point is to demonstrate that salvation is of God from start to finish. With that in view, C.J. Vaughan comments,

> Everyone who is eventually saved can only ascribe his salvation, from the first step to the last, to God's favour and act. Human merit must be excluded: and this can only be by tracing back the work far beyond the obedience which evidences, or even the faith which appropriates, salvation; even to an act of spontaneous favour on the part of that God who foresees and foreordains from eternity all his works.[1]

I think back on my own life. There was a time when the gospel didn't make any sense to me. Then, God called me. He opened my eyes. I repented of my sin and believed in Christ. And God justified me. That act was rooted in his foreknowledge and predestination of me. Now, I'm certain that he will glorify me because all those whom he foreknew he also glorified. Since that's true, I know I'm in God's hands. And, for this reason, I'm absolutely certain ("I know") God causes all things to work together for my good. Calvin writes,

> In times of adversity believers comfort themselves with the solace that they suffer nothing except by God's ordinance and command, for they are under his hand ... his solace, I say, is to know his Heavenly Father so holds all things in his power, so rules by his authority and will, so governs by his wisdom, that nothing can befall except he determine it.[2]

---

[1] C.J. Vaughan, *St. Paul's Epistle to the Romans* (Macmillan, 1885), 163.
[2] John Calvin, *Institutes of the Christian Religion*, ed. J.T. McNeill (Philadelphia: Westminster Press, 1960), 1:16:3.

49
All Things for Good (8:28–30)

Jacob had a hard life. He was forced to flee from his father's home because his brother hated him. He was humiliated in his uncle's home. He was cheated of the woman he loved. He was deceived into marrying another woman. He was forced to flee from his uncle's home, because his cousins resented him. He was grieved by the death of his wife Rachel in childbirth. He was grieved at the rape of his daughter Dinah. He was troubled by the murderous ways of his sons Simeon and Levi. He was troubled by the licentious ways of his son Judah, who fathered a child by his own daughter-in-law. He was robbed of his beloved son Joseph. His attitude in the midst of these circumstances is summed up in his cry, "All this has come against me" (Gen. 42:36).

Joseph, too, had a hard life. He was resented and hated by all of his brothers. He was stripped of his clothes and tossed into a pit like an animal. He was ignored as he pleaded with his brothers to help him. He was treated as a mere slave. He was transported to a foreign country (the land of Egypt), where he didn't know the language or culture. He was separated from all that was familiar to him. He was sold as a piece of merchandise into the house of Potiphar. He was hounded by a licentious woman—"bitter as wormwood, sharp as a two-edged sword" (Prov. 5:4). He was wrongfully accused. He was wrongfully imprisoned. His attitude in the midst of these circumstances is summed up in his cry, "God meant it for good" (Gen. 50:20).

Jacob and Joseph represent two very different outlooks on life. There are Christians who identify with Jacob. Perhaps that's you. You're experiencing affliction. Things aren't going your way. Your cry is Jacob's cry: "All this has come against me!" There are Christians who identify with Joseph. Perhaps that's you. You're experiencing affliction. Things aren't going your way. Your cry is Joseph's cry: "God means it for good!"

How do we account for these very different outlooks? Our outlook is determined by our understanding of 8:28, "And we know that for those who love God all things work together for good, for those who are called according to his purpose."

What is the meaning of "good"?

We often err in our definition of "good." Why? We define "good" according to the sensual instead of the spiritual, according to what we want instead of what we need, according to what makes us happy instead of what makes us holy, according to what's seen instead of what's unseen, according to what's temporal instead of what's eternal. What's the "good" in 8:28? It's God's purpose. According to 8:29, his purpose is to glorify himself by conforming us to the image of his Son. John Flavel expresses that so well: "The intent of the Redeemer's undertaking was not to purchase for his people riches, ease, and pleasures on earth; but to mortify their lusts, heal their natures, and spiritualize their affections; and thereby to fit them for the eternal fruition of God."[1] All things work to together for that good.

What is included under the banner of "all things"?

It includes prosperity: health, strength, friends, wealth, honour, etc. It also includes adversity: sickness, weakness, enemies, poverty, dishonour, etc. All things (prosperity and adversity) work together for our good. That's difficult to comprehend. The following illustration from Joel Beeke might help us.

> The life of a true Christian resembles the internals of a watch. Open a watch, and what do you see? You see that certain wheels, which turn in a counterclockwise direction, are attached to other wheels that are working in a clockwise direction. Your first thought may be that the watchmaker is either foolish or confused. But he is neither. Rather, he has so arranged the internals of this watch and put in a mainspring to govern all its wheels, that when wound, though one wheel turns clockwise and another counterclockwise, all work together to move the hands around the face of the watch at precisely the right speed. Many wheels appear to counteract each other, but they all work together for the identical purpose of revealing accurate time.[2]

Some circumstances in our life run clockwise. These are good providences that work for our good. Some circumstances in our life run counterclockwise. These are evil providences that work for our good. In this context, Paul's focus is upon adversity (8:18). How does adversity result in good? How does it conform us to the image of Christ? Thomas Watson provides some helpful

---

[1] Flavel, *Works*, 6:84.
[2] http://www.gospeltrumpet.net/uploads/3/1/6/5/31658911/4_-_all_things_working_together_for_good_-_romans8-28_-_dr_beeke.pdf

insights.[3]

First, it reveals our sin: "Water in the glass looks clear, but set it on fire, and the scum boils up" (Thomas Watson). When things are going our way, we begin to think we have it all together. Affliction, however, cures us of that fallacy. It shows us our sin. It reminds us of its ugliness. And that sight produces humility. In a word, God afflicts us in order to humble us.

Second, it destroys our sin: "There is much corruption in the best heart; affliction does by degrees work it out, as the fire works out the dross from the gold" (Thomas Watson). As Christians, we'll try to hide behind our righteousness—our service, our attendance, our niceness, our activity, etc. Affliction burns all of that away.

Third, it loosens our heart from the world: "When you dig away the earth from the root of the tree, it is to loosen the tree from the earth; so God digs away our earthly comforts to loosen our hearts from the earth" (Thomas Watson). As Christians, we struggle with not being of the world while being in the world. Unending earthly delights aren't good for us. Affliction loosens our attachment to this world. It helps us see that the world is a passing shadow.

Fourth, it increases our joy: "Afflictions are ensigns of glory, signs of sonship" (Thomas Watson). That's what Paul says in 8:17. God deals with us as sons. "For the Lord disciplines the one he loves, and chastises every son whom he receives" (Heb. 12:6). In the home, a lack of discipline is a sure sign of a lack of love. Parents discipline their children because they love them. The same is true in God's family.

Fifth, it increases our faith: "Being sanctified, afflictions bring us nearer to God" (Thomas Watson). Affliction causes us to look for help. When a child skins her knee, or loses her doll, or hears the thunder, she runs to her mom and dad. We're no different. Without affliction, it's business as usual. But affliction startles us from our self-reliance. In the end, this makes us happy because it causes us to seek fellowship with God.

Was it good that Joseph was sold as a slave into Egypt? As a circumstance, "no." But according to God's purpose, it was good for Joseph. Was it good that Daniel was persecuted? As a circumstance, "no." But according to God's purpose, it was good for Daniel. Was it good that David was the object of Saul's hatred? As a circumstance, "no." But according to God's purpose, it was good for David. Was it good that Naomi's husband and sons died? As a

---

[3] Thomas Watson, *All Things for Good* (Carlisle: Banner of Truth, 1994), 25–32.

circumstance, "no." But according to God's purpose, it was good for Naomi.

Why was it good for them? They learned humility, faith, hope, peace, and patience. Is it good that you're suffering? As a circumstance, it isn't good. According to God's purpose, it is good for you. As Thomas Watson explains, "As the hard frosts in winter bring on the flowers in the spring, and as the night ushers in the morning-star, so the evils of affliction produce much good to those that love God."

Conclusion

What's my response to the above?

First, *I should be challenged*. Can I say with the psalmist: "It is good for me that I was afflicted, that I might learn your statutes" (Ps. 119:71)? If I can't, something is wrong. It's a sin to murmur under God's yoke. I'm not talking about crying, struggling, or groaning. Affliction hurts. No one denies that. I'm talking about permitting affliction to affect our walk, our marriage, our ministry, our relationships, our worship, etc. We sin when affliction tarnishes the image of Christ instead of producing the image of Christ. I've quoted a great deal from Thomas Watson in this study. I want to refer to him once more. He writes, "There are no sins God's people are more subject to than unbelief and impatience." You see, when we lose sight of God's purpose in adversity, that's precisely what happens—we succumb to unbelief and impatience. That's terrible. Why? (1) It's an "ungrateful" sin. When we manifest unbelief and impatience in affliction, we've lost sight of what God has done in our lives. It's an expression of ingratitude. (2) It's an "irrational" sin. When we manifest unbelief and impatience in affliction, we've lost sight of how God works. And we've lost sight of what God promises. (3) It's an "aggravating" sin. When we manifest unbelief and impatience in affliction, we've made ourselves vulnerable to all sorts of sins. Impatience always fosters bitterness, anger, discouragement, rashness, harshness, etc. The opposite is true of the Christian, whose sight remains fixed upon God's purpose in affliction.

Second, *I should be comforted*. I hope we're encouraged by the knowledge of what God is doing through affliction. Let me conclude with another illustration from Joel Beeke:

> Consider as an example the story of a man who once found a cocoon of the emperor moth and took it home to watch it emerge. One day a small opening appeared. For several hours the moth struggled but couldn't

seem to force its body past a certain point. Deciding something was wrong, the man took scissors and snipped the remaining bit of cocoon. The moth emerged easily, its body large and swollen, the wings small and shriveled. The man expected that in a few hours the wings of the moth would unfurl in their natural beauty, but they did not. The moth spent its life dragging around a swollen body and shriveled wings. The struggle and pain necessary to pass through the tiny opening of the cocoon are God's way of forcing fluid from the body of a moth into the wings. The merciful snip of the scissors was, in reality, most cruel.

He adds, "Likewise, the Christian life is a struggle. It demands entrance through a narrow gate and a daily walk along a narrow path."[4]

---

[4] Beeke, *Overcoming the World*, 14.

50
Divine Sovereignty (8:28-30)

The *Westminster Confession of Faith* states: "There is but one only, living and true God, who is infinite in being and perfection, a most pure spirit, invisible, without body, parts, or passions; immutable, immense, eternal, incomprehensible, almighty, most wise, most holy, most free, most absolute." For centuries, this God has provided comfort to countless Christians. He's sovereign; thus, his control is absolute. He's immutable; thus, his will is certain. He's mighty; thus, his power is limitless. He's wise; thus, his plan is perfect. He's incomprehensible; thus, his providence is inscrutable. While not always understanding God's ways, Christians are certain he "causes all things to work together for good to those who love God, to those who are called according to his purpose."

Many people disagree with that. Why? They reason as follows: "If I affirm God is absolutely sovereign, then I must also believe that God ordains suffering and that he works suffering for good in the case of those who love him and for evil in the case of those who don't love him. If I believe that, then I can't believe God loves everyone in precisely the same way. And if I believe that, then I can't believe man is basically good. But, I do believe man is basically good, and I do believe God loves everyone in precisely the same way. Therefore, I can't affirm God is absolutely sovereign." And so, they suggest an alternative understanding of the relationship between God and human suffering. It stands upon three premises. (1) God's control is limited. (2) God loves everyone in precisely the same way. (3) Man is basically good.

In this study, we're going to respond to each of these premises. In so doing, we're going to be doctrinal and polemical. We have to be in order to be pastoral. If we're going to derive any pastoral comfort from the promise in 8:28, then we need to be clear when it comes to the God upon whom it stands.

The doctrine of God's absolute sovereignty
The doctrine of God's absolute sovereignty is our response to the notion that God's control is limited. As Paul affirms, "For from him and through him and to him are all things" (11:36). God alone is the cause, means, and purpose of

all things. God decrees absolutely everything that happens. That includes sin and suffering. Now, I know that fact normally raises two objections.

First, some people object: "If God controls sin and suffering, then he must be responsible for both. He decreed it; therefore, he's responsible for it." That's untrue. Why? When God decreed sin and suffering, he did so by a privative decree. A positive decree is something God has willingly predetermined to "perform" in time—all good things; for example, the creation. A privative decree is something God has willingly pre-determined to "permit" in time—all bad things; for example, the fall.

Second, some people object: "If God controls sin and suffering, then he must be in favour of both. He decreed it; therefore, he's in favour of it." That's untrue. Why? There are two ways of "willing." Here's an example. When a child disobeys his parents, they discipline him. Do his parents want to discipline their child? On the one hand, the answer is "yes." They want to drive foolishness from him. On the other hand, the answer is "no." They don't derive any pleasure from disciplining him. You see, it's possible to will in two different ways. Similarly, God wills in two different ways. In the Bible, there's a clear difference between God's will of decree (secret will) and God's will of disposition (revealed will). And it's possible for something to happen according to God's will of decree, yet against God's will of disposition. Let me give you two examples. (1) Was it God's will that Joseph's brothers sell him as a slave? In terms of God's will of disposition, the answer is "no." God didn't take any pleasure from that. However, in terms of God's will of decree, the answer is "yes." Joseph even says to his brothers: "As for you, you meant evil against me, but God meant it for good" (Gen. 50:20). (2) Was it God's will that godless men nail Christ to the cross? In terms of God's will of disposition, the answer is "no." God didn't take any pleasure from that. However, in terms of God's will of decree, the answer is "yes." Peter declares, "This Jesus, delivered up according to the definite plan and foreknowledge of God, you crucified and killed by the hands of lawless men" (Acts 2:23).

God is absolutely sovereign in that he decrees (or, foreordains) all that comes to pass. He wills "good" by a positive decree—that includes all that he "performs." He wills "evil" by a privative decree—that includes all that he "permits."

The doctrine of God's just liberty
The doctrine of God's just liberty is our response to the notion that God loves

Divine Sovereignty (8:29-30)

everyone in precisely the same way. According to 9:15, God says, "I will have mercy on whom I have mercy, and I will have compassion on whom I have compassion." Paul adds, "So then it depends not on human will or exertion, but on God, who has mercy."

That's a difficult truth to grasp. Let me begin by affirming that God does indeed love everyone. I'm not denying that for one moment. The Bible makes it very clear. You're his creature. He protects you. He prospers you. He sustains you. These are expressions of his love for you. More importantly, he calls to you. That's the general call. If you aren't a Christian, and you respond to his call at this very moment, he will receive you with open arms. He takes no pleasure in the destruction of the wicked. That's a wonderful love.

However, we dare not confuse that love with God's love for his Son and all those who are in his Beloved. Christ says, "I made known to them your name, and I will continue to make it known, that the love with which you have loved me may be in them, and I in them" (John 17:26). Does everyone possess Christ? No. Then, not everyone enjoys this love. Paul says, "Hope does not put us to shame, because God's love has been poured into our hearts through the Holy Spirit who has been given to us" (Rom. 5:5). Does everyone have the Holy Spirit? No. Then, not everyone enjoys this love. John says, "See what kind of love the Father has given to us, that we should be called children of God; and so we are" (1 John 3:1). Is everyone a child of God? No. Then, not everyone enjoys this love.

I love children and I love my daughters. Yet, you can't compare the two. No one thinks it's unfair of me to love my daughters in a different way than I love other children. Yet, the moment we make a distinction between God's common love for his creatures and his special love for his children, people think it's unfair.

We need to be careful. What does it mean to be fair? It means to give someone what he deserves. When the angels rebelled, God condemned them. He didn't make any provision for their salvation. Was that unfair? No. He gave them what they deserved. We're sinners. We're murderers. We're liars. We're idolaters. We're rebels. Does God owe us anything? No. God is at liberty to do whatever he wants with us. He isn't obligated to us. He isn't indebted to us. We deserve to be punished. God is at liberty to inflict that punishment now. Or, God is at liberty to delay that punishment until the future. Or, God is at liberty to save whomever he pleases from that punishment. God is at liberty to have mercy on whomever he will have mercy. That's God's just liberty.

The doctrine of man's total depravity

The doctrine of man's total depravity is our response to the notion that man is basically good. In 3:11, Paul declares, "No one seeks for God." In other words, no one chooses God. The reason no one chooses God is because no one can choose God. Now, people immediately object: "That means man doesn't have free will!" But that isn't what I'm saying. We need to begin by defining free will. Let's do so by asking three questions.

First, can God sin? You say, "No, of course not!" Well, doesn't he have free will? If he can't sin, then he doesn't have free will. But we know he does have free will. He's free to do whatever he wants. The point is this: he never wants to sin. In that sense, he can't sin. He can't do what's contrary to his nature.

Second, can Satan repent? You say, "No, of course not!" Well, doesn't he have free will? If he can't repent, then he doesn't have free will. But we know he does have free will. He's free to do whatever he wants. The point is this: he never wants to repent. In that sense, he can't repent. He can't do what's contrary to his nature.

Third, can man come to God? Christ says, "No" (John 6:44, 65). You say, "That means he doesn't have free will." But he does have free will. As in the two instances above, man is free to do whatever he wants. Here's the issue: he doesn't want God. And he will never choose what he doesn't want. He can't do what's contrary to his nature. As Paul says, "No one seeks for God."

You see, when it comes to man's free will, there are two main schools of thought. Both agree that we choose without any external constraint or compulsion. How do they differ? The first maintains that the will is free from internal motives. In other words, it's free from the mind's thoughts and the heart's affections. That means it possesses arbitrary power. The second maintains that the will isn't free from internal motives. In other words, it isn't free from the mind's thoughts and the heart's affections. That means it doesn't possess arbitrary power.

What does the Bible say about the mind? It's darkened. What does it say about the heart? It's hardened. What does that mean for the will? It's enslaved. It's free to choose without any external constraint or compulsion. It's completely free to choose whatever it wants. That's free will! The problem is this: it always "freely" chooses according to the dictates of a darkened mind and hardened heart (Eph. 4:17-19).

Conclusion

Those are three pivotal doctrines at the foundation of God's promise in 8:28. If we don't understand them, we won't understand the promise. What should we say to the Christian who has cancer? What should we say to the Christian who has lost a child? What should we say to the Christian who's imprisoned for the faith? What should we say to the Christian who has struggled with depression for years? What should we say to the Christian who has suffered an automobile accident? Do we say, "God isn't in control?" Do we say, "God didn't see that coming?" Do we say, "God is as upset about this as you are?" No! We declare, "God causes all things to work together for good to those who love God, to those who are called according to his purpose."

And we tell them about man's total depravity. The reason there's suffering in this world is sin. We live in a fallen world. It's only God's restraining grace that keeps this world from being worse than it is. Although difficult to believe, our situation is far better than we deserve.

And we tell them about God's just liberty. God has set his love upon them. He has called them. He has taken them as his child. He has adopted them into his family. He loves them as he loves his own Son. He has their best interests in view. He has their glorification in view.

And we tell them about God's absolute sovereignty. Before the foundation of the world, God decreed all that would come to pass in their lives. By a positive decree, he has willingly pre-determined to perform in time all good things in their lives. By a privative decree, he has willingly predetermined to permit in time all bad things in their lives. Thus, all suffering is according to God's will of decree. He has an unassailable plan to use it for their good.

We only grasp the significance of 8:28 if we grasp the God it stands upon. Again, in the words of the *Westminster Confession of Faith*, "There is but one only, living and true God, who is infinite in being and perfection, a most pure spirit, invisible, without body, parts, or passions; immutable, immense, eternal, incomprehensible, almighty, most wise, most holy, most free, most absolute."

51
Victory: Part 1 (8:31-39)

"What then shall we say to these things?" (8:31). Paul is thinking of the pastoral implications of everything he has said in chapter 8. There are four. In this study, we're going to consider two.

There's no opposition to God's power (8:31)
This truth is found in Paul's question in 8:31, "If God is for us, who can be against us?" Does the field of wheat have any chance against the tornado? Does the bed of flowers have any chance against the frost? Does the stack of kindling have any chance against the fire? There's inevitability in all of those scenarios. Why? The one object is no match for the other.

Paul is trying to impress upon us the fact that there's no match for God when it comes to our salvation because there's no opposition to his power. Job cries, "I know that you can do all things, and that no purpose of yours can be thwarted" (Job 42:2). As J. I. Packer states, "God's dominion is total: he wills as he chooses and carries out all that he wills, and none can stay his hand or thwart his plans."[1] God foreknew us; he set his love upon us before the creation of the world. God predestined us; he predetermined that we would be conformed to the image of his Son. God called us; he opened our hearts to embrace the gospel. God justified us; he declared us to be just in his sight. God glorified us; he completed his work of sanctification in us—it's a given. Clearly, salvation is a work of God's limitless power from start to finish. If that's true, who or what can be against us?

God works *irresistibly*. No one can hinder him. All the combined power and wisdom of humans and angels cannot stop him. God does whatever he wills. God works *autonomously*. His pleasure is his reason. He alone does whatever he wills. Everything he does is just and right and good because he does it. God works *effortlessly*. He does the hardest things with ease. He does the greatest things with the same ease that he does the least things. It's all the same to him. God works *independently*. He never requires a helping hand from any of his

---
[1] Packer, *Concise Theology*, 33.

creatures. He did not make us because he needed us, but because it was his pleasure to do so. He uses us because he chooses to use us.

The doctrine for us is this: *There's no opposition to God's power.* "If God be for us," says Martin Luther, "who is the Judge of all and whose omnipotence calls into being all things, no one can be against us, since everything that he has created must be subject to the Creator."[2] The Reformers coined a phrase as they stood against their enemies: *Deus pro nobis* (God for us). "If God is for us, who is against us?"

Some people might respond, "Satan." They think he's too strong. William Gurnall gives four facts concerning Satan's power that we would do well to remember.[3] (1) Satan is powerful. "Did God's eye slumber or wander one moment, there would need be no other flood to drown thee, yea, the whole world, than what would come out of this dragon's mouth." (2) Satan's power is a derived power. He's a mere creature. (3) Satan's power is a limited power. "He cannot do what he will, and he shall not do what he can." (4) Satan's power is a ministerial power. "It is appointed by God for the service and benefit of the saints." That's why Martin Luther wrote in his famous hymn:

> And tho this world, with devils filled, should threaten to undo us,
> We will not fear, for God hath willed his truth to triumph thru us.
> The prince of darkness grim, we tremble not for him.
> His rage we can endure, for lo, his doom is sure: One little word shall fell him.[4]

Before moving on, I want to make one additional comment—if nothing can be against us when God is for us, then nothing can be for us when God is against us. I believe the following is one of the most frightening verses in the entire Bible: "Behold, I am against you, O proud one, declares the Lord GOD of hosts, for your day has come, the time when I will punish you" (Jer. 50:31). The most terrifying thing isn't famine or terrorism or death. It's to hear God say, "I am against you!" If you aren't a Christian, and you die without God having forgiven you, you will hear him say, "I am against you. Your day has come, the time when I will punish you." That punishment is hell. But, it

---

[2] Luther, *Commentary on Romans*, 133.
[3] William Gurnall, *The Christian in Complete Armor: A Treatise of the Saints' War Against the Devil* (Carlisle: Banner of Truth, 1995), 1:146-147.
[4] Martin Luther, "A Mighty Fortress is Our God" in *The Hymnal for Worship and Celebration*, 26.

doesn't have to be that way. Hear these words: "There is therefore now no condemnation for those who are in Christ Jesus."

There's no limitation to God's grace (8:32)

This truth is found in Paul's question in 8:32, "He who did not spare his own Son but gave him up for us all, how will he not also with him graciously give us all things?" Here, Paul states two facts, and then draws a conclusion.

The first fact: God didn't spare his own Son
This statement takes us back to Genesis 22, where God commands Abraham to offer Isaac upon the altar: "Take your son, your only son Isaac, whom you love, and go to the land of Moriah, and offer him there as a burnt offering on one of the mountains of which I shall tell you" (Gen. 22:2). Abraham obeys. He's ready to plunge the knife into his son. But God speaks: "Do not lay your hand on the boy or do anything to him, for now I know that you fear God, seeing you have not withheld your son, your only son, from me" (Gen. 22:12). Isaac was Abraham's son—his only son, his beloved son. But Abraham didn't spare him. Similarly, Christ is God's Son—his only Son, his beloved Son. But God didn't spare him. There are two important details here.

First, *God didn't spare* his own Son. When Christ died for us, God didn't withhold one drop of wrath. There was no mercy. R.C. Sproul observes,

> The fullest manifestation of the curse is found in Jesus' cry from the cross about being forsaken. To be cursed of God is to be forsaken by God. Jesus' cry was not merely an expression of disillusionment or an imagined sense of forsakenness. For him to complete his work of redemption, he actually had to be forsaken. He had to receive the curse of the Father in his own person. The Father had to turn his back on his only begotten Son. The Father had to cover his face and not let Jesus see the light of his countenance.[5]

For Christ to be a curse, he had to bear the full measure of the curse—including hell.

Second, God didn't spare *his own Son*. The angels are God's sons by creation (Job 1:6). The saints are God's sons by adoption (Rom. 8:14–17). Christ is God's only begotten Son by nature. He's co-eternal, co-equal, and co-

---

[5] R.C. Sproul, *Loved by God* (Nashville: Word Publishing, 2001), 57.

essential with the Father. He's the Father's Beloved. At the time of his greatest distress, his Father didn't spare him. God heard Naaman when he cried for healing. He heard Hannah when she cried for a child. He heard Hagar when she cried for help. He heard the Ninevites when they cried for mercy. He heard Elijah when he cried for help. When Christ cries ("My God, My God, why have You forsaken Me?") there's deafening silence.

The second fact: God gave him up for us all
How can God pardon a guilty sinner? He does so "through the redemption that is in Christ Jesus, whom he put forward as a propitiation by his blood" (Rom. 3:24). The term "propitiation" is problematic for some because they have an inaccurate notion of what it means. In Greek lore, Prince Paris carries Princess Helen to Troy. The Greeks decide to go after her, but the winds are against them. And so, Agamemnon, the Greek general, slaughters his daughter as a sacrifice in order to mollify the gods. It works. None of the Greek gods possesses absolute power. Each possesses just enough power to make your life enjoyable or miserable. They're extremely temperamental—petty, jealous, and impetuous. If you don't give them enough attention, they become offended. They manipulate circumstances to hurt you. The only way to mollify them is sacrifice—the bigger the better. Propitiation, then, is the appeasing of a celestial hissy fit.

Regrettably, that's the sort of thing that often comes to mind when people hear that God "put forward Christ as a propitiation in his blood." But we need to remember that when we speak of the wrath of God, we aren't talking about an emotional outburst provoked by something external to him. We're simply talking about the holy revulsion of his being against whatever contradicts his holiness.

Christ bears God's wrath as he hangs upon Calvary's cross. He offers a penal substitutionary sacrifice. *Penal*: Christ paid a penalty. *Substitutionary*: Christ paid a penalty on our behalf. *Sacrifice*: Christ paid a penalty on our behalf to God.

The conclusion
Having stated those two facts, Paul draws his conclusion. If God has done the above, then there's no limit to what he'll give us. If God didn't spare his own Son but gave him up for us all, then all things belong to us. As Paul says elsewhere: "All things are yours ... and you are Christ's, and Christ is God's" (1

Cor. 3:22-23). If the purchasing price of our inheritance was Christ's blood, then we will most assuredly receive the inheritance.

The doctrine for us is this: *There's no limitation to God's grace.* "In giving his Son," notes John Stott, "He gave everything. The cross is the guarantee of the continuing, unfailing generosity of God."[6] Paul asks, "He who did not spare his own Son but gave him up for us all, how will he not also with him graciously give us all things?"

Some people might respond, "God has done his part, but I must do my part. I must believe. I must persevere. It depends on me, but my effort is too feeble." Yes, it's true—you must believe. Yes, it's true—you must persevere. But you only do so by God's grace! In one of his hymns, Thomas Kelly writes,

> Then we shall be where we would be,
> then we shall be what we should be;
> Things that are not now, nor could be,
> soon shall be our own.[7]

We must always remember the "already" and "not yet" realities to our salvation. I'm saved, yet I await my salvation. I'm redeemed, yet I await my redemption. I'm adopted, yet I await my adoption. It's all mine, but I haven't entered into the full enjoyment of it. I know I will because I have the Holy Spirit. Until then, I groan. When doubts arise, I look away from my feeble effort to the One who has done it all.

William Plumer recounts the following incident from the life of John Newton:

> In his old age, when he could no longer see to read, John Newton heard someone recite this text, "By the grace of God I am what I am." He remained silent a short time and then said, "I am not what I ought to be. Ah, how imperfect and deficient! I am not what I wish to be. I abhor that which is evil, and I would cleave to that which is good. I am not what I hope to be. Soon I shall put off mortality, and with mortality all sin and imperfection. Though I am not what I ought to be, what I wish to be, and what I hope to be; yet I can truly say, I am not what I once was—a slave to sin and Satan! I can heartily join with the apostle and

---

[6] Stott, *Message of Romans*, 255.
[7] Thomas Kelly, "Praise the Savior" in *The Hymnal for Worship and Celebration*, 75.

acknowledge—By the grace of God I am what I am!"[8]

---

[8] William Plumer, *The Grace of Christ; or, Sinners Saved by Unmerited Kindness* (Philadelphia: Presbyterian Board of Publication, 1853).

52
Victory: Part 2 (8:31-39)

"What then shall we say to these things?" (8:31). Paul is thinking of the pastoral implications of everything he has said in chapter 8. There are four. We've considered two: there's no opposition to God's power; and there's no limitation to God's grace. In this study, we're going to consider the remaining two.

There's no alteration to God's justice (8:33-34)
This truth is found in Paul's questions in 8:33-34, "Who shall bring any charge against God's elect? It is God who justifies. Who is to condemn? Christ Jesus is the one who died—more than that, who was raised—who is at the right hand of God, who indeed is interceding for us." Here, Paul describes Christ's threefold work as priest. (1) His crucifixion: Christ is "the one who died." He has paid the penalty for our sin. (2) His resurrection: Christ is "the one who was raised." God has accepted Christ's payment. (3) His intercession: Christ is "the one who is interceding for us." Christ is present at the right hand of God. As we read elsewhere, "He appears in the presence of God on our behalf" (Heb. 9:24). Again, "He is able to save to the uttermost those who draw near to God through him, since he always lives to make intercession for them" (Heb. 7:25).

In light of Christ's priestly work, we ask, "Who shall bring a charge against God's elect?"

Some people might respond, "My sin is too great!" Yes, your sin is great. However, your acceptance in God's sight isn't determined by what you've done or haven't done. It's determined by what Christ has done. We see that in Zechariah 3, where Joshua stands before God. Satan stands at Joshua's right hand, accusing him. But God rebukes Satan. Then, he says regarding Joshua, "Remove the filthy garments from him ... See, I have taken your iniquity away from you and will clothe you with festal robes." God accepts Joshua on the basis of an imputed righteousness, not an inherent righteousness. The same is true of us. God accepts us in Christ.

Satan still accuses us. He's persistent. He tries to make us doubt the satisfaction of God's justice in Christ. He tries to make us think that our acceptance with God depends upon us rather than Christ. How? Let me give you some examples. (1) Satan whispers, "You've succumbed to that sin again. You repented of it a few months ago. That makes your repentance meaningless. You're a hypocrite." In response, we must remember to distinguish between the "presence" and "dominance" of sin. A sin is dominant when we have no desire to mortify it. (2) Satan whispers, "Your affections are so cold. If you're one with Christ, then why don't you evidence greater delight in God. Your lack of these affections can only mean one thing: You're a hypocrite." In response, we must remember that we don't evaluate our affections by a moment in time, but over a period of time. We don't discern a plant's growth by watching it at one particular moment, but by observing it over time. (3) Satan whispers, "You've been struggling to pray and study in private, yet you attend all of the church meetings. If you were sincere, you'd be more consistent in your private pursuit of God. You're a hypocrite." In response, we must discern if we struggle in our use of spiritual duties or if we willfully neglect spiritual duties. There's a difference. (4) Satan whispers, "You sin in your thoughts. You do this even when engaged in worship. Is it possible that such thoughts can be present where grace reigns? You're a hypocrite." In response, we must remember to ask ourselves: Do we consent to such thoughts? Or, do we fight against them?

In these (and many other) ways, Satan tries to make us doubt the satisfaction of God's justice in Christ. Paul makes it clear, however, that no one can bring a charge against us. Why? Christ died for us. Christ was raised for us. Christ intercedes for us. Therefore, Christ has satisfied God's justice in full. There's no changing that for those who are in Christ. If you struggle with believing it, please listen to these words from John Bunyan:

> One day, as I was passing in the field, and that too with some dashes on my conscience, fearing lest yet all was not right, suddenly this sentence fell upon my soul, "Thy righteousness is in heaven;" and methought withal, I saw, with the eyes of my soul, Jesus Christ at God's right hand; there, I say, is my righteousness; so that wherever I was, or whatever I was a-doing, God could not say of me, "He wants My righteousness," for that was just before him. I also saw, moreover, that it was not my good frame of heart that made my righteousness better, nor yet my bad frame that made my righteousness worse; for my righteousness was Jesus Christ himself, the same yesterday, and today, and forever.[1]

---

[1] Bunyan, *Works*, 1:67.

There's no separation from God's love (8:35-39)

This truth is found in 8:35-39, "Who shall separate us from the love of Christ?" That question is followed by another, in which Paul identifies seven things that a Christian may think separates him from the love of Christ: tribulation, distress, persecution, famine, nakedness, danger, and sword. If any of these things are happening to me, I might be tempted to conclude that Christ doesn't love me. If he cared for me, then he wouldn't let me experience these things. Paul corrects such thinking in 8:36 by quoting Psalm 44:22, "For your sake we are being killed all the day long; we are regarded as sheep to be slaughtered."

Why do we suffer these things? Paul says, it's "for [God's] sake!" Suffering doesn't separate us from the love of Christ. Suffering doesn't mean he has abandoned us. On the contrary, the reason we suffer these things is because Christ loves us. That was Paul's point in 8:17. As sons of God, we can expect to experience the same treatment experienced by the Son of God. We don't view these things as defeats. Rather, we overwhelmingly conquer in these things. That means we win a glorious victory. What's the victory? "If indeed we suffer with him so that we may also be glorified with him" (8:17). Why are we victorious? It's because Christ loves us.

Therefore, "I am convinced," says Paul, that no "created thing" will be able to separate us from the love of God, which is in Christ. Paul's point is that nothing has the power to separate us from Christ's love.

Some people might respond, "My love is too weak!" Yes, it is. However, it doesn't depend upon your love. It depends upon God's love. Paul has already spoken of God's love in 5:5-8. Its *source* is the Father: "the love of God has been poured out within our hearts" (5:5). Its *pledge* is the Spirit: "through the Holy Spirit" (5:5). Its *revelation* is the Son: he died for us while we were "helpless" (5:6), "ungodly" (5:6), "sinners" (5:8), and "enemies" (5:10). Nothing can separate us from that love. Separation means division (or, divorce). When couples divorce, they separate. But Christ never divorces his bride. It's an eternal union, based upon an eternal love.

Paul prays that we may "know the love of Christ which surpasses knowledge" (Eph. 3:19). Its value surpasses knowledge in that it covers all our sins and it doesn't depend upon anything in us. As a matter of fact, we spoil God's love when we think it's induced by anything in us. As R.C. Sproul puts it: "God does not love us because we are lovely. He loves us because Christ is lovely. He loves us in Christ."[2] We find an example of that in David's love for Mephibosheth. It wasn't anything in Mephibosheth that prompted that love. It was on account of Jonathan that David loved Mephibosheth. The same is true of God's love for us. He loves us because we're one with his Beloved.

Conclusion

Frederick Lehman provides a fitting conclusion:

> Could we with ink the ocean fill and were the skies of parchment made,
> were ev'ry stalk on earth a quill and ev'ry man a scribe by trade,
> to write the love of God above would drain the ocean dry,
> nor could the scroll contain the whole tho stretched from sky to sky.[3]

---

[2] Sproul, *Loved by God*, 35.
[3] Frederick Lehman, "The Love of God" in *The Hymnal for Worship and Celebration*, 67.

Section 4:
Election (9:11–11:36)

53
Great Sorrow (9:1-6)

We come to the fourth section in Paul's epistle to the Romans: *Election* (9:1-11:36). He's ready to address an issue that has been lingering since chapter 3. I want you to imagine you're a first-century Christian, living in Rome, listening to this letter read in a gathering of a church. Given what Paul has said at the end of chapter 8, what are you thinking?

I know what it means to be called according to God's purpose (8:28-39). I understand the golden chain of salvation. And I understand the implications of that golden chain; namely, there's no opposition to God's power, no limitation to God's grace, no alteration to God's justice, and no separation from God's love. Amen. I love it. This is extremely encouraging.

I know the Jews are accursed (9:1-3). The vast majority of them have rejected the gospel. As a result, they're accursed. They're cut off from Christ. I know this is true. There's a community of Jews in Rome. They have their synagogue. A few of them have received Christ and joined themselves to this church. But the majority of them are hostile.

I know the Jews are privileged (9:4-5). After the tower of Babel, God permitted the nations to go their own way. He chose Abraham, Isaac, and Jacob. He chose Israel. He entrusted his oracles to them. Paul enumerates their privileges, dividing them into three sections based upon three relative clauses. (1) "To whom belongs" (9:4): "the adoption as sons" (the filial relationship with God, established at the time of the Exodus); "the glory" (the cloud that descended upon the tabernacle); "the covenants" (God's covenants with the patriarchs); "the giving of the law" (the Mosaic covenant); "the temple service" (the rites and ceremonies associated with the law); and "the promises" (God's promises to the patriarchs). (2) "Whose are the fathers" (9:5): Abraham, Isaac, and Jacob. (3) "From whom is the Christ according to the flesh, who is over all, God blessed forever" (9:5).

I'm a little perplexed (9:6). God glorified those whom he justified. He justified those whom he called. He called those whom he predestined. He predestined those whom he foreknew. He promises to work all things together for their good. He promises that nothing can separate them from his love in

Christ. But the vast majority of the Jews are accursed. Aren't they God's chosen people? If they're God's chosen people (yet separated from God's love), then perhaps those who are called according to God's purpose can be separated from his love. What does that mean for me?

Paul responds to this "apparent" dilemma by affirming: "But it is not as though the word of God has failed" (9:6). He gives three arguments to prove it. These arguments unlock the entire section. (1) "For not all who are descended from Israel belong to Israel" (9:6-10:21). (2) "God has not rejected his people whom he foreknew" (11:1-24). (3) "All Israel will be saved" (11:25-32).

What's Paul doing in these three arguments? We need to understand the basics of logic. In logic, we derive a conclusion from certain premises. Let me give you an example. First premise: fire consumes. Second premise: I'm flammable. Conclusion: fire is dangerous. If I err in one of my premises, then what happens to my conclusion? It's wrong. Let me illustrate. First premise: fire consumes. Second premise: I'm not flammable. Conclusion: fire isn't dangerous. That's how Paul presents his three arguments. What's their first premise? All physical Jews are heirs of the Abrahamic covenant. What's their second premise? Most Jews are accursed. What's their conclusion? God hasn't kept his promise, and, therefore, he's unfaithful. Paul challenges their first premise. Simply put, it's wrong.

What is the cause of Paul's great sorrow?
The cause of Paul's "great sorrow and unceasing anguish" is the spiritual condition of his fellow Jews. In a word, they're accursed. They're separated from the very thing he has just celebrated in 8:39, "the love of God."

I want to stress the fact that this entire section must be interpreted in light of Paul's "great sorrow." It's important we grasp that. Why? Simply put, there's serious disagreement as to what Paul is saying in these chapters. For example, in 9:13, he quotes Malachi 1:2-3, where God declares, "Jacob I loved, but Esau I hated." This verse is at the centre of much controversy. Does it refer to God's election of nations for the fulfillment of certain historical roles (i.e., Israel and Edom) or does it refer to God's election of individuals for salvation (i.e., Jacob and Esau)? The answer to that question must be determined by the context. What's the context? Well, we know that Paul is expressing his sorrow at the spiritual condition of his fellow countrymen. Furthermore, we know that he's seeking to explain that the "accursed" condition of his kinsmen doesn't mean that God's promise has failed. Here's my point: Paul doesn't express "great sorrow and unceasing grief" in 9:2 because his kinsmen have lost their historical role. Paul doesn't wish to be "accursed" in 9:3 so that his kinsmen might regain their historical role. Clearly, Paul has something of far greater significance in view; namely, the eternal destiny of their souls. Therefore, what he says in 9:13 (and, for that matter, throughout the entire section) must address that issue. If it doesn't, then it makes no sense.

That's all I'm going to say about the subject for now. Again, I simply want us to keep in mind Paul's "great sorrow" because it's an important key for interpreting this chapter.

What do we learn from Paul's great sorrow?
This question arises from Paul's statement in 9:3, "For I could wish that I myself were accursed and cut off from Christ for the sake of my brothers, my kinsmen according to the flesh." That's quite a striking declaration. Paul has just explained that, for those in Christ, there's no separation from God's love (8:35-39). Now he says that if such a thing were possible, he would wish it upon himself if it would mean the salvation of his "kinsmen." Commenting on this verse, Martin Luther writes, "It seems incredible that a man would desire to be damned, in order that the damned might be saved."[1]

How can Paul say such a thing? I believe the answer is found in what he has declared in chapters 1-8. Paul is overwhelmed by the glory of God as revealed in the gospel. As J.N. Darby states in one of his hymns:

> And is it so—I shall be like thy Son?
> Is this the grace, which he for me has won?
> Father of glory, thought beyond all thought!
> In glory, to his own blest likeness brought![2]

What a blessed hope! For Paul, the thought that anyone might miss out on this great salvation is unbearable. He's all too aware of the horror that awaits those who reject Christ.

In hell, the sinner loses all the comforts of earthly possessions: "As he had come naked from his mother's womb, so will he return as he came. He will take nothing from the fruit of his labor that he can carry in his hand. This also

---

[1] Luther, *Lectures in Romans*, 380; quoted in Stott, *The Message of Romans*, 264.
[2] J.N. Darby, "I Shall Be Like Thy Son" in *Hymns of Worship and Remembrance*, 195.

is a grievous evil—exactly as a man is born, thus will he die" (Eccl. 5:15-16). At death, people are stripped of everything that they've enjoyed in this life. Their homes are gone. Their cottages are gone. Their leisure activities are gone. Their favourite sports teams are gone. Their art is gone. Their music is gone. Their family heirlooms are gone. Their favourite sceneries are gone. Their hobbies are gone. There will be nothing to provide any comfort in hell. There will be nothing to provide any pleasure in hell.

In hell, the sinner loses all the comforts of family and friends: "For when he dies he will carry nothing away; his glory will not go down after him" (Ps. 49:17). The context of this verse is the glory of a man's house—his family. At death, all familial ties are lost. In addition, all friendships are lost. In hell, people will not receive any comfort from their spouse. They will not receive any comfort from their children. They will not receive any comfort from their parents. They will not receive any comfort from their siblings. They will not receive any comfort from their friends. These relationships will be meaningless. The presence of friends and family will not ease their pain; on the contrary, it will only increase their pain.

In hell, the sinner gains the most intense pain imaginable: "And the smoke of their torment goes up forever and ever, and they have no rest, day or night" (Rev. 14:11). The sinner will "be thrown into the outer darkness. In that place there will be weeping and gnashing of teeth" (Matt. 8:12). In the Bible, hell is described as fire. Why? Fire speaks of hell's intensity. In hell, the sinner becomes the object of God's intense hatred and wrath. In hell, the sinner falls into the hands of God, who is a "consuming fire" (Heb. 12:29).

Above all else, in hell the sinner loses God: "Depart from me, you cursed, into the eternal fire prepared for the devil and his angels" (Matt. 25:41). This is why hell is so painful—it's a total and final departure from God. At death, the sinner loses the dearest father, the wisest guide, the strongest shield, the greatest good, the closest friend, the richest grace, the highest honour, the kindest comfort, the finest beauty, the deepest truth, and the sweetest love. At death, the sinner loses the Lord of life, the Lord of light, the Lord of glory, the Lord of Lords. At death, the sinner loses the God of hope, the God of grace, the God of comfort, the God of peace, the God of gods. The sinner loses the only source of happiness and contentment—the One in whose presence is fullness of joy and the One in whose right hand are pleasures forevermore (Ps. 16:11). As Robert Bolton notes, this is "the more horrible part of hell," for sinners lose "God's glorious presence" and, therefore, are separated from "bliss above."[3]

Conclusion

I don't believe for one moment that we're supposed to wish to be accursed for the salvation of others. However, I do believe we need something of Paul's zeal for the lost. We need to be overwhelmed by the glory of God as revealed in the gospel. We need to be overwhelmed by the horror of hell—eternal separation from God.

> What would happen if believers could stand before the cross and realize more fully what was really happening there? Overwhelmed by the dimensions of their salvation, they would become compulsive worshippers. They would never stop marvelling at the wonderful grace of Jesus, and would talk about him to anyone who would listen. Day and night, they would be unashamedly enthusiastic about the One who called them out of darkness into his marvellous light. Worldly ambitions would perish as they gave themselves without reserve to Christ and his service. The world would be evangelized.[4]

---

[3] Robert Bolton, *The Four Last Things: Death, Judgment, Hell, Heaven* (1830; repr., Pittsburgh: Soli Deo Gloria, 1994), 82.

[4] MacDonald, *My Heart, My Life, My All*, 12.

54
God's Purpose of Election (9:6-13)

As we saw in the last study, Paul anticipates a problem in 9:1-5. This problem emerges because of two apparently irreconcilable facts. The first concerns the Jews' condition: they're accursed (9:1-3). The second concerns the Jews' privilege: they're the descendants of Abraham (9:4-5). The problem is this: How can they be accursed if they're the descendants of Abraham? Didn't God promise to be the God of Abraham's descendants forever? Has God reneged on his promise? Has God's word failed?

In 9:6, Paul responds, "But it is not as though the word of God has failed." He proceeds to prove it by presenting three arguments: (1) "Not all who are descended from Israel belong to Israel" (9:6-10:21); (2) "God has not rejected his people whom he foreknew" (11:1-24); and (3) "All Israel will be saved" (11:25-32). That's the general outline we're going to follow as we make our way through these chapters.[1]

Now we begin with Paul's first argument. Does the fact that the Jews are accursed mean that God's word (or, promise) has failed? No, definitely not! The word of God hasn't failed. How do we know? Paul tells us: "For not all are children of Abraham because they are his offspring" (9:6-7). In other words, there's an Israel within Israel. To put it another way, there's a spiritual Israel within ethnic Israel.

This distinction between Abraham's physical and spiritual descendants shouldn't surprise us. Paul has already referred to it on two occasions. (1) In 2:28-29, he says that there's a difference between those who are circumcised outwardly ("in the flesh" and "by the letter") and those who are circumcised inwardly ("of the heart" and "by the Spirit"). The former are Abraham's physical descendants, whereas the latter are Abraham's spiritual descendants. (2) In 4:9-12, Paul says that the blessed man is the justified man. Is this blessed man circumcised or uncircumcised? Paul turns to Abraham for an answer: "Faith was credited to Abraham as righteousness ... not while circumcised,

---

[1] See John Piper, *The Justification of God: An Exegetical & Theological Study of Romans 9:1-23* (Ada, MI: Baker Academic, 1993).

but while uncircumcised" (4:9-10). God promised Abraham that in his seed all of the nations of the earth would be blessed. Abraham believed God, and God imputed righteousness to him. Then, God sealed it with circumcision. This means that Abraham is the father of all who aren't circumcised yet believe and the father of all who are circumcised yet believe (4:11-12). In other words, the true descendants of Abraham are those who believe.

All of this is made perfectly clear in Galatians 3:16 and 3:29, where Paul writes, "Now the promises were made to Abraham and to his offspring. It does not say, 'And to offsprings,' referring to many, but referring to one, 'And to your offspring,' who is Christ ... And if you are Christ's, then you are Abraham's offspring, heirs according to promise." Returning to 9:6-7, Paul's argument is now obvious: the fact that the Jews are accursed doesn't mean that God's word has failed. How could it? After all, God's promises weren't given to Abraham's physical descendants but to his spiritual descendants.

Paul doesn't leave it at that. He produces two pieces of evidence to prove his argument. (1) The first piece of evidence is the case of Isaac and Ishmael (9:7-9). They were both physical descendants of Abraham. Were they both saved? No. Isaac was saved, but Ishmael was accursed. Does that mean God's promise to Abraham concerning his descendants failed? No. Why? Ishmael wasn't a child of promise (i.e., spiritual descendant), whereas Isaac was (9:8). (2) The second piece of evidence is the case of Jacob and Esau (9:10-13). They were both physical descendants of Abraham. Were they both saved? No. Jacob was saved, but Esau was accursed. Does that mean God's promise to Abraham failed? No. Why? Esau wasn't a child of promise (i.e., a spiritual descendant), whereas Jacob was (9:11).

And so, the sons (Isaac and Ishmael) and the grandsons (Jacob and Esau) of Abraham clearly prove that there's a difference between his spiritual and physical descendants. "It is not the children of the flesh who are children of God, but the children of the promise are regarded as descendants" (9:8). This distinction continues throughout Israel's history, meaning "they are not all Israel who are descended from Israel" (9:6). Therefore, the accursed state of the majority of the Jews in no way implies that God's word has failed.

We'll return to Paul's first argument in the next study. For now, however, I want us to focus on a doctrine that's pivotal to his argument. We find it in 9:11-12, where he says, "Though they were not yet born and had done nothing either good or bad—in order that God's purpose of election might continue, not because of works but because of him who calls—she was told, 'The older will serve the younger.'" I want you to notice six things about the example of Jacob and Esau.

God chooses to love Jacob and hate Esau (9:13)
Jacob is the object of God's covenant love. Esau isn't. But God most certainly loves Esau. We must differentiate between God's love for his *creatures* (his general love as Creator) and God's love for his *children* (his special love as Redeemer). When we speak of God's general love for his creatures and his special love for his children, we're speaking of two different things. "See what kind of love the Father has given to *us*, that *we* should be called children of God" (1 John 3:1).

God's choice is between twins (9:10)
In the case of Isaac and Ishmael, I suppose we could reason as follows. "Isaac's mother is Rebecca. Ishmael's mother is Hagar. That's why God chooses Isaac, not Ishmael." But we can't reason like that in the case of Jacob and Esau. They're twins, meaning they have the same father and mother. For all intents and purposes, they're the same.

God's choice is before birth (9:11)
God's choice is independent of their actions. Esau was a terrible sinner, but he was no worse than Jacob. Jacob was selfish in his relationship with Esau (Gen. 25:29-34), weak in his relationship with Rebekah (Gen. 27:6-17), deceitful in his relationship with Isaac (Gen. 27:18-29), and rebellious in his relationship with God. God's choice certainly wasn't based on Jacob's good works.

God's choice is contrary to all that differentiates them (9:12)
There's one difference between Jacob and Esau: birth order. But God reverses this distinction, in order to demonstrate that there's nothing in Esau and Jacob that determines his choice.

God's choice is rooted in his purpose of election (9:11)
Paul doesn't say that God has no reasons, but that his reasons aren't in us. God chose Jacob over Esau, in order to teach that he's sovereign in dispensing his mercy. "I will have mercy on whom I have mercy, and I will have compassion on whom I have compassion."

God's choice guarantees that works play no role in salvation (9:11)

Every conceivable human factor is excluded. Salvation rests completely on God. Does the fact that the Jews are accursed mean that God's word (promise) has failed? No. God's promise wasn't given to Abraham's physical descendants but to his spiritual descendants (the elect).

Now, I'm aware that the "popular" view of election within today's evangelicalism is this: God foresaw those who would believe in him. Hence, his choice of them is based upon their choice of him. In other words, divine election isn't active. Personally, I don't see how we can possibly reconcile such a notion with what Paul says in 9:11. Nor do I see how we can reconcile this "popular" view with what Paul says in 9:16, "It does not depend on the man who wills or the man who runs, but on God who has mercy."

I'm also aware that some people sidestep this entire issue by simply denying that these verses have anything to do with salvation. They argue that Paul is taking about the historical roles of nations (Israel and Edom), not the salvation of individuals (Jacob and Esau). However, as I explained in the previous study, such a notion is irreconcilable with Paul's "great sorrow" (9:1-3). Paul doesn't express "great sorrow and unceasing grief" because Israel has lost its historical role. He doesn't wish to be "accursed, separated from Christ" because Israel has lost its historical role. No. Paul is upset because his kinsmen are accursed. His entire purpose in this chapter is to show that this doesn't mean that God's word has failed. If Paul is speaking of historical roles in 9:6-13, then I fail to see what these verses have to do with his overall argument.

Finally, I'm aware that some people avoid the issue of election by arguing that the term doesn't have anything to do with salvation. They maintain that it (along with the term *predestination*) refers to service or blessing. In other words, God chooses us for service or blessing but never for salvation. Such a notion is problematic given what Paul says in 2 Thessalonians 2:13, "But we ought always to give thanks to God for you, brothers beloved by the Lord, because God chose you as the first fruits to be saved, through sanctification by the Spirit and belief in the truth."

With that said, I believe J. I. Packer provides a very helpful definition of the doctrine of election when he writes,

> Before creation God selected out of the human race, foreseen as fallen, those whom he would redeem, bring to faith, justify, and glorify in and through Jesus Christ. This divine choice is an expression of free and

sovereign grace, for it is unconstrained and unconditional, not merited by anything in those who are its subjects.[2]

This doctrine is central to Paul's argument. As a matter of fact, it's central to everything he says in these chapters.

Conclusion

Many years ago, A.W. Pink wrote a book entitled *The Sovereignty of God*. It cost him dearly. After it was published, many churches and conferences wouldn't invite him to preach any more. Many people accused him of neglecting the balance between God's sovereignty and man's responsibility. He replied:

> The fact is that those who undertake to expound the responsibility of man are the very ones who have lost the "balance of truth" by ignoring very largely the sovereignty of God. It is perfectly right to insist upon the responsibility of man, but what of God?—has he no claims, no rights? A hundred such works as this are needed, and ten thousand sermons would have to be preached throughout the land on this subject, if the "balance of truth" is to be regained.[3]

Nothing has changed. In a church in which people have only ever heard of man's responsibility, any mention of God's sovereignty is viewed as an imbalance. In a sea of apathy, zeal is labelled fanaticism. In a sea of worldliness, discipline is labelled legalism. In a sea of Semi-Pelagianism, the doctrine of election is labelled "extreme," "dangerous," or "unbalanced." Personally, I believe this doctrine has been sorely neglected for one simple reason: people don't like it. Why? They don't want to hear this: "It is he who sits above the circle of the earth, and its inhabitants are like grasshoppers" (Is. 40:22). But if we're going to be faithful to Scripture, we can't avoid this doctrine.

First, it establishes the simple gospel. Martyn Lloyd-Jones expresses it like this: "All other doctrines derive from this. You can have no doctrine if this is not right ... If this is not understood then neither will the doctrines of justification, sanctification and glorification be understood aright."[4] Simply put, the entire order of salvation rests upon the doctrine of election. That makes it extremely important. Without the doctrine of election, I'm forced to believe that

---

[2] Packer, *Concise Theology*, 149.
[3] A.W. Pink, *The Sovereignty of God* (London: Banner of Truth, 1961), 11.
[4] Quoted in Iain Murray, *David Martyn Lloyd-Jones: The Fight of Faith 1939 to 1981* (Edinburgh: Banner of Truth, 1990), 239.

salvation is ultimately controlled by me. Why am I a Christian? I received Christ. Why did I receive Christ? God called me. The Holy Spirit gave me eyes to see and ears to hear. Why did God call me? God decreed it by his grace and for his glory. Why did God decree it? "He has mercy on whomever he wills, and he hardens whomever he wills" (9:18). The alternative leads to justification by works.

Second, it emphasizes the grace of God. He set his love upon us before the foundation of the world (Eph. 1:3). God doesn't say he loves you because you're useable, profitable, wonderful, or adorable. He says he loves you because he loves you. Be encouraged.

Third, it evokes praise and thanksgiving. "What do you have that you did not receive?" (1 Cor. 4:7). This condition of heart cultivates humility, compels service, encourages forgiveness, and promotes holiness.

> Sovereign grace o'er sin abounding! Ransomed souls, the tidings swell;
> Tis a deep that knows no sounding; Who its breadth or length can tell?
> On its glories, on its glories, let my soul for ever dwell.

> On such love, my soul, still ponder, Love so great, so rich, so free;
> Say, while lost in holy wonder, Why, O Lord, such love to me?
> Hallelujah! Hallelujah! Grace shall reign eternally.[5]

---

[5] John Kent, "Sovereign Grace O'er Sin Abounding" in *Hymns of Worship and Remembrance*, 29.

55
The Objections: Part 1 (9:14-23)

In 9:1-5, Paul presents a problem. It emerges because of two apparently irreconcilable facts. The first fact concerns the Jews' condition (9:1-3); simply put, they're accursed. The second fact concerns the Jews' privilege (9:4-5); simply put, they're Abraham's descendants. Here's the problem: How do we reconcile their condition with their privilege? Has God abandoned his people? Has God's promise failed?

In 9:6, Paul responds: "But it is not as though the word of God has failed." The idea that God's promise has failed stands upon a false assumption; namely, God's promises were given to Abraham's physical descendants. They weren't. Paul makes it clear: "It is not the children of the flesh who are the children of God, but the children of the promise are counted as offspring" (9:8). God's promises were given to Abraham's spiritual descendants.

In 9:7-13, Paul provides the evidence. The first piece of evidence is God's choice of Isaac, not Ishmael (9:7-9). Both were Abraham's sons. Were both saved? No. Did God's word fail? No. Why? Ishmael wasn't a child of promise; Isaac was. The second piece of evidence is God's choice of Jacob, not Esau (9:10-13). Both were Abraham's grandsons. Were both saved? No. Did God's word fail? No. Why? Esau wasn't a child of promise; Jacob was. That proves Paul's point in 9:6. The Jews' accursed condition doesn't mean that God's word has failed. Why? God never promised that the physical descendants of Abraham would be saved.

Now, in 9:14-23, we enter a new stage in Paul's argument. He knows that people will struggle with what he has just said about God's choice of Isaac over Ishmael and God's choice of Jacob over Esau. Basically, they will make two objections.

God is unjust in choosing (9:14-18)
For starters, some people will say that God is unjust in choosing one over the other. They will reason as follows: "God chose Isaac over Ishmael and Jacob over Esau without taking into account anything in them. The sole reason God chooses people for salvation is so that his purpose according to his choice will

stand. If that's true, God is unjust! There must be something in those who are saved that sets them apart from those who aren't saved. Salvation must ultimately depend upon something they do that others don't do. Otherwise, God is unjust and unfair."

Paul responds to this objection with two arguments. In both, he quotes an OT text. The quotations begin with the preposition *for* (1:15, 17). In both, he derives a conclusion from the OT text. The conclusions begin with the expression *so then* (1:16, 18). Paul's purpose is to prove that the doctrine of election doesn't mean that God is unjust.

The first OT text is Exodus 33:19, "*For* he says to Moses, 'I will have mercy on whom I have mercy, and I will have compassion on whom I have compassion'" (9:15, italics added). In the original context, Moses prays, "Please show me your glory" (Exod. 33:18). God responds, "I will make all my goodness pass before you and will proclaim before you my name 'The LORD'" (Exod. 33:19). What's this goodness that will pass before Moses? What's this name that will be proclaimed before Moses? God tells us: "I will be gracious to whom I will be gracious, and I will show mercy on whom I will show mercy" (Exod. 33:19). That means God's glory or God's name is his inclination to show mercy and his freedom to do so as he pleases. In other words, God's glory (or, God's name) is his freedom to have mercy on whomever he pleases apart from any reason outside of his own purpose. The conclusion is this: "*So then* it depends not on human will or exertion, but on God, who has mercy" (9:16, italics added).

The second OT text is Exodus 9:16, "*For* the Scripture says to Pharaoh, 'For this very purpose I have raised you up, that I might show my power in you, and that my name might be proclaimed in all the earth'" (9:17, italics added). What does that mean? It means God's activity in Pharaoh's life is ultimately determined by God's purpose, not Pharaoh's willing or running. The conclusion is this: "*So then* he has mercy on whomever he wills, and he hardens whomever he wills" (9:18, italics added).

These two examples serve to demonstrate that the doctrine of election doesn't mean that God is unjust. On the contrary, it confirms his justice (or, righteousness). God's glory (or, God's name) is his freedom to have mercy on whomever he pleases apart from any reason outside of his own purpose. People most certainly possess free will. They're free to choose whatever they want. Because of their sin, they never want God. Therefore, they never choose God. That means God must intervene if anyone is to be saved. In choosing Isaac,

Jacob, and Moses, he gives them what they don't deserve: mercy. In not choosing Ishmael, Esau, and Pharaoh, he gives them what they do deserve: wrath. How does that make God unjust? It doesn't.

R.C. Sproul provides a helpful illustration:

> Suppose ten people sin and sin equally. Suppose God punishes five of them and is merciful to the other five. Is this injustice? No! In this situation five people get justice and five get mercy. No one gets injustice. What we tend to assume is this: If God is merciful to five, he must be equally merciful to the other five. Why? He is never obligated to be merciful. If he is merciful to nine of the ten, the tenth cannot claim to be a victim of injustice. God never owes mercy.[1]

God is unjust in condemning (9:19-23)

Next, some people will say that God is unjust in condemning. They will reason as follows: "Salvation doesn't depend on the man who wills or runs, but on God who has mercy. And the only thing that matters is God's purpose. If that's true, God is unjust. After all, 'Who resists his will?' God is responsible for the salvation of Isaac, Jacob, and Moses. Likewise, God is responsible for the damnation of Ishmael, Esau, and Pharaoh. That means we're all a bunch of robots. That can't be so! My will must be the determining factor in my salvation or else God is unjust and unfair."

Paul responds by rebuking those who question God: "Who are you, O man, to answer back to God?" (9:20). Then, he asserts God's right to do whatever he wants with his creatures. In the eternal plan of redemption, God's all-encompassing purpose is the revelation of his glory. Before the creation of the world, God saw man in his fallen condition by man's own free choice. From humanity, God chose some to salvation: vessels "for honourable use" (9:21). God passed over others: vessels "for dishonourable use" (9:21). In the former, he purposes to reveal his glory (grace and mercy) by bestowing upon them what they don't deserve. In the latter, he purposes to reveal his glory (justice and wrath) by bestowing upon them what they do deserve. In regards to this latter group, he also purposes to reveal his patience by enduring them in the present, that is, by withholding his final judgment while bestowing his common grace upon them.

That doesn't make us robots. We willfully reject God's revelation because

---

[1] R.C. Sproul, *The Holiness of God* (Wheaton: Tyndale House, 1998), 127-128.

we're sinners (1:18-3:20). God doesn't force us to sin against our will. He willingly permits us to do so. To reveal the glory of his justice and wrath, he willingly permits some to continue to do so. To reveal the glory of his grace and mercy, he calls some to salvation. How does that make us robots? How does that violate man's free will? How does that make God unjust?

Conclusion

As we conclude, I want to affirm three important lessons from these verses.

First, *these verses show us how we can know for certain if our doctrine of election is biblical.* If our doctrine of election doesn't lead to the objections in 9:14 and 9:19, then it's unbiblical. Let me illustrate—the popular notion that God's election is simply his "knowing beforehand" those who will choose him doesn't lead to the objections in 9:14 and 9:19. It doesn't lead anyone to ask, "Is there injustice on God's part?" Therefore, it doesn't faithfully represent what Paul is teaching in these verses. Why? What Paul teaches in these verses causes people to object. If my doctrine of election doesn't cause people to object along the lines articulated in these verses, then it clearly isn't Paul's doctrine of election. It isn't biblical.

Second, *these verses show us why people struggle with the doctrine of election.* They don't appreciate God's just liberty. As Paul says, "So then it depends not on human will or exertion, but on God, who has mercy" (9:16). Many people object, "That's unfair!" Why do they object? Iain Murray gets to the heart of the matter when he says, "Man unhumbled before God believes that God has no right to give to any what he will not equally give to all."[2] But what does it mean to be fair? It means to give someone what he deserves. We're sinners. We deserve to be punished. God is at liberty to inflict that punishment now. God is at liberty to delay that punishment until the future. God is at liberty to save whomever he pleases from that punishment. He's free to do as he pleases because he doesn't owe anything to anyone. Think about it. Do we call Christ unfair because he chose to raise Lazarus from the dead while leaving others in the grave? Do we call Christ unfair because he chose to heal one man beside the pool of Bethesda while ignoring the multitude of sick around him? Do we call Christ unfair because he blesses whomever he chooses? Do we call Christ unfair because he imparts life to whomever he chooses? We struggle with the concept of God's "just liberty" because we fail to grasp the seriousness of our

---

[2] Iain Murray, *Revival and Revivalism: The Making and Marring of American Evangelicalism 1750-1758* (Edinburgh: Banner of Truth, 1994), 181.

sin. God doesn't owe anything to anyone. God isn't obligated to anyone.

Third, *these verses show us the peril of minimizing the doctrine of election.* As we see in Exodus 33, God equates his glory with his freedom to bestow mercy on whomever he pleases. This should serve as a serious warning to those who deny (and perhaps even despise) this doctrine. When we deny the absolute sovereignty of God in salvation, we rob him of his glory.

56
The Objections: Part 2 (9:14–23)

We're going to look (one more time) at God's "purpose of election" as Paul expounds it in Romans 9. I want to begin by making five remarks concerning Paul. My prayer is that these will shed some light on the passage.

Paul aims to explain the gospel. As far as he's concerned, the doctrine of election establishes the simple gospel. Without the doctrine of election, I'm forced to believe that my salvation is ultimately determined by me. Paul shows that the reason I'm saved isn't found in me, but God. He makes it clear that it's impossible to preserve justification by grace alone through faith alone in Christ alone without the doctrine of election. If the determining factor resides within us, it isn't all of grace.

Paul is convinced that truth matters. He tackles some of the Bible's most difficult theological concepts. Many Christians don't think doctrine is important. They think it's possible to grow spiritually without doctrine. They think it's possible to grow a healthy church without doctrine. "Doctrine? I couldn't care less." We should care. Blurry notions about God produce blurry Christians.

Paul is committed to God's glory. He delights in the sovereignty of God. He insists upon God's rule over his creatures. He insists upon God's just liberty when it comes to his governance of his creatures. He insists upon God's freedom to do as he pleases with his creatures. God (not man) is Paul's starting point. His entire paradigm for thinking rests on this premise: God is the only sovereign.

Paul is an example of heart-felt evangelistic zeal. "I could wish that I myself were accursed and cut off from Christ for the sake of my brothers, my kinsmen according to the flesh" (9:3). It's incredible when we think of how the Jews treated Paul. "Five times I received at the hands of the Jews the forty lashes less one. Three times I was beaten with rods. Once I was stoned" (2 Cor. 11:25–26). Add to this list trials and imprisonment, slander and innuendo, malice and contempt.

Paul is pastoral in his approach. He's deeply theological and doctrinal because he's deeply pastoral and practical. At the end of the previous chapter, Paul says that nothing can "separate us from the love of God in Christ Jesus our Lord" (8:39). He's determined to prove it.

In the last study, we considered two objections to the doctrine of election: (1) God is unjust in choosing (9:14); and (2) God is unjust in condemning (9:19). In this study, I want to add seven more objections. These usually arise in my discussions with people who reject this doctrine.

The doctrine of election makes God arbitrary

This objection goes like this: "If God chose Isaac (not Ishmael) and Jacob (not Esau), so that his purpose according to his choice would stand (9:11), then God is arbitrary. If God dispenses mercy on whomever he pleases without any motive outside of himself, then God is arbitrary. How does God decide who's a vessel of wrath and who's a vessel of mercy (9:22-23)? On what basis does he make that choice? If there's no identifiable reason, then he's arbitrary. And that's a disturbing thought!"

I agree that the doctrine of election "appears" to make God arbitrary. However, we must keep three facts in mind. (1) We know that God isn't arbitrary. Neither is he capricious, erratic, whimsical, or impulsive. (2) We know that God is good. He always does what's right. (3) We don't know why God chooses some people and passes over others.

It's at this point that we enter the realm of mystery. God hasn't revealed to us why he chooses some and passes over others. Admittedly, we don't understand it. But that doesn't mean it isn't true. We don't understand the doctrine of the Trinity, yet we believe it. We don't understand the doctrine of the incarnation, yet we believe it. Similarly, we don't understand the doctrine of election, yet we believe it. We must always remember that we don't need to understand something for it to be true. Our understanding isn't the measure of truth.

The doctrine of election makes God unloving

This objection goes like this: "According to 1 John 4:16, God is love. This necessarily means that it's impossible for God to act toward man in an unloving way. God's treatment of man must always be an expression of love. If God loves Jacob, but not Esau, then God is acting in a way that's inconsistent with his nature. Besides, doesn't the Bible teach that God loves everyone?"

This objection arises because people fail to distinguish between God's common love for his creatures and God's special love for his children. The Bible teaches that God loves his creatures (Matt. 5:45; Acts 14:17; Rom. 2:4).

However, the Bible also makes it clear that God loves his children. (1) Christ says, "I made known to them your name, and I will continue to make it known, that the love with which you have loved me may be in them, and I in them" (John 17:26). According to this verse, God loves those in whom Christ dwells. Does Christ dwell in everyone? No. Then, not everyone enjoys this love. (2) Paul says, "Hope does not put us to shame, because God's love has been poured into our hearts through the Holy Spirit who has been given to us" (Rom. 5:5). According to this verse, God loves those to whom the Holy Spirit is given. Is the Holy Spirit given to everyone? No. Then, not everyone enjoys this love. (3) John says, "See what kind of love the Father has given to us, that we should be called children of God" (1 John 3:1). According to this verse, God loves his children. Is everyone called a child of God? No. Then, not everyone enjoys this love.

When God says, "Jacob I loved, but Esau I hated" (9:13), He's referring to his special love for his children. Jacob was a child of God. Esau wasn't. But God most certainly loved Esau. This is his common love for all people.

The doctrine of election contradicts God's will that all men be saved

This objection goes like this: "If God has chosen some people to be saved, then how can it be God's will for all people to be saved? The Bible says it's God's will for all people to be saved. Therefore, it can't be true that he wills the salvation of only the elect."

The answer to this objection is found in the distinction that exists between God's "will of decree" (his secret will) and God's "will of disposition" (his revealed will). We see this distinction, for example, when it comes to Christ's crucifixion. Was Christ's crucifixion God's will? Yes, it was God's will, in terms of his will of decree. No, it wasn't God's will, in terms of his will of disposition. God wanted it to happen (his will of decree) yet didn't want it to happen (his will of disposition). As Jonathan Edwards explains,

> When a distinction is made between God's revealed will and his secret will, or his will of command and decree, "will" is certainly in that distinction taken in two senses. His will of decree is not his will in the same sense as his will of command is. Therefore, it is no difficulty at all to suppose, that the one may be otherwise than the other.[1]

---

[1] Quoted in John Piper, "Are There Two Wills in God?" in *Still Sovereign: Contemporary Perspectives on Election, Foreknowledge, and Grace*, ed. T. Schreiner and B. Ware (Grand Rapids: Baker Books, 2000).

And so, God asks, "Have I any pleasure in the death of the wicked, declares the Lord GOD, and not rather that he should turn from his way and live?" (Ezek. 18:23). The answer is "No." God doesn't take any pleasure in anyone's death and destruction. On the contrary, he wills that all men be saved. That's his will of disposition (or, command). However, when we speak of the doctrine of election, we don't have God's "will of disposition" in view, but his "will of decree."

The doctrine of election negates man's free will

This objection goes like this: "Man possesses free will. If he doesn't, then he's a robot. If he's a robot, then he can't be held accountable for what he does. Yet Paul says that God hardened Pharaoh's heart. Plus, God prepared 'vessels of wrath' for destruction. It seems that God is active in all of this. So, how can man have free will?"

By way of solution, we must define what we mean by *free will*. Here are three questions to help us. (1) Can God sin? "No," you say. Well, I ask, "Doesn't he have free will?" If God can't sin, then he doesn't have free will. But we know that he does have free will—he's free to do whatever he wants. The point is this: he can't sin because he doesn't want to sin. (2) Can Satan repent? "No," you say. Well, I ask, "Doesn't he have free will?" If Satan can't repent, then he doesn't have free will. But we know that he does have free will—he's free to do whatever he wants. The point is this: he can't repent, because he doesn't want to repent. (3) Can man come to God? "No," I say. Well, you ask, "Doesn't he have free will?" If he can't come to God, then he doesn't have free will. But we know that he does have free will—he's free to do whatever he wants. The point is this: he can't come, because he doesn't want to come.

You see, to have free will is to be free from external constraints and compulsions. In that sense, man most certainly possesses free will. However, man's free will isn't free from the inclination of his own heart. Man always willingly chooses according to his depraved heart. We see this in the example of Pharaoh. When God hardens Pharaoh, what does he do? He doesn't stop Pharaoh from doing something he wants to do. He doesn't make Pharaoh do something he doesn't want to do. He willingly permits Pharaoh to do precisely what he wants to do. When God prepares vessels of wrath before the foundation of the world for destruction (9:22), what does he do? He doesn't stop them from doing something they want to do. He doesn't make them do something they don't want to do. He willingly permits them to do precisely what they want to do.

And so, God is sovereign. His will of decree is absolute. However, God doesn't violate man's free will in carrying out his decrees. God's election doesn't prevent anyone from being saved. In passing over some, God doesn't prevent them from being saved. Man's sin prevents him from being saved!

Christ declares that we must come to him (John 6:35). In other words, we must believe in him, abide in him, and rest in him. However, Christ also declares that we can't "come" to him (John 6:44, 65). In other words, we can't believe in him, abide in him, or rest in him. So, in effect, Christ declares, "You must come to me, but you can't come to me." A misunderstanding of this statement always leads to one of two errors.

The first error is called "voluntarism" (also known as *Semi-Pelagianism* or *Arminianism*). Some people accept Christ's words "You must come to me" while rejecting his words "You can't come to me." They think that since Christ says we must believe, we can believe. They ignore what Christ says about man's inability to believe. Essentially, they think that God has done all he can in making salvation possible. Now he's completely passive as he waits for us to make a decision.

The second error is called "determinism" (also known as *Hyper-Calvinism*). Some people accept Christ's words "You can't come to me" while rejecting his words "You must come to me." They think that since Christ says we can't believe, it doesn't matter what we do. They go so far as to affirm that we're totally passive in salvation. They ignore the fact that Christ says we must believe. As a result, they're reluctant to call upon people to do just that.

I reject these two errors. I affirm the whole truth: "We must come to Christ, but we can't come to Christ." This statement perplexes people because they fail to discern the nature of free will. We possess free will: the ability to choose what we want. We're never coerced or compelled by external forces. Therefore, we're responsible for our choices. As we've seen, we must believe in Christ in order to be saved. The problem is this: we don't want to believe. We can't come to Christ, because we don't want to come to Christ. For this reason, God must draw us to Christ.

Turning to John 6, that's precisely what we find. Christ declares, "All that the Father gives me will come to me, and whoever comes to me I will never cast out. ... For this is the will of my Father, that everyone who looks on the Son and believes in him should have eternal life, and I will raise him up on the last day" (John 6:37-40). Here Christ makes it clear that we must believe in him for eternal life. No one is prevented from believing. However, no one will believe, because of sin. For this reason, God must act first. As Christ says, "All that the Father gives me will come to me."

The doctrine of election is an impediment to prayer

This objection goes like this: "If God has chosen some to be saved, then why bother to pray? It doesn't make any difference."

When we take the time to think about it, we discover that it's this objection that doesn't make any sense. The real question is this: If God isn't sovereign in salvation, why bother to pray? If he isn't sovereign, what are we asking him to do when we pray for someone's salvation? Aren't we asking him to do something we don't believe he does (or, has any right to do)? As John Owen explains:

> For a man to lie praying, with earnestness and fervency, for that which is in his own power, and can never be effected but by his own power, is ridiculous; and they do but mock God who pray unto him to do that for them which they can do for themselves, and which God cannot do for them but only when and as they do it themselves. Suppose a man to have a power in himself to believe and repent; suppose these to be such acts of his will as God does not, indeed cannot, by his grace work in him, but only persuade him thereunto, and show him sufficient reason why he should so do,—to what purpose should this man pray that God would give him faith and repentance?[2]

Rather than impede prayer, the doctrine of election actually stimulates prayer. Aware that salvation is of God, we're driven to pray that he will illuminate the mind, soften the heart, turn the will, and stir the conscience. We're driven to pray that he will be merciful to sinners.

The doctrine of election is an impediment to evangelism

This objection goes like this: "If God has chosen some to be saved, then why bother to evangelize? It doesn't make any difference."

Contrary to popular belief, the doctrine of election actually stimulates evangelism. Knowing that salvation is entirely dependent upon God, we're confident that he will save according to his will. Our responsibility is simply to

---

[2] Owen, *Works*, 3:312.

proclaim "Whosoever will, may come!" Let me add—God doesn't command people to figure out if they're numbered among the elect. He commands people to repent and believe in Christ. If we were sick in the hospital, and the doctor prescribed medicine for us, we wouldn't waste any time trying to figure out if it was God's will for us to get better before taking that medicine. We would take the medicine without a moment's hesitation. So it is in the matter of salvation. God offers salvation right now. Christ is willing to receive any sinner who repents and believes right now. God's election doesn't prevent anyone from being saved. We possess free will. If we choose not to repent and believe, we have done so of our own free will. And we're responsible for that decision.

The doctrine of election produces abrasive Christians
This objection goes like this: "I know people who believe in God's sovereignty in salvation. They're not very likeable. As a matter of fact, they're downright abrasive. Where this doctrine takes hold, it's often accompanied by an arrogant spirit, an intolerant spirit, and an uncompassionate spirit. Therefore, I don't think it can be true."

Sadly, there's some truth to this objection. However, it must be understood that it isn't the doctrine of election that produces abrasive Christians. It's the doctrine of election "misunderstood" or "misapplied" that produces abrasive Christians. That happens when the doctrine of election isn't guarded and balanced with two Biblical truths.

The first is this: the truth of divine pity in God's estimation of man. God loves people. In their attempt to protect God's special love for his children, some downplay God's common love for his creatures. That's a mistake of gigantic proportions. We must be careful to maintain the distinction between God's special and common love. However, we must not do so at the expense of God's common love. We must not lose sight of the reality of that love. We must not lose sight of the depths of that love. We must not lose sight of the greatness of that love. That love should cause us to love our fellow man. When the truth of divine pity in God's estimation of man is lost sight of, the doctrine of election becomes ugly and those who hold to it become abrasive.

The second is this: the truth of divine sincerity in God's invitation to man. God wills (will of disposition) the salvation of everyone. God invites everyone to believe in Christ. God accepts everyone who believes. God wants us to proclaim that good news to everyone. God wants us to proclaim it openly and freely. We must be careful to maintain the distinction between the general and effectual calls. However, we must not do so at the expense of the general call. When the truth of divine sincerity in God's invitation to man is lost sight of, the doctrine of election becomes ugly and those who hold to it become abrasive.

Conclusion

Admittedly, I have been somewhat polemical in this study. So, I want to end on a more pastoral note. Here are three pastoral implications of the doctrine of election.

First, *the doctrine of election should comfort the troubled heart*. How could God love someone like me? How could God forgive someone like me? What is there in me that might make me acceptable in God's sight? If God's election of me depends upon him seeing something in me, I have no hope. But, praise God! It doesn't depend upon anything in me. "So then it depends not on human will or exertion, but on God, who has mercy" (9:16).

Second, *the doctrine of election should humble the proud heart*. Paul asks, "What do you have that you did not receive?" (1 Cor. 4:7). The answer is, "Nothing!" The only thing that distinguishes the believer from the unbeliever is God's good pleasure. Where would you and I be without God's sovereign grace?

Third, *the doctrine of election should encourage the concerned heart*. Is there no hope for your unsaved spouse? Is there no hope for your unsaved child? Is there no hope for that poor sinner? Given man's sinful condition, election is the only hope. As John Arrowsmith says,

> Election, having once pitched upon a man, will find him out and call him home, wherever he be. It called Zacchaeus out of accursed Jericho; Abraham out of idolatrous Ur of the Chaldees; Nicodemus and Paul, from the College of the Pharisees, Christ's sworn enemies; Dionysius and Damaris, out of superstitious Athens. In whatsoever dunghills God's elect are hid, election will find them out and bring them home.[3]

---

[3] Quoted in Thomas, *A Puritan Golden Treasury*, 84.

57
God's People (9:24-29)

God forgives us our sin and declares us to be just in his sight. How does he do that? He unites us to Christ. What belongs to us (our sin) is reckoned to Christ, and he paid its penalty at the cross. What belongs to Christ (his righteousness) is reckoned to us. This means that we're clothed in Christ's righteousness. As a result, we're no longer condemned (8:1). Moreover, there isn't anything that can "separate us from the love of God in Christ Jesus our Lord" (8:39).

In 9:1-5, Paul presents a problem. God promised Abraham, "And I will establish my covenant between me and you and your offspring after you throughout their generations for an everlasting covenant" (Gen. 17:7). Despite that promise, most of the descendants of Abraham (the Jews) are separated from God's love. Has God failed to keep his promise? Has God's word failed?

In 9:6, Paul declares the solution: "It is not as though the word of God has failed." He presents three arguments to prove it. We're in the midst of considering the first: "Not all who are descended from Israel belong to Israel" (9:6-10:21). You see, the notion that God's word has failed rests upon a false premise: God's promise was given to Abraham's physical descendants. It wasn't. As Paul affirms elsewhere, "Now the promises were made to Abraham and to his offspring. It does not say, 'And to offsprings,' referring to many, but referring to one, 'And to your offspring,' who is Christ ... And if you are Christ's, then you are Abraham's offspring, heirs according to promise" (Gal. 3:16, 29).

In 9:7-13, Paul proves it by producing two pieces of evidence. (1) Abraham had two physical sons: Isaac and Ishmael. Were both saved? No. Does this mean God's word failed? No. Why? Ishmael wasn't a child of promise; Isaac was. (2) Isaac had two physical sons: Jacob and Esau. Were both saved? No. Does this mean God's word failed? No. Why? Esau wasn't a child of promise; Jacob was. That distinction continues throughout Israel's history. There's clearly an Israel within Israel. To put it another way, there's a spiritual Israel within ethnic Israel. There are spiritual descendants of Abraham (children of promise) and there are physical descendants of Abraham (children of flesh).

In 9:14-23, Paul addresses several objections. He knows some people will struggle with what he says about God choosing Isaac over Ishmael and God choosing Jacob over Esau. He knows this will raise two objections. (1) God is unjust in choosing. To put it another way, it isn't fair to choose one and not the other. Paul responds by quoting two OT texts. The first is Exodus 33:19, which shows that God's glory or God's name is his freedom to bestow mercy on whomever he pleases apart from any motive outside of his own purpose. Paul draws a conclusion in 9:16, "So then it depends not on human will or exertion, but on God, who has mercy." The second text is Exodus 9:16, which shows that God's activity in Pharaoh's life is ultimately determined by God's purpose, not Pharaoh's willing or running. Paul draws a conclusion in 9:18, "So then he has mercy on whomever he wills, and he hardens whomever he wills." (2) God is unjust in condemning. After all, who resists his will? Paul responds to this objection by appealing to God's all-encompassing purpose: the revelation of his glory. Before the creation of the world, God saw humanity in its fallen state. From humanity, God chose "vessels for honourable use" and vessels "for dishonourable use" (9:21-23). In the former, he purposed to reveal the glory of his grace and mercy. In the latter, he purposed to reveal the glory of his justice and wrath.

Now, in 9:24-29, Paul develops the implications of his argument. There are two.

God calls his people from among the Gentiles (9:24-26)
According to the book of Hosea, God enters into a marriage covenant with Israel at Mt. Sinai. However, Israel commits spiritual whoredom by worshipping idols. God says that he's going to punish Israel. He declares his intention to do so in the names he gives to Hosea's three children (Hos. 1:4-9). The first is *Jezreel*: "God scatters (or, sows)." The second is *Lo-Ruhamah*: "Not loved." The third is *Lo-Ammi*: "Not my people." In a word, God disowns Israel.

But the prophecy doesn't end there. God promises, "Yet the number of the children of Israel shall be like the sand of the sea, which cannot be measured or numbered. And in the place where it was said to them, 'You are not my people,' it shall be said to them, 'Children of the living God'" (Hos. 1:10). God repeats this promise, declaring, "And I will have mercy on No Mercy, and I will say to Not My People, 'You are my people'; and he shall say, 'You are my God'" (Hos. 2:23).

God's People (9:24-29)

In 9:24-26, Paul quotes these texts from Hosea. What's interesting is this: he doesn't apply them to the salvation of the Jews but to the salvation of the Gentiles. At one time, the Gentiles weren't God's people. Now, they're numbered among God's people. In a word, those Gentiles who believe are Abraham's descendants: children of promise.

God calls his people from among the Jews (9:27-29)

In the book of Isaiah, God expresses his displeasure with Israel. The Israelites have broken his covenant. They've worshipped false gods. As a result, God sends the Assyrians to invade their land and destroy their cities. The Assyrian invasion of the northern kingdom is devastating. It results in the large-scale deportation of Israelites to Assyria and other places.

However, God preserves a remnant. If he hadn't, Israel would have been completely destroyed: "If the LORD of hosts had not left us a few survivors, we should have been like Sodom, and become like Gomorrah" (Isa. 1:9). At the time of the Assyrian invasion, the Israelites were numerous. However, only a remnant was spared:

> A remnant will return, the remnant of Jacob, to the mighty God. For though your people Israel be as the sand of the sea, only a remnant of them will return. Destruction is decreed, overflowing with righteousness. For the Lord GOD of hosts will make a full end, as decreed, in the midst of all the earth (Isa. 10:21-23).

In 9:27-29, Paul applies these texts from Isaiah to the situation in his own day. The Jews are numerous—like the sand of the sea. However, only a remnant is saved. Only a remnant is numbered among the people of God. Those Jews who believe are Abraham's descendants: children of promise.

Conclusion

Paul expands on this theme (the inclusion of believing Jews and Gentiles in the people of God) in Ephesians 2:11-22. He begins by describing our past condition as Gentiles. (1) We were "separated from Christ" (v. 12). In Romans 9:5, Paul says that Christ "according to the flesh" is from the Jews. In other words, Christ himself was a Jew. (2) We were "alienated from the commonwealth of Israel" (v. 12). In Romans 9:4, Paul says that "the promises" belong to the Jews. The Gentiles knew nothing of the rights and privileges of citizenship in the Israelite community. (3) We were "strangers to the covenants of promise"

(v. 12). In Romans 9:4, Paul says that "the covenants" belong to the Jews. They possessed the Abrahamic and Davidic covenants (Gen. 15:18-21; 17:7-8; 26:1-5; 28:10-17; 2 Sam. 7:14-15). (4) We were "without God in the world" (v. 12). In Romans 9:4, Paul says that "the glory" belongs to the Jews. This refers to the cloud that led the nation and filled the tabernacle (Ex. 16:10; 40:34).

To sum up, we were without "hope" (v.12). But Paul doesn't end there. He declares, "But now in Christ Jesus you who once were far off have been brought near by the blood of Christ" (v. 13). The expressions *far off* and *near* are extremely significant. As William Hendriksen explains,

> In the old dispensation, Jehovah (in a sense) had his dwelling in the temple. That temple was in Jerusalem. Israel, therefore, was "nearby." On the other hand, the Gentiles were "far away." Not only was this true literally, but even more so in a spiritual sense: the Gentiles generally lacked the true knowledge of God.[1]

As Gentiles, we were "far off." But Christ has brought us near. How? According to Ephesians 2:13-18, he has made both groups (Jews and Gentiles) into one. He has broken down the barrier of the dividing wall, he has made the two (Jews and Gentiles) into one new man. He has reconciled them both (Jews and Gentiles) in one body to God, he has preached peace to those who were far away (Gentiles) and those who were near (Jews), and he has given us access in one Spirit to the Father.

How did Christ accomplish all that? He did so by "killing the hostility" (v. 16). What is this? It's "the law of commandments contained in ordinances" (v. 15). How did Christ destroy it? Notice the threefold description—by his "blood" (v. 13), his "flesh" (v. 15), and "the cross" (v. 16). At the cross, Christ satisfied and fulfilled the demands of the law. As a result, he abolished the enmity. There is now peace between God and us in Christ. And there is now peace between Jews and Gentiles in Christ.

This brings us to our present condition in Ephesians 2:19-22. We're no longer "strangers and aliens"; rather, we're "fellow citizens with the saints" and we're of "God's household." (1) This temple's foundation is "the apostles and prophets." (2) This temple's corner stone is "Christ Jesus." (3) This

---

[1] William Hendriksen, *New Testament Commentary: Galatians and Ephesians* (Grand Rapids: Baker Books, 1987), 131.

God's People (9:24–29)

temple's occupant is God. We're being "built together into a dwelling of God in the Spirit."

The significance of these verses for us is tremendous. At one time, we were alienated from God. Because of our sin, God called us "Lo-Ruhamah" ("Not loved") and "Lo-Ammi" ("Not My people"). But what happened? Simply this: Christ "made peace through the blood of his cross" (Col. 1:20). Christ became sin for us. God punished Christ in our place. As a result, we have peace with God. God no longer calls us "Not loved" but now calls us "My beloved." God no longer calls us "Not my people" but now calls us "My people." We're God's beloved and God's people because we're one with Christ. Christ's purity is ours, however filthy we might be. Christ's dignity is ours, however vile we might be. Christ's wisdom is ours, however foolish we might be. Christ's righteousness is ours, however unrighteous we might be. Christ says, "the glory that you have given me I have given to them" (John 17:22). And God loves us with the love with which he loves his Son. We are called "sons of the living God" (Rom. 9:26). Surely, we can sing:

> Behold, what love, what boundless love, the Father hath bestowed
> On sinners lost, that we should be now called the sons of God!
> No longer far from him, but now by "precious blood" made nigh;
> Accepted in the "Well-beloved," near to God's heart we lie.[2]

---

[2] Robert Boswell, "Boundless Love" in *Hymns of Worship and Remembrance*, 5.

58
A Stone of Stumbling (9:30–10:3)

In Romans 10:2, Paul says, "For I bear them witness that they have a zeal for God, but not according to knowledge" According to the *Oxford Dictionary*, zeal is "great energy or enthusiasm for a cause or aim." We see it in sports, politics, etc. In the verses we're studying, Paul says that the Jews have "a zeal for God." In other words, they have great energy and enthusiasm when it comes to God. They celebrate their feasts, give their tithes, bring their offerings, follow their rules, practice their ceremonies. They have "a zeal for God." However, Paul says it's without "knowledge."

We see the same thing in Islam. Muslims believe they must adhere to five "pillars" in order to be saved. (1) They must recite their creed: "There is no God but Allah and Mohammed is his prophet." (2) They must pray at five set times each day. (3) They must give alms to certain religious and humanitarian groups. (4) They must fast, especially during the month of Ramadan. (5) They must make a pilgrimage to Mecca at least once in their lifetime. What devotion! What zeal! But it's zeal without knowledge.

We see the same thing in Roman Catholicism. Alison and I served as missionaries in Portugal for five years. We lived near a town called Fatima, where Mary allegedly appeared in the early 1900s. There's a pilgrimage to Fatima twice each year. Some think it will restore justifying grace. You see, according to Roman Catholicism, justifying grace is infused into the soul at baptism. Baptized people must co-operate with that justifying grace in order to become righteous. If they commit mortal sin, they lose that grace. To get it back, they must perform penance. Penance involves works of satisfaction. That means they must do something that makes it fitting for God to restore justifying grace. And so, some people actually crawl on their knees to Fatima. What devotion! What zeal! But it's zeal without knowledge.

All false religions (although different in form) are the same in substance, in that they're based on two fundamental errors in thinking. (1) They don't understand what God requires from man. They think the determining factor in salvation is what they do. In other words, they think God determines whether they're saved or damned on the basis of their works. If their good works outweigh their bad works, they're saved. But if their bad works outweigh their good works, they're damned. (2) They don't understand that man is unable to please God. They think they possess the ability to do good works in order to merit salvation. They think God makes certain demands, sets certain requirements, or establishes certain laws. And they think it's within their power to do whatever God requires in order to be saved.

That's precisely Paul's point concerning the Jews in 9:30-10:3. Do you remember the context? (1) Paul presents the problem in 9:1-5. If God promised to be the God of Abraham's descendants, why are most of the Jews accursed? (2) Paul declares the solution in 9:6, "It is not as though the word of God has failed." (3) Paul presents his first argument in 9:6, "For not all who are descended from Israel belong to Israel." There's a difference between Abraham's physical and spiritual descendants. (4) Paul provides the evidence in 9:7-13. Isaac was saved; Ishmael wasn't. Jacob was saved; Esau wasn't. Yet they were all physical descendants of Abraham. (5) Paul addresses the objections in 9:14-23. God isn't unjust in choosing Isaac and Jacob over Ishmael and Esau. His glory is his freedom to bestow mercy on whomever he pleases apart from any external motive. (6) Paul develops the implications in 9:24-29. Both believing Jews and believing Gentiles are numbered among God's people—Abraham's spiritual descendants.

Now, in 9:30-10:21, Paul draws his conclusion. It's this: the fact that most of the Jews are accursed isn't God's fault; on the contrary, it's their fault. In 9:30-10:3, Paul explains why.

The Jews are ignorant of what God wants (9:30-32)

> What shall we say, then? That Gentiles who did not pursue righteousness have attained it, that is, a righteousness that is by faith; but that Israel who pursued a law that would lead to righteousness did not succeed in reaching that law. Why? Because they did not pursue it by faith, but as if it were based on works. They have stumbled over the stumbling stone.

What does God want from us? Perfect righteousness. How do we get it? The Jews think we get it by works. They think the law shows them what they must do and can do. They think the righteousness God requires is their righteousness. And so, they work for it.

The Jews are ignorant of what man needs (10:3)
"For, being ignorant of the righteousness of God, and seeking to establish their own, they did not submit to God's righteousness." The Jews don't understand man's inability to please God. And so, they seek to establish their own righteousness. What's wrong with that? Paul tells us way back in 1:29, man is "filled with all manner of unrighteousness." The Jews don't see it.

Owing to their ignorance, the Jews stumble over Christ (9:32-33)
"Behold, I am laying in Zion a stone of stumbling, and a rock of offense; and whoever believes in him will not be put to shame." Here Paul quotes Isaiah 8:14 and 28:16. What's the context? The Assyrians are going to sweep over the land of Israel like a flood. There's only one place of refuge: God. He's a rock. For those who trust in anyone or anything other than God to save them from the Assyrians, the rock will become a cause of offence. The floodwaters will sweep them against it. Paul says that the rock is Christ. God's judgment is coming. All those who believe in Christ are saved. All those who don't believe in Christ will strike against him. That's what has happened to the Jews. They know God requires righteousness but they don't understand whose righteousness that is. They think it's their righteousness, to be produced by their works. It isn't. It's Christ's righteousness, to be received by faith.

Conclusion
Very little has changed today. Most people still make the same two mistakes the Jews made. (1) They don't understand what God requires from man. (2) They don't understand that man is unable to please God. Those two errors are at the foundation of every religion except Christianity.

According to the Christian faith, God is righteous. He requires righteousness (perfect obedience) from us. We can't give him that. We don't have the ability to give him that. God gave the law to prove it. The law says we must love God with all our heart, soul, mind, and strength. We disobey that commandment every moment of every day. The law also says we must love our neighbour as ourselves. Yet we're full of envy and jealousy. We're full of anger and bitterness and resentment. Therefore, we must look elsewhere for the righteousness that God requires. Paul says, "But now the righteousness of God has been manifested apart from the law" (3:21). What righteousness is that? It's Christ! When I believe in Christ, God credits Christ's righteousness to me. That's why Paul says, "The righteous shall live by faith" (1:17).

Paul knows what he's talking about when he says that the Jews "have a zeal for God, but not according to knowledge" (10:2). Prior to his conversion, he was the same way (Phil. 3:6). One day, however, the light went on. He saw his inability to please God. And he believed in Christ. From that moment, his desire was to "be found in [Christ], not having a righteousness of my own that comes from the law, but that which comes through faith in Christ, the righteousness from God that depends on faith" (Phil. 3:9).

There are a number of lessons to be taken from these verses.

First, *legalism arises when we explain God's acceptance of us in terms of merit.* The Jews tried to establish their own righteousness as the basis for God's acceptance of them (10:3). That's legalism. The moment we identify something in us as the cause of God's acceptance of us, we've fallen prey to legalism. And so, the person who says "God must be pleased with the fact that I go to church every Sunday" is a legalist. The person who says "God must be pleased with the amount of money I give to the church" is a legalist. The person who says "God, I thank you that I am not like other men, extortioners, unjust, adulterers, or even like this tax collector. I fast twice a week; I give tithes of all that I get" (Luke 18:11-12) is a legalist.

Second, *legalism may exist in practice even if grace is preached in theory.* It's easy to proclaim the primacy of grace yet live as though human effort is the determining factor in salvation. We can fool ourselves. What the Jews viewed as grace Paul called legalism. What the Roman Catholics viewed as grace Martin Luther called legalism. Is it possible that what many view today as grace is actually legalism?

Third, *it's possible to possess zeal without knowledge.* How do we explain the zeal of Jews, Muslims, Mormons, or Catholics? At times, such zeal can be troubling. Why? We reason to ourselves, "They seem so sincere. They must really believe what they say they believe. Maybe they're right." We need to remember that it's possible to be sincerely wrong.

Fourth, *it's impossible to possess knowledge without zeal.* We act on what we know. Richard Baxter says, "Zeal is the fervor or earnestness of the soul: its first subject is the will and affections, excited by the judgment; and thence it appears in the practice. It is not a distinct grace or affection, but the vigor and liveliness of every grace, and their fervent operations."[1]

Fifth, *it's a comfort to know that those who believe in Christ will not be*

---

[1] Richard Baxter, *The Practical Works of Richard Baxter* (1846; repr., Morgan: Soli Deo Gloria, 2000), 1:382.

disappointed. That's what Paul says in 9:33 and 10:11, quoting from Isaiah 28:16. Why won't we be disappointed? Because God accepts us in the Beloved. We're united with Christ. What's ours is his: God has reckoned our sin to Christ, and Christ has satisfied God's justice by dying on the cross. What's his is ours: God has reckoned Christ's righteousness to us. "By faith," writes E. Hopkins, "we are united to Christ; by that union, we truly have a righteousness; and upon that righteousness, the justice of God as well as his mercy, is engaged to justify and acquit us."[2] And so, we sing:

> Mine is the sin, but thine the righteousness,
> Mine is the guilt, but thine the cleansing blood;
> Here is my robe, my refuge, and my peace—
> Thy blood, thy righteousness, O Lord, my God.[3]

---

[2] Quoted in Handley Moule, *Thoughts on Union with Christ* (London: Seeley & Co. Limited, 1885), 126.

[3] Horatius Bonar, "Here, O My Lord, I See Thee Face to Face" in *The Hymnal for Worship and Celebration*, 325.

59
Abounding in Riches (10:4-13)

In simple terms, a fanatic is someone whose zeal isn't based on knowledge. In 10:2, Paul basically calls the Jews *fanatics*: "For I bear them witness that they have a zeal for God, but not according to knowledge." What don't they understand? According to 9:30-10:3, they don't understand how to get righteousness. They think they can establish their own righteousness. They're wrong. How can they possibly establish their own righteousness? Man is totally depraved. Man's righteousness, therefore, is unacceptable in God's sight. The man who tries to produce his own righteousness is only accumulating a heap of filthy rags. He must get righteousness from somewhere other than himself. Where? The answer is Christ. Man can receive Christ's righteousness by faith. The Jews don't understand that. As a result, they stumble over the stumbling stone.

Whose fault is that? That's a good question, seeing as Paul ascribes their error to a lack of knowledge (i.e., ignorance). How can they be held responsible for something they don't know? To answer that, we need to remember that there are two types of ignorance. (1) There's such a thing as *unwillful* ignorance. There are things we don't know because we lack the information. There are lots of things I don't know because no one has ever told me. That isn't my fault. (2) There's such a thing as *willful* ignorance. There are things we don't know because we lack the inclination. In other words, we possess the information, but we don't like it. That's our fault. We have an example of this in 1:20-23, where Paul says that man has the necessary revelation to know God. Yet man doesn't worship God. Why? He doesn't like God. And so, he willfully supresses God's revelation. Man professes to be wise, but he's really a fool. That's willful ignorance.

In the case of the Jews, they have zeal for God, "but not according to knowledge." Is that an *unwillful* or *willful* ignorance? In 10:4-13, Paul proves that it's a willful ignorance. Can we blame them? Can we blame them for thinking they needed to establish their own righteousness? After all, God gave them the law. What else were they supposed to think? Paul wants to clear this up once and for all.

The nature of righteousness (10:4)

What's God's righteousness? It's Christ. In 10:4, Paul says, "For Christ is the end of the law for righteousness to everyone who believes." How is Christ the end of the law? (1) He's the end of the law in that he fulfilled its requirement. The law requires perfect obedience. Christ obeyed it perfectly. That's known as his *active* obedience. (2) Christ is the end of the law in that he fulfilled its penalty. Anyone who breaks the law must die. Christ bore that penalty on the cross. That's known as his *passive* obedience.

Those who believe in Christ partake of his obedience. First, they partake of Christ's active obedience. Christ's righteousness is reckoned to them. Second, they partake of Christ's passive obedience. Their sin is reckoned to Christ. In that way, he's "the end of the law for righteousness to everyone who believes."

The imputation of righteousness (10:5-10)

In these verses, Paul explains the wrong way and the right way of getting righteousness.

The wrong way: the righteousness based on law

In 10:5, Paul refers to Leviticus 18:5, where God says to Israel: "You shall therefore keep my statutes and my rules; if a person does them, he shall live by them." In the context, God says that man must fulfill the law in order to be righteous. However, God doesn't say that man can fulfill the law. That's where the Jews become confused. They think they can produce their own righteousness by their works—obeying the law. They're wrong. Back in 3:20, Paul declares, "For by works of the law no human being will be justified in his sight, since through the law comes knowledge of sin."

The right way: the righteousness based on faith

In 10:6-8, Paul quotes Deuteronomy 30:12-14. The man of faith doesn't say, "Who will ascend into heaven? (that is, to bring Christ down)." Why? He knows Christ came down at the time of his humiliation. The man of faith doesn't say, "Who will descend into the abyss? (that is, to bring Christ up from the dead)." Why? He knows Christ came up at the time of his exaltation. And so, what does the man of faith say? He confesses with his mouth Jesus as Lord and believes in his heart that God raised him from the dead (10:9). In other words, the man of faith doesn't seek to establish his own righteousness by his own effort. Rather, he looks to Christ—namely, what he accomplished by his humiliation and exaltation.

The proclamation of righteousness (10:11-13)

In 10:11, Paul quotes Isaiah 28:16, "Everyone who believes in him will not be put to shame." In 10:13, Paul quotes Joel 2:32, "Everyone who calls on the name of the LORD will be saved." In between these two quotations, Paul makes his point: "There is no distinction between Jew and Greek" (10:12). In short, the gospel is universal. God bestows his "riches on all who call on him" (10:12).

Conclusion

If Christ has done everything, then there's nothing left to do. Christ lived the life we were required to live. Christ died the death we were condemned to die. We believe in Christ. We don't contribute anything to the gospel. I pray we'll understand that we don't make a deal with God. We don't give him faith and obedience so that he'll give us salvation and happiness. There's no deal. Even our faith is God's gift to us. The gospel isn't about what we can or can't do, but about what God has done in Christ. "For there is no distinction between Jew and Greek; for the same Lord is Lord of all, bestowing his riches on all who call on him" (10:12).

Christ abounds in "riches" in that he pays all our debts. When we're united with him, our debt becomes his. What debt? Death! He has paid that debt in full at the cross.

Christ abounds in "riches" in that he satisfies all our wants. When we're united with him, our wants become his. Do we want grace, righteousness, wisdom, peace, and joy? He's full of these.

Christ abounds in "riches" in that he carries all our burdens. When we're united with him, our burdens become his. He strengthens us and sustains us by his grace.

Christ abounds in "riches" in that he sanctifies all our afflictions. When we're united with him, our afflictions become his. He governs them for our good.

Christ abounds in "riches" in that he defeats all our enemies. When we're united with him, our enemies become his. He has conquered the grave, the flesh, the devil, and the world. These are conquered foes for those who are in Christ.

Christ abounds in "riches" in that he guarantees our inheritance. When we're united with him, what's his becomes ours. We're heirs of God and joint heirs with Christ.

60
Hearing the Word (10:14-21)

Over the years, God has used a number of verses from Paul's epistle to the Romans to speak to me at important junctures in my life (e.g., 1:16; 2:5; 3:25; 5:1; 8:28; 9:18). Close to twenty years ago, he used 10:17, "So faith comes from hearing, and hearing through the word of Christ." I want to explain *how*. But, first, I need to set the verse's context. What's happening in this chapter? Paul is explaining the Jews' unbelief.

First, Paul affirms that they stumble over Christ (9:30-10:4). They do so because they insist on putting their righteous where his righteousness belongs.

Second, Paul responds to an objection (10:5-13). Is it possible they stumbled over Christ because they were *misinformed*? Paul shows that Moses proclaimed "the righteousness based on faith." To prove it, he applies three citations from Deuteronomy 30:12-14 to Christ.

Third, Paul responds to an objection (10:14-21). Is it possible they stumbled over Christ because they were *uniformed*? Paul handles this objection in three distinct stages.

Paul explains how people are saved (10:14-15)
There are five steps. (1) "Everyone who calls on the name of the Lord will be saved" (10:13). (2) "How are they to call on him in whom they have not believed?" People only call on Christ when they believe in Christ (10:14). (3) "How are they to believe in him of whom they have never heard?" People only believe in Christ when they hear of Christ (10:14). (4) "How are they to hear without someone preaching?" People only hear of Christ when they hear a preacher (10:14). (5) "How are they to preach unless they are sent?" People only hear a preacher when God sends one (10:15).

So, Paul sums up *how* people are saved in five words: sending, preaching, hearing, believing, and calling.

Paul applies his explanation to the Jews (10:15-21)
How do we explain the Jews unbelief? How do we explain the fact that they stumbled over Christ? Is it possible there was a breakdown somewhere in this

five-step process?

Was there a lack of *sending*? No. "How beautiful are the feet of those who preach the good news!" (Isa. 52:7; 10:15). God sent preachers throughout Israel's history, culminating in the apostles.

Was there a lack of *preaching*? No. "Lord, who has believed what he has heard from us?" (Isa. 53:1; 10:16). The Jews repeatedly hardened their hearts to God's messengers. The same thing happened in the apostles' day.

Was there a lack of *hearing*? No. "Their voice has gone out to all the earth, and their words to the ends of the world" (Ps. 19:4; 10:18). They possess God's revelation. They're without excuse.

Was there a lack of *understanding*? No. "I will make you jealous of those who are not a nation; with a foolish nation I will make you angry" (Deut. 32:21; 10:19). "I have been found by those who did not seek me; I have shown myself to those who did not ask for me" (Isa. 65:1; 10:20). Who are the "foolish" people who didn't seek God? Who are the people who didn't "seek" God? The Gentiles. Yet, salvation has come to them. The Jews were the informed people who possessed the oracles of God.

And so, why didn't they believe? In short, they're "a disobedient and contrary people" (10:21).

Conclusion

"So faith comes from hearing, and hearing through the word of Christ" (10:17). I want to explain *how* God has used this verse (in its context) at different junctures in my life.

He used it to free me from the treadmill of methods, programs, and techniques
Why did the Jews reject the gospel? "All day long I have held out my hands to a disobedient and contrary people" (10:21). Why do people today reject the gospel? The same reason: they're "disobedient and contrary." You might not think this is important, but I suggest to you that it's very important. Why?

One of the most popular misconceptions today is that people reject the gospel because the message isn't engaging. It isn't sophisticated enough. It isn't relevant enough. It isn't hip enough. When we adopt this thinking, we jump on the endless treadmill of methods, programs, and techniques, thinking to ourselves: "If only we were doing something different, people would believe the gospel." That's why there are innumerable books, seminars, and conferences on what we need to do to make the message more effective.

God freed me from this way of thinking many years ago. He used this verse to do so. The problem isn't the message. The problem is man's sinful heart.

He used it to point me to a very simple strategy for church growth
Sending, preaching, hearing, believing, and calling. This is how people come to saving faith. This is how people walk by faith. What are the implications? It means the Bible is the only means of cultivating faith. Saving faith requires that we hear the Bible. We must explain and apply the Bible. We need messages filled with the Bible.

This is my strategy for church growth. This is my strategy for evangelism. This is my strategy for sanctification. This is my strategy for discipleship. This is my strategy for dealing with broken marriages, wayward children, and substance abuse. This is my strategy for dealing with bereavement, persecution, rejection, and every other form of affliction. We need *faith*. It's the answer to everything. Faith comes by hearing, and hearing by the Word of Christ.

As Calvin says, "This is a remarkable passage with regard to the efficacy of preaching; for Paul testifies that by it faith is produced … when it pleases the Lord to work, it becomes the instrument of his power."[1] If that's true, what are the implications?

It means something for the preacher. He must be careful to proclaim the Word. "For our appeal does not spring from error or impurity or any attempt to deceive, but just as we have been approved by God to be entrusted with the gospel, so we speak, not to please man, but to please God who tests our hearts" (1 Thess. 2:3-4).

It means something for the sermon. Our sermons must be expositional. We must seek to explain and apply God's Word. We don't need to apologize for that. We don't make God's Word relevant. It's relevant, because it's God's Word. "All Scripture is breathed out by God and profitable for teaching, for reproof, for correction, and for training in righteousness, that the man of God may be complete, equipped for every good work" (2 Tim. 3:16-17).

It means something for the listener. We must give our full attention to God's Word. We should be in prayer for God's blessing upon his Word. We should be diligent to act upon all that we hear. We should seek to be "effectual doer[s]" of the Word (James 1:25).

It means something for the church. Here's the only acceptable strategy for

---

[1] Calvin, *Epistle to the Romans*, 401.

church growth: "I planted, Apollos watered, but God gave the growth. So neither he who plants nor he who waters is anything, but only God who gives the growth" (1 Cor. 3:6-7).

Most of what I've just said is rejected by large segments of today's church. Worldliness has destroyed our ability to discern and digest God's Word. We've entertained ourselves in the world to such an extent that we're on the brink of spiritual imbecility. We downplay preaching and teaching. We downplay content. We dismiss doctrine as too academic and theology as too abstract. We speak of the need to be relevant and practical. And all we're doing is confirming what Jonathan Edwards wrote so many years ago: "The person who is in a worldly condition is not able to judge spiritual realities properly."[2]

He used it to protect me from the oppressive effects of hyper-Calvinism
There's nothing outside of man that prevents him from calling upon God. When a person rejects the call, refuses to subject himself to God's righteousness, and stumbles over the stumbling stone, he does so of his own free will. He confirms that he's "disobedient and contrary."

If anyone is saved, the cause is God's sovereignty. If anyone is condemned, the cause is man's obstinacy. Here are two things we must never lose sight of.

First, the truth of divine pity in God's estimation of man. We must be careful to maintain the distinction between God's special and common love. However, we must not do so at the expense of God's common love. We must not lose sight of the reality of that love. We must not lose sight of the depths of that love. We must not lose sight of the greatness of that love. That love should cause us to love our fellow man. When the truth of divine pity in God's estimation of man is lost sight of, the doctrine of election becomes ugly.

Second, the truth of divine sincerity in God's invitation to man. God wills (i.e., his will of command) the salvation of everyone. God invites everyone to believe in Christ. God accepts everyone who believes in Christ. God commands us to proclaim that good news to everyone. God wants us to proclaim it openly and freely. We must be careful to maintain the distinction between the general and effectual calls. However, we must not do so at the expense of the general call. When the truth of divine sincerity in God's invitation to man is lost sight of, the doctrine of election becomes ugly.

We want to stand in the tradition of Charles Spurgeon, William Cary,

---

[2] Jonathan Edwards, *Faith Beyond Feelings: Discerning the Heart of True Spirituality*, ed. J.M. Houston (Portland: Multnomah Press, 1984), 104.

Andrew Fuller, George Mueller, etc.

He used it to preserve me from the fog of restless experimentalism
If the framework by which we understand spirituality is unbiblical, then our conclusions regarding the Christian life and Christian growth will be unbiblical. How do we understand spirituality?

In the "platonic" world view, reality consists of a material realm (imperfection, shadow, unreal, changeable) and a spiritual realm (perfection, form, real, unchangeable). Man is stuck in both. His body resides in the material world while his spirit resides in the spiritual world. Spiritual growth, therefore, comes through the spirit's direct communion with God. We must realize God's presence. This has impacted the church. The majority of people think they can experience God directly, apart from the mind. It has led us to a frantic search for a spiritual experience that will assure us that we have a relationship with God.

Scripture comes alive when God's Spirit touches our spirit as we read/study/listen. We must, therefore, engage Scripture with the mind. "I rejoice at your word like one who finds great spoil" (Ps. 119:162).

He used it to show me what people must do to be saved
Bartimaeus cries, "Have mercy on me!" (Mark 10:47-48). The verb is *keradzo*. It means to scream. It's the term used to describe the screaming of demon-possessed people. It's in the imperfect, meaning he continually screams. If someone were to scream like this right now, we'd dial 911. Bartimaeus is hysterical. He knows he has no merit of his own. He knows what he deserves. He screams for mercy. People only cry like that when they're desperate. In one of our hymns, we sing, "Nothing in my hand I bring, simply to Your cross I cling." Based on those words, C.J. Mahaney writes:

> "Nothing in my hand I bring." Lord, I bring nothing to you. I do not bring to you my own righteousness. What a joke that would be! How repulsive even the thought of that must be to you. No, nothing, nothing in my hands do I bring, except my sin in need of forgiveness. I come to you in spiritual poverty and helplessness, looking to you for the grace that flows from the fountain filled with Your holy blood. "Simply to Your cross I cling." O Lord Jesus Christ, I wrap my arms and the entirety of my heart around Your cross! Thank You, Jesus, that you loved

me! Thank you that you gave yourself for me! I rejoice in your love and acceptance of me.[3]

---

[3] C.J. Mahaney, *Christ Our Mediator* (Sisters: Multnomah Publishers, 2004), 94.

61
Chosen by Grace (11:1-6)

As we embark on a new chapter, I think it's important to review what Paul is trying to accomplish in this section: *Election* (9:1-11:36). In this epistle, he unfolds the doctrine of justification by grace alone through faith alone in Christ alone. His teaching culminates in that tremendous declaration in 8:39, "[Nothing] in all creation will be able to separate us from the love of God in Christ Jesus our Lord." As we've seen, that statement raises a perplexing question: How do we explain the state of the Jews? For the most part, they're separated from God's love. They're accursed. But didn't God make them a promise? If so, has God's word failed? If so, why should we believe God?

Simply put, there are two important issues at stake here. (1) God's faithfulness is at stake. Moses declares, "God is not man, that he should lie, or a son of man, that he should change his mind. Has he said, and will he not do it? Or has he spoken, and will he not fulfill it?" (Num. 23:19) Well, didn't God make a promise to Abraham concerning the salvation of his descendants? Aren't most of those descendants accursed? Doesn't that mean God has changed his mind? Doesn't that undermine any notion of God's faithfulness? (2) Man's faith is at stake. Paul declares, "No unbelief made [Abraham] waver concerning the promise of God, but he grew strong in his faith as he gave glory to God, fully convinced that God was able to do what he had promised" (Rom. 4:20-21). God made a promise. Abraham believed God. Paul exhorts us to follow Abraham's example. Why should we if God doesn't keep his promises? Why should we if God might change his mind?

Do you see what's at stake? Paul does. It's an issue that in many respects has plagued him since 3:3, where he wrote, "What if some were unfaithful? Does their faithlessness nullify the faithfulness of God?" He gave the issue just a cursory glance at that point. But in chapters 9-11 he deals with it head on. Simply put, Paul can't avoid the issue any longer. He must address it because a great deal hangs upon it.

His solution to the "apparent" problem is summed up in one statement in 9:6, "It is not as though the word of God has failed." He proves it by way of three arguments. (1) "Not all who are descended from Israel belong to Israel"

(9:6-10:21). (2) "God has not rejected his people whom he foreknew" (11:1-24). (3) "All Israel will be saved" (11:25-32).

For some time, we've been considering Paul's first argument: "Not all who are descended from Israel belong to Israel." How does he unpack that argument? (1) He provides the evidence (9:7-13). (2) He addresses the objections (9:14-23). (3) He develops the implications (9:24-29). (4) He draws the conclusion (9:30-10:21). In short, God's word hasn't failed. Rather, God's purpose according to election stands. He's doing exactly what he promised. He isn't to blame for the Jews' condition. On the contrary, they're to blame. As God declares, "All day long I have held out my hands to a disobedient and contrary people" (10:21).

In this study, we move into Paul's second argument: "God has not rejected his people whom he foreknew" (11:1-24).

The problem (11:1)

He begins in 11:1 by stating the problem: "I ask, then, has God rejected his people?" It's true that God has stretched out his hands to an obstinate people—the Jews (10:21). And it's true that they have willingly rejected him. Does this mean that God has rejected his people? If it does, then the word of God has failed.

The solution (11:1-2)

Paul responds, "By no means!" What's the basis for Paul's confident assertion? "For I myself am an Israelite, a descendant of Abraham, a member of the tribe of Benjamin. God has not rejected his people whom he foreknew" (11:1-2). Paul makes the point that foreknowledge and rejection are incompatible. What's God's foreknowledge? Many people suggest that it's God's knowledge in advance of those who will choose him or obey him or love him or believe in him. In this context, that simply can't be. Why? In 11:4-5, Paul makes it clear that those whom God foreknew are those whom he has kept for himself. They're "a remnant, chosen by grace." If God's foreknowledge is dependent upon something we do, we undermine the essence of God's grace. You see, Paul doesn't say God foreknew that we would choose something or believe something or do something. Paul says God foreknew *us* just as he predestined us, called us, justified us, and glorified us (8:29-30).

And so, the vast majority of the Jews have refused to submit themselves to God's righteousness. They've literally stumbled over the stumbling stone.

They've fallen. They're accursed. However, that doesn't mean God has rejected his people whom he foreknew. Not one of his elect from within Israel has been lost. Paul is a case in point. If God has totally rejected the Jews, then Paul couldn't be a Christian. But he is a Christian. Obviously, therefore, God hasn't totally rejected the Jews.

The evidence (11:2-6)
Now, Paul appeals to an illustration as proof of what he has said in 11:1-2. It's the story of Elijah, as found in 1 Kings 19:10-18. Ahab and Jezebel were on the throne. Israel had succumbed to Baal worship. The situation was desperate. From Elijah's perspective, the entire nation was accursed. But God told him, "I have kept for myself seven thousand men who have not bowed the knee to Baal" (11:4). In other words, God had preserved a remnant: "his people whom he foreknew"—his elect (11:2). He hadn't totally rejected Israel. Similarly, says Paul, God had preserved a remnant in his day (11:5-6). He hadn't totally abandoned the Jews. Paul's point is that no one should be surprised by that. After all, it was the same way in Elijah's day.

Conclusion
What do we learn from these verses?

First, *we learn that God's purposes are oftentimes hidden from view.* Elijah has a tremendous showdown with the prophets of Baal on Mt. Carmel. What a victory! However, Jezebel is now seeking his life. Elijah thinks he's alone. He thinks he's the only one who hasn't bowed the knee to Baal. From his perspective, the situation in Israel is all doom and gloom. He falls into such depths of despair—a feeling of helplessness and hopelessness. And he wants to die (1 Kings 19:1-4). Here's the question: What's wrong with Elijah? Simply this: he's lost sight of the fact that God's will is secret. Elijah doesn't know what God is doing in the midst of Israel's apostasy. Why doesn't he know? Because he doesn't know the end from the beginning. And God hasn't seen fit to tell him! Rather than acknowledging the fact that God's purposes are sovereign and that God more often than not keeps those purposes to himself, Elijah succumbs to the depths of despair.

What's the lesson for us? It should challenge us to trust in God's secret will. Moses declares, "The secret things belong to the LORD our God, but the things that are revealed belong to us and to our children forever, that we may do all the words of this law" (Deut. 29:29). When we lose sight of that, we become discouraged. Perhaps there's something happening in your life that you can't explain. You can't see any reason for it. You don't have a clue how it's going to work for your good. You don't have any idea how God is going to glorify himself in it. None of that should surprise you. God's purposes are oftentimes hidden from view. We would do well to remember God's words to Habakkuk: "Look among the nations, and see; wonder and be astounded. For I am doing a work in your days that you would not believe if told" (Hab. 1:5).

Second, *we learn that God's grace is sovereign grace.* Why did a remnant exist in Elijah's day? God's gracious choice! Why did a remnant exist in Paul's day? God's gracious choice! Why does a remnant exist today? God's gracious choice! That's precisely what Paul said back in 9:16, "So then it depends not on human will or exertion, but on God, who has mercy."

What's the lesson for us? It should challenge us to think seriously about the nature of God's grace. Why? We can't fully appreciate the nature of God's grace without a biblically informed doctrine of election. As long as we look for the determining factor in salvation in us, we undermine God's grace. If we make God's election dependent upon anything in us, we compromise God's grace. And we unwittingly alter the essence of the gospel.

Third, *we learn that we should be amazed that we're numbered among God's people.* God tells Elijah: "I have kept for myself seven thousand" (11:4). Out of how many? Millions! Why these seven thousand? We don't know.

What's the lesson for us? It should challenge us to ask, "Why did God choose and call me?"

> Lord, how is it that I, unworthy I, should be chosen, when others are rejected; that I should be called when others are neglected; that I, who came into the world with the same rage against you and godliness, and did many a day run with others to the same excess of riot, should turn about, be in love with holiness, and run the ways of your commandments; when many others still wallow in their wickedness, and are every hour hastening unto hell? Lord, how is it that you have revealed yourself to me, and not to the world?[1]

What a humbling thought! May the wonder of God's sovereign grace draw forth worship from our hearts!

---

[1] Swinnock, *Works*, 5:254.

How sweet and holy is the place with Christ within the doors,
Where everlasting love displays the choicest of her stores!
With joyful hearts we raise our song, as those who have been blest;
Each one thus cries with thankful tongue: Lord, why am I a guest?
Why was I made to hear thy voice, and enter while there's room,
When thousands make a wretched choice, and rather starve than come?
'Twas the same love that spread the feast, that sweetly forced us in:
Else we had still refused to taste, and perished in our sin.[2]

---

[2] Isaac Watts, "How Sweet and Holy Is the Place" in *Hymns of Worship and Remembrance*, 158.

62
When Grace Isn't Grace (11:7-10)

In 3:3, Paul asks, "What if some were unfaithful? Does their faithlessness nullify the faithfulness of God?" By "some," Paul means the Jews. For the most part, they didn't believe in Christ. This raises a problem. Aren't they the descendants of Abraham? Aren't they the heirs of the Abrahamic covenant? Aren't they the people of God? If so, does their unbelief nullify God's faithfulness? Paul responds, "By no means!" (3:4). However, he doesn't provide much of an explanation. Instead, he waits until chapters 9-11, where he gives three arguments to prove that God's faithfulness isn't compromised by the fact that most of the Jews are accursed.

In logic, we derive a conclusion from certain premises. If I err in one of our premises, then what happens to our conclusion? It's wrong. That's how Paul presents his three arguments. In the first, beginning in 9:6, Paul challenges the logic of those who say God is unfaithful. What's their first premise? All Jews are heirs of the Abrahamic covenant because they're Abraham's physical descendants. What's their second premise? Most Jews are accursed. What's their conclusion? God hasn't kept his promise, and, therefore, he's unfaithful. What's Paul's argument? He challenges their first premise. In effect, he says, "You're wrong to assume that all Jews are heirs of the Abrahamic covenant simply because they're Abraham's physical descendants. 'This means that it is not the children of the flesh who are the children of God, but the children of the promise are counted as offspring'" (9:8). Paul proves it by appealing to Isaac, Ishmael, Jacob, and Esau. There has always been a spiritual Israel within ethnic Israel. There have always been spiritual descendants in the midst of the physical descendants. The heirs of the Abrahamic covenant have always been those who are chosen. If that's our first premise, then we won't arrive at a wrong conclusion concerning God's faithfulness.

In his second argument, beginning in 11:1, Paul again challenges the logic of those who say God is unfaithful. What's their first premise? All Jews are God's people because they're Abraham's physical descendants. What's their second premise? Most Jews are accursed. What's their conclusion? God has rejected his people, and, therefore, he's unfaithful. What's Paul's argument?

He challenges their first premise. In effect, he says, "You're wrong to assume that all Jews are God's people simply because they're Abraham's physical descendants. God's people are those whom he foreknew. 'God has not rejected his people whom he foreknew.'" And Paul proves it by appealing to Elijah. There has always been a spiritual remnant within Israel. There have always been a people of God within Israel. The people of God have always been those who are chosen. If that's our first premise, then we won't arrive at a wrong conclusion concerning God's faithfulness.

In the last study, we started to look in detail at Paul's second argument (11:1-24). (1) Paul states the problem in 11:1. Most of the Jews are accursed. Has God rejected his people? Is God unfaithful? (2) Paul declares the solution in 11:2. God hasn't rejected his people whom he foreknew. Paul himself is an Israelite. (3) Paul presents the evidence in 11:2-6. He appeals to Elijah to demonstrate that just as there was a remnant in Elijah's day, there's a remnant in his day. This remnant is "chosen by grace."

In this study and the next, we're going to consider the implications of Paul's argument. There are two: (1) Israel has stumbled (11:7-10); and (2) Israel hasn't stumbled so as to fall (11:11-24). We begin with the first. Essentially, Paul makes three points.

What Israel is seeking, it has not obtained (11:7)

What were the Jews seeking? We already know the answer to that. They were seeking to establish their own righteousness (10:3). Therefore, they refused to "submit to God's righteousness" (10:3). Therefore, they "stumbled over the stumbling stone"—Christ (9:32).

But those who were chosen obtained it (11:7)

The "chosen" are the remnant according to God's gracious choice. They're those whom God foreknew; those whom he foreknew, he predestined; those whom he predestined, he called; those whom he called, he justified; and those whom he justified, he glorified (8:29-30). They don't seek to establish their own righteousness. They know they're sinners. Therefore, they believe in Christ, and God imputes Christ's righteousness to them.

And the rest were hardened (11:7-10)

In 11:8, Paul quotes Isaiah 29:10, "God gave them a spirit of stupor, eyes that would not see and ears that would not hear, down to this very day." This "spirit of stupor" (or, slumber) is spiritual insensitivity: eyes that do not see and ears that do not hear. In 11:9-10, Paul quotes Psalm 69:22, "Let their table become a snare and a trap, a stumbling block and a retribution for them; let their eyes be darkened so that they cannot see, and bend their backs forever." What's the table? According to Calvin, it's "whatever is desirable and happy in life."[1] David prays that this might turn out to the ruin and destruction of the ungodly. Furthermore, he prays that their eyes might be "darkened" and their backs might be "bent" (bondage). Paul applies all this to the state of the Jews. God had hardened them.

It's extremely important to remember that this spiritual insensitivity is self-induced before it becomes divine judgment. In 10:4-21, Paul makes it perfectly clear that the Jews alone are to blame for their condition. They're "a disobedient and contrary people" (10:21). Therefore, God's hardening of the Jews is judicial. We find the term *harden* back in 9:18 in reference to Pharaoh. When God hardened Pharaoh's heart, what did he do? He didn't stop Pharaoh from doing something he wanted to do. He didn't make Pharaoh do something he didn't want to do. He willingly permitted Pharaoh to do what was already in his heart. When God hardened the "rest" (11:7), what did he do? He didn't stop them from doing something they wanted to do. He didn't make them do something they didn't want to do. He willingly permitted them to do what was already in their hearts.

Conclusion

I want to affirm four lessons from the above.

First, *the unbeliever never finds what he's seeking* (11:7). The Jews were seeking to establish their own righteousness by their own effort. They failed. Everyone is like that by nature. Everyone has a belief system. Although these systems differ in form, they're exactly the same in substance. By that I mean they're based on the same two fundamental errors in thinking. (1) They don't understand what God requires from man. They think the determining factor in salvation is what they do. They think God determines whether they're saved or damned on the basis of their works. (2) They don't understand that man is unable to please God. They think they possess the ability to do good works in order to merit salvation. That's what the Jews thought. That's why they stumbled over the stumbling stone: Christ. And that's why people continue to

---

[1] Calvin, *Epistle to the Romans*, 419.

stumble over the stumbling stone in our day.

Second, *the unbeliever is in a deep sleep* (11:8). I've had a couple of operations on my knees. Each time, I had a full anaesthetic. It amazes me how someone under anaesthetic is completely desensitized to stimuli. You can't feel anything. And you can't awaken yourself from that sleep. Similarly, God has given to man "a spirit of stupor, eyes that would not see and ears that would not hear" (11:8). When it comes to spiritual truth, people are completely insensible.

Third, *the unbeliever is in a state of bondage* (11:10). (1) He can't know God: "The natural person does not accept the things of the Spirit of God, for they are folly to him, and he is not able to understand them because they are spiritually discerned" (1 Cor. 2:14). (2) He can't come to God: "No one can come to me unless the Father who sent me draws him" (John 6:44). (3) He can't obey God: "For the mind that is set on the flesh is hostile to God, for it does not submit to God's law; indeed, it cannot" (Rom. 8:7). (4) He can't speak one good word: "You brood of vipers! How can you speak good, when you are evil? For out of the abundance of the heart the mouth speaks" (Matt. 12:34). (5) He can't do one good deed: "I am the vine; you are the branches. Whoever abides in me and I in him, he it is that bears much fruit, for apart from me you can do nothing" (John 15:5).

Fourth, *God's grace is sovereign grace*. It has to be, for if man were left to himself, no one would be saved. (1) God's gracious choice is eternal. God chose us before the foundation of the world (Eph. 1:4). (2) God's gracious choice is immutable: "But God's firm foundation stands, bearing this seal: 'The Lord knows those who are his'" (2 Tim. 2:19). (3) God's gracious choice is unto salvation through sanctification: "But we ought always to give thanks to God for you, brothers beloved by the Lord, because God chose you as the first fruits to be saved, through sanctification by the Spirit and belief in the truth" (2 Thess. 2:13). (4) God's gracious choice is according to the mere pleasure of his will: "So then it depends not on human will or exertion, but on God, who has mercy" (Rom. 9:16). (5) God's gracious choice is designed for the praise of his glory (Eph. 1:5-6).

> Sov'reign grace o'er sin abounding,
> Ransomed souls, the tidings swell;
> 'Tis a deep that knows no sounding,
> Who its breadth or length can tell?
> On its glories, on its glories,

let my soul forever dwell![2]

---

[2] John Kent, "Sovereign Grace O'er Sin Abounding" in *Hymns of Worship and Remembrance*, 29.

63
A Remnant, Chosen by Grace (11:11-24)

As I've mentioned on several occasions, chapters 9-11 consist of three arguments in which Paul defends God's faithfulness. At present, we're considering the second argument. Paul unfolds it in four steps. (1) He states the problem (11:1). If God has rejected his people, he's unfaithful. (2) He declares the solution (11:2). God hasn't rejected his people whom he foreknew. (3) He presents the evidence (11:2-6). God called a remnant in Elijah's day, and he has called a remnant in Paul's day. These are God's people. (4) He considers the implications: first, Israel has stumbled (11:7-10); and, second, Israel hasn't stumbled so as to fall (11:11-24). Now we arrive at the second implication.

The question (11:11)
In 11:7-10, Paul states that Israel has stumbled. The Jews have stumbled over the stumbling stone (9:32). Why? They were seeking to establish their own righteousness (10:3). That raises a question: "Did they stumble in order that they might fall?" In other words, "Is their stumbling permanent?"

The answer (11:11-15)
"By no means!" Israel hasn't stumbled so as to fall. On the contrary, Israel's stumbling has a threefold purpose. (1) "Through their trespass salvation has come to the Gentiles" (11:11). That's confirmed throughout the Book of Acts. Repeatedly, Paul preaches to the Jews. When they reject his message, he turns to the Gentiles. (2) "Through their trespass salvation has come to the Gentiles, so as to make Israel jealous" (11:11). God will provoke the Jews to jealousy by saving the Gentiles. (3) "Now if their trespass means riches for the world, and if their failure means riches for the Gentiles, how much more will their full inclusion mean!" (11:12). Again, "For if their rejection means the reconciliation of the world, what will their acceptance mean but life from the dead?" (11:15). What does Paul mean in these verses? Simply this: the Jews' rejection of the gospel resulted in the salvation (or, reconciliation) of the world; that is, the gospel has gone out to the Gentiles (1:8). If that's what the Jews' rejection of the gospel has accomplished, what will the Jews' acceptance

of the gospel accomplish? It will be "life from the dead" (11:15).

The analogy (11:16-24)
Paul draws out the significance of this implication by way of analogy. The purpose of this analogy is to support Paul's assertion that God has a purpose in Israel's stumbling.

The analogy explained (11:16-17)
Paul says, "If the dough offered as first fruits is holy, so is the whole lump, and if the root is holy, so are the branches" (11:16). The dough and root point to Abraham (4:1; 9:7; 11:1). The lump and branches are the Jews. Paul says the lump is holy by virtue of its relationship to the dough, and the branches are holy by virtue of their relationship to the root. Paul's point, therefore, is that the Jews are holy because of their relationship with Abraham.

In order to understand what Paul means, we must define the term *holy*. Clearly, he isn't talking about internal holiness. He has already made it clear that the Jews aren't saved simply because they're physical descendants of Abraham. If he's now saying that they're internally holy because they're physical descendants of Abraham, then he's guilty of contradicting himself. That can't be. This holiness, therefore, isn't internal but external. Because the Jews are the physical descendants of Abraham, they enjoy all the external privileges of God's covenant with Abraham (9:4-5). In that sense, they're holy.

When the Jews rejected Christ, they lost that external holiness. They were broken off from the root. They lost the external privileges of God's covenant with Abraham. And God took wild branches (Gentiles) and grafted them into the vine. They "now share in the nourishing root of the olive tree" (11:17).

The analogy applied (11:18-24)
Paul draws out two lessons from the above analogy.

The first lesson is this: Don't be arrogant, but believe! (11:18-20). Some Gentiles might say, "Branches were broken off so that I might be grafted in" (11:19). In other words, "I must be pretty special." "Nonsense!" says Paul. "You were grafted in according to God's good pleasure. Don't make the same mistake as the Jews! But believe!"

The second lesson is this: Don't be careless, but fear! (11:20-24). Although the Jews enjoyed external holiness by virtue of their relationship with Abraham, very few truly believed. Now, the Gentiles are grafted in. They'd

A REMNANT, CHOSEN BY GRACE (11:11-24)

better not make the same mistake as the Jews. If God cut the Jews off for unbelief, he will do the same to the Gentiles without a moment's hesitation. In effect, Paul says, "Don't make the same mistake as the Jews! But fear!"

Conclusion

From these verses, we learn four important truths.

First, *we learn that external holiness doesn't save anyone*. According to 11:16-17, the Jews were holy (externally) by virtue of their relationship with Abraham. They were his physical progeny. As a result, they partook of the external privileges of the covenant. However, most of them failed to believe. Now, as Gentiles, we partake of "the nourishing root of the olive tree." But we must make certain to believe. No one is saved by association. We can think in terms of our children. We raise them in the church. From an early age, they hear the preaching of God's Word. They see the ordinances. They experience Christian fellowship. But this external holiness is no guarantee that they'll become holy internally.

My fear is that many people who are raised in Christian homes become comfortable with external holiness. It's familiar. They can't imagine life without it. But they never personalize it. They're never born again. But they're too accustomed to the externals of Christianity to leave it. What happens? The church becomes filled with people who hold to a form of godliness while denying its power (2 Tim. 3:5).

Second, *we learn why apostasy is so easy*. How is it that someone who is raised in a church and who memorizes Bible verses, serves at camp, and teaches Sunday school can leave it all behind? It's possible when none of it is internalized. They partake of the "nourishing root of the olive tree," but they never embrace it with the heart. Eventually prosperity allures him away or adversity scares him away. John Bunyan describes the process like this:

> 1. They draw off their thoughts, all that they may, from the remembrance of God, death, and judgment to come. 2. Then they cast off by degrees private duties, as closet-prayer, curbing their lusts, watching, sorrow for sin, and the like. 3. Then they shun the company of lively and warm Christians. 4. After that, they grow cold to public duty, as hearing, reading, godly conference, and the like. 5. Then they begin to pick holes, as we say, in the coats of some of the godly, and that devilishly, that they may have a seeming colour to throw religion behind their backs. 6. Then they begin to adhere to, and associate themselves with carnal, loose, and

wanton men. 7. Then they give way to carnal and wanton discourses in secret; and glad are they if they can see such things in any that are counted honest, that they may the more boldly do it through their example. 8. After this, they begin to play with little sins openly. 9. And then being hardened, they show themselves as they are. Thus being launched again into the gulf of misery, unless a miracle of grace prevent it, they everlastingly perish in their own deceiving.[1]

I've seen it more times than I care to remember. I've seen it in many churches. I'm not trying to discourage you, but warn you. Apostasy is easy. It's easy because it's possible to partake of the rich root without ever truly believing or fearing.

Third, *we learn why we are to fear God.* All we have is a result of God's grace. Where would we be without God's gracious choice? Doesn't that make you fear God? It should. According to John Bunyan, such fear,

Begets and continues in the soul a great reverence for God, his word and ways, keeping it tender, and making it afraid to turn from them, to the right hand or to the left, to any thing that may dishonour God, break its peace, grieve the Spirit, or cause the enemy to speak reproachfully.[2]

Fourth, *we learn that the saints are secure.* Many people think these verses teach the very opposite. Many people think these verses teach that Christians can lose their salvation. They say that it's possible to be in the vine (to be a Christian) and then be severed for unbelief. As with most errors, this assertion is based on a misunderstanding of Scripture. When interpreting these verses, we need to keep two facts clearly in mind. (1) Who are the branches? The natural branches are Jews. The wild branches are Gentiles. Paul isn't talking about individuals. He's talking about groups. (2) What is holiness? It isn't internal, but external. Paul is talking not about inward change but about external privilege. Paul is talking not about union with Christ but about union with the people of God.

If we understand those two facts, then we see that these verses in no way imply that Christians can lose their salvation. As a matter of fact, it would be completely absurd if they did, given the fact that Paul's main point is to prove that foreknowledge and rejection are incompatible. Those whom God

---

[1] Bunyan, *Pilgrim's Progress*, 177–178.
[2] Bunyan, *Pilgrim's Progress*, 173.

foreknew, he predestined, called, justified, and glorified (8:29-30). Has God rejected his people? How can he reject his people? Can a Christian lose his salvation? How? It's an absurdity. Such a notion reveals a complete misunderstanding of the gospel. God is faithful. He can't reject his people whom he foreknew.

64
A Mystery (11:25-32)

William Greenhill states, "Man's faith may fail him sometimes, but God's faithfulness never fails him."[1] Paul understands the importance of God's faithfulness to the Christian. And he knows that some people might question God's faithfulness because of the Jews' unbelief. He expresses that very thing in 3:3, "What if some were unfaithful? Does their faithlessness nullify the faithfulness of God?" Why would the Jews' unbelief nullify God's faithfulness? Well, aren't the Jews God's people? And aren't most of the Jews accursed? Doesn't that imply that God isn't faithful? Paul gives his answer in 9:6-11:32. It consists of three arguments: (1) "Not all who are descended from Israel belong to Israel" (9:6-10:21); (2) "God has not rejected his people whom he foreknew" (11:1-24); and (3) "All Israel will be saved" (11:25-32). We're going to complete our study of Paul's arguments by looking at the third. As we do, we must keep two things in view.

The first is Paul's time references (11:5, 13-14, 29-32). He isn't describing an apocalyptic expectation, but a present reality that directly shaped and impacted his ministry. It's a present reality that had tremendous pastoral application, which Paul addresses in chapters 12-13.

The second is Paul's central argument. In chapters 9-11, he's demonstrating that God's word hasn't failed by proving that God's promises were never directed to the nation of Israel as a whole, but to the remnant chosen by grace.

The mystery stated (11:25-27)
Here Paul states a mystery that consists of three truths.[2]

First, "a partial hardening has come upon Israel" (11:25). Paul has already mentioned this in 11:7, "Israel failed to obtain what it was seeking. The elect obtained it, but the rest were hardened." They willfully rejected Christ. God, in turn, gave them over to greater spiritual insensibility. Elsewhere, Paul says, "But their minds were hardened. For to this day, when they read the old

---
[1] Quoted in Thomas, *A Puritan Golden Treasury*, 122.
[2] See Sam Storms, *Kingdom Come: The Amillennial Alternative* (Fearn, UK: Christian Focus, 2013), 303-334.

covenant, that same veil remains unlifted, because only through Christ is it taken away" (2 Cor. 3:14). Despite this hardening, there's a remnant (11:7).

Second, this partial hardening of Israel will continue "until the fullness of the Gentiles has come in" (11:25). Paul has already alluded to this in 11:11, "Through their trespass salvation has come to the Gentiles." We see this happening in the book of Acts. Repeatedly, Paul preaches to the Jews. Upon their rejection, he turns to the Gentiles. Israel's partial hardening will continue until God's elect from among the Gentile nations are gathered. There's a purpose to Israel's partial hardening: the fullness of the Gentiles. The term "until" doesn't refer to a point of time after which something else is going happen. It refers to a goal—a termination point.

Third, once the fullness of the Gentiles has come in, "all Israel will be saved" (11:26). Paul has already said that in 11:12, "Now if their trespass means riches for the world, and if their failure means riches for the Gentiles, how much more will their full inclusion mean!" Similarly, in 11:15 he writes, "For if their rejection means the reconciliation of the world, what will their acceptance mean but life from the dead?"

There's a huge debate concerning the meaning of "Israel" in 11:26. I'm not about to enter into all the details. Let me state it simply for you. (1) On the one hand, some believe *Israel* is spiritual Israel. It's the spiritual Israel within ethnic Israel that Paul mentions back in 9:6-7. (2) On the other hand, some believe *Israel* is ethnic Israel. John Murray writes, "It is exegetically impossible to give to 'Israel' in this verse any other denotation than that which belongs to the term throughout this chapter."[3]

We need to be clear on two things. First, the phrase "in this way" means "similarly" or "in such manner" or "in accordance with this pattern." Evidently, Paul is making a comparison. He isn't telling us *when* "all Israel" will be saved, but *how* "all Israel" will be saved. Second, the phrase, "the fullness of the Gentiles," refers to the full number of the elect from among the Gentiles throughout history. The phrase, "all Israel," refers to the full number of the elect from among the Jews throughout history. It's the "full inclusion" of which Paul speaks in 11:12. And so, when "the fullness of the Gentiles" is complete, we can be certain that "the fullness of the Jews" will be complete too.

In 11:26-27, Paul says the Deliverer will come to Zion (Isa. 59:20). He will

---

[3] Murray, *Epistle to the Romans*, 96.

remove ungodliness from Jacob. He will take away their sins (Jer. 31:34). Paul quotes Isaiah 27:9; 59:20-21 to affirm that Christ came to accomplish all this at his first advent. Christ takes away his people's sins.

The mystery supported (11:28-32)
Regarding the gospel, they're God's enemies, for your sake. Regarding election, they're God's beloved, for their forefathers' sake. Who are *they*? They're "all Israel" (11:26). They're the "full inclusion" of believing Jews. While they reject the gospel, they're God's enemies. When they accept the gospel, they become God's beloved. Their acceptance of the gospel is rooted in God's election. It's a certainty.

Paul gives two reasons why we can be sure it will come to pass.

The first is God's faithfulness (11:28-29). The Jews are hostile toward the gospel. For that reason, they're enemies. However, the Jews are the physical descendants of Abraham, Isaac, and Jacob, whom God chose. This doesn't guarantee their salvation. Paul has made that clear throughout chapters 9-11. He isn't about to contradict himself now. He's simply making the point that God has chosen, at some point, to bestow salvation upon his people from among the Jews for the sake of the patriarchs. In that sense, they're beloved.

The second reason is God's mercy (11:30-32). Because of disobedient Jews, God showed mercy to disobedient Gentiles. Because of his mercy to disobedient Gentiles, God shows mercy to disobedient Jews. "For God has consigned all to disobedience, that he may have mercy on all," says Paul (11:32). The first part of that verse takes us back to 3:9-20, where Paul declares that Jews and Gentiles are condemned in God's sight. The second part of the verse reveals that God is merciful to Jews and Gentiles. The Greek is *tous pantes*—the all. Paul is referring to all those Jews and Gentiles whom he will save, as expressed throughout this chapter.

Conclusion
Do you see Paul's overall argument? We can summarize it as follows. (1) There's a "spiritually elect remnant" within a "physically ethnic nation" (9:6-13; 11:1-10). (2) This "remnant" is extended to include the elect from among the Gentiles (9:24-29; 11:11-24). (3) The solution to the apparent dilemma, therefore, is that this "remnant" (consisting of the elect from among Jews and Gentiles) is the object of God's covenantal promises. (4) God's word hasn't failed. (5) Therefore, "I am sure that neither death nor life, nor angels

nor rulers, nor things present nor things to come, nor powers, nor height nor depth, nor anything else in all creation, will be able to separate us from the love of God in Christ Jesus our Lord" (8:38).

As we conclude, let me point you to what Paul says in 11:29, "The gifts and the calling of God are irrevocable." What an encouragement! Why? This means that God is faithful. He's faithful because he's unchangeable. As the hymn writer says, "We blossom and flourish as leaves on the tree, and wither and perish—but nought changeth thee."[4]

J.I. Packer explains that God's life doesn't change: "God alone has immortality" (1 Tim. 6:16). In addition, God's character doesn't change: "Every good gift and every perfect gift is from above, coming down from the Father of lights, with whom there is no variation or shadow due to change" (James 1:17). God's truth doesn't change: "The grass withers, the flower fades, but the word of our God will stand forever" (Isa. 40:8). God's purposes don't change: "The counsel of the LORD stands forever, the plans of his heart to all generations" (Ps. 33:11). And God's Son doesn't change: "Jesus Christ is the same yesterday and today and forever" (Heb. 13:8).[5]

Because God is unchangeable, he's faithful. Because God is faithful, he's trustworthy in all that he promises. "God is not man, that he should lie, or a son of man, that he should change his mind. Has he said, and will he not do it? Or has he spoken, and will he not fulfill it?" (Num. 23:19). Paul has proved this very thing in chapters 9-11. The accursed condition of the Jews doesn't undermine God's faithfulness. As promised, God has saved (and will save) his people. God's promise hasn't failed.

---

[4] Walter Chalmers Smith, "Immortal, Invisible" in *The Hymnal for Worship and Celebration*, 25.

[5] Packer, *Knowing God*, 81-85.

65
The Depth of God's Knowledge (11:33–36)

The psalmist declares, "On the glorious splendor of your majesty, and on your wondrous works, I will meditate" (Ps. 145:5). That's precisely what I want us to do by looking at one of the greatest doxologies in Scripture: Romans 11:33–36.

"Oh, the depth of the riches and wisdom and knowledge of God!" (11:33). Here, Paul identifies three "depths." (1) There's the depth of God's riches. That takes us back to 10:22, where Paul says that God abounds in riches for all who call on him. If you turn to God in faith and repentance, you can be absolutely certain he will receive you. How can you be so certain? The depth of the riches of his grace and mercy is immeasurable. (2) There's the depth of God's wisdom. God's wisdom is his skilful performance of all things. (3) There's the depth of God's knowledge. God's knowledge is his understanding of all things.

Still in 11:33, Paul expands upon the depth of God's wisdom and knowledge, declaring: "How unsearchable are his judgments and how inscrutable his ways!" In other words, it's impossible to plumb the depth of God's wisdom and knowledge. They're too deep. God is infinite; therefore, his wisdom and knowledge are infinite.

In 11:34–35, Paul stresses that fact, asking, "For who has known the mind of the Lord, or who has been his counselor? Or who has given a gift to him that he might be repaid?" Here, Paul quotes two OT texts. (1) The first text is Isaiah 40:12–14:

> Who has measured the waters in the hollow of his hand and marked off the heavens with a span, enclosed the dust of the earth in a measure and weighed the mountains in scales and the hills in a balance? Who has measured the Spirit of the LORD, or what man shows him his counsel? Whom did he consult, and who made him understand? Who taught him the path of justice, and taught him knowledge, and showed him the way of understanding?

(2) The second text is Job 41:11, "Who has first given to me, that I should repay him? Whatever is under the whole heaven is mine." In a word, God's

wisdom and knowledge are beyond our comprehension.

In 11:36, Paul develops that fact, stating, "For from him and through him and to him are all things." Here, Paul uses three prepositions to explain the relationship between God and creation. (1) "From [*ex*] him ... are all things." That means God is the source from which all things exist. (2) "Through [*dia*] him ... are all things." That means God is the means through which all things exist. (3) "To [*eis*] him are all things." That means God is the end for which all things exist. To sum up, all things exist for his glory.

And so, Paul completes his doxology, declaring, "To him be glory forever. Amen." I want to meditate upon the glorious splendour of God's majesty. Now we begin with his knowledge.

God knows

There are three things that set God's knowledge apart from ours.

First, God's knowledge is independent. He doesn't obtain his knowledge from outside of himself. We do. Everything we know comes from outside of ourselves. It comes from parents, teachers, siblings, preachers, books, or whatever. God isn't like us. "Who has measured the Spirit of the LORD, or what man shows him his counsel?" (Isa. 40:13).

Second, God's knowledge is infallible. He doesn't err in his knowledge. We do. There are countless things we think we know, but we don't really. There are countless things we think we know, but we're actually wrong. God isn't like us. "The LORD of hosts has sworn: 'As I have planned, so shall it be, and as I have purposed, so shall it stand'" (Isa. 14:24).

Third, God's knowledge is immutable. He doesn't change in his knowledge. We do. We change in at least two ways: we learn, and we forget. We do these two things every day. Our knowledge is in a constant state of flux. God isn't like that. "Many are the plans in the mind of a man, but it is the purpose of the LORD that will stand" (Prov. 19:21).

God knows all things

That's a direct quote from 1 John 3:20, "God is greater than our heart, and he knows everything." In our day, we have witnessed an explosion of knowledge. This explosion is seen, for example, on the Internet. We have an incredible amount of knowledge at our fingertips. Yet our knowledge is still a mere drop in the ocean in comparison to God's. He knows what was, what is, what will be, what can be, and what can't be. By one pure, simple, eternal act of his

The Depth of God's Knowledge (11:33-36)

infinite understanding, God knows all things perfectly, immediately, and distinctly—at every moment. He's "perfect in knowledge" (Job 37:16). He knows all things fully and immediately.

God knows all things past, present, and future
God is beyond the realm of time. Therefore, his knowledge of all things is an ever present. He declares,

> Remember the former things of old; for I am God, and there is no other; I am God, and there is none like me, declaring the end from the beginning and from ancient times things not yet done, saying, My counsel shall stand, and I will accomplish all my purpose (Isa. 46:9-10).

God knows all things possible
When I awoke this morning, I was immediately faced with several choices. I could have rolled over and fallen back to sleep. I could have got up on the left side of the bed. I could have got up on the right side of the bed. I could have gone for a shower. I could have gone for breakfast. I could have eaten several different things for breakfast. I could have worn one of three or four different pairs of pants, six or seven different shirts, and maybe twenty different ties. I could have left home at any time between 7:30 and 8:00. I could have taken one of four or five different routes to get to the college. I could have parked in one of roughly thirty different parking spaces. And it goes on. Here's the amazing thing: God knows my every decision. And God knows my every potential decision. And God knows the result of my every potential decision. And God knows my every potential decision that would have arisen from all of my potential decisions. God knows all of that for every single human being who has ever lived.

If that isn't amazing enough, consider for a moment that God knows what his power can do. His power is infinite. Therefore, God's knowledge of possible things is infinite.

Conclusion
"Oh, the depth of the riches and wisdom and knowledge of God! How unsearchable are his judgments and how inscrutable his ways!" (11:33). In a word, he is omniscient. Our awareness of this should have a practical effect upon us.

First, *it should challenge the unbeliever.* If you aren't a Christian, the depth of God's knowledge should terrify you. Why? "And no creature is hidden from his sight, but all are naked and exposed to the eyes of him to whom we must give account" (Heb. 4:13). One day, you'll give an account to God, who knows absolutely everything about you. He declares, "For my eyes are on all their ways. They are not hidden from me, nor is their iniquity concealed from my eyes" (Jer. 16:17). There's no such thing as secrecy when it comes to your sin. "You have set our iniquities before you, our secret sins in the light of your presence" (Ps. 90:8). If your life and your every word, deed, and thought were put on display for all to see, how embarrassed would you be? They are on display—before God! Do you understand how desperately you need Christ? You need him to pay the penalty for your sin. And you need him to give you his righteousness so that you can stand before "him to whom we must give an account."

Second, *it should challenge the believer.* (1) God's knowledge should curb our sin. "Does not he see my ways and number all my steps?" (Job 31:4). Does that frighten me? When a child knows what his parents expect yet disobeys when they aren't looking, that's sin. When a child knows what his parents expect yet disobeys when they're looking, that's open defiance. We do that all the time when we sin in God's sight. (2) God's knowledge should govern our thoughts. We think our thoughts are our personal domain. But God says, "I know the things that come into your mind" (Ezek. 11:5). He knows every jealous thought, every nasty thought, every lustful thought, and every proud thought. All of this shows us that we must strive to live *coram deo*: before the face of God. We must strive to impress upon ourselves the depth of God's knowledge, the fact that his eyes move to and fro throughout the whole earth (2 Chron. 16:9).

Third, *it should comfort the believer.* (1) God knows our circumstances: "For he knows our frame; he remembers that we are dust" (Ps. 103:14). That means he knows our afflictions, infirmities, and sorrows. (2) God knows our sins. He knew my sins before the foundation of the world, yet he loved me and predestined me to be conformed to the likeness of his Son. He knew my sins when he sent his Son to die on the cross, yet he loved me and gave his Son for me. He knew my sins when I became a Christian, yet he loved me and called me and justified me. He knows my sins at present, yet he continues to love me. As Paul says, "The Lord knows those who are his" (2 Tim. 2:19). Here's the amazing thing: he loves us anyway.

66
The Depth of God's Wisdom (11:33–36)

In the last study, we considered the depth of God's knowledge. In this study, we're going to consider the depth of God's wisdom. What's the difference between the two? God's knowledge is his understanding of all things. God's wisdom is his ability to use his knowledge to produce the best results through the best means.

According to Stephen Charnock, God's wisdom possesses six properties.[1] (1) God is wise "necessarily." "God does make himself wise, no more than he makes himself God." In other words, he's wise because he's God: "With God are wisdom and might; he has counsel and understanding" (Job 12:13). (2) God is wise "originally." "He goes not out of himself to search wisdom." In other words, he isn't dependent upon anything for his wisdom: "Whom did he consult, and who made him understand?" (Isa. 40:14). (3) God is wise "perfectly." "There is no cloud upon his understanding." In other words, everyone is foolish in comparison to him: "Even in his servants he puts no trust, and his angels he charges with error" (Job 4:18). (4) God is wise "universally." "His wisdom orders all things, so that nothing is done but what is fit and convenient, and agreeable to so excellent a Being." In other words, God's wisdom extends to all things: He "works all things according to the counsel of his will" (Eph. 1:11). (5) God is wise "perpetually." "It is a wisdom infinite, and therefore without increase or decrease in itself." In other words, his wisdom isn't subject to change: "The counsel of the LORD stands forever, the plans of his heart to all generations" (Ps. 33:11). (6) God is wise "incomprehensibly." "A splendor more dazzling to our dim minds than the light of the sun to our weak eyes." In other words, God's wisdom exceeds our grasp: "Can you find out the deep things of God? Can you find out the limit of the Almighty?" (Job 11:7). (7) God is wise "infallibly." "As nothing can resist the efficacy of his will, so nothing can countermine the skill of his counsel." In other words, God never errs in his wisdom: "No wisdom, no understanding, no counsel can avail against the LORD" (Prov. 21:30).

---

[1] Charnock, *Attributes of God*, 1:509–513.

We see the depth of God's wisdom in his great works.

We see the depth of God's wisdom in creation

The psalmist declares, "O LORD, how manifold are your works! In wisdom have you made them all; the earth is full of your creatures" (Ps. 104:24). God's wisdom is seen in creation's variety, beauty, harmony, and complexity.

> Traces of the wisdom of God can be seen in the natural creation, but the full revelation will stretch out through eternity. Take the universe, for instance. A recent scientific article said that it is so finely tuned that the odds of achieving it by chance "would be the same as throwing an imaginary microscopic dart across the universe to the most distant quasar and hitting a bull's-eye one millimeter in diameter." The human body is a masterpiece of divine wisdom and engineering. For example, one writer observed, "The brain has been called an enchanted loom. Somehow it is able to take the shifting electric signals from 252 million rods and cones in man's eye and, moment by moment, weave these tiny snippets of information into a tapestry portrait of what is before him." Similarly, the DNA, which is the basis of heredity, "is so narrow and so compacted that all the genes in all my body's cells would fit into an ice cube; yet if the DNA were unwound and joined together end to end, the strand could stretch from the earth to the sun and back more than four hundred times."[2]

Surely, we can say with the psalmist, "I praise you, for I am fearfully and wonderfully made. Wonderful are your works; my soul knows it very well" (Ps. 139:14).

We see the depth of God's wisdom in providence

God governs all things. He governs the universe: all its stars and galaxies. He governs the earth in its orbit around the sun. He governs the earth as it spins on its axis. He governs the clouds as they float across the sky. He governs the rain as it replenishes the earth. He governs the seasons. He governs the harvests. He governs every plant that bears fruit. He governs the migration of geese. He governs the hibernation of bears. He governs the death of every sparrow. He governs every raindrop and snowflake. He governs every atom. In a word, he "upholds the universe by the word of his power" (Heb. 1:3). John Brown writes,

---

[2] MacDonald, *Alone in Majesty*, 136–137.

The Depth of God's Wisdom (11:33-36)

The term "uphold" seems to refer both to preservation and government. "By him the worlds were made"—their materials were called into being, and arranged in comely order; and by him, too, they are preserved from running into confusion, or reverting back into nothing. The whole universe hangs on his arm; his unsearchable wisdom and boundless power are manifested in governing and directing the complicated movements of animate and inanimate, rational and irrational beings, to the attainment of his own great and holy purposes; and he does this by the word of his power, or by his powerful word. All this is done without effort or difficulty. He speaks and it is done; he commands, and it stands fast.[3]

What wisdom! What's amazing about God's providence is that it includes everything. There is nothing that falls outside the parameters of his control. He "works all things according to the counsel of his will" (Eph. 1:11).

We see the depth of God's wisdom in redemption

In the words of Jonathan Edwards, "God had a design of glorifying himself from eternity; yea, to glorify each person in the Godhead ... and the principal means that he adopted was this great work of redemption."[4] Edwards proceeds to break down this plan into three stages. (1) From the fall to the incarnation, God performed those things that were preparatory to Christ's coming. (2) From the incarnation to the resurrection, Christ procured and purchased redemption. (3) From the resurrection to the end of the world, God accomplishes the great effect of his purpose.

In the unfolding of this plan, we behold God's "manifold wisdom" (Eph. 1:8; 3:10). We see it in many ways. Let's consider just for a moment the incarnation. (1) In Christ, we have "deity and humanity" united. Christ is one person in two natures, containing the perfections of God and the weaknesses of man. (2) In Christ, we have "precept and penalty" satisfied. Christ's active obedience satisfies God's precept, whereas Christ's passive obedience satisfies God's penalty. (3) In Christ, we have "justice and mercy" secured. Christ satisfies God's justice and secures God's mercy. (4) In Christ, we have "suffering and victory" harmonized. Christ suffered the shame of the cross. In so doing, he won the victory over sin.

---

[3] Quoted in A.W. Pink, *An Exposition of Hebrews* (Grand Rapids: Baker Books, 2004).
[4] Edwards, *Work of Redemption, Works*, 1:536.

Conclusion

By way of application, I can think of eight lessons that arise from our consideration of God's wisdom.

First, *we should make God's wisdom a frequent object of our meditation.* As Stephen Charnock remarks,

> Who can contemplate the sparklings of this perfection in the variety of the works of his hands, and the exact government of all his creatures, without a raised admiration of the excellency of his Being, and a falling flat before him, in a posture of reverence to so great a Being?[5]

Second, *we should see the folly of probing too deeply into the depth of God's wisdom.* "He reveals deep and hidden things; he knows what is in the darkness, and the light dwells with him" (Dan. 2:22). This should guard us against straying beyond the boundaries of God's revelation in Scripture. "Let us learn," says John Calvin, "to make no searchings respecting the Lord, except as far as he has revealed himself in the Scriptures; for otherwise we shall enter a labyrinth, from which the retreat is not easy."[6]

Third, *we should see the arrogance that lies behind our sin.* We sin against God, who is all-wise. "Because your heart is proud, and you have said, 'I am a God, I sit in the seat of the gods, in the heart of the seas,' yet you are but a man, and no God, though you make your heart like the heart of a God" (Ezek. 28:2).

Fourth, *we should desist from growing impatient in affliction.* "Will any teach God knowledge?" (Job 21:22). We must recognize that God's wisdom isn't man's wisdom, and God's ways aren't man's ways. God's plan is best. He never makes a mistake. Therefore, we should trust him.

Fifth, we *should derive great comfort from God's wisdom.* (1) We should be comforted in affliction (Rom. 8:28). (2) We should be comforted in temptation (2 Peter 2:9). (3) We should be comforted in delays or denials in prayer (Rom. 8:26). (4) We should be comforted when surrounded by enemies (Job 5:13; Prov. 21:30; 1 Cor. 1:25).

Sixth, *we should strive to be wise.* Being wise doesn't mean that we'll be able to explain God's providence, but that we'll trust in the God of providence. J.I. Packer explains:

---

[5] Charnock, *Attributes of God*, 1:669.
[6] Calvin, *Epistle to the Romans*, 445.

The Depth of God's Wisdom (11:33–36)

To drive well, you have to keep your eyes skinned to notice exactly what is in front of you. To live wisely, you have to be clear-sighted and realistic—ruthlessly so—in looking at life as it is. Wisdom will not go with comforting illusions, false sentiment, or the use of rose-coloured spectacles. Most of us live in a dream world, with our heads in the clouds and our feet off the ground; we never see the world, and our lives in it, as they really are. This deep-seated, sin-bred unrealism is one reason why there is so little wisdom among us—even the soundest and most orthodox of us.[7]

Seventh, *we should pursue God's wisdom*. How? (1) We must learn to fear God: "The fear of the LORD is the beginning of wisdom, and the knowledge of the Holy One is insight" (Prov. 9:10). (2) We must learn to receive God's Word: "I have more understanding than all my teachers, for your testimonies are my meditation" (Ps. 119:99).

Eighth, *we should worship God, for "who has known the mind of the Lord?"*

He formed the stars, those heavenly flames,
He counts their numbers, calls their names:
His wisdom's vast, and knows no bound,
A deep where all our thoughts are drowned.[8]

---

[7] Packer, *Knowing God*, 112.
[8] Samuel Worcester, *The Psalms, Hymns, and Spiritual Songs of the Reverend Isaac Watts* (Boston: Crocker & Brewster, 1840), 280.

67
The Depth of God's Sovereignty: Part 1 (11:36)

Does it look like God rules? We may be tempted to think that things are out of control. Yet the Bible teaches that God is in control. David declares, "Yours, O LORD, is the greatness and the power and the glory and the victory and the majesty, for all that is in the heavens and in the earth is yours. Yours is the kingdom, O LORD, and you are exalted as head above all" (1 Chron. 29:11). That's the doctrine of God's sovereignty. It's a truth that we must repeatedly affirm.

> The doctrine of God's sovereignty lies at the foundation of Christian theology, and in importance is perhaps second only to the Divine Inspiration of the Scriptures. It is the centre of gravity in the system of Christian truth; the sun around which all the lesser orbs are grouped; the cord upon which all other doctrines are strung like so many pearls, holding them in place and giving them unity. It is the plumb line by which every creed needs to be tested; the balance in which every human dogma must be weighed. It is designed as the anchor for our souls amid the storms of life. The doctrine of God's sovereignty is a Divine cordial to refresh our spirits. It is designed and adapted to mould the affections of the heart, and to give a right direction to conduct. It produces gratitude in prosperity and patience in adversity. It affords comfort for the present and a sense of security respecting the unknown future. It is, and it does, all and much more than we have just said, because it ascribes to God—the Father, the Son, and the Holy Spirit—the glory which is his due, and places the creature in his proper place before him—in the dust.[1]

Paul provides a succinct description of God's sovereignty in 11:36, "For from him and through him and to him are all things." Quite simply, that means God is the cause of all things. Now, when we speak of causality, we must make some distinctions. We can see these distinctions in the case of a sculpture. What causes it? Aristotle identifies five causes. (1) The "material" cause is the substance. It's impossible to make a sculpture without some substance: wood, ice, or stone. (2) The "formal" cause is the plan. There must be a

---

[1] Pink, *Sovereignty of God*, 139.

picture in the artist's mind that he's seeking to reproduce in the sculpture. (3) The "final" cause is the purpose. Why is the artist making the sculpture? It may be for his pleasure. It may be for a gift. It may be for someone who has paid him to do so. (4) The "efficient" cause is the sculptor. The sculpture doesn't appear by itself. Someone must actually make it. (5) The "instrumental" cause is the tools. The sculptor uses a hammer and chisel.

Now, we can apply the above to what Paul says in 11:36, "For from him and through him and to him are all things." (1) "From him." This means that God is the "efficient" cause: the source from which all things exist. (2) "Through him." This means that God is the "instrumental" cause: the means through which all things exist. (3) "To him." This means that God is the "final" cause: the end for which all things exist.

In a word, this world is the stage on which God displays his glory. "Worthy are you, our Lord and God, to receive glory and honour and power, for you created all things, and by your will they existed and were created" (Rev. 4:11).

These "things" include the heavens
"And the sun stood still, and the moon stopped, until the nation took vengeance on their enemies" (Josh. 10:13). Here, the Israelites are pursuing the Amorites. Joshua asks God to give them more time in order to defeat their enemies. God causes the sun to stand still. You see, God governs the heavens. Every sunrise and every sunset testifies to God's sovereignty.

These "things" include the elements
"Peace! Be still" (Mark 4:39). Christ utters these words as he and his disciples find themselves in the midst of a terrible storm at sea. Quite literally, he rebukes the wind and the waves. And the storm disappears. Clearly, God governs the elements. He sends the rain, snow, ice, and wind. Every raindrop and snowflake testify to God's sovereignty.

These "things" include the plants
"It is as I told Pharaoh; God has shown to Pharaoh what he is about to do" (Gen. 41:28). Here, Joseph interprets Pharaoh's dream. There's going to be seven years of plenty, followed by seven years of famine. This is what God is about to do. God governs the plants. He causes every tree to bud and every flower to bloom. Every blade of grass testifies to God's sovereignty.

The Depth of God's Sovereignty: Part 1 (11:36)

These "things" include the animals
"And the ravens brought him bread and meat in the morning, and bread and meat in the evening, and he drank from the brook" (1 Kings 17:6). God sent ravens to feed Elijah while he was hiding from Ahab. Similarly, God led the animals into the ark. He prevented the lions from harming Daniel. He caused the donkey to rebuke Balaam. God governs the animals. Every squirrel collecting nuts, every robin making its nest, every raccoon going through your garbage, and every hawk circling in search of prey testifies to God's sovereignty.

These "things" include the nations
"And he made from one man every nation of mankind to live on all the face of the earth, having determined allotted periods and the boundaries of their dwelling place" (Acts 17:26). He spread the nations from Babel over the face of the earth. He governed the rise and fall of Egypt, Assyria, Babylon, Persia, Greece, and Rome. God governs the nations. Every nation's rise and fall testifies to God's sovereignty.

These "things" include people
"In him we live and move and have our being" (Acts 17:28). God governed every detail of the lives of Adam, Noah, Abraham, Joseph, and David. God governs people. Every birth, breath, decision, and action is in the palm of his hand. "You do not know what tomorrow will bring. What is your life? For you are a mist that appears for a little time and then vanishes. Instead you ought to say, 'If the Lord wills, we will live and do this or that'" (James 4:14–15). Every human life testifies to God's sovereignty.

These "things" include angels
"Then the LORD commanded the angel, and he put his sword back into its sheath" (1 Chron. 21:27). Because of his pride, David dares to number the Israelites. God sends an angel to punish Israel. Throughout the Bible, we see God sending his angels to do his will. God governs angels. Every angel testifies to God's sovereignty.

These "things" include demons
"Now the Spirit of the LORD departed from Saul, and a harmful spirit from the Lord tormented him" (1 Sam. 16:14). God rejected Saul as king because of his disobedience. And God sent a demon to torment Saul the rest of his days.

God sent a demon to deceive Ahab and Jehoshaphat. God sent a demon to trouble Abimelech and the men of Shechem. God governs demons. Every demon testifies to God's sovereignty.

These "things" include calamity

"I am the LORD, and there is no other. I form light and create darkness; I make well-being and create calamity; I am the LORD, who does all these things" (Isa. 45:6–7). We see it in the flood. We see it time and time again throughout the Bible. God governs calamity. Years ago, I watched an interview of several survivors of a devastating tsunami. One dared to blame nature. Another dared to blame fate. Yet every calamity testifies to God's sovereignty.

These "things" include war

"Woe to, Assyria, the rod of my anger; the staff in their hands is my fury! Against a godless nation I send him, and against the people of my wrath I command him, to take spoil and seize plunder, and to tread them down like the mire of the streets" (Isa. 10:5-6). God sends the Assyrians to destroy Israel. God orchestrates every conflict of which we read in the Bible. God governs wars. God's will is being done in Afghanistan, Iraq, and Sudan. Every war testifies to God's sovereignty.

These "things" include disease

"Jesus answered, 'It was not that this man sinned, or his parents, but that the works of God might be displayed in him'" (John 9:3). Christ's disciples want to know why this particular man is blind. The answer is God. God governs disease. Every cold and every flu, every germ and every virus, and every form of cancer testifies to God's sovereignty.

These "things" include death

"Since his days are determined, and the number of his months is with you, and you have appointed his limits that he cannot pass" (Job 14:5). Rachel died while giving birth. Samson died while fighting the Philistines. Sisera died while sleeping in Jael's tent. Absalom died while hanging from a tree. God governs death. You won't live one moment longer than God has appointed for you. Every death testifies to God's sovereignty.

These "things" include evil
"The LORD has made everything for its purpose, even the wicked for the day of trouble" (Prov. 16:4). God raised up Pharaoh, Ahab, Pilate, and Judas. God raised up the Philistines, Amorites, Assyrians, and Chaldeans. Why? He accomplished his purpose by the very evil they willingly committed. God governs evil. Evil testifies to God's sovereignty.

These "things" include blessing
"Every good gift and every perfect gift is from above, coming down from the Father of lights, with whom there is no variation or shadow due to change" (James 1:17). God governs blessing. Every child, every day, every meal, every marriage, every friend, and every comfort testifies to God's sovereignty.

These "things" include salvation
"So then it depends not on human will or exertion, but on God, who has mercy" (Rom. 9:16). God chose Isaac, not Ishmael. God chose Jacob, not Esau. God was merciful to Moses, not Pharaoh. God governs salvation. Every Christian testifies to God's sovereignty.

Conclusion
Truly, Isaac Watts had a glimpse into the depth of God's sovereignty when he wrote:

> Ten thousand ages ere the skies were into motion brought;
> All the long years and worlds to come, stood present to his thought:
> There's not a sparrow or a worm, but's found in his decrees,
> He raises monarchs to their throne and sinks them as he please.[2]

This glimpse of God's sovereignty should grip us. How? First, *it should correct our thinking.* This doctrine places God where he belongs, and it places man where he belongs. There's no other truth in the Bible that reveals the nature of man's sin quite like God's sovereignty. No one objects to God's love, God's faithfulness, or God's righteousness. I've never had anyone get annoyed with me for preaching about God's love or God's faithfulness or God's righteousness or even God's wrath. But God's sovereignty! That's a different matter entirely. Why? It places us in the dust. It makes everything of God and

---

[2] https://www.ccel.org/ccel/watts/psalmshymns.II.99.html.

nothing of us. It makes God significant in every possible way. It makes us completely insignificant. For this reason, the carnal man detests God's sovereignty.

Second, *it should cause us to stand in wonder.* "Yours, O LORD, is the greatness and the power and the glory and the victory and the majesty, for all that is in the heavens and in the earth is yours. Yours is the kingdom, O LORD, and you are exalted as head above all" (1 Chron. 29:11). We should stand in wonder because this great God became a man.

> The marvel which staggered Isaiah was that the despised, rejected, humiliated, bruised, wounded, pierced, broken, unresisting, meek and lowly, suffering sin-bearer whom he saw "led as a lamb to the slaughter" was the very One whom he had earlier seen surrounded by overwhelming heavenly splendor, sitting on the glory-flashing throne, reigning in super-sovereignty over all nations and centuries! His omnipotent sovereignty which could crush a million alpha-stars underfoot and never feel them; that sovereignty which governs all worlds and all beings; that sovereignty incarnates itself in the person of Jesus, descends from that ineffable throne of glory, and hangs on that gory, felon's cross as the lamb which bears away the sin of the world![3]

Third, *it should stir us to action.* "He shall seduce with flattery those who violate the covenant, but the people who know their God shall stand firm and take action" (Dan. 11:32). What action? We should fear him. We should obey him. We should trust him. We should thank him. We should praise him. We should cry with Paul: "To him be glory forever. Amen" (11:36).

Fourth, *it should impart comfort to us.* "Of all God's marvels transcendent, this wonder of wonders I see, that the God of such infinite greatness should care for the sparrows—and me" (Mabel Brown Denison).[4]

---

[3] J. Sidlow Baxter, *The Master Theme of the Bible: Grateful Studies in the Comprehensive Saviorhood of Our Lord Jesus Christ* (Wheaton: Tyndale, 1973), 80.

[4] Source unknown.

68
The Depth of God's Sovereignty: Part 2 (11:36)

In 11:36, Paul says that "from him and through him and to him are all things." This truth has provided comfort to countless Christians in the midst of suffering. God is sovereign; therefore, his control is absolute. God is immutable; therefore, his will is certain. God is mighty; therefore, his power is limitless. God is most wise; therefore, his plan is perfect. God is incomprehensible; therefore, his providence is inscrutable. With this God before them, Christians (while not always understanding his ways) are certain he "causes all things to work together for good" (8:28).

A few years ago, open theism emerged to challenge this view of God's sovereignty, suggesting it was pastorally deficient. According to open theists, all that God foreknows must certainly occur, since it's impossible for anyone to choose anything other than what God foreknows. This would make God alone responsible for human suffering. For this reason, proponents of open theism affirm that it's necessary to "limit" God. In short, God isn't absolutely sovereign; he isn't immutable; he isn't infinite in power and knowledge. On the contrary, he's limited. Among other things, this means that God doesn't know the future, but reacts as events unfold. They consider this to be a reasonable explanation for the relationship between God and human suffering. They argue that if my view of God's sovereignty is correct, then God's foreknowledge means suffering necessarily occurs, and, therefore, God is responsible for it. They believe that God's openness frees him from this charge. He has no control over human suffering because he's as much a part of unfolding events as we are. For open theists, this realization supposedly provides comfort in the midst of suffering.

One of the key proponents of open theism was the late Clark Pinnock, who provides the following definition of the movement:

> Our understanding of the Scriptures leads us to depict God, the sovereign Creator, as voluntarily bringing into existence a world with significantly free personal agents in it, agents who can respond positively to God or reject his plans for them ... God rules in such a way as to uphold the created structures and, because he gives liberty to his creatures, is

happy to accept the future as open, not closed, and a relationship with the world that is dynamic, not static. We believe that the Bible presents an open view of God as living and active, involved in history, relating to us and changing in relation to us. We see the universe as a context in which there are real choices, alternatives and surprises. God's openness means that God is open to the changing realities of history, that God cares about us and lets what we do impact him. Our lives make a difference to God—they are truly significant.[1]

How do open theists defend their position? They do so theologically and philosophically.

The theological argument
Theologically, they argue that the Bible teaches that God has limits. Their proof texts fall into two broad categories. (1) They maintain that the Bible teaches that God learns. By way of example, they appeal to the story of Abraham and Isaac in Genesis 22. God wants to know if Abraham fears him, so he commands Abraham to offer Isaac as a sacrifice. Abraham demonstrates his faithfulness. In response, God declares, "Now I know that you fear God" (Gen. 22:12). For open theists, this sort of "divine" learning experience occurs throughout Scripture, thus proving that God has no foreknowledge of human decisions. (2) They maintain that the Bible teaches that God repents. They point to the example of the flood. When God creates humanity, he has no idea that people are going to sin so grievously. When he sees what happens, he regrets "that he had made man on the earth" (Gen. 6:6). Consequently, he's forced to make the best of a situation that he never foresaw. According to open theists, this happens all the time because God isn't privy to what people are going to do until they decide to do it.

Before moving on to their philosophical argument, let me respond briefly to the above. (1) As for Genesis 22:12, this verse doesn't mean that God learns. It depicts what's known as *peirastic* irony. God knows exactly what he's going to do. He knows exactly what Abraham is going to do. He's simply testing him. (2) As for Genesis 6:6, this verse doesn't mean that God would have done something different if he'd only foreseen the negative effects of sin. It simply means he views man's sin as terrible. He genuinely grieves over man's

---

[1] Clark Pinnock, Richard Rice, John Sanders, William Hasker, and David Basinger, *The Openness of God: A Biblical Challenge to the Traditional Understanding of God* (Downers Grove: InterVarsity, 1994), 103-104.

The Depth of God's Sovereignty: Part 2 (11:36)

sin. But God doesn't regret like we regret: "And also the Glory of Israel will not lie or have regret, for he is not a man, that he should have regret" (1 Sam. 15:29).

The philosophical argument
Philosophically, open theists argue that God's foreknowledge is inconsistent with human free will. William Hasker explains,

> If God knows already what will happen in the future, then God's knowing this is part of the past and is now fixed, impossible to change. And since God is infallible, it is completely impossible that things will turn out differently than God expects them to. But this means that the future event God knows is also fixed and unalterable, and it cannot be true of any human being that they are both able to perform a certain action and able not to perform that action.[2]

Simply put, this philosophical argument has three components. (1) Human freedom only exists if the future is completely open. (2) The future isn't completely open if God knows it. Why? People lack the freedom to do anything other than what God knows. (3) God can't know the future. Why? It's contingent upon choices, which don't exist until they occur.

I've organized my response to open theism's philosophical argument under four headings.

The doctrine of free will
We've been down this road before, so we can be brief. When it comes to free will, there are two main schools of thought. Both agree that we choose without any external compulsion. How do they differ? The first maintains that the will is free from internal motives and desires. In other words, it's free from the mind's thoughts and the heart's affections. It possesses arbitrary power. This means that we don't know why the will chooses what it chooses. The second maintains that the will isn't free from internal motives and desires. In other words, it isn't free from the mind's thoughts and the heart's affections. It doesn't possess arbitrary power. This means that we do know why the will chooses what it chooses.

Open theists hold to the first. We hold to the second. Why? Well, what

---
[2] William Hasker, *Providence, Evil and the Openness of God* (New York: Routledge, 2004), 103-104.

does the Bible say about the mind? It's darkened. What does it say about the heart? It's hardened. What does this mean for the will? It means that it's an enslaved free will. It's perfectly free to choose, but it always does so according to the darkened mind and the hardened heart. God knows this. And God knows exactly what man will choose by his own free will in every situation. "The LORD saw that the wickedness of man was great in the earth, and that every intention of the thoughts of his heart was only evil continually" (Gen. 6:5).

The doctrine of concurrence
Upon this doctrine of free will, we place the doctrine of concurrence. When it comes to performing an action, there's a difference between *motion* and *motive*. An action's motion in and of itself is never sinful. It's the motive that determines whether or not an action is good or bad. Let me give you a couple of examples. (1) Is it sinful to speak? In terms of motion, it's never sinful to speak. In terms of motive, it may be sinful to speak. When Jacob told Isaac that he was Esau, did he sin? His motion of speaking wasn't sinful. It was his motive that made his speaking sinful. (2) Is it sinful to drink? In terms of motion, it's never sinful to drink. In terms of motive, it may be sinful to drink. When Samson became drunk from drinking too much wine, did he sin? His motion of drinking wasn't sinful. It was his motive that made his drinking sinful.

Where does an action's motion come from? The answer is God. Where does an action's motive come from? The answer is man. This means that God is the first cause and man is the second cause in all actions. That's the doctrine of concurrence.

The doctrine of divine decrees
Upon the doctrines of free will and concurrence, we place the doctrine of divine decrees. Again, I've mentioned this before, so I can be brief. The Bible affirms that God decrees everything that happens. By a positive decree, he wills that which is good. This means that he effects all good things, such as creation. By a privative decree, he wills that which is evil. This means that he willingly permits all evil things, such as the fall.

Now, this doesn't mean that God approves of the evil that he willingly permits. We must distinguish between his will of decree and his will of disposition. It's possible for something to happen according to God's will of decree yet against his will of disposition. When God willingly permits evil, he doesn't contradict his revealed will (i.e., his disposition toward evil), but approves of the good that he aims at in permitting it.

The biblical evidence

How do we know that the above three doctrines are true? We find them throughout the Bible. Let's consider the following examples. (1) Was it God's will that Joseph's brothers sold him as a slave in Egypt (Gen. 50:19-20)? (2) Was it God's will that Pharaoh prevented the Israelites from leaving Egypt (Ex. 4:21)? (3) Was it God's will that Samson married a Philistine woman (Judges 14:1-4)? (4) Was it God's will that David numbered the Israelites (2 Sam. 24:1; 1 Chron. 21:1)? (5) Was it God's will that the Babylonians invaded Judah (Hab. 1:6)? (6) Was it God's will that Judas betrayed Christ (John 6:70-71)? (7) Was it God's will that men crucified Christ (Acts 2:23)?

The answer to all of these questions is "yes" and "no." In terms of his will of decree, God willed all of these things. In terms of his will of disposition, God didn't will any of these things. (1) In these examples, we see the doctrine of divine decrees. God's will is done—even in the evil that's committed! Does that make God responsible for it? No! He ordains evil by a privative decree. He willingly permits in time what he decrees in eternity. (2) In these examples, we see the doctrine of concurrence. How could God be certain that these events would come to pass? The answer: he's the first cause of all things. All motion derives from God. Does that make God responsible for evil? No! An action is good or bad according to the motive for which it's performed. (3) In these examples, we see the doctrine of free will. God holds all involved responsible for the evil they commit. How can he do that if he decreed it? Quite simply, he didn't force them to do anything. He willingly permitted them to do precisely what was in their hearts.

Conclusion

As already stated, the main impetus behind open theism is pastoral—to provide comfort in the midst of adversity. Yet, in relation to Romans 8:28, John Sanders (another proponent of open theism) admits, "God is working to accomplish good in all things," nevertheless, "the purposes of God meet with resistance, and even God does not always get what he wants."[3] I fail to see how such a concept of God provides comfort in suffering. Bruce Ware comments,

---

[3] John Sanders, *The God Who Risks: A Theology of Providence* (Downers Grove: InterVarsity, 1998), 127-128.

"At the most, the God of open theism commits himself to doing his best to trying within his significant limitations to work things out for the good of his own." Thus, he asks,

> How pastorally, spiritually, and existentially adequate is the counsel offered by openness proponents? At the heart of the pastoral counsel offered to suffering people by open theists is this claim: God did not bring about your suffering, so don't blame God for it; instead, be encouraged because he feels as badly about the suffering you are enduring as you do.[4]

Ironically, this means that open theism is weakest where it claims to be strongest—pastorally.

---

[4] Bruce Ware, *God's Lesser Glory: The Diminished God of Open Theism* (Wheaton: Crossway Books, 2000), 207.

Section 5: Application (12:1–15:13)

69
A Living Sacrifice (12:1)

We arrive at the fifth section in Paul's epistle to the Romans: *Application* (12:1-15:13). He begins, "I appeal to you therefore, brothers, by the mercies of God, to present your bodies as a living sacrifice, holy and acceptable to God, which is your spiritual worship." I want to break Paul's statement down into five parts.

"Therefore"
What's so significant about this word? It implies that what Paul is about to say builds on what he has already said. In chapters 1-11, he explains the gospel. In effect, he says, "This is what we believe." In chapters 12-15, he applies the gospel. In effect, he says, "This, then, is how we should live."

Paul's approach points to a very important lesson: *doctrine is foundational to practice*. This necessarily means that doctrine is practical. As A.W. Pink notes,

> The substitution of so-called "practical" preaching for the doctrinal exposition which it has supplanted is the root cause of many of the evil maladies which now afflict the church of God. The reason why there is so little depth, so little intelligence, so little grasp of the fundamental verities of Christianity, is because so few believers have been established in the faith through hearing the doctrines of grace expounded.[1]

If we're going to grow beyond elementary things, then we must cultivate an appetite for doctrinal exposition. What doctrine has Paul expounded in the first eleven chapters?

In his first section, *Condemnation* (1:18-3:20), he explains that we need righteousness. He takes us into God's courtroom to show us that need. The judge is God. The accused is humanity. The accusation is unrighteousness. The witnesses are General and Special Revelation. The Gentiles have rejected God's revelation in Creation. The Jews have rejected God's revelation in

---

[1] Pink, *Sovereignty of God*, 138.

Scripture. The verdict is guilty. The sentence is death.

In his second section, *Justification* (3:21-5:21), Paul declares that God justifies sinners. (1) Justification is by grace alone. In other words, it's a gift. Christ's death satisfied God's justice, thereby appeasing God's wrath and securing God's mercy. (2) Justification is through faith alone. It isn't by works. We don't merit justification in any way. (3) Justification is in Christ alone. We're justified because we're united with Christ. Our sin is reckoned to him; he pays its penalty on our behalf. His righteousness is reckoned to us; he fulfills the law on our behalf. Union with Christ is central to this. There are two federal heads. We were united to Adam under the covenant of works. By his one transgression, there resulted condemnation to all those who are one with him. Now, we're united to Christ under the covenant of grace. By his one act of obedience, there resulted justification of life to all those who are one with him.

In his third section, *Sanctification* (6:1-8:39), Paul explains that union with Christ deals with the power of sin in addition to the penalty of sin. In chapter 6, he speaks of two masters: sin and righteousness. We're no longer enslaved to sin but now are enslaved to righteousness. In chapter 7, he speaks of two marriages: law and grace. We're no longer married to the law but now are married to grace (i.e., Christ). In chapter 8, he speaks of two minds: flesh and Spirit. We no longer walk according to the flesh but now walk according to the Spirit.

In the fourth section, *Election* (9:1-11:36), Paul answers a question: Does the Jews' separation from God's love mean that God is unfaithful? He responds, "It is not as though the word of God has failed" (9:6). He proves it by way of three arguments. (1) They aren't all Israel who are descended from Israel (9:6-10:21). (2) God hasn't rejected his people whom he foreknew (11:1-24). (3) All Israel will be saved (11:25-32). From these arguments emerges the doctrine of election: "So then it depends not on human will or exertion, but on God, who has mercy" (9:16).

As Paul reflects upon these great doctrines, he's overwhelmed. This leads him to his doxological celebration in 11:33-36, where he speaks of the depth of God's riches, God's knowledge, God's wisdom, and God's sovereignty. "To him be glory forever. Amen." Now, he says, "Therefore." In other words, if we know this gospel and this God (chapters 1-11), it will change us. In chapters 12-15, Paul explains how.

A Living Sacrifice (12:1)

"I appeal to you, brothers"
This is an expression of urgency. When we say to someone, "I urge you not to do that," we're trying to communicate that we're serious. We might say "I beg you" or "I plead with you." And so, it's evident that Paul is seeking to convey a sense of urgency. In effect, he says, "You must listen to what I'm about to say. This is serious. This is crucial. I'm going to tell you how you should live. You must understand this. This will save you from a life of disappointment. This will save you from a life of frustration. This will help you live in a manner that pleases God. This will help you live a meaningful life."

We desperately need to hear the contents of these chapters. Far too many Christians are frustrated and disappointed. Far too many suffer from apathy and monotony. Paul knows that (if heeded) what he's about to say will rescue us from all that. This is urgent.

"By the mercies of God"
Paul appeals to the mercies of God as the supreme motive for listening to him. In the Greek, the term *mercy* is in the plural, *mercies*. What are these mercies? We find them in the first eleven chapters. To mention a few: (1) God foreknew us before the foundation of the world. (2) God predestined us to adoption as sons. (3) God redeemed us by the blood of his Son. (4) God called us. (5) God justified us. (6) God reconciled us to himself. (7) God poured out his Spirit upon us. (8) God made us one with Christ. (9) God made us co-heirs with Christ. (10) God freed us from the bondage of sin. (11) God freed us from the curse of the law. (12) God grants us free access to himself. (13) God calls us his sons. (14) God promises to work everything together for our good. (15) God promises that nothing will separate us from his love. (16) God sanctifies us. (17) God will glorify us.

These are the mercies of God. What makes them mercies? They're mercies because we don't deserve them. But it's more than that. They're mercies because we deserve the exact opposite. If I give all that I have to a poor man, that isn't really mercy. If I give all that I have to a poor man who attacks me, who resents me, who slanders me, who neglects me, who hates me, that's mercy! God has been merciful to us. He has bestowed all these blessings upon us—sinners, who had rejected him. Paul says this should motivate us.

> The secular world never understands Christian motivation. Faced with the question of what makes Christians tick, unbelievers maintain that Christianity is practiced only out of self-serving purposes. They see

Christians as fearing the consequences of not being Christians (religion as fire insurance), or feeling the need of help and support to achieve their goals (religion as crutch), or wishing to sustain a social identity (religion as a badge of respectability). No doubt all these motivations can be found among the membership of churches: it would be futile to dispute that. But just as a horse brought into a house is not thereby made human, so a self-seeking motivation brought into the church is not thereby made Christian, nor will holiness ever be the right name for religious routines thus motivated. From the plan of salvation, I learn that the true driving force in authentic Christian living is, and ever must be, not the hope of gain, but the heart of gratitude.[2]

If we truly understand the mercies of God, we won't require any additional motive to heed what Paul says next.

"To present your bodies as a living sacrifice, holy and acceptable to God"
This statement raises two questions. First, what are we to present? The answer is our bodies. In the OT, the body of the sacrifice was placed on the altar. Similarly, we're to offer our bodies to God. That refers to our complete person. It includes our eyes (all that we see), ears (all that we hear), hands (all that we do), brains (all that we think), and hearts (all that we feel). We're to offer our complete person to God. We're bombarded with a very simple message in our day: personal gratification will make us happy. Paul says the opposite: personal sacrifice (not gratification) is the key to the Christian life. Sacrifice is commitment. It's turning our lives over to God—not just our money, time, talents, etc. It's exchanging our will for God's will. This is captured in the following words by George Mueller: "As a young man, I had a great many ambitions, but there came a day when I died to all those things, and I said, 'Henceforth, Lord Jesus, not my will but Thine,' and from that day God began to work in and through me."[3]

Second, how are we to offer our bodies as a sacrifice? (1) It must be a living sacrifice. In the OT, the sacrifices were dead. We have died in Christ. Now, we live in Christ. (2) It must be a holy sacrifice. The OT sacrifices had to be without spot or blemish. We too must seek to be holy. (3) It must be an acceptable sacrifice. The burnt offering in the OT was a "soothing aroma" to God (Lev. 1:13). Our sacrifices are made acceptable in Christ.

---

[2] J.I. Packer, *Rediscovering Holiness* (Ann Arbor: Servant Publications, 1992), 75.
[3] Source unknown.

"Which is your spiritual worship"

This is a tricky statement. The NIV reads: "spiritual act of worship." The AV reads: "reasonable service." The noun can be translated "service" or "worship." The adjective can be translated "spiritual" or "reasonable." Therefore, the phrase can be translated "reasonable service," "spiritual service," "reasonable worship," or "spiritual worship." Which is it? I think *service* and *worship* express the same thing. And I think *reasonable* is preferable to *spiritual* because of what Paul says in 12:2 about being "transformed by the renewal of your mind."

Presenting our bodies to God as a sacrifice is reasonable because of what Paul says in the first eleven chapters. Given the mercies of God, it's only reasonable that we should seek to live for him. James Boice gives the following example of "reasonable" worship.

> William Borden came from a wealthy privileged family, was a graduate of Yale University, and had the promise of a wonderful and lucrative career before him. But he felt a call to serve God as a missionary in China and left for the field even though his family and friends thought him a fool for going. After a short time away and even before he reached China, Borden contracted a fatal disease and died. He had given up everything to follow Jesus. He died possessing nothing in this world. But Borden of Yale did not regret it. We know this because he left a note as he lay dying that said, "No reserve, no retreat, and no regrets." Like so many others, he found the service of Christ to be eminently reasonable, and he gained a lasting reward.[4]

Conclusion

Given the mercies of God, it's only reasonable that we give our all to him. Let me conclude with the words of a well-known hymn that sums up beautifully what we've considered in this study.

> When I survey the wondrous cross on which the Prince of Glory died,
> My richest gain I count but loss, and pour contempt on all my pride.
> Forbid it, Lord, that I should boast, save in the cross of Christ, my God;
> All the vain things that charm me most, I sacrifice them to his blood
> See, from his head, his hands, his feet, sorrow and love flow mingled down;
> Did e'er such love and sorrow meet, or thorns compose so rich a crown?

---

[4] James M. Boice, *Romans: The New Humanity* (Grand Rapids: Baker Books, 1995), 1521.

The Obedience of Faith

Were the whole realm of nature mine, that were an off'ring far too small;
Love so amazing, so divine, demands my soul, my life, my all.[5]

---

[5] Isaac Watts, "When I Survey the Wondrous Cross" in *Hymns of Worship and Remembrance*, 189.

70
A Renewed Mind (12:2)

Horatius Bonar remarks,

> Associating too much and too intimately with the world, we have in a great measure become accustomed to its ways. Hence our tastes have been vitiated, our consciences blunted, and that sensitive tenderness of feeling which ... shrinks from the remotest contact with sin, has worn off and given place to an amount of callousness of which we once, in fresher days, believed ourselves incapable.[1]

One of the problems with "intimacy with the world" is that it renders us incapable of seeing ourselves as we really are. It's a way of thinking that deprives us of spiritual discernment.

That's why this verse is so important: "Do not be conformed to this world, but be transformed by the renewal of your mind, that by testing you may discern what is the will of God, what is good and acceptable and perfect" (12:2). I want to break it down into three parts.

"Do not be conformed to this world"

Here, the term "world" is *aion* (age). We find it in various places in the NT. "Where is the one who is wise? Where is the scribe? Where is the debater of this age? Has not God made foolish the wisdom of the world?" (1 Cor. 1:20). "Let no one deceive himself. If anyone among you thinks that he is wise in this age, let him become a fool that he may become wise" (1 Cor. 3:18). "In their case the God of this world has blinded the minds of the unbelievers, to keep them from seeing the light of the gospel of the glory of Christ, who is the image of God" (2 Cor. 4:4). "Christ gave himself for our sins to deliver us from the present evil age, according to the will of our God and Father" (Gal. 1:4). "In which you once walked, following the course of this world" (Eph. 2:2). "For the grace of God has appeared, bringing salvation for all people, training us to renounce ungodliness and worldly passions, and to live self-controlled,

---

[1] Horatius Bonar, *Words to Winners of Souls* (Phillipsburg: P&R Publishing, 1995), 31–32.

upright, and godly lives in the present age" (Titus 2:11-12).

"This age" is the world, the flesh, the kingdom of darkness, or the seed of the serpent. It's a way of *thinking* and *behaving*. David Wells explains, "Worldliness is that system of values and beliefs, behavior and expectations, in any given culture that have at their centre the fallen human being and that relegate to their periphery any thought about God."[2] According to 1 John 2:16, it bears three marks. First, there's the lust of the flesh (hedonism): excessive sensual pleasure. Second, there's the lust of the eyes (materialism): greed for possessions. Third, there's the boastful pride of life (humanism): man's unbridled arrogance. In the words of John Trapp, these three are the "worldling's trinity."[3]

We aren't to be "conformed" to this world. Simply put, we don't belong to "this age" but to "the age to come." We're one with Christ, who's "not of the world" (John 17:14). He refused to pray for the world: "I am not praying for the world but for those whom you have given me, for they are yours" (John 17:9). He opposed the world: "Now is the judgment of this world; now will the ruler of this world be cast out" (John 12:31). Clearly, there's open hostility between Christ and the world. If we belong to Christ, it's inconceivable that we could align ourselves with what he hates. (1) Conformity to the world is *adultery*. We're married to Christ. If our hearts go after the world, then we're guilty of spiritual whoredom. (2) Conformity to the world is *idolatry*. We worship Christ. If our hearts go after the world, then we're guilty of worshipping it. (3) Conformity to the world is *enmity*. We love Christ. If our hearts go after the world, then we're guilty of embracing that which hates Christ. James warns, "You adulterous people! Do you not know that friendship with the world is enmity with God? Therefore whoever wishes to be a friend of the world makes himself an enemy of God" (James 4:4). Likewise, John warns, "Do not love the world or the things in the world. If anyone loves the world, the love of the Father is not in him" (1 John 2:15).

For this reason, we must strive to be nonconformists. Elsewhere, Paul says, "But far be it from me to boast except in the cross of our Lord Jesus Christ, by which the world has been crucified to me, and I to the world" (Gal. 6:14). To be a nonconformist is to mortify the world.

---

[2] David Wells, *God in the Wasteland: The Reality of Truth in a World of Fading Dreams* (Grand Rapids: W.B. Eerdmans, 1994), 29.

[3] Quoted in Thomas, *A Puritan Golden Treasury*, 310.

Consider the man who lived at the top of a mountain. He needed to hire someone to take his daughter up and down the mountain each day for school. So he interviewed various candidates, asking them, "How close can you come to the edge without going over?" The first man said, "I can come within twelve inches and not go over the edge." The second claimed, "I can come within six inches of the edge." The third boasted he could come within an inch. But the fourth said, "I don't know, because I'll be hugging the other side. I will stay as far away from the edge as I can." You know who got the job.[4]

And so, we resist temptations to excessive eating and drinking. In addition, we resist sexual immorality. That includes adultery, pornography, immodesty, and whatever. Furthermore, we strive to avoid all that stirs the lust of the flesh, the lust of the eyes, and the pride of life. We don't allow ourselves to be under bondage to anything (1 Cor. 3:17; 6:12; 9:27).

"But be transformed by the renewing of your mind"
From the Greek term for "transform" is *metamorphoo*, from which we derive the word *metamorphosis*. We use it to describe the transformation of a caterpillar into a butterfly. We find it in three other places in the NT. "And he was transfigured before them, and his face shone like the sun, and his clothes became white as light" (Matt. 17:2; Mark 9:2-3). "And we all, with unveiled face, beholding the glory of the Lord, are being transformed into the same image from one degree of glory to another. For this comes from the Lord who is the Spirit" (2 Cor. 3:18). Paul has in view our renewal in the likeness of Christ whereby we reflect God's glory. That work commenced at regeneration and continues until glorification.

Paul says we're transformed by the renewing of our minds. The Holy Spirit illuminates our minds to behold God's glory in Christ. Once our minds are illuminated, our affections are rightly ordered. Love is removed from sin and set upon God. Desire and delight follow. Once our affections are rightly ordered, our wills are liberated. Yet this process is ongoing. Therefore, we must grow in the grace and knowledge of Christ. Paul prays that "the eyes of our hearts" might be enlightened, so that we may "know" (Eph. 1:18). Again, "From the day we heard, we have not ceased to pray for you, asking that you may be filled with the knowledge of his will in all spiritual wisdom and understanding" (Col. 1:9).

---

[4] Beeke, *Overcoming the World*, 120.

How do we renew our minds? Christ prays, "Sanctify them in the truth; your word is truth" (John 17:17). Paul writes, "Christ loved the church and gave himself up for her, that he might sanctify her, having cleansed her by the washing of water with the word" (Eph. 5:25-26). Sanctification is the Holy Spirit's work. He sanctifies us by the Word. Our duty, therefore, is to get ourselves under the Word. We do that by reading and studying, by praying and meditating, by listening to sermons, by reading good books, and by fellowshipping with Christians. As a result, we grow in our understanding of God's glory in the gospel. The Holy Spirit impresses that glory upon our hearts. Our affections are rightly ordered, and we delight to do God's will.

"So that you may prove what the will of God is"
There's God's secret will—his will of decree. And there's God's revealed will—his will of disposition. Which is Paul talking about here? He's referring to God's revealed will. In the context, I think he primarily has in view the commandment in 12:1, "Present your bodies as a living sacrifice, holy and acceptable to God." We're to turn our lives over to God. We're to exchange our will for his will. Let me remind you again of the words of George Mueller: "As a young man, I had a great many ambitions, but there came a day when I died to all those things, and I said, 'Henceforth, Lord Jesus, not my will but Thine,' and from that day God began to work in and through me."

We're to prove three things. (1) We're to prove that God's will is good. It's good because it's conducive to our happiness. (2) We're to prove that God's will is acceptable. That means it's pleasing. (3) We're to prove that God's will is perfect. It isn't lacking in anything. When we reach the end of our lives, we will be satisfied. I don't know of any Christian who has looked back on his life wishing he had indulged in the world.

Conclusion
To be a Christian is to be a nonconformist. It means to be separate from the world. Many professing Christians are perfectly happy in this world. Why? According to David Wells,

> The fundamental problem in the evangelical world today is not inadequate technique, insufficient organization, or antiquated music, and those who want to squander the church's resources bandaging these scratches will do nothing to stanch the flow of blood that is spilling from its true wounds. The fundamental problem in the evangelical world

today is that God rests too inconsequentially upon the church. His truth is too distant, his grace is too ordinary, his judgment is too benign, his gospel is too easy, and his Christ is too common.[5]

---

[5] Wells, *God in the Wasteland*, 30.

71
Sober Judgment (12:3-8)

Paul begins this chapter with these words: "I appeal to you therefore, brothers, by the mercies of God, to present your bodies as a living sacrifice, holy and acceptable to God, which is your spiritual worship" (12:1). In light of what God has done for us, it only makes sense that we should live for him. But what does this "living sacrifice" look like? Paul answers that question in 12:2-15:12. Basically, it consists of (1) renewing our minds (12:2); (2) exercising sober judgment (12:3-8); (3) loving without hypocrisy (12:9-21); (4) submitting to authority (13:1-7); (5) obeying the law (13:8-14); and (6) keeping the peace (14:1-15:12).

We've already looked at the first. In this study, we're going to look at the second.

A Wrong Way of Thinking

"For by the grace given to me I say to everyone among you not to think of himself more highly than he ought to think" (12:3). Here, Paul addresses one of our greatest problems: pride. "It is," says Thomas Manton, "a lifting up of the heart above God and against God and without God."[1]

How are we supposed to think about ourselves? The Bible stresses two foundational truths. (1) The first can be summed up in the expression *human dignity*. We were created in the image of God. For this reason, every human being has intrinsic worth. We respect human life. We value human life. We protect human life. Humans are of inestimable value because God created them in his own image. That's human dignity. (2) The second can be summed up in the expression *human depravity*. We were created in the image of God. Yet that image has been corrupted. The natural image of God (understanding, affections, and will) remains, but the moral image of God (knowledge, righteousness, and holiness) is gone. And so, Paul says, "I know that nothing good dwells in me" (7:18). That's human depravity.

That's a hard sale in today's church. Why? It's contrary to what we hear

---
[1] Quoted in Thomas, *A Puritan Golden Treasury*, 223.

outside the church, and it's often contrary to what we hear inside the church. The popular view today is that we're inherently good and that we have intrinsic value apart from God. This view upholds the perfectibility of human nature. That's the underlying premise for the "self" movement. But the Bible asserts the opposite. Yes, on the one hand, it affirms human dignity—we were made in the image of God. However, it also affirms human depravity—we're corrupt in all that we do, say, think, and feel. We will never deal with our pride until we grasp that basic truth.

A right way of thinking
"For by the grace given to me I say to everyone among you not to think of himself more highly than he ought to think, but to think with sober judgment, each according to the measure of faith that God has assigned" (12:3). If we have sound judgment, then we'll believe what the Bible says about God and us. And this will produce humility. How?

First, it will produce *natural* humility. Adam and Eve possessed this humility before the fall. What is it? It arises when we perceive our littleness as a creature. God is naturally excellent. When we compare ourselves to God's natural excellence, we see our littleness. We're weak in comparison to God's power. We're foolish in comparison to God's wisdom. We're ignorant in comparison to God's knowledge. We're dependent in comparison to God's sovereignty.

Second, it will produce *moral* humility. Adam and Eve didn't possess this humility before the fall. What is it? It arises when we perceive our vileness as a sinner. God is morally excellent. When we compare ourselves to God's moral excellence, we see our sinfulness. "Woe is me! For I am lost; for I am a man of unclean lips, and I dwell in the midst of a people of unclean lips; for my eyes have seen the King, the LORD of hosts!" (Isa. 6:5).

In short, humility flows from a sight of God. As Bruce Ware explains:

> In a culture saturated with the esteem of the "self" and marred by the decline of Deity, we stand in need of beholding God for who he is. We need desperately to be humbled and amazed at the infinite splendor of his unrivaled greatness and the unspeakable wealth of his lavish goodness. We must marvel at his blinding glory and fall astonished at his benevolent grace. If we are to escape the cult of self and find, instead, the true meaning of life and the path of true satisfaction, if we are to give God the glory rightly and exclusively owed to him—that is, if we are to

know what truly promotes both our good and his glory—we must behold God for who he is.[2]

Paul adds that this right way of thinking means that we think "according to the measure of faith that God has assigned" (12:3). According to James Boice, the expression *measure of faith* can be interpreted in three ways. (1) It may be our faith in God, meaning we shouldn't think we trust God more than we really do. (2) It may be *the* faith, meaning we should think of ourselves according to what the Bible teaches. (3) It may be our individual gifts that are received by faith, meaning we should think of ourselves in accordance with the specific gifts God has given us.[3] Boice argues for the third interpretation. I agree with him. Why? It leads naturally to what Paul says about the church and its members in 12:4-8.

The unity of the Church (12:4-5)
"For as in one body we have many members, and the members do not all have the same function, so we, though many, are one body in Christ, and individually members one of another" (12:4-5). In a previous study, we spoke of the doctrine of union with Christ. The Holy Spirit unites us to Christ, thereby making us one with him. As we noted, the Bible uses three metaphors to describe that union: husband and wife (Eph. 5:25-32), vine and branches (John 15:1-5), head and body (Eph. 5:22-24). These three metaphors unfold what it means to be in union with Christ. The third also points to our union with each other. By virtue of our union with Christ, we are "members in one body."

Christ speaks of this in John 17. He gives us three truths concerning this unity. (1) Its source is God: "Holy Father, *keep* them" (17:11). There's no appeal to produce or create this unity. As a matter of fact, people can't produce this unity. Why? It comes from God. (2) Its object is believers: "Holy Father, keep *them*" (17:11). Who is Christ talking about? They're those who have been drawn to Christ (17:6) and given to Christ (17:6). (3) Its nature is spiritual: "that they may be one, even as we are one" (17:11).

The plurality of its members (12:5)
"We, though many, are one body in Christ, and individually members one of

---

[2] Bruce Ware, *God's Greater Glory: The Exalted God of Scripture and the Christian Faith* (Wheaton: Crossway Books, 2004), 9.
[3] Boice, *Romans*, 1569-1570.

another" (12:5). Plurality implies diversity. And diversity means that there are differences. I'm not talking about differences in doctrine. There's only one faith that was once for all delivered to the saints (Jude 1:3). I'm talking about differences that exist among individuals arising from nationality, ethnicity, age, social status, and education.

In terms of nationality, Angolans and Canadians are different. They have different histories. They have different collective experiences. They have different cultural traditions. In terms of gender, men and woman are different. They view things differently. They value things differently. In terms of age, children and adults are different. They have different likes and dislikes. They're at different levels of maturity. In terms of social status, the upper class and lower class are different.

This diversity is more prevalent in the North American church today than it has ever been. It isn't uncommon to find in many churches a traditional service and a contemporary service. In other words, there's a service for the old and a service for the young. It isn't uncommon to find Chinese churches, Korean churches, and Dutch churches. It isn't uncommon to find churches that are upper class and churches that minister to the lower class. People will naturally gravitate to those who think like they do. Despite this diversity, we're one in Christ.

The variety of its gifts (12:6-8)

"Having gifts that differ according to the grace given to us" (12:6). Before we look specifically at the gifts, I want to make three general remarks based upon what we read in Romans 12:3-8, 1 Corinthians 12:12-27, and Ephesians 4:1-13. (1) The source of spiritual gifts is God triune. In Romans 12, God the Father is in view. In Ephesians 4, God the Son is in view. In 1 Corinthians 12, God the Spirit is in view. (2) The purpose of spiritual gifts is to build up the Church. Paul makes that clear in Ephesians 4. The gifts serve to build up the body of Christ. This means that growth is impossible without these spiritual gifts. (3) There are a variety of gifts. Does the NT provide an exhaustive list? I don't know. But it certainly stresses the fact that there are many different kinds of spiritual gifts.

In our text, Paul mentions seven. (1) *Prophesying*. A prophet is a spokesperson who mediates between God and man by proclaiming the mind of God. That may be done publicly or privately. Paul includes a qualifying parameter: "in proportion to our faith" (12:6). The possessive pronoun isn't in the

Greek. I'm inclined to think that Paul is speaking of "the faith," meaning a prophet speaks according to the standard, namely, God's Word. As Micaiah declares, "As the LORD lives, what my God says, that I will speak" (2 Chron. 18:13). (2) *Serving*. Paul is likely thinking of hands-on ministries. (3) *Teaching*. A teacher is someone who expounds God's Word. It was said of Ezra that he "had set his heart to study the Law of the LORD, and to do it and to teach his statutes and rules in Israel" (Ezra 7:10). This may be done publicly or privately. (4) *Exhorting*. This is someone who comes alongside another, in order to encourage, warn, counsel, or comfort. (5) *Giving*. Paul is primarily thinking in terms of finances. (6) *Leading*. This includes elders but isn't exclusive to elders. Leadership takes place at many different levels and in many different ways. (7) *Showing Mercy*. We show mercy by doing good to the soul of others: counselling, encouraging, warning, exhorting, teaching, correcting, etc. We also show mercy by doing good to the body of others: giving, serving, suffering, etc.

Conclusion
We have a tendency to think that everyone should be like us. The teacher thinks everyone should be interested in the conjugation of Greek verbs. The evangelist thinks everyone should go door to door distributing tracts. The server thinks everyone should cut grass or shovel snow. The exhorter thinks everyone should see things as clearly as he does. The one who shows mercy thinks everyone should volunteer in a soup kitchen. This is a mistake. We must refrain from expecting everyone to do what we do. We must learn to value one another and thank God for one another's gifts. Plus, we must be content with the gifts God has given us.

In this regard, Martin Luther writes,

> Horace, the heathen [*poet*], said: "The lazy ox wants to bear the saddle, while the horse wants to plow." No one is satisfied with his calling, but praises those who walk in other ways ... Those who are qualified (for a certain work) detest it; those who are unfit, long for it.[4]

Rather than thinking "This is what God has given me to do. I'm going to do it," we often wish that we were doing something else. We must desist from thinking that way. We need to remember that "in a healthy human body all the

---

[4] Luther, *Commentary on Romans*, 172.

parts function harmoniously and interdependently for the good of the whole body."[5]

It's easy to preach, give, serve, or show mercy for the wrong reason. Rather than seeking to please God, we may really be seeking to impress others. William Gurnall comments, "So far as pride prevails, the man prays, preaches, etc., rather to be thought good by others, than to do good to others."[6] How can we combat this tendency? Again, in the words of Gurnall, "Make this sin as black and ugly as you can possibly to your thought, that when it is presented to you, you may abhor it the more."[7]

---

[5] Bruce, *Romans*, 214.
[6] Gurnall, *Christian in Complete Armor*, 1:193.
[7] Gurnall, *Christian in Complete Armor*, 1:198.

72
Genuine Love (12:9-16)

According to Paul, our love is to be "genuine" (12:9). The term is *anupokritos*, which means "without a mask." In Greek drama plays, actors wore masks to depict their characters' emotions. An actor might actually have been feeling something entirely different from the emotion depicted by his mask. The mask might have been sad, but he was really happy. The mask might have been happy, but he was really sad. The mask wasn't necessarily a true reflection of the person wearing it. Paul is saying that we shouldn't wear masks. We do. Oftentimes, the outside doesn't reflect the inside. Oftentimes, what we do doesn't reflect what we feel.

In 1 Peter 1:22, Peter speaks of "sincere" love. According to James Boice, the English word *sincere* comes from two Latin words: *sine cera* (without wax). In the ancient world, merchants would use wax to hide cracks in pottery so that they could sell their merchandise at a higher price.[1] Years ago, my wife's father bought a used car. Within a few days, he had problems with it. So he took it to a garage. The mechanic looked at it and told him it had been in a serious accident. The car was a piece of junk with a new paint job. That's what these merchants would do. They would use wax to hide defects. More reputable merchants would hang a sign over their pottery—*sine cera* (without wax)—to inform their customers that their merchandise was genuine.

Our love for our fellow believers is to be *sine cera*. But Paul doesn't leave it at that. He adds two qualifying expressions: "abhor what is evil; hold fast to what is good" (12:9). These are important given the confusion surrounding the nature of love. Many people equate love with permissiveness. But Paul tells us that to love is to abhor what's evil and cling to what's good. What's "good"? Paul tells us back in 12:2, the will of God is "that which is good and acceptable and perfect." This means that we're to cling to God's will. The verb *cling* means to glue or cement together. It's used to describe the marriage relationship: a man shall "be joined" to his wife and the two shall "become one flesh" (Matt. 19:5). We love people by clinging to what is good—by

---

[1] Boice, *Romans*, 1591.

upholding God's will for their lives.

What does this look like?

"Love one another with brotherly affection" (12:10)

The Greek term for "brotherly love" is *filadelfia*. It refers to the affection that exists between members of the same family. Believers are a family. Despite differences, disagreements, and disappointments, they're devoted and committed to one another.

"Outdo one another in showing honour" (12:10)

This is difficult to do because we're so susceptible to envy. According to Jonathan Edwards, "Envy is a disposition natural in men, that they love to be uppermost; and this disposition is directly crossed, when they see others above them."[2] I was reminded of this recently in the book of Esther. For starters, Haman resents Mordecai's prosperity. He reflects on his own material prosperity and privilege, yet he declares, "All this is worth nothing to me, so long as I see Mordecai the Jew sitting at the king's gate" (Esther 5:13). In addition, Haman hates Mordecai's person. "And Haman went out that day joyful and glad of heart. But when Haman saw Mordecai in the king's gate, that he neither rose nor trembled before him, he was filled with wrath against Mordecai" (Esther 5:9).

We're susceptible to this sin. Thus, Paul writes, "Do nothing from selfish ambition or conceit, but in humility count others more significant than yourselves. Let each of you look not only to his own interests, but also to the interests of others" (Phil. 2:3-4). We're to treat others as valuable. We're to prefer to serve them rather than be served by them.

"Do not be slothful in zeal, be fervent in spirit, serve the Lord" (12:11)

Other words for "zeal" include *eagerness*, *earnestness*, and *diligence*. To be "fervent" is to boil over. We find this term in only one other place in the NT—Apollos was fervent in his preaching and teaching (Acts 18:25). Likewise, we're to be fervent in serving the Lord. This means that we shouldn't do things half-heartedly. The one who serves doesn't pack it in when the job is half done. The one who teaches doesn't prepare his sermon on Saturday evening. The one who exhorts doesn't encourage people and then forget about

---

[2] Edwards, *Charity and Its Fruits*, 112.

them. The one who gives doesn't do so sporadically but consistently. The one who leads is on top of things. The one who shows mercy doesn't know anything about half measures.

One of our problems today is that we have a terrible tendency to do only what's necessary to get by—nothing more. Many of us went through school like that. Many of us approach work like that. Many of us approach church like that. Many of us approach our marriages like that. Many of us serve the Lord just like that. In so doing, we rob one another of what is rightfully ours. God gives gifts so that they might be used "fervently" for the edification of his church.

"Rejoice in hope" (12:11)
In the Bible, the word *hope* refers to a confident expectation—something we know is going to happen. Paul writes, "But our citizenship is in heaven, and from it we await a Saviour, the Lord Jesus Christ, who will transform our lowly body to be like his glorious body, by the power that enables him even to subject all things to himself" (Phil. 3:20-21). That's our hope. It's a great cause of joy. It's contagious. It's encouraging to be around people who have their hope fixed on God.

"Be patient in tribulation" (12:12)
The term for "tribulation" is *thlipsis*. It refers to a "pressing." There are many pressings in life. Many of them are self-inflicted. Many of them are not. I recently met with a Christian brother who's passing through a difficult time of "pressing." The shadows are dark and deep. Yet, he perseveres. To persevere means "to remain in a place instead of leaving it." Despite his circumstances, he will not be moved. His faith in God is unshakeable.

"Be constant in prayer" (12:12)
Consider the following passages of Scripture. "All these with one accord were devoting themselves to prayer" (Acts 1:14). "They devoted themselves to prayer" (Acts 2:42). "Continue steadfastly in prayer" (Col. 4:2). Prayer is an expression of genuine love, as we intercede for one another.

"Contribute to the needs of the saints and show hospitality" (12:13)
Elsewhere, Paul says, "So then, as we have opportunity, let us do good to everyone, and especially to those who are of the household of faith" (Gal. 6:10).

We should contribute to the needs of unbelievers; however, generosity really begins at home—the church. We should be looking for ways to help Christians who are in need. One very practical way of meeting the needs of others in the ancient world was hospitality. We too should practice hospitality. It's interesting that the Greek word for "practice" means "to hunt or pursue." In other words, we're to actively pursue hospitality.

"Rejoice with those who rejoice, weep with those who weep" (12:15)
We see it in Christ—his compassion, kindness, humility, meekness, and patience in his dealing with the diseased, the tormented, the despised, and the ridiculed. We see these things manifested in his forbearing and forgiving.

Similarly, we're called to seek to understand the inner world of other people. What's happening in his life? What's she going through? Now, let me say this. If your first thought, as you read those words, was "Amen. I wish someone would empathize with me. I wish someone would reach out to me. I wish someone would come alongside me," you now know what your greatest problem is. It's you! Paul doesn't command me to think about how others could (and perhaps should) be ministering to me, but how I should be ministering to others. That's the point of the entire passage. Stop thinking about yourself!

Empathy is a great way to break down barriers, disarm hostility, and remove suspicion. Do we find this difficult? There are only three possible reasons why. (1) We're too consumed with ourselves—this distances us. (2) We're too critical of others—this hardens us. (3) We're too resentful toward others—this embitters us.

"Live in harmony with one another" (12:16)
What is "harmony"? It doesn't mean we seek "peace at all costs." A local church isn't to tolerate doctrinal evil or moral evil in its midst. However, neither is it to tolerate disputes which are caused by envy, bitterness, or misunderstanding. We must actively seek peace within the body, recognizing that we're one. Every decision should be based in large measure upon what brings peace to the church without compromising the truth.

How do we do this? We cultivate sober judgment. Those who are discontent, unhappy, resentful, proud, and agitated sow the seeds of discord wherever they go. But those who are at peace keep the peace. They're objective is to extinguish anger, strife, and division. "A significant portion of peacemaking has to do not with actively doing anything, but with just leaving things alone.

A peacemaker often need not actually take positive action, but merely refrain from disturbing the peace."[3] One of our greatest callings isn't to make peace where there's trouble, but to refrain from making trouble where there's peace.

**"Do not be haughty, but associate with the lowly.
Never be wise in your own sight" (12:16)**

Who are the "lowly"? They're those from whom we don't receive anything. We don't receive any financial benefit, social benefit, intellectual benefit, or personal benefit. We're to make a point of associating with them. To do this, we can't be "haughty." There are three common forms of pride. (1) The self-infatuated wants praise. (2) The self-glorified assumes everyone wants him to be the centre of attention. (3) The self-preoccupied can think of nothing other than himself—his self-love masquerades as self-effacing.

Is that us? We must look to Christ who "humbled himself" (Phil. 2:8). "To see a poor man, traveling the country, hungry, thirsty, weary, accompanied by poor men ... Who would have ever thought that this was the Creator of the world, the Prince of the kings of the earth?"[4] Paul exhorts us: "Have this mind among yourselves, which is yours in Christ Jesus" (Phil. 2:5).

Conclusion

I want to take three lessons from the above.

First, *we see the importance of self-examination.* "If anyone says, 'I love God,' and hates his brother, he is a liar; for he who does not love his brother whom he has seen cannot love God whom he has not seen" (1 John 4:20). Do I love others, especially God's children? If I don't see at least a glimmer of this kind of love in me, then I don't have any grounds for calling myself a Christian. Flowing from our love for God is love for God's people. With this love before him, John Flavel asks us to examine ourselves: "Is it thus with you? Do you sympathize with the affairs and concernments of Christ in the world? Or, care you not which way things go with the people of God, and gospel of Christ, so long as your own affairs prosper, and all things are well with you?"[5]

Second, *we see the importance of mortifying pride (and her three sisters: envy, malice, and bitterness).* "For where jealousy and selfish ambition exist, there

---

[3] Terry Johnson, *When Grace Transforms: The Character of Christ's Disciples Put Forward in the Beatitudes* (Ross-shire: Christian Focus, 2008).
[4] Flavel, *Works*, 2:230.
[5] Flavel, *Works*, 2:338.

will be disorder and every vile practice" (James 3:16). Have I ever felt uncomfortable at the prosperity or advancement or blessing of another? Have I ever thought to myself that it would be a comfort to me if that person were brought down? If so, I need to mortify that sin.

Third, *we see the importance of genuine love.*

> If I speak in the tongues of men and of angels, but have not love, I am a noisy gong or a clanging cymbal. And if I have prophetic powers, and understand all mysteries and all knowledge, and if I have all faith, so as to remove mountains, but have not love, I am nothing. If I give away all I have, and if I deliver up my body to be burned, but have not love, I gain nothing (1 Cor. 13:1-3).

Jonathan Edwards makes the point that "excellent privileges" (e.g., great grasp of doctrine, great singing voice, great teaching ability, or great organizational skill) are nothing without love. He also makes the point that "excellent performances" (e.g., giving to the poor or witnessing to unbelievers) are nothing without love.[6]

When we abound in God's mercies, we cultivate genuine love. The local church becomes a family of believers characterized by compassion, kindness, humility, meekness, and patience (Col. 3:12). Moreover, the local church "puts on love, which binds everything together in perfect harmony" (Col. 3:14).

---

[6] Edwards, *Charity and Its Fruits*, 26-65.

73
Active Compassion (12:17-21)

What should Christians do when they encounter or experience evil? When a Christian is imprisoned for the faith? When a Christian is the victim of a violent crime? When a Christian is abused or neglected? When a Christian is vilified or ridiculed? That's what we want to consider as we turn to 12:17-21. For the sake of clarity, I need to make four preliminary remarks.

We need to look at what comes before these verses. In chapters 1-11, Paul makes it clear that salvation is a river flowing one way. It's all mercy. God's mercy is like a rushing river. We're God's elect. We're God's possession. God is the author of our salvation from start to finish. He purchased us, redeemed us, and adopted us. God holds us with a strong arm, even when we feel little joy and sense little assurance. God carries us with a mighty hand, even when we limp through life barely able to see beyond our struggles. God's mercies abound toward his people. What does this mean for the commands in these verses (12:17-21)? This isn't a system of ethics. This isn't a course in morals. This is mercy in action. Mercy experienced is mercy expressed.

We need to look at what comes after these verses. "But if you do wrong, be afraid, for he does not bear the sword in vain. For he is the servant of God, an avenger who carries out God's wrath on the wrongdoer" (13:4). We need to go back in time to understand this statement. In the days of Noah, God sends a flood, destroying humanity. After the flood, God enters into a covenant with Noah, the new head of humanity. God promises to give, sustain, and preserve life. "Whoever sheds the blood of man, by man shall his blood be shed, for God made man in his own image" (Gen. 9:6). Here, God establishes the foundational principle for all law and order: the sanctity of human life. In addition, he imparts to humanity the responsibility for establishing law and order upon this principle. Obedience requires government. And government bears the sword. Why's this important? It means that, in 12:17-21, Paul isn't thinking on a judicial level, but a personal level.

We need to look at the historical context behind these verses. Paul writes to people who live in the midst of a totalitarian regime. His society knows nothing of "inalienable rights"—life, liberty, and the pursuit of happiness. His society knows nothing of religious freedom. Paul's commands become even more radical when we consider that the recipients of this letter live in a world in which life is cheap, justice is brutal, and violence is common. This is important. We face the temptation of thinking that no one has seen what we've seen, no one has faced what we've faced, and no one has experienced what we've experienced. Really? Some of the believers, belonging to the church at Rome, will be human torches at Nero's garden parties.

We need to look at the governing principle over these verses. "I appeal to you therefore, brothers, by the mercies of God, to present your bodies as a living sacrifice, holy and acceptable to God, which is your spiritual worship" (12:1). God claims all of us. As we face different circumstances in life, we must make a choice between two options. (1) What will promote my comfort? (2) What will promote God's glory? When we encounter evil, our chief concern must be this: How am I going to glorify God in this particular circumstance? If that isn't our starting point, then Paul's commands in these verses will seem alien to us.

With all that said, what should Christians do when we they encounter or experience evil? "Bless those who persecute you; bless and do not curse them" (12:14). We need to keep three things in view.

Our responsibility (12:17-18)

According to what Paul says in these verses, we have three responsibilities when we face evil.

We respond selflessly

"Repay no one evil for evil" (12:17). Paul isn't saying we shouldn't pursue justice (if it's attainable). Justice isn't evil. According to Jonathan Edwards, Paul's command means four things.[1] (1) It means that evil should be borne without doing anything to avenge ourselves. This doesn't mean that we don't reprove evil. It means that we don't gratify the bitter spirit that's in our hearts. (2) It means that evil should be borne with the continuance of love in the heart. It shouldn't affect how we feel about people. (3) It means that evil should be borne without losing the repose of our own souls. We shouldn't become agitated. (4) It means that evil should be borne for the sake of peace. We see all of these in the case of David's reaction to Saul's persecution. David didn't seek to avenge himself despite several opportunities to do so. David never lost

---

[1] Edwards, *Charity and Its Fruits*, 71-74.

his love for Saul. David never lost his self-control when it came to his dealings with Saul. David desired peace.

We behave honourably
"Give thought to do what is honourable in the sight of all" (12:17). "Keep your conduct among the Gentiles honourable, so that when they speak against you as evildoers, they may see your good deeds and glorify God on the day of visitation" (1 Peter 2:12).

We live peaceably
"If possible, so far as it depends on you, live peaceably with all" (12:18). It isn't always possible. Why? It isn't possible when God's glory or God's truth are at stake. Paul's main point is that the absence of peace should never be our fault, and we should never take our own revenge (12:19-20).

Our certainty (12:19)
What happens when justice miscarries? Or, what happens when evil is permitted within the judicial system? In a word, what happens when it looks like the perpetrators of evil are going to get away with it? We remind ourselves of an absolute certainty. In the end, no one gets away with anything. Although it might seem that those who abuse and misuse others escape the consequences of their actions, Paul assures us that God is a glorious Avenger. "Vengeance is mine, I will repay" (See Deut. 32:35, 43; Isa. 59:17; Nah. 1:2). John Murray provides a helpful explanation of what this means:

> Here we have what belongs to the essence of piety. The essence of ungodliness is that we presume to take the place of God, to take everything into our own hands. It is faith to commit ourselves to God, to cast all our care on him and to vest all our interests in him. In reference to the matter in hand, the wrongdoing of which we are the victims, the way of faith is to recognize that God is judge and to leave the execution of vengeance and retribution to him. Never may we in our private personal relations execute the vengeance which wrongdoing merits.[2]

We should never usurp God's prerogative. It's faith to commit ourselves to God. It's faith to vest all our interests in him. It's faith to recognize that he's the judge. It's faith to leave the execution of justice to him.

---

[2] Murray, *Epistle to the Romans*, 95.

On one occasion, Paul writes, "Alexander the coppersmith did me great harm; the Lord will repay him according to his deeds" (2 Tim. 4:14). Paul has no recourse under the law. So how does he respond? Undoubtedly, he responds selflessly, behaves honourably, and lives peaceably. Undoubtedly, he offers Alexander conditional forgiveness. But without repentance, forgiveness is impossible. And so, Paul assures himself that God "will repay him according to his deeds."

Our strategy (12:20-21)
Rather than taking revenge, we should show kindness to our enemy "for by so doing [we] will heap burning coals on his head" (12:20). As Augustine remarks, "We must understand these words thus: We should incite those who have hurt us to repentance by doing them good. For such 'coals of fire,' that is, good deeds, have the power to consume his spirit, or to grieve him."[3] What is our goal when we respond selflessly, behave honourably, and live peaceably? (1) In the case of those who persist in evil, our goal is their condemnation. We show kindness to them, in order to heap "burning coals" on them (12:20). (2) In the case of those who repent of evil, our goal is their salvation. We show kindness to them, in order to overcome evil with good (12:21).

"Do not be overcome by evil, but overcome evil with good" (12:21). To be overcome by evil means to respond to evil with evil, that is, to fight back. And that's the most natural thing for a sinful human being to do. A proper self-perspective will help us to resist when we're tempted to retaliate. Jonathan Edwards says, "A humble spirit disinclines us to indulge resentment of injuries; for he that is little and unworthy in his own eyes, will not think so much of an injury offered to him as he that has high thoughts of himself."[4]

Conclusion
An unwillingness to destroy the desire for revenge breaks down the door to the heart, leaving it wide open for other sins to enter. An unwillingness to mortify the desire for revenge reveals deep-rooted pride and prevents spiritual growth and maturity. An unwillingness to smother the desire for revenge belittles God's grace as displayed in the gospel. At the foot of the cross, we're humbled. In the shadow of the cross, Christ engenders meekness, enabling us to seek the good of others. When we contemplate the cross, we're crushed to the ground.

---

[3] Quoted in Luther, *Commentary on Romans*, 178.
[4] Edwards, *Charity and Its Fruits*, 79.

We're overwhelmed by God's love for us. And we're compelled to extend compassion to others, even the worst people.

74
Grateful Submission (13:1-7)

I want to begin back in 12:1-2,

> I appeal to you therefore, brothers, by the mercies of God, to present your bodies as a living sacrifice, holy and acceptable to God, which is your spiritual worship. Do not be conformed to this world, but be transformed by the renewal of your mind, that by testing you may discern what is the will of God, what is good and acceptable and perfect.

Here, Paul appeals to the mercies of God as the supreme motive for obeying him. How do we respond to God's mercies?

We respond with a consecrated body (12:1). Paul says we're to present our bodies as living sacrifices to God. This includes our complete person. We're bombarded with a very simple message in our day: personal gratification will make us happy. Paul says the opposite: personal sacrifice (not gratification) is the key to the Christian life. It's exchanging our will for God's will.

We respond with a renewed mind (12:2). Paul says we're to be transformed by the renewal of our minds. What's wrong with our minds? Our perception of reality is severely limited and twisted. It dictates our thoughts, desires, affections, words, values, and actions. How are our minds renewed? We set our minds on Christ—all we are and will be in him. We think in an entirely new way. Who am I? What am I doing? Where am I going? What do I want? What do I value? We immerse ourselves in God's Word, so that it determines our answers to these questions.

What does a consecrated body and a renewed mind look like? It touches everything. Christianity isn't a series of truths. It's one truth that shapes our entire life. (1) How we relate to ourselves: sober judgment (12:3-8). (2) How we relate to believers: genuine love (12:9-16). (3) How we relate to enemies: active compassion (12:17-21). (4) How we relate to leaders: grateful submission (13:1-7).

And that brings us to our text. As Christians, we're called to glorify God in every area of our lives: personal, familial, vocational, recreational, social, and political. Yet, we rarely talk about the political (at least not in a constructive way). Why? Many of us view politics as taboo. There are two main reasons for this.

The first reason is historical. Many of us believe politics are taboo because of what we think happened in the past. In the fourth century, the Emperor Constantine made Christianity the official religion of the Roman Empire. He convened church councils, appointed church bishops, and debated church doctrines. Athanasius (the bishop of Alexandria) wrote a letter to the Emperor expressing his concern:

> Intrude not yourself into ecclesiastical matters, neither give commands to us concerning them; but learn them from us. God has put into your hands the kingdom, to us he has entrusted the affairs of his church. And as he who would steal the Empire from you would resist the ordinance of God, so likewise fear on your part lest by taking upon yourself the government of the church, you become guilty of a great offence. It is written, "Render unto Caesar the things that are Caesar's, and unto God the things that are God's." Neither therefore is it permitted to us to exercise an earthly rule, nor have you any authority to burn incense.[1]

It was too little too late. In the days of Constantine, the church and the state became intertwined. When the Roman Empire split in the fifth century, the church split with it. In the East, the Orthodox Church arose, with its centre at Constantinople. Today, it's the state church in countries such as Russia, Greece, and Macedonia. In the West, the Roman Catholic Church arose, with its centre at Rome. Today, it's the state church in countries such as Italy, Portugal, and Spain. At the time of the Reformation, the relationship between church and state continued. In Scandinavia, there was the Lutheran Church. In Switzerland, there was the Reformed Church. In Scotland, there was the Presbyterian Church. In England, there was the Anglican Church. The independent church movement only blossomed with the Great Ejection in 1662. This gave rise to the Baptists and Congregationalists. In the last two centuries, we've witnessed the emergence of numerous independent churches and denominations. But for 1,300 years, the church and state were intertwined. Many Christians look back at that relationship with horror. They see a tremendous amount of compromise and corruption. Consequently, they have an uneasy feeling about politics.

---

[1] Athanasius, *A Library of Fathers of the Holy Catholic Church, Anterior to the Division of East and West* (Oxford: John Henry Parker, 1843), 258.

The second reason is eschatological. Many of us have a negative view of politics because of what we think will happen in the future. J.N. Darby popularized the view that everything (even the church) is in ruin. Thus, the faithful remnant gathers to await the rapture. This view influences a person's approach to life. F.W. Newman explains:

> The importance of this doctrine is, that it totally forbids all working for earthly objects distant in time ... For instance, if a youth had a natural aptitude for mathematics, and he asked, ought he to give himself to study, in hope that he might diffuse a serviceable knowledge of it, or possibly even enlarge the boundaries of the science? My friend (Darby) would have replied, that such a purpose was very proper, if entertained by a worldly man. Let the dead bury their dead; and let the world study the things of the world ... But such studies cannot be eagerly followed by the Christian, except when he yields to unbelief.[2]

What's the point of dedicating oneself to the study of mathematics when everything is in ruin? What's the point of applying oneself to a career in science when everything is in ruin? What's the point of committing oneself to social efforts when everything is in ruin? What's the point of concerning oneself with politics when everything is in ruin? According to this school of thought, God isn't working through these things. God isn't glorified in these things. So, what's the point? To engage in such pursuits is to think that God is actually working through them, when, in actual fact, he isn't. For many, this thinking undermines social and political involvement. They have an uneasy feeling about politics.

When we put these two together, we see why many Christians keep politics at arm's length, failing to see it as a sphere in which they should glorify God. We rarely talk about the subject. Yet the Bible addresses the subject.

Back in Genesis 9:6, we read, "Whoever sheds the blood of man, by man shall his blood be shed, for God made man in his own image." We all know the context of this verse. God sends the flood, destroying all of humanity except Noah's family. Afterward, he enters into a covenant with Noah, the head of humanity. He promises to give, sustain, protect, and preserve life. In making these promises, he reveals his glorious generosity. According to the *Oxford Dictionary*, generosity is "freely giving more than is necessary or expected."

---

[2] Quoted in Iain Murray, *The Puritan Hope: Revival and the Interpretation of Prophecy* (Edinburgh: Banner of Truth, 1998), 203.

At times, we do this. A few years ago, the government issued a commemorative coin for Terry Fox. We call Terry Fox generous because he gave more than was necessary. However, the term *generosity* takes on a whole new significance when a person freely gives not merely more than is necessary but contrary to what is deserved. That's what God does in this covenant.

God makes this covenant with sinners. Before and after the flood, he declares, "Every intention of the thoughts of [man's] heart [is] only evil continually" (Gen. 6:5; see also 8:21). In other words, man is sinful—inherently, totally, and continually. Yet God makes a covenant with humanity. God gives, sustains, protects, and preserves life. One of the ways in which he fulfills these promises is through the institution of human government: "Whoever sheds the blood of man, by man shall his blood be shed, for God made man in his own image." Here, God establishes the foundational principle for law and order: the sanctity of human life. And he imparts to humanity the responsibility to establish law and order upon this principle. This requires government. Therefore, human government is God-ordained. With that context in place, we can turn to our passage.

The command (13:1)

"Let every person be subject to the governing authorities." Paul writes to people living under a totalitarian regime. His society knows nothing of inalienable rights: life, liberty, and the pursuit of happiness. His society knows nothing of religious freedom. Paul's commands become even more radical when we consider that the recipients of this letter live in a world in which life is cheap, justice is brutal, and violence is common. Paul commands them to be subject to the governing authorities.

The reasons (13:1-4)

"Let every person be subject to the governing authorities." Why? Paul gives three reasons. First, "For there is no authority except from God, and those that exist have been instituted by God" (13:1). Whoever refuses to submit to the government "resists what God has appointed" (13:2). Paul's point is simple. Human government is a divine institution. To oppose human government is to oppose God (1 Kings 12:15; Jer. 27:6; Dan. 2:21; John 19:10). In short, we're to "be subject to the governing authorities" because it's right. Second, "For rulers are not a terror to good conduct, but to bad" (13:3). Again, Paul's point is simple. Human government is a divine institution. It exists to punish bad behaviour and reward good behaviour. In short, we're to "be subject to the governing authorities" because it's wise. If we obey the law, we have no reason to fear. Third, "For he is God's servant for your good" (13:4). Human government restrains man's sin, acting as a deterrent.

The examples (13:5-7)
For these three reasons, we submit. But what does this look like? Paul gives four examples. (1) We render "taxes" (13:6-7). Government officials deserve to receive financial remuneration. (2) We render "customs" (13:7). These payments go toward public services—the construction of roads and ports, the maintenance of security forces, the provision of public services, etc. (3) We render "fear" (13:7). This is our attitude toward their laws. (4) We render "honour" (13:7). This is our attitude toward their persons.

The questions
Our submission to governing authorities is a manifestation of godliness because it's done in the fear of God. Now, this normally leads to two questions.

First, what if our leaders are ungodly? This doesn't negate the function of government. James Boice explains, "The many failures of human government, which are the failures of human beings themselves, must not blind us to the truth that government is nevertheless directly and divinely appointed."[3] As a manifestation of his benevolence, God uses the ungodly to maintain a measure of restraint over man's sin. This is his common grace. This is part of his covenant with Noah. We should be extremely thankful for it.

Second, what if our leaders require us to do something ungodly? The Bible teaches us that there's a limit to our submission. When ordered to cease preaching, Peter declares, "We must obey God rather than men" (Acts 5:29). This means we willingly submit to our government unless it requires us to violate God's law.

Conclusion
Man possesses understanding, affections, and will—this is the natural image of God in man. These faculties are marked by knowledge, righteousness, and holiness—this is the moral image of God in man (Eph. 4:24; Col. 3:10). At the time of the fall, man lost the moral image of God. However, he maintained the

---

[3] James M. Boice, *Genesis 1-11* (Grand Rapids: Baker Books, 2002), 381.

natural image of God. This is the basis for the sanctity of human life. We don't murder people. Why? They're made in God's image. We don't abort babies. Why? They're made in God's image. We don't euthanize the elderly. Why? They're made in God's image. We don't permit doctors to help the ill to commit suicide. Why? They're made in God's image. Human life is precious because humans are made in the image of God. This gives dignity to every person. This gives value to every person. This is the basis of God's love for every person. Therefore, God protects life by giving man the right to execute judgment upon those who disregard the sanctity of human life.

To a great extent, Canada has lost this understanding of the sanctity of human life because it has lost its moral compass. It revels in the Charter of Rights and Freedoms. It claims to be a just society. In actual fact, Canada has demonstrated time and time again that it's quickly losing sight of this foundational principle: the sanctity of human life. The reason this country has lost its moral compass is because it lacks citizens who know God.

> In a declining cultural and moral environment, such as our own, the greatest need is not for more laws or even for a greater spiritual sensitivity on the part of unbelievers, but rather for confession of sin and a deep moving of the Spirit of God among God's people.[4]

As Christians, we must live in the fear of God. As we do so, we will have an impact upon our society. As Christians, we should be the best citizens. We should be the best husbands, fathers, wives, mothers, workers, neighbours, and friends. Why? Godliness is practical.

---

[4] Boice, *Genesis 1-11*, 384.

75
Glorifying the King (13:1-7)

The gospel is the power of God for salvation to everyone who believes (1:16). It's powerful because it does what nothing else can do. It saves. God's hyperplentiful grace in Christ abounds toward the most sinful, rebellious, antagonistic, depraved individuals. This gospel is transformative. That's Paul's point in 12:1-15:13. This transformation even effects how we relate to our governing authorities. That's Paul's point in 13:1-7.

The command (13:1). "Let every person be subject to the governing authorities."

The reasons for grateful submission (13:1-4). The first is divine authority. We're to "be subject to the governing authorities" because it's right. The second is human society. We're to "be subject to the governing authorities" because it's wise.

The examples of grateful submission (13:5-7). We pay "taxes." We pay "revenue." We pay "respect." We pay "honour."

I want to expand on this. Why? Politics creates a lot of confusion and frustration. I'm not interested in answering every question or resolving every issue. I'm interested in ensuring that we're glorifying God in our approach to politics. I want to give you five words of encouragement.

I encourage you to think biblically

It's interesting (and telling) that Paul never remarks on current events. He lives in the midst of the Roman Empire—surrounded by political intrigue, social upheaval, international turmoil, class conflict, and religious controversy. Yet he never utters a word about any of it. How unlike today's church! I think there's one main reason for this difference. For Paul, there's no correlation between the advancement of God's kingdom and the advancement of any earthly kingdom. There's no correlation between the furtherance of God's kingdom and the furtherance of any particular political agenda.

Paul is far more concerned about our personal humility than our civil liberty. He's far more concerned about our unmortified sins than our inalienable rights. Paul sees human pride as a far greater threat than political injustice. He sees the transforming effects of the gospel as far more significant than the apparatus of politics. He sees Christ ruling by his Word and Spirit as far more powerful than any earthly leader, party, or country.

Many Christians think this country's present condition is the result of a political problem. As a result, they think the solution for this country's present condition is political. It isn't. Only the biblical gospel rescues people from sin, death, and hell. Only the biblical gospel lifts people out of the muck and mire. Only the biblical gospel transforms people. Only the biblical gospel alters the course of societies. As Christians, our chief calling isn't to win back our country. Our chief calling is to preach biblically and to live biblically.

I encourage you to listen carefully
A certain narrative has captured the minds of many believers. Here it is. There was a time when our country was close to a utopian state, but we've been caught in a terrible downward spiral ever since. We need to get back to what we were. Personally, I believe this is a misleading (if not, false) narrative, which leads to a spirit of negativity—an attitude of settled disgruntlement. Two ingredients poison the mix even more.

The first is a conspiratorial mindset. I'm referring to those people who live in a state of self-induced paranoia—an irrational fear of the hidden hand.

The second is an apocalyptic mindset. I'm referring to those people who handle prophetic biblical texts as if they were a crystal ball through which they can ascertain the significance of current events.

These factors have converged to produce a perfect storm. This kind of thinking is gospel truth within vast segments of evangelicalism. As a matter of fact, to question the validity of this so-called gospel truth is akin to the unpardonable sin. For many, adherence to this so-called gospel truth has become the hallmark of what it means to be a Christian. Some politicians are preying on this distorted and twisted misrepresentation of the Christian faith. We need to listen carefully.

I encourage you to pray regularly
Paul says we're to pray "for kings and all who are in high positions" (1 Tim. 2:2). Why? (1) "That we may lead a peaceful and quiet life." The word "quiet" means "restfulness unmarred by disturbance." The word "peaceful" means "the stillness that accompanies restfulness." (2) "That we may live godly and dignified in every way."

We pray to God that our governing authorities grant us the freedom to live peacefully, so that we can pursue godliness. It's important to remember the historical setting. Who's in power? The Roman Emperor! He dictated how people lived their lives. He maintained his power by military force. He accumulated wealth. He required worship. Yet, the believers in Ephesus are to pray for him, as they're to pray for all their leaders. Why? God rules over all. "The king's heart is a stream of water in the hand of the LORD; he turns it wherever he will" (Prov. 21:1).

I encourage you to vote prudently
As Christians, we've lost sight of the origins of democracy. In the seventeenth century, Charles I ruled England in conjunction with Parliament—elected officials from among the gentry and aristocracy. Charles wanted to rule without Parliament. He did so for eleven years. Eventually, he was forced to assemble Parliament in order to raise money to pay an indemnity for a war he had started with Scotland. Parliament seized the opportunity to make certain demands. This led to civil war. Parliament won. Charles was executed. Oliver Cromwell ruled for a few years as Lord Protector. When he died, Parliament restored Charles II. James II followed, again asserting royal absolutism. So, Parliament offered the throne to James's daughter, Mary, who was married to William of Orange. In 1689, they were crowned king and queen of England on the condition that they accept a set of constitutional principles enacted by Parliament. This laid the foundation for constitutional monarchy in England, which in turn laid the foundation for our democracy.

Compare that history of democracy in Britain with the rest of the world. Most of the kings in southern Europe maintained power by governing on the principle of royal absolutism. Louis XIV proclaimed, "I am the state." Most of these monarchs were eventually overthrown in bloody revolutions and replaced with dictatorships, in France, Portugal, Italy, Spain, etc. These dictatorships only gave way to democracies in the twentieth century. Since then, the West has tried to spread democracy throughout the world—with very limited success. Why? A democratic form of government is established upon one basic principle: the sanctity of human life. This is lacking in Islamic countries, Hindu countries, Buddhist countries, and animistic countries. It will soon be lacking in secular countries—the West. My point is this: as Christians, we dare not take democracy for granted. We have a tremendous responsibility to vote in the fear of God. How?

We acknowledge God's revealed will for human government. Its main responsibility isn't to provide education, establish social programs, ensure retirement savings, strengthen labour unions, sponsor the arts, provide foreign aid, subsidize universities, help the homeless, build houses, establish daycare, or anything like that. First and foremost, the government exists for the maintenance of law and order—the protection of human life, based upon the sanctity of human life. God has established human government for the good of humanity. It's a manifestation of his common grace. We should be interested in making sure that it serves the purpose for which it was intended. We should vote accordingly.

I encourage you to submit gratefully
These verses are liberating (13:1-7). They provide wisdom for our day. We don't have to agree with, comment on, or respond to every decision the government makes. We're called to be good citizens. We should be the best husbands, fathers, wives, mothers, workers, neighbours, and friends. In a word, we should be the best at the roles in which God places us. Why? Godliness is practical. Paying our income tax is an act of worship. Parking in designated spots is an act of worship. Adhering to an emissions' test is an act of worship. Observing building codes is an act of worship. Honouring immigration laws is an act of worship. Buying a hunting license is an act of worship. Obeying laws is an act of worship. In short, grateful submission to our governing authorities is an act of worship.

76
Fulfilling the Law (13:8-14)

What is the law? That's a tricky question because the word *law* is used in various ways in the NT. At times it refers to the Pentateuch: the first five books of the OT. At times it refers to the Mosaic Covenant, which was established between God and Israel at Mt. Sinai. At times it refers to the moral law.

What's the moral law? A law is whatever God commands. Many of God's commandments are *limited*. (1) Some are limited to certain individuals. For example, God commanded Abraham to sacrifice his son, Isaac. He doesn't command everyone to do that. It isn't an eternal and universal commandment. (2) Some are limited to certain nations. For example, God commanded Israel to destroy the Canaanites. He doesn't command everyone to do that. It isn't an eternal and universal commandment. (3) Some are limited to certain circumstances. For example, God commanded Israel to celebrate the seven feasts of Jehovah. He doesn't command everyone to do that. It isn't an eternal and universal commandment.

What distinguishes the moral law is that it's eternal and universal. This means that it applies to all people in all places at all times. Why? It's inherently good. And everyone is under obligation to keep the moral law, because they have an inherent knowledge of it (2:14).

The moral law is found throughout the Bible. We have a fairly complete summary of it in the Decalogue as found in Exodus 20:1-17. The Decalogue, in turn, is summed up in two commandments as found in Matthew 22:36-40. Here, Christ says we're to love God with all our heart, soul, mind, and strength. That's another way of saying "You shall have no other gods before me." Christ also says we're to love our neighbour as ourselves. That's another way of saying "You shall not covet." This means that the essence of the law is love.

It's this law that Paul has in mind in 13:8-14. What is its purpose?

To condemn us
Paul makes that clear in this letter (3:20; 4:15; 5:20; 7:9). Personally, he thought all was well with his soul (Phil. 3:6). However, the time came when he

died. Why? The law showed him his sin. According to the law, it's a sin to covet. Paul realized that he was guilty of coveting. If he was guilty of coveting, then he didn't love his neighbour as himself. If he didn't love his neighbour as himself, then he didn't love God. He realized that he was condemned in God's sight.

To lead us to Christ
In Galatians 3:24, Paul says, "So then, the law was our guardian until Christ came, in order that we might be justified by faith." We read God's law. As a result, we see our sin. We see the nature of our sin—it permeates us. We see the power of our sin—it controls us. As Martin Luther says, "These precepts are given that proud and blind man might, by them, learn the disease of his own *spiritual* impotency."[1] We're humbled by our inadequacy and inability. We're ready for help. And we find that help in Christ. He was born under the law (Gal. 4:4-5), and he did two things that correspond to our twofold need. (1) He bore the curse of the law. God reckons our sin to Christ. On that basis, God forgives us. (2) He obeyed the law. God reckons Christ's righteousness to us. On that basis, God declares us to be just.

To guide us
When the law is viewed as a ladder to heaven (a righteousness of works), then it stands in an antithetical relationship to the gospel (a righteousness of grace). That's true. But we must not allow this antithetical relationship to detract from a positive view of the law—as an expression of God's eternal will. The law isn't a reaction to humanity's fall; nor is it merely an aspect of Israel's religion. On the contrary, the law is permanent in the plan of God. According to Calvin, the law is useful to believers in that: (1) it gives a clearer understanding of God's will for their lives; and (2) it continues to convict, thereby cultivating a sense of need within them.[2]

Contrary to popular misconception, this use of the law doesn't lead to legalism. In the New Covenant, Jeremiah speaks of God putting his law within his people (Jer. 31:31-33) whereas Ezekiel speaks of God putting his Spirit within them (Ezek. 36:26-27). An appreciation of the relationship between the law and the Spirit is pivotal. Because they're born of the Spirit, believers love God with all their heart, soul, and mind, thereby fulfilling the law (Lev. 19:18;

---
[1] Luther, *Bondage of the Will*, LVII.
[2] Calvin, *Institutes*, 2:12.

Deut. 6:3-5; 10:12-13; Matt. 22:37-40; Rom. 10:13). As Christians, we have the Holy Spirit within us. He writes the law upon our hearts. This means that he causes us to love God. Because we love God, we want to know his will. Because we love God, we want to do his will. We find his will expressed in his law. Obedience, therefore, isn't an attempt to obtain a meritorious standing before God; rather, it's the fruit of love for God.

How we fulfill the law (13:8-10)
"Owe no one anything, except to love each other." This statement flows from the previous verse where Paul says we're to "pay to all what is owed to them" (13:7). He isn't saying we shouldn't incur debts, but we must repay our debts. There's only one debt we can't repay—the love we owe to others. How's this a debt? We don't owe love to people because of what they've done for us, but because of what God has done for us. "God shows his love for us in that while we were still sinners, Christ died for us" (5:8).

Christ exchanged wealth for poverty and majesty for humility. He exchanged a throne for a manger and a crown of glory for a crown of thorns. He exchanged the admiration of angels for the rejection of humans. He was ridiculed, harassed, betrayed, arrested, and condemned. He was pierced with thorns and scourged with cords. He climbed a shameful cross. "Shredded flesh against unforgiving wood, iron stakes pounded through bone and wracked nerves, joints wrenched out of socket by the sheer dead weight of the body, public humiliation before the eyes of family, friends, and the world—that was the death of the cross."[3] Through it all, Christ never hurled screams of rage toward the heavens. He never hurled threats of defiance toward the crowds. He never uttered sobs of self-pity. He never claimed his rights. He never championed his feelings. He never promoted his interests. He never demanded his comforts. He never even considered himself. He gave himself as a sacrifice to God.

As Christians, we're beggars who've found food to satisfy our hunger. We're rebels who've found pardon and forgiveness. We're the diseased and deformed who've found healing. We're the unclean and untouchable who've found cleansing. We're the dead who've found eternal life. That's why we're to love.

---

[3] Greg Gilbert, "The Gospel: God's Self-Substitution for Sinners" in *Don't Call It a Comeback*, ed. Kevin DeYoung (Wheaton: Crossway Books, 2011), 72.

THE OBEDIENCE OF FAITH

We love by doing no wrong in the sight of God
In 13:9, Paul quotes the last four of the Ten Commandments (Exod. 20:13-17). His point is that loving our neighbour means we're committed to our neighbour's well-being. In 13:10, Paul summarizes his point as follows: "Love does no wrong to a neighbor." I love my neighbour by not committing adultery (13:9; Exod. 20:14). I love my neighbour by not murdering (13:9; Exod. 20:13). I love my neighbour by not stealing (13:9; Exod. 20:15). I love my neighbour by not coveting (13:9; Exod. 20:17).

We love by pursuing for our neighbour what we want for ourselves
In 13:9, Paul actually quotes the second of the two greatest commandments: "You shall love your neighbor as yourself." What do we want? That's what we should want for our neighbour. How do we want it? That's how we should want it for our neighbour. Do you want respect? Respect others. Do you want help? Help others. Do you want compassion? Be compassionate toward others. Are you lonely? Befriend someone. Are you upset? Comfort someone. Are you hungry? Feed someone. Are you vulnerable? Protect someone. And do all these things with the same zeal and enthusiasm you'd do them for yourself. "You shall love your neighbor as yourself."

Why we fulfill the law (13:11-14)
In 13:11, Paul says, "you know the time." In other words, we're to obey Paul's command to love our neighbour because of what we know about "the time." What do we know? (1) We know "the hour is come for you to awake from sleep" (13:11). (2) We know that "salvation is nearer to us now than when we first believed" (13:11). (3) We know that "the night is far gone; the day is at hand" (13:12). What's Paul saying? He appears to have in view the "now" and "not yet" realities of our salvation. As we know, the Bible divides history into "this age" and "the age to come." Christ inaugurated "the age to come" at his first advent. It overlaps with "this age." It will do so until the consummation of God's kingdom.

That day is fast approaching. Given that fact, Paul makes three appeals—all are double sentences, the negative and positive aspects of the appeal forming an antithesis.

First, "Let us cast off the works of darkness and put on the armor of light" (13:12). What is the armor of light? Paul tells us in 1 Thessalonians 5:8. It consists of faith, hope, and love. When these are present, we cast off the works of darkness.

Second, "Let us walk properly as in the daytime" (13:13). Paul gives three categories of sinful desires: (1) "orgies and drunkenness"—inordinate desire for stimulation; (2) "sexual immorality and sensuality"—inordinate desire for pleasure; and (3) "quarreling and jealousy"—inordinate desire for attention.

Third, "Put on the Lord Jesus Christ, and make no provision for the flesh, to gratify its desires" (13:14). The word "provision" means "forethought." We aren't to think about anything that will lead to sinful desire. We aren't to think about anything that might give rise to any of the things in 13:13. Rather, we're to put on Christ. We've already put on Christ (6:3). We're legally righteous in God's sight. Now, we must live as though we're clothed by him. We must remember who we're wearing. Putting on Christ is the way we keep from making provision for the flesh. It's the way we kill these sinful thoughts.

And so, the fact that "the day is at hand" (13:12) should cause us to heed the three commands in 13:12-14. If we heed these three commands, then we'll seek to love our neighbour as ourselves, thereby fulfilling the law (13:8-10).

Conclusion
Paul wants us to possess a biblical view of time. He wants us to maintain this perspective at all times. And he wants us to live accordingly. "Teach us to number our days that we may get a heart of wisdom" (Ps. 90:12). We're to live as though "the day" has arrived. What's really important? What really matters? What will last? What will perish? How should we then live? Paul has told us in 12:1-13:10.

77
Keeping the Peace (14:1-15:12)

Legalism arises when we view God's commands as conditions to be fulfilled by us rather than the implications of God's mercy lived out in us. Here's what we must always keep in mind:

First, God offers Christ to sinners. We don't need to fulfill any conditions. We don't need to get our act together before we can receive Christ. We don't need to meet a certain standard before we can receive Christ. We don't need to be sorry enough, ashamed enough, good enough, or holy enough, before we can receive Christ.

Second, when we receive Christ, we take possession of all the benefits that are found in him. To be united to Christ is justification. To be united to Christ is adoption. To be united to Christ is reconciliation. To be united to Christ is sanctification. To be united to Christ is glorification.

Third, we glorify God by obeying him. God says to us: "I didn't choose you because of who you are. I chose you by sovereign grace. You didn't earn my favour then, and you can't earn my favour now. But I want you to grow in your knowledge of me and your love for me. And I want you to obey me. Don't divorce my commands from who I am! They're an expression of my love for you. In commanding you, I'm not depriving you of anything. In commanding you, I'm not destroying your joy. On the contrary, I have your joy in view. My glory and your joy are inseparable. Both are found in obedience. I know what's best for you, and I want what's best for you. Trust me and obey me!"

We're debtors to God's mercy. When we get this, we respond with a consecrated body and a renewed mind (12:1-2). And these will be evident in how we relate to ourselves (12:3-8), believers (12:9-16), enemies (12:17-21), rulers (13:1-7), neighbours (13:8-10), desires (13:11-14), and opinions (14:1-15:12).

We've considered the first six. In this study, we arrive at the seventh. I want to "ease" into it by making a number of statements. Please pay close attention to what I'm doing here.

I know Christians who play sports on a Sunday afternoon, and I know Christians who don't because they think it's a violation of the Sabbath.

I know Christians who play cards and dominoes, and I know Christians who don't because of their association with the occult.

I know Christians who watch football, and I know Christians who don't because they find the cheerleaders to be degrading to women.

I know Christians who celebrate Christmas, and I know Christians who don't because of its historical association with pagan festivities.

I know Christians who vacation at the beach, and I know Christians who don't because too many people are dressed inappropriately.

I know Christians who read Ernest Hemingway, and I know Christians who don't because his books don't reflect a biblical worldview.

I know Christians who lift weights, and I know Christians who don't because they think it's motivated by vanity.

I know Christians who watch "I Love Lucy," and I know Christians who don't because it conveys a spirit of feminism in seminal form.

I know Christians who study the martial arts, and I know Christians who don't because of their origins in eastern spirituality.

I know Christians who drink beer and wine in moderation, and I know Christians who don't because they believe the devil is in every bottle.

I know Christians who own a gun (or, guns), and I know Christians who don't because they can't picture Jesus carrying a gun.

I know Christians who worship with songs drawn from a vast array of sources, and I know Christians who only sing the psalms because it's the church's hymn book.

I know Christians who believe all church services should integrate all ages, and I know Christians who don't because there are educational goals corresponding to certain stages of spiritual and intellectual development.

I know Christians who use the internet, and I know Christians who don't because it's used in morally repugnant ways.

I know Christians who hunt deer, and I know Christians who don't because they think it's cruel and, therefore, a flagrant abuse of God's creation.

I know Christians who think babies should be borne in a hospital, and I know Christians who think babies should be borne at home.

I know Christians who have no problem with women wearing pants, makeup, or earrings, and I know Christians who are opposed to such things because of their overt worldliness.

I know Christians who allow their kids to dress up in morally inoffensive costumes and collect candy on Halloween, and I know Christians who don't because of its association with evil.

I know Christians who think there are many ways to educate their children, and I know Christians who think there's only one God-approved and God-ordained way and we dare not deviate from it.

I know Christians who dance (or, at least, think they can), and I know Christians who are opposed to all dancing.

I know Christians who watch movies at the cinema, and I know Christians who are opposed to the cinema because of the garbage that's shown there.

I know Christians who adhere to a certain dress-code for Sunday worship, and I know Christians who don't believe such things are necessary.

And I could go on.

Now, I say this tongue-in-cheek: I hold the *right* position on all of these issues. Here's my dilemma: I'm a member of a local church in which some people clearly hold the *wrong* position. What am I going to do? (1) I could make it my mission to convert everyone to my point of view. (2) I could force the church to take a stand on all of these issues. (3) I could act upon my convictions without giving a moment's thought to what anyone else thinks. (4) I could try to find a church where everyone agrees with me on everything. (5) I could gather my wife and children around me on a Sunday morning and worship at home.

What am I going to do? The struggle is never going away. There will always be an issue (or, issues). Paul helps us to work through this struggle by prescribing three remedies:

Remedy #1 (14:1-12): "Don't judge your brother; welcome him!"
Remedy #2 (14:13-23): "Don't destroy your brother; edify him!"
Remedy #3 (15:1-12): "Don't ignore your brother; honour him!"

That's where we're going. In this study, I simply want to give you the major principles that emerge from these verses. By the time we arrive at 15:12, I want us to be able to say (at the very least) the following.

I have opinions that offend someone in my church (14:1)

These are matters of conscience to which the Bible doesn't speak directly or definitively. When we take a position on such issues, we potentially offend someone. We must recognize this. We must also recognize that, when it comes to these opinions, the most important thing isn't winning an argument, defending a position, or enforcing uniformity. The most important thing is maintaining unity.

I accept that people are in different stages of spiritual growth (14:1)

Paul speaks of "weak" and "strong" Christians. The difference between them is their understanding of their relationship to the OT ceremonial law. For weak Christians, it's binding. For strong Christians, it isn't binding. They're at different stages in their understanding of Scripture. It isn't a reflection of how spiritual they are. It isn't a reflection of how much they love the Lord. They're simply at different places as they grow in their understanding of the Christian faith.

I welcome my brothers and sisters as they stand in Christ (14:1, 3)

James Boice writes,

> Christ is served when we understand that we are accepted by God through the work of Jesus Christ alone and are therefore able joyfully to accept and love all others for whom Jesus died. These other believers may be wrong in many respects, in our opinion. But we will know that we are all nevertheless part of one spiritual body, the body of Christ, and that we belong together with all other Christians as together we seek to live for Christ and bear a strong witness for him in this world.[1]

All believers (no matter their opinions) are fully and equally loved, accepted, cherished, and welcomed by their Father. Thus, I must not make my acceptance of my fellow believers contingent on how they score on my list of opinions. 100%—I welcome you! 80%—I welcome you, but I'll be watching you! 60%—I'll pray for you! 40%—I'm not sure you're saved!

I am convinced in my own mind (14:5)

How do I become convinced in my own mind about something to which the Bible doesn't speak directly or definitively? I think we need to work through four questions. (1) Can I do this to God's glory? "So, whether you eat or drink, or whatever you do, do all to the glory of God" (1 Cor. 10:31). (2) Is it worthy of someone in whom the Holy Spirit dwells? "Or do you not know that your body is a temple of the Holy Spirit within you, whom you have from God? You are not your own" (1 Cor. 6:19). (3) Does it edify? "All things are lawful, but not all things build up" (1 Cor. 10:23). (4) Does it enslave me? "All things are lawful for me, but I will not be enslaved by anything" (1 Cor. 6:12). In a word,

---

[1] Boice, *Romans*, 1780.

can I thank God for this?

I am committed to pursuing what makes for peace and edification (14:19)
There's a connection between peace and edification. The latter is impossible without the former. (1) I want peace. How will what I say and do affect others? What's in the best interest of others? What's in the best interest of the church? Will this create unnecessary problems? (2) I want edification. Will my actions, decisions, opinions in some way adversely affect someone else's spiritual walk?

I embrace silence as one of the best ways to make peace (14:22)
There are times when I must keep my opinions between God and me. If I recognize something is disputable, then I need to be convinced of my opinion, and then keep it to myself.

I am chiefly concerned about pleasing others (15:2-3)
This is simple. It reduces everything to one basic issue. Do I love Christ enough to imitate him by thinking of others before me? What impact will this have on my fellow believer? How will he interpret this? Who might be offended by this? Will this create dissension or confusion or division? What are the consequences? If I everyone did what I did, what would be the repercussions?

Conclusion
The governing principles for working through "opinions" are established at the Council of Jerusalem (Acts 15:23-29). Some of the Jews want to impose certain rites and rituals upon Gentiles. What's the Council's decision? They ask the Gentile Christians to "abstain from things sacrificed to idols and from blood and from things strangled and from fornication" (Acts 15:29). Please notice three important facts concerning this decision. (1) It upholds the truth of the gospel. There's no mention of any of these things as being necessary to salvation. The gospel isn't compromised by refraining from these things. (2) It shows concern for the consciences of the weak. Three of the four stipulations concern the ceremonial law. The point is this: What's at risk if you abstain from these things? Nothing! What's it going to cost you to abstain from these things? Nothing! Then, for the sake of peace, it would be a good idea if you refrained. (3) It upholds the truth of Christian liberty. In the letter, the apostles clearly state, "Some ... have disturbed you" (Acts 15:24)—that is,

the weak have disturbed the strong. The Council makes it clear that the weak are in the wrong. In effect, this decision sets the stage for instructing the weak. The expectation is that the weak will grow into maturity.

78
Remedy 1: Don't Judge! Welcome! (14:1-12)

Paul knows a problem is festering within the church at Rome. He identifies the problem in 14:1 as "opinions" (ESV), "disputable matters" (NIV), "doubtful disputations" (AV). What's he talking about? Some eat only vegetables, while others don't (14:2). Some observe festival days, while others don't (14:5). Some avoid unclean foods, while others don't (14:14). Some refuse to drink wine, while others don't (14:21). Paul divides these two groups into "weak" and "strong" (14:1; 15:1). The difference stems from their understanding of the ceremonial law.

First, there are "strong" Christians. They understand that the ceremonial law is a shadow. They have no problem leaving Judaism behind. They recognize that it had served its purpose. They know that they aren't expected to obey all of those commandments concerning foods and days.

Second, there are "weak" Christians. (1) Some are Jews. For hundreds of years, they had lived with the ceremonial law. It's part of their psyche. Do you remember the story of Daniel? He was taken into exile in Babylon. He was chosen to be educated for three years in the Chaldean language and literature, so that he might serve in the king's court. He was allotted food and drink from the king's table. "But Daniel made up his mind that he would not defile himself with the king's choice food or with the wine which he drank" (Dan. 1:8). So, what did he do? He asked for permission to abstain. He asked for vegetables. Do you see how difficult it might have been for some of the early Jewish converts to let go of the ceremonial law? (2) Some are Gentiles. They esteem the Jews. After all, the Jews possess the oracles of God. They worship at the temple. They observe numerous festivals. All of these things came from God. If the Jews say it's necessary to observe the ceremonial law, then they must be right. It sure looks godly.

Do you see the problem that's festering? On one side, there are "weak" Christians. On the other side, there are "strong" Christians. The weak judge the strong: "They must not be very spiritual. If they were, they wouldn't think like that." Meanwhile, the strong despise the weak: "They must not be very spiritual. If they were, they wouldn't think like that." These two groups are on a collision course. Unless something is done, there are only two possible results. The first is cold war: they'll claim their territories and then avoid each other. The second is civil war: they'll tear each other apart.

This is a recurring issue within the church. I'm thinking particularly of matters of conscience to which the Bible doesn't speak directly or definitively. All of us assume a position on such matters. All of us assume our position is correct. And so, when we meet believers who don't see things the way we do, what are we going to do? Paul prescribes three remedies. In this study, we're going to look at the first. Here, Paul forbids the strong from despising the weak, and he forbids the weak from judging the strong. Why? He gives three reasons.

God has welcomed my brother (14:3)
"Let not the one who eats despise the one who abstains, and let not the one who abstains pass judgment on the one who eats, for God has welcomed him." My brother is chosen, predestined, called, justified, and glorified. He's as loved, accepted, cherished, and welcomed by God as I am. Therefore, I must not make my acceptance of him contingent on how he scores on my list of opinions.

God has redeemed my brother (14:4-9)
God is my brother's Master (14:4). God will uphold (accept) my brother on the judgment day (14:4). My brother is fully convinced in his own mind as to his opinions (14:5). My brother is motivated by a desire to honour God (14:6). This is crucial. I don't want us to miss this. Both the weak and strong act in faith. Both the weak and strong act from gratitude. Both the weak and strong act for God's glory. My brother lives for God because he belongs to God (14:7-8). My brother is Christ's possession (14:9).

God will judge my brother (14:10-12)
Please notice the word "all" in 14:10. A day is coming when we'll "all" stand before God's judgment seat. Please notice the word "every" in 14:11. A day is coming when "every" knee will bow before God. Please notice the word "each" in 14:12. A day is coming when "each" one will give an account. This has two implications for the current discussion.

First, I must realize that I'm not appointed to judge my brother on these matters. He has a Master to whom he'll give an account.

Second, I must realize that I'm going to stand before God's judgment seat.

Remedy 1: Don't Judge! Welcome! (14:1-12)

I'm going to bow my knee. I'm going to give an account of my life. All that to say: God will judge me according to my works. If I've been judgmental toward others, contemptuous toward others, unmerciful toward others, uncharitable toward others, these things will be made evident on the judgment day. And these things will testify to the fact that I know nothing of God's mercy. These things will testify to the fact that I'm a fake.

Conclusion
John Stott summarizes this first remedy as follows.[1] Christ died to be our Saviour. Christ rose to be our Lord. Christ is coming to be our Judge. We belong to Christ; therefore, matters of conscience are between us and him. Our duty is to welcome one another. I want to mention three lessons.

I need to be careful how I apply this text (14:4)
Some people will twist what Paul says in these verses in order to justify doctrinal error or moral laxity. They'll think to themselves: "According to Paul, the most important thing is that we get along. Therefore, it doesn't matter what we believe or how we live. We're to accept one another—no questions asked." More often than not, when people talk like that, they mean that we should turn a blind eye to what people believe and how people live. That's a misapplication of these verses.

Paul isn't saying that we should accept people no matter what they believe. Some of the Galatians suggest that circumcision is necessary for salvation. How does Paul respond? He doesn't encourage them to accept one another. What does he say? He rebukes them (Gal. 1:6-9).

Paul isn't saying that we should accept people no matter how they live. The Corinthians tolerate an individual in their midst who's guilty of immorality. How does Paul respond? He doesn't encourage them to accept one another. He rebukes them (1 Cor. 5:1-5).

I need to pursue a God-centred way of thinking and living (14:6)
Isn't it amazing how Paul relates great theological truths to petty problems festering within the church at Rome? We have two groups struggling over meat and wine. What does Paul do? He takes them to Christ's crucifixion, resurrection, present reign, and future judgment. Grasping these great truths, our chief

---

[1] Stott, *Message of Romans*, 373.

concern is to be God's honour. Do we act in faith? Do we act out of gratitude? Do we act for God's glory?

I need to nurture a joy-inducing appreciation of my identity in Christ (14:8)
Christ purchased me (14:8-9). He welcomes me (14:3). He will uphold me (14:4).

> Our whole salvation is in Christ. If we seek redemption, it's found in his passion; if forgiveness, in his condemnation; if remission of the curse, in his sacrifice; if purification, in his blood; if reconciliation, in his suffering; if newness of life, in his resurrection. Let us drink our fill from this fountain.[2]

Because of our sin, we are cut off from God. But, when we come to Christ in childlike dependence, and look to him alone to save us, God receives us in Christ—his Beloved. And this is the sweetest truth known to man.

---

[2] Calvin, *Institutes*, 2:16:19.

79
Remedy 2: Don't Destroy! Edify! (14:13-23)

Let me begin with three questions to make sure we're all on the same page.

First, why is Paul concerned about what's happening in the church at Rome? He's concerned that a fight is brewing over "opinions" (14:1). There are two groups: weak and strong. The weak judge the strong while the strong despise the weak. They're on a collision course.

Second, what does Paul mean by opinions? He isn't talking about biblical doctrine or moral behaviour. He's referring to disputes that arise over the application of the OT law. This is timely because it deals with a perennial issue. How are we going to handle differences that arise over matters of conscience to which the Bible doesn't speak directly or definitively?

Third, how does Paul proceed? I want you to notice a few things. Paul acknowledges that one group is right, and one group is wrong (15:1), but he doesn't actually attempt to prove that either of these groups is right or wrong. Paul is focused on something he considers to be more important—how they can worship together without devouring one another. To that end, he gives three remedies. We've considered the first: "Don't judge! Welcome!" Now, we turn our attention to the second: "Don't destroy! Edify!" Paul provides three reasons to obey this command.

It's consistent with what it means to love God's people (14:15-16)
"For if your brother is grieved by what you eat, you are no longer walking in love. By what you eat, do not destroy the one for whom Christ died. So do not let what you regard as good be spoken of as evil." If I do something that I know will grieve my brother, then I'm not really loving God's people (12:9-10). Rather, I'm acting from self-interest, and I'm actually harming the one for whom Christ died. Christ gave up his life to save my brother. Can I not give up some of my opinions for my brother's good? Christ sacrificed everything to save my brother. Can I not sacrifice some of my liberties for my brother's good? Christ surrendered everything to save my brother. Can I not surrender some of my preferences for my brother's good?

It's consistent with what it means to esteem God's kingdom (14:17)

"For the kingdom of God is not a matter of eating and drinking but of righteousness and peace and joy in the Holy Spirit." If I do something that I know will grieve my brother, then I'm not really esteeming God's kingdom. Instead, I'm turning something trivial into something pivotal. Are my freedoms the most important thing in the Christian life? Are my preferences the most important thing in the Christian life? No. The most important thing is righteousness, peace, and joy. Am I willing to tear down God's work in others for the sake of my opinions?

It's consistent with what it means to seek God's acceptance (14:18-19)

"Whoever thus serves Christ is acceptable to God and approved by men. So then let us pursue what makes for peace and for mutual upbuilding." If I do something that I know will grieve my brother, then I'm not really seeking God's acceptance. I'm ignoring what he explicitly identifies as pleasing in his sight. Am I interested in pleasing myself or pleasing God? Is my concern to satisfy my desires or build up the body of Christ? Is my objective to do what I want or help people grow in the grace and knowledge of Christ?

Conclusion

All those who are part of God's kingdom are righteous. Obviously, this means that the unrighteous are excluded.

> Do you not know that the unrighteous will not inherit the kingdom of God? Do not be deceived: neither the sexually immoral, nor idolaters, nor adulterers, nor men who practice homosexuality, nor thieves, nor the greedy, nor drunkards, nor revilers, nor swindlers will inherit the kingdom of God" (1 Cor. 6:9-10).

We're unrighteous by birth. This means that none of us will inherit the kingdom on our own merit. It's crucial that we understand this. If we don't, the gospel doesn't make any sense. The gospel addresses our most fundamental problem. I'm unrighteous. How do I get the righteousness I need to enter the kingdom of God? "O LORD, who shall sojourn in your tent? Who shall dwell on your holy hill? He who walks blamelessly and does what is right and speaks truth in his heart" (Ps. 15:1-2). I must believe in Christ. God takes my unrighteousness and reckons it to Christ. God takes Christ's righteousness and reckons it to me. As a result, I have peace with God.

Remedy 2: Don't Destroy! Edify! (14:13-23)

The sin is on the Saviour laid, 'tis in his blood sins debt is paid;
Stern justice can demand no more, and mercy can dispense her store.
The sinner who believes is free, can say: "The Saviour died for me;"
Can point to the atoning blood, and say: "This made my peace with God."[1]

In Christ, God isn't a terrifying Judge but a loving Father. He isn't a condemning God but a pardoning God. He isn't a threatening God but a welcoming God. God's wrath is removed. Christ has swallowed it all. He has left nothing for us. Our peace with God is such that he loves us as if we had never been the object of his wrath.

Does this gospel shape our approach to our fellow believers? Are we pursuing what makes for peace and edification in the church? For people who don't really grasp the gospel, opinions become insurmountable obstacles because everything is riding on them. The instinct to look down on another Christian over his "opinions" is one of the most obvious signs of a heart from which legalism has not yet been fully banished. It implies that I have merited the grace of God more than my brother has.

But, when we live in the light of the gospel, we pursue what makes for peace and edification in the church.

---

[1] Albert Midlane, "The Perfect Righteousness of God" in *Hymns of Worship and Remembrance*, 332.

80
The Kingdom of God (14:17)

In chapter 14, Paul says that there are two kinds of Christians in the church at Rome. (1) There are "strong" Christians. They understand their relationship as Christians to the ceremonial law. They're aware of the fact that OT laws governing certain foods and days are no longer binding. (2) There are "weak" Christians. They don't understand their relationship as Christians to the ceremonial law. They aren't aware of the fact that OT laws governing certain foods and days are no longer binding.

Because of this difference in understanding, the weak Christians judge the strong Christians: "They must not be very spiritual. If they were, they wouldn't do that." Meanwhile, the strong Christians judge the weak Christians: "They must not be very spiritual. If they were, they would do that." Paul knows that these two groups are on a collision course. And so, he prescribes three remedies. (1) Don't judge! Welcome one another! (2) Don't destroy! Edify one another! (3) Don't ignore! Honour one another!

In the midst of these remedies, Paul provides a wonderful description of the kingdom of God. It's found in 14:17, "For the kingdom of God is not a matter of eating and drinking but of righteousness and peace and joy in the Holy Spirit." What is the kingdom of God? In the Bible, this expression is used in two ways.

At times, it refers to God's "providential" kingdom. He's the King of creation. As David declares, "Yours, O LORD, is the greatness and the power and the glory and the victory and the majesty, for all that is in the heavens and in the earth is yours. Yours is the kingdom, O LORD, and you are exalted as head above all" (1 Chron. 29:11).

At times, it refers to Christ's "spiritual" kingdom. He's the King of the church. One day, he will rule over his people in the new heaven and earth. For now, he rules by his Spirit in the hearts of his people. That's what Paul has in mind in this verse. He says three things about this kingdom.

The kingdom of God is righteousness

All those who are part of God's kingdom are righteous. Obviously, this means that the unrighteous are excluded. Paul declares,

> Or do you not know that the unrighteous will not inherit the kingdom of God? Do not be deceived: neither the sexually immoral, nor idolaters, nor adulterers, nor men who practice homosexuality, nor thieves, nor the greedy, nor drunkards, nor revilers, nor swindlers will inherit the kingdom of God (1 Cor. 6:9-10).

(1) Are you an adulterer? "But I say to you that everyone who looks at a woman with lustful intent has already committed adultery with her in his heart" (Matt. 5:28). (2) Are you a thief? Do you take things that aren't yours? Do you fudge on your income tax? Do you take credit for other people's ideas? Do you misuse your time at work? Do you give God what is rightfully his? (3) Are you a coveter? Are you envious of others? Do you wish you had that person's wealth? Do you wish you had that person's job? Do you wish you had that person's beauty? Do you wish you had that person's notoriety? (4) Are you an idolater? "Put to death therefore what is earthly in you: sexual immorality, impurity, passion, evil desire, and covetousness, which is idolatry" (Col. 3:5). Have you ever experienced an evil desire? Have you ever experienced greed?

We're adulterers, thieves, coveters, and idolaters. We're unrighteous. This poses a serious problem because Paul makes it clear that the unrighteous will not "inherit the kingdom of God" (1 Cor. 6:9-10). This means that none of us will inherit the kingdom on our own merit.

It's crucial we understand this. Why? If we don't, the gospel doesn't make any sense. Ray Comfort gives a very helpful illustration of this. There are two men on a plane. The flight attendant approaches the first man, hands him a parachute, and tells him that the flight will be more enjoyable if he puts it on. He complies. Before long, he finds the parachute uncomfortable. It's hot and bulky. No one else on the plane is wearing a parachute. People are staring and snickering. And so, he takes it off. The flight attendant approaches the second man, hands him a parachute, and tells him to put it on because the plane is going to crash. He complies. The parachute is uncomfortable. It's hot and bulky. No one else on the plane is wearing a parachute. People are staring and snickering. He doesn't care. Nothing is going to take that parachute away from him. Why? He's convinced he needs it.[1]

Do you see the point? We can invite people to come to Christ, telling them that it will make them happy, or it will fill a void in their life, or it will solve all their problems. And they may decide to try Christ. But, sooner or later, the trials of this life will drive them away or the pleasures of this world will lure them away. Why? They aren't convinced they need the gospel. Why? Because they aren't aware of their sin.

The true gospel addresses man's fundamental problem—his sin. Until people feel their sin, the gospel is irrelevant to them. I'm unrighteous. How do I get the righteousness I need to enter the kingdom of God? I must believe in Christ. God takes my unrighteousness and reckons it to Christ. God takes Christ's righteousness and reckons it to me. That's the doctrine of justification.

The kingdom of God is peace
All those who are part of God's kingdom enjoy peace. This is the result of Christ's righteousness. "Therefore, since we have been justified by faith, we have peace with God" (Rom. 5:1). You may recall that the term *peace* means binding together what has been separated. Because of our sin, we were separated from God. But Christ made "peace by the blood of his cross" (Col. 1:20). Now, we're bound together with God.

> The perfect righteousness of God is witnessed in the Saviour's blood;
> 'Tis in the cross of Christ we trace his righteousness, yet wondrous grace.
> God could not pass the sinner by, his sin demands that he must die;
> But in the cross of Christ we see how God can save us righteously.
> The sin is on the Saviour laid, 'tis in his blood sins debt is paid;
> Stern justice can demand no more, and mercy can dispense her store.
> The sinner who believes is free, can say: "The Saviour died for me;"
> Can point to the atoning blood, and say: "This made my peace with God."[2]

What a wonderful truth! At one time, we were God's enemies. We were children of wrath. We were at war with God. But now we have peace with God.

---

[1] Ray Comfort, *God Has A Wonderful Plan for Your Life: The Myth of the Modern Message* (Bellflower: Living Waters Publications, 2010), 69–71.

[2] Albert Midlane, "The Perfect Righteousness of God" in *Hymns of Worship and Remembrance*, 332.

The kingdom of God is joy

All those who are part of God's kingdom experience joy in the Holy Spirit. This is the result of peace. I've been saved from God's wrath. I've been spared an eternity in hell. I've been redeemed from slavery to sin. I've been forgiven. I've been justified—clothed in Christ's righteousness. I've been adopted into God's family. I've been sealed with the Holy Spirit of promise. I've been granted eternal life. That's the cause of my joy. This joy can't be quenched by opposition or affliction. This joy transcends my circumstances.

> Several years ago, while preaching in the United States, I stayed in the home of a very successful young couple who were surrounded with the trappings of success and growing wealthier by the day. They were enthusiastic members of a church which majored in an effervescent approach to all its activities and my hosts seemed to be on a permanent "high." As the husband started the car before leaving for church one night there was a startled squeal from under the bonnet. When he opened it up, their pet cat was sitting there, looking decidedly frightened and minus several patches of fur. Instantly, my hosts were in a frenzied panic. All their confidence and cheerfulness vanished. Frankly, they were in worse shape than the cat! It took several hours before they recovered and the whole incident was a bizarre illustration of how flimsy and fragile happiness is when divorced from true blessedness and of the truth of Thomas Watson's assertion that "Blessedness does not lie in externals."[3]

Christian joy isn't related to life's circumstances. It's rooted in peace with God.

Conclusion

Joy is the restoration of our relationship with God. And it only comes by way of the cross. "Therefore, since we have been justified by faith, we have peace with God through our Lord Jesus Christ ... and we exult in hope of the glory of God" (Rom. 5:1-2). In Christ, divine communion is restored. And we enjoy true peace of mind—joy.

---

[3] John Blanchard, *The Beatitudes for Today* (Epsom: Day One Publications, 1999), 56.

81
Remedy 3: Don't Ignore! Honour! (15:1-12)

In one of his hymns, William Cowper, writes:

Seeing the law by Christ fulfilled and hearing his pardoning voice,
Changes a slave into a child and duty into choice.[1]

I want to take just a few moments to ponder Cowper's statement.

What do we see? We see "the law by Christ fulfilled." God has a law. It requires us to love him with all our heart, soul, mind, and strength, at all times in all places, under all conditions. We don't. We've broken God's law. Therefore, we're under its curse (penalty)—eternal death. Mercifully, that isn't the end of the story. We see Christ fulfilling what the law requires by obeying its commands (in his life) and paying its penalty (in his death). He does both of these things on behalf of his people.

What do we hear? We hear "His pardoning voice." God is willing to forgive us on the basis of Christ's fulfillment of the law. He has obeyed its commands, and he has paid its penalty. Therefore, God is prepared to change the verdict from condemned to justified, and he's prepared to change the sentence from eternal death to eternal life. Forgiveness doesn't mean God acts like nothing happened, nor does it mean that he lessens the consequences of our sins. It means that he dissolves the obligation to punishment on the basis of Christ's work.

What's the result? It's twofold. (1) It changes "a slave into a child." In other words, it changes our legal standing before God. We move from a position of alienation to reconciliation, from estranged to welcomed, from wrath to mercy. In sum, we draw near to God. (2) It changes "duty into choice." God's law becomes to us what it always was—the will of a good God. In Christ, God's commands aren't conditions to be fulfilled but implications to be enjoyed.

Seeing the law by Christ fulfilled and hearing his pardoning voice,

---
[1] https://hymnary.org/text/no_strength_of_nature_can_suffice.

Changes a slave into a child and duty into choice.

In many ways, that's what we have seen in Paul's epistle to the Romans. In chapters 1-11, we see "the law by Christ fulfilled and hear his pardoning voice." This changes us from slaves to children. In chapters 12-15, we see that in Christ "duty becomes a choice." In 14:1-15:4, Paul explains in detail what this duty looks like when it comes to disagreements among believers arising from "opinions." Remedy #1: Don't judge! Welcome! (14:1-12). Remedy #2: Don't destroy! Edify! (14:13-23). Remedy #3: Don't ignore! Honour! (15:1-12). We've considered the first two. In this study, we arrive at the third.

An obligation to fulfill (15:1-2)
"We who are strong have an obligation to bear with the failings of the weak, and not to please ourselves. Let each of us please his neighbor for his good, to build him up." We have an "obligation." Because of God's love for us, we have an obligation to love each other. Because of God's love for us, we have an obligation to please each other. Paul isn't suggesting we're supposed to be people-pleasers. We're to please people as long as it's for their good. Anything that will build them up is for their good.

We see the importance of this obligation to the present discussion. Believers in the church at Rome disagree over "opinions"—specifically, what they eat and drink. Strong believers need to remember that they're under "obligation" to love weak believers. They need to apply this command: "Let each of us please his neighbor for his good, to build him up." This is an extremely important principle when it comes to handling differences that arise over matters of conscience to which the Bible doesn't speak directly or definitively.

We see the importance of this obligation when it comes to life decisions. Where should I live? Where should I work? How should I use my finances? How should I use my home? How should I use my time? When facing these (and other) life decisions, we need to apply this command: "Let each of us please his neighbor for his good, to build him up." When making these decisions, we're usually driven by the wrong question: What do I want? But the Christian life isn't about what we want. It isn't about our rights, comforts, dreams, interests, or goals. The Christian life is about determining how we can please others for their good, to build them up, even if it means denying self.

We see the importance of this obligation in the context of the church. How do I determine the extent of my involvement, the measure of my service, the

Remedy 3: Don't Ignore! Honour! (15:1-12)

depth of my commitment? Do I serve, or don't I serve? Do I attend, or don't I attend? How do I make decisions, view differences, and resolve problems? I need to apply this command: "Let each of us please his neighbor for his good, to build him up."

We see the importance of this obligation in the context of the home. How do I view my spouse? How do I view my children? How do I decide what to do with my time? How do I make decisions? We need to apply this command: "Let each of us please his neighbor for his good, to build him up."

That's tough. As a matter of fact, it's near impossible. Who can live like that? I don't live like that. I need help. And that brings us to the second point.

An example to follow (15:3-5)

"For Christ did not please himself." To prove it, Paul quotes Psalm 69:9, "The reproaches of those who reproached you fell on me." This psalm depicts a righteous man who endures undeserved suffering. The NT quotes it seven times, and always applies it to Christ. He was willing to endure underserved suffering. He was willing to deny himself for the good of others.

Christ exchanged wealth for poverty. He exchanged majesty for humility. He exchanged a throne for a manger. He exchanged a crown of glory for a crown of thorns.

> He stood upon even ground with God, he was co-equal and co-essential and co-substantial with his Father, yet for all that he took on flesh. He stripped himself of the robes of his glory, and covered himself with the rags of our humanity. He who was numbered among the persons of the Trinity is numbered among transgressors (Isa. 53:12).[2]

Christ did not "please himself." Rather, he gave himself for sinners—for our "good." We're to imitate his selflessness.

"For whatever was written in former days was written for our instruction, that through endurance and through the encouragement of the Scriptures we might have hope" (15:4). This verse almost seems like a footnote, but it's much more than that. Paul stresses our obligation in 15:1-2. He gives us the motivation to obey in 15:3. And now, he gives us the means to obey in 15:4. I'm going to give you five statements to help you grasp his point. (1) We hear, read, and study the Bible: its commands and promises. (2) When we obey the

---
[2] Thomas Watson, *A Body of Divinity* (1890; repr., London: Banner of Truth, 1958), 137.

Bible's commands, we experience endurance. (3) When we believe the Bible's promises, we experience encouragement. (4) Endurance and encouragement lead to hope. (5) Hope kindles love. (6) Love compels us to fulfill our obligation to please our neighbours for their good, to build them up.

We can't do this in our own strength. And so, Paul prays, "May the God of endurance and encouragement grant you to live in such harmony with one another, in accord with Christ Jesus, that together you may with one voice glorify the God and Father of our Lord Jesus Christ" (15:5). For Paul, everything is a means to this end: God's glory. The question the world should ask, as it looks at a local church, is this: "How do these people get along?" The result of a Christ-like attitude in humility is unity and harmony in worship, to the glory of God.

An appeal to obey (15:7-12)
"Therefore welcome one another as Christ has welcomed you, for the glory of God" (15:7). Christ served the Jews by coming to fulfill the promises given to the patriarchs (15:8). In so doing, he brought salvation to the Gentiles (15:9). Paul proves it by making three points. (1) The Gentiles praise God (15:9-11). (2) This praise is rooted in OT prophecy: 15:9 (Ps. 18:49), 15:10 (Deut. 32:43), and 15:11 (Ps. 117:1). (3) This praise is possible because of Christ: 15:12 (Isa. 11:10).

In many ways, this brings us to the pinnacle of Paul's argument in this epistle. Since chapter 1, he has been laying the foundation for this moment. Jews and Gentiles share the same condemnation (3:9), the same judgment (2:9-10), the same gospel (1:16-17), the same regeneration (2:28-29), the same justification (3:29-30), the same father (4:11-12), the same promise (9:6-8), the same calling (9:22-24), the same tree (11:17), and the same mercy (11:32). What's the conclusion? "God shows no partiality" (2:11). Therefore, we're to welcome one another as Christ has welcomed us (15:7).

Conclusion
This is one of the most precious truths in all of Scripture: "Christ has welcomed you, for the glory of God" (15:7). Despite our sin, he accepted us. Despite our rebellion, he accepted us. Despite our animosity, he accepted us. Sin has marred us beyond recognition. It has brought us under God's condemnation. Mercifully, Christ came to bear our sin and shame. He was humiliated, that we might be exalted; condemned, that we might be justified; rejected, so

that we might be accepted. While on the cross, he satisfied God's offended justice. When we receive him through faith, his forgiveness supersedes our sinfulness; his merit eclipses our guilt; and his righteousness hides our vileness. His mercies wipe away our sins.

Centuries ago, many Scottish pulpits had a small brass plate fastened to the top, with these words engraved: "Sir, we would see Jesus." It was a reminder to the preacher to stay on topic—to remember why he was in the pulpit; namely, to point people to Christ. When we gaze upon Christ, the One who loved us and gave himself for us, we're crushed to the ground. We're humbled. Only then are we ready to "welcome one another as Christ has welcomed [us]" (15:7).

82
Abounding in Hope (15:13)

I've been engaged in pastoral ministry since 1995. During that time, I've seen a few things and I've noticed a few trends. One of the most troubling is the increased prevalence (among God's people) of despair—the utter loss of hope.

All of us have experienced discouragement because of issues related to work, marriage, children, finances, health. For most, it dissipates over time. For some, it doesn't dissipate. It deepens. It takes root, assumes control, clouds vision, impairs function. It morphs into despair, and manifests itself in apathy, anxiety, insomnia, hypersomnia, irritability, emotional instability, cognitive impairment, and (in some cases) self-harm and suicide.

The psychiatrist approaches despair through a biological lens. He might diagnose the individual's despair as arising from clinical depression or bipolar disorder. He then offers a pharmaceutical remedy. Indeed, medication might very well prevent the individual from falling deeper into despair. That's a good and necessary thing. But the psychiatrist can't offer any lasting remedy.

The psychologist approaches despair through an existential lens. He might diagnose the individual's despair as arising from past or present trauma, or from repressed anger, sorrow, passion, creativity, or sexuality. He then offers a therapeutic remedy. He encourages the individual to find some meaning in the pain, the misery, and the suffering. He encourages the individual to harness the power of his repressed true self, while recommending a vast array of coping mechanisms for day-to-day problems. But the psychologist can't offer any lasting remedy.

I'm not saying that despair is never associated with a biochemical or physiological crisis, but that (despite whatever else might be going on) it's almost always a spiritual crisis. Despair is the utter loss of hope. The only remedy for an utter loss of hope is to abound in hope—the life-changing certainty that someday we'll have all that God has promised.

Hope is fueled by the conviction that God is able to do what he has promised (4:18-21)

God gives Abraham a promise. (1) Abraham believes *against hope* (4:19). He considers two undeniable facts: "his own body, which is as good as dead"; and "the barrenness of Sarah's womb." He knows they're well beyond childbearing age. (2) Abraham believes *in hope* (4:20-21). He considers his God. He deduces certain unalterable truths. He's God Most High, the Possessor of heaven and earth. Therefore, there's nothing that will prevent God from keeping his promise.

What do we learn from Abraham? We need to *reflect* on God rather than *react* to circumstances. What are the three most common affirmations concerning God in the Bible? He is good. He is able. He is faithful.

The little girl stands at the pool's edge. She's wearing her goggles, water wings, and other floaty devices. Her father is already in the water with his arms outstretched, urging her to jump. "I'll catch you." Will she jump? It depends on her answers to three questions. (1) Is he *good*? Does he have my best interest in view? (2) Is he *strong*? Does he possess the necessary upper body strength to catch me? (3) Is he *faithful*? Does he keep his word? If the little girl is confident of her answers to these three questions, she trusts her father and she will jump into his arms. If, however, she has any doubts concerning her father's goodness, strength, or faithfulness, she won't jump.

God is good, able, and faithful. He's able to do what he has promised. He upholds "all things by the word of his power" (Heb. 1:3). He rules the universe fully and completely, from the smallest particles dancing in the beam of sunlight to the greatest stars burning in the distant galaxies above. Our God isn't merely mighty, but almighty. Our God has never encountered difficulty—let alone impossibility. "None can stay his hand or say unto him, 'What have you done?'" (Dan. 4:35).

Hope is rooted in the assurance that we have peace with God through Jesus Christ (5:1-10)

We have "peace with God" (5:1). This isn't an emotion, but a condition. At one time, we were the objects of his wrath. But now, we're the recipients of his grace. This peace is attained through Christ (5:1, 2, 9, 10, 11). Because of Christ, we no longer have any reason to fear the sting of death, terror of judgment, torment of hell, or wrath of God. Christ has swallowed it all. Our peace with God is such that he loves us as if we had never been the object of his wrath.

As a result, "we rejoice in hope of the glory of God" (5:2).

> So dear, so very dear to God, more dear I cannot be;
> The love where with he loves the Son: Such is his love to me!
> Why should I ever fretful be, since such as God is mine?
> He watches o'er me night and day, and tells me Mine is thine.[1]

This is difficult to take to heart. Why? We tend to measure God's love by our circumstances. Did God love Joseph? He spent years in jail. Did God love Naomi? She buried a husband and two sons. Did God love Jonathan? He died on a lonely hill at the edge of a Philistine sword. Did God love David? He spent years fleeing from Saul. Did God love Paul? He suffered shipwrecks, imprisonments, and beatings.

Here's what we must grasp. There's something far worse than losing our job, health, money, reputation, friends, spouse, or even our life. What's worse than losing these things? Losing God "at whose right hand are pleasures forevermore" (Ps. 16:11). What's the great promise in Scripture? The sum and substance of all the promises? "I will be their God, and they shall be my people" (Jer. 31:33). This promise is heaven—the very heaven of heavens. God alone is blessedness, and this is what Christ has purchased for us. "For Christ also suffered once for sins, the righteous for the unrighteous, that he might bring us to God" (1 Peter 3:18). When we come to him through Christ, he becomes ours. His power is ours to protect us; his wisdom is ours to direct us; his mercy is ours to pity us; his grace is ours to pardon us; his love is ours to refresh us; his joy is ours to satisfy us. On top of all this, he's "our God forever and ever" (Ps. 48:14). He isn't our God for a day, week, month, or year, but "forever and ever." He isn't our God for a thousand years, but "forever and ever." He isn't our God for a million years, but "forever and ever." Truly we can say, "Blessed are the people whose God is the LORD" (Ps. 144:15).

Hope is fixed on the glory that will be revealed to us (8:18-25)

"The sufferings of this present time are not worth comparing to the glory that is to be revealed" (8:18). Someday we'll have all that God has promised: a glorified soul without sin; a glorified body with decay; a renewed earth. Far eclipsing these, we'll see God in the face of Christ. Augustine says that experiencing the presence of God will be like a torrent of pleasure. All the pleasant

---

[1] Horatius Bonar, "A Mind at Perfect Peace" in *Choice Hymns of the Faith*, 258.

memories and experiences in this life are signposts of what's coming.

C.S. Lewis ends the Chronicles of Narnia as follows:

> And for us this is the end of all the stories, and we can most truly say that they all lived happily ever after. But for them it was only the beginning of the real story. All their life in this world and all their adventures in Narnia had only been the cover page: now at last they were beginning Chapter One of the Great Story, which no one on earth has read: which goes on forever: in which every chapter is better than the one before.[2]

Do we understand that this life is but a prologue? Investments can evaporate, houses can crumble, jobs can disappear, relationships can sour, and health can fail. Hope doesn't run from these realities—no matter how unpleasant. It faces reality, while remaining fixed on what will be. As the anchor steadies the ship in the midst of the storm, so hope keeps us steady in the storms of life. We can hope when the pain is chronic, the illness is incurable, and the cancer is inoperable; when the persecution is unavoidable; when the relationship has turned poisonous; when the days are oppressively grey, and sadness has set in like a thick fog, hiding all from view; when the horror of sin overwhelms like a tsunami; when the foundations of society begin to crumble, and we fear for what the future might hold; when we begin to feel our own mortality with the passing of the years.

Hope is fixed on the return of Christ, resurrection from the dead, full and final deliverance from sin, renovation of the entire cosmos, and prospect of eternal joy. Hope makes this future certainty a present reality. It penetrates the shadows. It's immune to every illness, every threat, every grief, every worry, every challenge, and every loss.

Hope is cultivated through the encouragement of the Scriptures (15:4)
"For whatever was written in former days was written for our instruction, that through endurance and through the encouragement of the Scriptures we might have hope." How do the Scriptures cultivate hope?

Its commands provide encouragement: "If anyone would come after me, let him deny himself and take up his cross and follow me" (Matt. 16:24). We know that the cross is the way to the crown.

Its doctrines provide encouragement: "God works all things according to

---

[2] C.S. Lewis, *The Last Battle* (New York: HaperCollins, 2000), 210.

the counsel of his will" (Eph. 1:11). We know that God's providence extends to all things, in all places, at all times. We aren't the victims of random events.

Its examples provide encouragement: "Behold, we consider those blessed who remained steadfast. You have heard of the steadfastness of Job, and you have seen the purpose of the Lord, how the Lord is compassionate and merciful" (Jas. 5:11-12). We know that God has watched over his people since the beginning of time.

Its principles provide encouragement: "Oh, the depth of the riches and wisdom and knowledge of God! How unsearchable are his judgments and how inscrutable his ways!" (Rom. 11:33). We know that his ways aren't our ways. We judge our circumstances by our finite understanding, while he judges all things by one infinite act of understanding.

Its promises provide encouragement: "And we know that for those who love God all things work together for good, for those who are called according to his purpose" (Rom. 8:28).

A word of counsel: we must be clear as to what God has promised. Confusion reigns in this regard, and it feeds despair. God hasn't promised us immunity from debilitating illness, or immunity from civil strife, or immunity from personal loss, or immunity from death. He hasn't promised us a perfect family, perfect career, or perfect life. He hasn't promised us a life free of disorder, discomfort, danger, or discouragement. I've met numerous disappointed and disillusioned Christians struggling with despair because they're convinced God has let them down. God has promised to remember our sins no more. He has promised to work all things together for our spiritual good. He has promised to never forsake us. He has promised to preserve us from ultimate evil. He has promised to bestow a wonderful inheritance upon us.

When difficulties arise, our emotions often take over, exasperating the problem. Years ago, I was flying in the front seat of a Caravan over the country of Angola. As we passed through dense cloud and lost all visibility, I turned to the pilot, and somewhat sheepishly asked, "What now?" His response: "What do you mean, 'What now'? I keep doing what I always do. I trust this plane's guidance systems." The temptation for any pilot in the midst of thick cloud is to fall back on his senses. If he does, it will always get him into trouble. When in the cloud (i.e., difficult times in life), far too many of us decide to navigate by our feelings. The result is always disastrous. We must trust God's guidance system: his precepts and promises. Faith is fixed on objective historical facts and objective biblical promises—not subjective emotional feelings.

As Martin Luther expressed it:

> Feelings come and feelings go, and feelings are deceiving;
> My warrant is the Word of God, naught else is worth believing.[3]

Hope abounds by the power of the Holy Spirit (15:13)
"May the God of hope fill you with all joy and peace in believing, so that by the power of the Holy Spirit you may abound in hope." As we take hold of the gospel, we're filled with joy and peace, and the Holy Spirit causes us to abound in hope. In other words, he makes God's truth come alive to us.

In *The Pilgrim's Progress*, Christian and Hopeful (a fellow pilgrim) notice a pleasant meadow that appears to run parallel to the path they're traveling. Thinking it will ease their difficult journey, they decide to climb over the wall to walk in the meadow. Initially, all's well, but soon the storm gathers, the sky darkens, and the rain descends. By morning, they're completely lost and no longer in a position to find the path. To make matters worse, they stumble upon Giant Despair, who captures them, beats them, and imprisons them in Doubting Castle, where all hope is lost. After languishing for days, they decide to spend the night in prayer. As day breaks, Christian cries, "What a fool am I, thus to lie in a stinking dungeon, when I may as well walk at liberty? I have a key in my bosom, called *Promise*, that I am persuaded will open any lock in *Doubting Castle*."[4] Within moments, Christian and Hopeful are unlocking chains and doors. Free of Giant Despair and Doubting Castle, they scramble back to the narrow way.

Few things are more important for the Christian life than hope. We must "hold fast to the hope set before us" (Heb. 6:18). It's "a sure and steadfast anchor of the soul" (Heb. 6:19).

> Will your anchor hold in the storms of life,
> when the clouds unfold their wings of strife?
> When the strong tides lift, and the cables strain,
> will your anchor drift or firm remain?
> We have an anchor that keeps the soul,
> steadfast and sure while the billows roll,
> Fastened to the Rock which cannot move,

---

[3] https://hymnary.org/text/for_feelings_come_and_feelings_go.
[4] Bunyan, *Pilgrim's Progress*, 134.

grounded firm and deep in the Saviour's love.[5]

---

[5] https://hymnary.org/text/will_your_anchor_hold_in_the_storms_of_l.

Conclusion (15:14–16:27)

83
A Healthy Christian (15:14-16)

In 1:17, Paul introduces his main theme: "The righteous shall live by faith." In the rest of the epistle, he explains what he means by that. We've followed his explanation through five major sections: *Condemnation* (1:18-3:20); *Justification* (3:21-5:21); *Sanctification* (6:1-8:39); *Election* (9:1-11:36); and *Application* (12:1-15:13). In 15:14-16:27, Paul draws his epistle to a close. As he does, he touches on three subjects: (1) his ministry (15:14-21); (2) his plans (15:22-33); and (3) his greetings (16:1-24).

At the outset of his concluding remarks, Paul inserts a word of clarification. He says he has written "very boldly" on some points (15:15). So what? Why does he feel the need to say this? He knows some of the members of the church at Rome might be tempted to ask: "Who does Paul think he is? He didn't start this church. He doesn't belong to this church. He doesn't hold any leadership position in this church. He has never even visited this church. How dare he write so boldly to us?"

And so, Paul takes a moment to clear up any potential misunderstanding. How? He does two things.

Paul points to their maturity (15:14)
"I myself am satisfied about you, my brothers, that you yourselves are full of goodness, filled with all knowledge and able to instruct one another." Paul says he's satisfied (persuaded or convinced) about them. What specifically?

They're "full of goodness"
In effect, Paul is saying: "I've given you dozens and dozens of commandments. I've told you to offer yourselves to God as living sacrifices. I've told you to be transformed by the renewal of your minds. And I've told you in very specific terms what this will look like. My zeal in exhorting you might give you the erroneous impression that I think you're a bunch of backsliders who need constant correcting and admonishing. Let me clarify. I know you're full of goodness. Goodness is part of the fruit of the Spirit (Gal. 5:22). And I see it in your desire to please God above all else."

They're "filled with all knowledge"
In effect, Paul is saying: "I've sent you an exhaustive treatise on what it means for the righteous to live by faith. I've explained the doctrine of justification in relation to sanctification and election. I've demonstrated that the gospel is rooted in the OT Scriptures. I've tackled some really thorny issues. I've attempted to unravel some complex theological issues. I've added a long list of exhortations. This might give you the erroneous impression that I think you're completely clueless. Let me clarify. I know you're filled with all knowledge. I know you understand the Christian faith, and I know you live the Christian faith."

They're able "to instruct one another"
In effect, Paul is saying: "I've written a long letter, including a detailed explanation and application of the gospel. At several places, I've entered into your personal lives. I've dedicated a significant amount of space to telling you how to get along with each other. This might give you the erroneous impression that I think you're incompetent—incapable of ministering to one another. Let me clarify. I don't think you're deficient in this area. I know you care for one another. I know you watch over one another. I know you're able to instruct one another."

In sum, Paul has written "very boldly" on some points. But he doesn't want them to misinterpret his boldness. Hence, he explains that he's satisfied about them—namely, their maturity.

Paul points to his ministry (15:15-16)
Paul says he's "a minister of Christ Jesus to the Gentiles" (15:16). Looking around that statement, we learn three things about his ministry.

He ministers "because of the grace given him by God" (15:15)
What does Paul mean by this? Christ appoints the apostles as an extension of his ministry. Therefore, they minister under his authority. Paul reminds his readers of this fact. "I've been 'very bold' on some points, but I'm simply fulfilling my calling as an apostle of Christ."

He ministers "in the priestly service of the gospel of God" (15:16)
What does Paul mean by this? He offers himself as a living sacrifice to God (12:1). This includes his ministry. He preaches the gospel as an act of worship.

He writes to them as an act of worship. "I've been 'very bold' on some points, but I'm simply ministering as an offering to God."

He ministers "so that the offering of the Gentiles may be acceptable" (15:16)
What does Paul mean by this? He probably has Isaiah 66:20 in mind: "And they shall bring all your brothers from all the nations as an offering to the LORD ... to my holy mountain Jerusalem." Paul wants to contribute to that end. "I've been 'very bold' on some points, but I'm simply attempting to present you as an acceptable offering to God."

In sum, Paul has written "very boldly" on some points. But he doesn't want them to misinterpret his boldness. Hence, he reminds them that he's simply fulfilling his ministry.

Conclusion
From all that I want to suggest five marks of a healthy Christian.

A healthy Christian encourages others (15:14)
What happens when we encourage people? Encouragement stimulates the desire to grow. Encouragement stifles criticism and condemnation. Encouragement testifies to God's work. Encouragement magnifies the grace of God. Tim Challies writes,

> One day it occurred to me that I was going to have to discipline myself to encourage others. And so I took the strange and seemingly artificial step of scheduling time to do it. It sounds strange, I know, but I opened up my calendar and created a five-minute appointment recurring every three days. The appointment simply said "Encourage!" And so, every third day, while I was hard at work, a little reminder would flash up on my screen: "Encourage!" And I would take the opportunity to phone a friend or send an email to someone. This felt very artificial. But as time went on, it became quite natural. And I soon found that I no longer felt the same spirit of discouragement within me.[1]

A healthy Christian applies God's truth (15:14)
That's what we find in Paul's threefold description of this church. They're full of goodness. They're filled with all knowledge. They're able to instruct

---

[1] Tim Challies, "Holiness of Character," Challies, December 26, 2007. https://www.challies.com/articles/holiness-of-character/

one another. These are people who live out the contents of 12:1-15:13. These are people whose lives are shaped and molded by the mercies of God.

A healthy Christian knows how to speak boldly (15:15)
At times, we need to speak boldly. Our struggle is in knowing *how* to speak boldly. Here are four principles taken from Paul's example in this letter: (1) Make sure the reason is significant, not trivial; (2) Make sure the goal is edification, not demolition; (3) Make sure the tone is humble, not proud; (4) Make sure the context is thanksgiving, not griping.

We should be able to admonish one another. James Boice asks,

> Do we love the Lord enough to talk about him naturally and often? Do we love others enough to bring spiritual truths into daily conversation? Do we care for Christians enough to point them in the right direction when we see that they are deviating from or falling short of it?[2]

A healthy Christian views ministry as an offering to God (15:16)
Why do I preach? Why do I teach Sunday school? Why do I serve as a Care Group leader? Why do I participate in a mission trip? Why do I help at the kids' camp? Etc. We serve as an offering to our God. That realization keeps us from discouragement. It protects us against criticism or whatever else might dampen our ministry.

A healthy Christian keeps the gospel at the centre of everything (15:16)
For Paul, this entire epistle is the gospel. But what's the starting point? What must I grasp whereby everything else falls into place? "Blessed is the one whose transgression is forgiven; whose sin is covered. Blessed is the man against whom the LORD counts no iniquity" (Ps. 32:1-2; Rom. 4:7-8). Happiness is found in a relationship with the living God grounded in forgiveness. The only way we'll ever know true happiness it to be welcomed by God. The only way we'll ever be welcomed by God is when we say to him: "Lord, don't look at me. Look at your Son who stands at your right hand, because I have put all of my trust in him."

---

[2] Boice, *Romans*, 1851.

84
Holy Ambition (15:17-21)

In 15:14, Paul begins his rather lengthy conclusion by offering a word of clarification. He says he has written "very boldly" on some points. And so? Well, the members of the church at Rome might be tempted to ask: "Who does Paul think he is? He didn't start this church. He doesn't belong to this church. How dare he speak like that to us?" And so, Paul takes a moment to clear up any potential misunderstanding. How? First, he points to their maturity (15:14). Second, he points to his ministry (15:15-16).

In 15:17-21, Paul continues to talk about his ministry, mentioning two details.

Paul talks about his success (15:17-19)
"In Christ Jesus, then, I have reason to be proud of my work for God" (15:17). Paul attributes the success of his ministry to Christ. How does Christ work through Paul?

First, Christ works "by word and deed" (15:18). Paul preaches the Word. His starting point isn't reason or experience. He isn't interested in thinking or feeling his way to God. He believes God has spoken. He believes the Bible is divine revelation, not human speculation. And so, he preaches God's Word. Paul also lives the Word. He knows his doctrine is only as compelling as his conduct. His teaching is only as compelling as his behaviour.

Second, Christ works "by the power of signs and wonder" (15:19). What does this mean? Elsewhere, Paul writes, "The signs of a true apostle were performed among you with utmost patience, with signs and wonders and mighty works" (2 Cor. 12:2). He blinded the magician (Acts 13), healed the cripple (Acts 14), and expelled the demon (Acts 16). We read that God performed "extraordinary miracles by the hands of Paul, so that even handkerchiefs or aprons that had touched his skin were carried away to the sick, and their diseases left them and the evil spirits came out of them" (Acts 19:11-12). All of this served to confirm his apostolic authority.

Third, Christ works "by the power of the Spirit of God" (15:19). Paul reminds the Thessalonian believers: "Our gospel came to you not only in word, but also in power and in the Holy Spirit and with full conviction" (1:5). That is to say, the Spirit of God made the Word of God come alive to them.

Paul's point is that Christ is the only reason why his ministry has been successful. He has preached the gospel from Jerusalem to Illyricum (the Balkans). Does he mean that he has preached the gospel to every single individual in that geographical region? No. Does he mean that he has established local churches in every single town in that geographical region? No. His point is that there is now a gospel witness throughout the region.

Paul's success leads naturally to the second thing he says about his ministry.

Paul talks about his strategy (15:20-21)
"And thus I make it my ambition to preach the gospel, not where Christ has already been named, lest I build on someone else's foundation, but as it is written, 'Those who have never been told of him will see, and those who have never heard will understand.'" God didn't call Paul to build on another man's foundation. He called him to lay the foundation. He called him to proclaim Christ where he has not yet been named. For this reason, Paul plans to leave his present sphere of service. He wants to preach the gospel to those who've never heard.

This is why Paul is making plans. For years, he has used Antioch as his base of operation. From there, he has launched three missionary journeys, taking him through Turkey and Greece. He's done in that region. Now, he's planning to visit Rome, so that he can make it his new base of operation as he looks to the western part of the empire—Spain.

Conclusion
What are we to make of Paul's holy ambition? We need to be careful. We don't share Paul's apostleship, Paul's calling, or Paul's gifts. It would be wrong for us to think as follows: "Paul preached the gospel across Europe. So, I should preach the gospel across Europe." We aren't Paul. So how are we to imitate his holy ambition? I have four suggestions.

We should make it our ambition to boast in Christ (15:17)
Whatever our ministry, we must acknowledge our complete dependence on Christ. Paul writes, "I worked harder than any of them [i.e., the other apostles], though it was not I, but the grace of God that is within me" (1 Cor.

15:10). There's an interesting story in John 21. The disciples spend the whole night fishing without catching anything. At dawn, Christ appears and says to them: "Cast the net on the right-hand side of the boat and you will find a catch." They're unable to haul in their nets because of the number of fish. What was the difference between their first and second attempts at fishing? They were the same nets. They were the same fishermen. They were the same boats. It was the same lake. The difference was Christ.

We should make it our ambition to bring people to obedience (15:18)
What's the great commission (Matt. 28:19-20)? "To make disciples." "To baptize." "To teach them to observe all that I have commanded you." We haven't truly evangelized people until they've become obedient. This is an amazing thing—to watch people grow in obedience, to watch them become more like Christ, to watch them persevere through trials, to watch them abound in hope, to watch them pursue purity, to watch them honour God in their callings. Whatever the nature of our ministry, I trust our ambition is to bring people to obedience. This is what it means to present an acceptable offering to God.

We should make it our ambition to serve in the power of the Holy Spirit (15:19)
The longer I engage in ministry, the more I realize our need for miracles. The longer I preach, the more I realize my need for miracles. What do I mean by that? How else are we going to see the conversion of the wayward child, the restoration of the broken marriage, the healing of the festering wound, the comforting of the troubled soul, the sustaining of the ill and dying, the humbling of the hard-hearted, the breaking of addiction, etc. We're engaged in a supernatural work. I pray we understand it's futile without miracles. We accomplish nothing apart from the power of the Holy Spirit working through our feeble efforts.

We should make it our ambition to preach Christ to the unreached (15:20)
We aren't all called to take the gospel to those who've never heard. God has called us to something and equipped us accordingly. We should accept it, celebrate it, and fulfill our calling faithfully. That said, we can't very well claim to be a "loving" people if we aren't in some way involved in taking the gospel to those who've never heard.

According to the statistics, approximately 27% of the world's population still doesn't have access to an indigenous evangelical church. That means there are roughly 1.5 billion people without a clear gospel witness. What about the rest of the world? What about our own country? "How long will you love delusions (vain words) and seek after lies?" (Ps. 4:2). All around us, people are chasing delusions. Does this move us?

> Years I spent in vanity and pride,
> Caring not my Lord was crucified
> Mercy there was great, and grace was free;
> Pardon there was multiplied to me;
> There my burdened soul found liberty, At Calvary.[1]

Do we give? Do we pray? Do we weep? We need to re-capture something of the spirit of the apostle Paul in 15:20. He was preoccupied with God's ambition for the spread of his glory.

---

[1] William Newell, "At Calvary" in *Celebrating Grace Hymnal*, 589.

85
Fullness of Blessing (15:22-33)

I assume all of us have places that hold special significance for us. It might be a home, yard, porch, café, park, church, beach, or even a cemetery. The place might be significant because of the amount of time we spent there. It might be significant because of a momentous event that occurred there—a vacation, birth, engagement, etc. It might be significant because of a person we associate with it. Whatever the reason, it stands out in our minds. I have to believe that, for the apostle Paul, one such place was located somewhere on the road between Jerusalem and Damascus. Prior to arriving at this particular place, he had been struggling for some time with the ugliness of his sin. Much of his struggle stemmed from the tenth commandment: "You shall not covet" (7:7). For years, Paul had attached his happiness to something other than God. Power? Prestige? By his own account, he had become a "violent aggressor"—a person who deliberately mistreats others for the purpose of hurting and humiliating them (1 Tim. 1:13). He was an absolute mess. And yet, at some point on the road between Jerusalem and Damascus, Christ visited him, called him, saved him, and transformed him. Years later, reflecting on the incident, he writes, "The grace of our Lord overflowed for me" (1 Tim. 1:14). What did this overflowing grace look like in Paul's life?

In 15:22-33, we catch a glimpse. Paul tells us that his ministry in the eastern empire is complete. He has proclaimed the gospel and established churches from Jerusalem to Illyricum. Now, he's making plans.

Paul plans to visit Jerusalem, so that he can assist the poor (15:25-27)
During his missionary travels, Paul has been collecting an offering from other churches to assist the poor in the church at Jerusalem (1 Cor. 16:1-4; 2 Cor. 8:1-9:15; Gal. 2:10). Why can't the church at Jerusalem help its own poor? Circumstances must be such that they don't have the means. And so, Paul has collected an offering. He intends to deliver it personally to the church at Jerusalem.

Those who know the overflowing grace of God will assist the poor. We see the importance of this back in 12:9-13. The more we appreciate God's mercy toward us, the more we'll ask ourselves two questions. (1) "What do you have that you did not receive?" (1 Cor. 4:7). How much have I received? (2) "What shall I render to the LORD for all his benefits to me?" (Ps. 116:12). How much can I give?

Paul plans to visit Rome, so that he can strengthen the church (15:24, 28-29)
Paul wants to enjoy this church's company for a season. And he wants to be a blessing to them. Back in 1:11, he says that he wants to impart some spiritual gift to strengthen them. Undoubtedly, he has in mind his "preaching." For Paul, the church is an opportunity to minister to others.

Those who know the overflowing grace of God will serve the church. We see the importance of this back in 12:6-8. When we're lost in self-forgetting happiness in Christ, our goal is always Christ's glory. Often times, we look at the church the wrong way, assuming it exists for us—to meet our needs and satisfy our demands. But the church is actually the context in which we express our gratitude for God's mercy by ministering to others.

Paul plans to visit Spain, so that he can evangelize the lost (15:24, 28)
Paul intends to use Rome as his base of operations to reach the western empire just as he had used Antioch as his base of operations to reach the eastern empire. Back in 1:14, he declares, "I am under obligation both to Greeks and to barbarians, both to the wise and to the foolish." The term *obligation* means to owe. Paul is indebted to hand over the gospel. And so, he preaches the gospel to all people without discrimination.

Those who know the overflowing grace of God will evangelize the lost. The second question of the Heidelberg Catechism is this: "How many things are necessary for you to know, so that you may live and die happily?" The answer is threefold. First, I must know how great my sins and miseries are. Second, I must know how I may be delivered from all my sins and miseries. Third, I must know how I shall express my gratitude to God for such deliverance. One of the principal ways we express it is in seeking the lost.

Paul prays (15:30-33)
Having laid out his plans, Paul urges the church at Rome to pray for him (15:30-32). There are essentially three requests (1) So that he might be delivered from trouble in Judea (15:31). He means the Jews, who are seeking an opportunity to kill him. (2) So that the offering might be accepted by the saints

in Jerusalem (15:31). Perhaps he's worried that they might be offended by this offering. They might consider it a handout. Or, perhaps he's worried that the Jerusalem church won't receive an offering from the Gentile churches. They might consider it an offence. (3) So that he might come to them in joy and find refreshing rest in their company (15:32).

We know that God answers this prayer. (1) God does deliver Paul from trouble in Judea (Acts 21:30; 22:22; 23:10-16). The Jews try desperately to kill him. Through a series of events, God protects him. (2) God does make the offering acceptable to the church at Jerusalem (Acts 21:17). The Jerusalem church gladly receives Paul and, by inference, his offering. (3) God does lead Paul to Rome (Acts 25:11-12). According to several early church fathers, Paul is released from his imprisonment in Rome. He visits Spain. He's re-arrested. Shortly thereafter, he's martyred.

Paul ends this account of his plans with a brief benediction: "May the God of peace be with you all. Amen" (15:33). How fitting! God is the only source of peace in the believer's life. Why? "He is unchangeable, and who can turn him back? What he desires, that he does. For he will complete what he appoints for me, and many such things are in his mind" (Job 23:13-14).

Conclusion

What do we learn from Paul's example?

Like Paul, we should immerse our plans in prayer. We should plan while praying "by God's will." James writes,

> Come now, you who say, "Today or tomorrow we will go into such and such a town and spend a year there and trade and make a profit"—yet you do not know what tomorrow will bring. What is your life? For you are a mist that appears for a little time and then vanishes. Instead you ought to say, "If the Lord wills, we will live and do this or that" (James 4:13-15).

Some people ask, "If God does what he desires with me, then why bother praying?" This question reveals a misunderstanding of prayer. Many people believe that the purpose of prayer is to get God to do what they want him to do. In actual fact, the purpose of prayer is to bring ourselves into line with his will for us. John Stott remarks, "The struggle involved in prayer lies in the process of coming to discern God's will and to desire it above everything else."[1]

Like Paul, we should remember that God's ways aren't our ways. "The heart of man plans his way, but the LORD establishes his steps" (Prov. 16:9). "Many are the plans in the mind of a man, but it is the purpose of the LORD that will stand" (Prov. 19:21). We must view hindrances as part of God's plan. Oftentimes, God prevents us from doing something or going somewhere. We may not understand it at the time. Paul, for example, wanted to visit Rome. But God prevented him. Eventually, Paul did make it to Rome—as a prisoner. I'm not sure that's what he had planned, but it's what God had directed.

Like Paul, we should learn to accept our current circumstances. Paul was willing to accept God's plans for him. That's known as contentment. We dare not confuse contentment with apathy. If I'm apathetic, I don't care what happens. If I'm content, I care what happens, while trusting in God. Many people (including Christians) struggle to find contentment. Why? They're constantly looking for something bigger and better—always peering around the next bend. In so doing, they become their our own worst enemy.

Like Paul, we should trust God. Did Paul have doubts as he sat in a prison cell, as he endured beatings, as he lost friends and colleagues, as he battled false teachers? Perhaps, but he knew that God would complete what he had appointed for him. He trusted God. What an example for us! "And we know that for those who love God all things work together for good, for those who are called according to his purpose" (8:28).

---

[1] Stott, *Message of Romans*, 390.

86
Striving in Prayer (15:30-33)

In 15:14, Paul begins to wrap up his epistle. He acknowledges that he has written "very boldly" on some points (15:15). He has touched on lots of doctrines and commands. He doesn't want his audience to take unnecessary offense from his boldness. And so, he assures them of two things: their maturity (15:14) and his ministry (15:15-16).

Paul's mention of his ministry leads him to say a couple of things about his success (15:17-19) and his strategy (15:20-21). His mention of his strategy leads him to share his threefold plan: he wants to visit Jerusalem (to assist the poor), then Rome (to serve the church), and then Spain (to evangelize the lost) (15:22-29). His mention of his threefold plan then leads him to urge the church to pray for him (15:30-33).

Why we pray (15:30)
"I appeal to you, brothers, by our Lord Jesus Christ and by the love of the Spirit." Paul uses the term "appeal" (ESV) or "beg" (NKJV). The same word is found in 12:1. Just as Paul appeals to the Roman Christians to present themselves to God as living sacrifices, so he appeals to them to pray earnestly for his ministry. He gives two motives (or, incentives).

The first: "by our Lord Jesus Christ." Paul is reminding them of who Christ is. In a word, he's Lord. "All authority in heaven and on earth has been given to me" (Matt. 28:18). He rules the universe for the good of his church. Do you see how important this is for Paul's first request: "that I may be delivered from the unbelievers in Judea" (15:31)? His enemies are powerful, influential, and numerous. Who's Paul? Who can deliver him? Christ alone.

The second: "by the love of the Spirit." Paul is reminding them of the love that God has poured into their hearts through the Holy Spirit (5:5). Do you see how important this is for Paul's second request: "that my service for Jerusalem may be acceptable to the saints" (15:31)? Paul expects the Holy Spirit to work powerfully and lovingly in the lives of these believers so that they'll receive him. Who can change minds and soften hearts? The Holy Spirit.

What an incentive to pray! God has a ruling Son and a loving Spirit, who are able to do far more abundantly than all we ask or think.

How we pray (15:30)

"I appeal to you, brothers, by our Lord Jesus Christ and by the love of the Spirit, to strive together with me in your prayers to God on my behalf." In short, we "strive." Why? There are a host of things that keep us from prayer: the cares of the world; the schemes of the devil; and the lusts of the flesh. Striving arises from a burden. That's why crises drive us to our knees. The phone rings at two in the morning with bad news. We're on our knees. The test results come back. It doesn't look good. We're on our knees. But why isn't it like that all the time? We need to see how critical things really are. All human effort lies prostrate before the throne of God's providence.

What we pray (15:31-32)

In 15:32, Paul inserts an important phrase in his prayer: "by God's will." He has plans. He prays that those plans will come to fruition, but he knows that God's will must be done. That teaches us how to pray. In the words of Thomas Manton, "Prayer is the offering up of our desires to God, in the name of Christ, for such things as are agreeable to his will." And so, we pray that ...

God blesses the preaching and teaching of his Word, and creates in us an insatiable appetite for his Word.

God guards us from any scandal that would sully our witness, and keeps us from error, idolatry, apathy, and worldliness.

God cultivates discipleship among us, to such a degree that it becomes normal and natural—fathers discipling sons, mothers discipling daughters, friends discipling friends.

God enables us to share the gospel boldly, regularly, and faithfully, and stirs in us an eagerness, earnestness, fearlessness, and willingness to proclaim the good news of salvation.

God equips us to do good in our various callings, and turns us into the best husbands, fathers, wives, mothers, workers, bosses, neighbours, friends, and citizens, as we seek to live as an act of worship—the death of self in the interest of Christ-likeness.

God turns our homes into places of gospel-centredness whereby it's evident in the relationship between husband and wife, parent and child.

God strengthens us to love our enemies—even those who persecute us.

God shows us that the most dangerous threat to us isn't the sin in this world, but the sin in our hearts.

God maintains our unity, and stirs in us a love for people who share nothing in common with us except their love of Christ.

God stirs us to give consistently, faithfully, joyfully, and sacrificially, and nurtures in us a zeal for the spread of his glory among the nations.

God sustains us in the darkest nights, enabling us to see that we only reach the heights of blessedness through the valleys of despair and that temporal suffering isn't worth comparing to future glory.

God convinces us to value everything according to his eternal glory, not our earthly happiness.

Conclusion

Paul concludes his prayer with these words: "May the God of peace be with you all. Amen" (15:33). This title "God of peace" is a description of God as he stands in relation to his people (16:20; 2 Cor. 13:11; Phil. 4:9; 1 Thess. 5:23; 2 Thess. 3:16).

First, it's a description of God as our King. He's the "God of peace" by virtue of providence. God keeps all things in existence, causes all things to act as they do, and directs all things to their appointed end. He governs the snowflake and the supernova. This brings peace. "The peace of God is that eternal calm which lies far too deep in the praying, trusting soul to be reached by any external disturbances" (A.T. Pierson).[1]

Second, it's a description of God as our Father. He's the "God of peace" by virtue of salvation. "We have peace with God through our Lord Jesus Christ" (5:2). We're no longer God's enemies. This peace is achieved by Christ's atoning work on the cross. We stand on a firm foundation: God's grace to us in Christ. Therefore, we approach God as our reconciled Father. In Christ, the sinful failings of our best actions aren't scrutinized by a severe Judge, but accepted by a loving Father. In Christ, we draw near to God with comfort and confidence. In Christ, we pray to God with boldness. In Christ, we cry out to God as children cry out to their father.

---

[1] Source unknown.

87
Final Greetings (16:1-24)

We're in the midst of Paul's conclusion. We've considered his ministry (15:14-21) and his plans (15:22-33). In this chapter, we're going to consider his greetings (16:1-24). In 2 Timothy 3:16, Paul affirms, "All Scripture is breathed out by God and profitable." I think we can put that statement to the test as we look at Paul's comments in 16:1-24.

Are these verses inspired?
There are those who believe that Paul's epistle to the Romans ends with his benediction in 15:33, "May the God of peace be with you all. Amen." They argue that Paul wrote his letter and made copies to send to other churches. He made one of these copies for the church at Ephesus. To that copy, he added an appendix, in which he greets the believers in that church. Some people believe that's what we have in chapter 16. Why do they think that?

F.F. Bruce identifies four main reasons.[1] Let me paraphrase them for you. (1) In these verses, Paul sends personal greetings to twenty-six individuals and five households. If these personal greetings are directed to the church at Rome, how does he know so many people in a place that he has never visited? Ephesus, on the other hand, is a church well known to Paul. (2) In these verses, Paul sends personal greetings to Priscilla and Aquila (16:3). From Acts 18:26 and 1 Corinthians 16:19, we know that they live in Ephesus. If this personal greeting is directed to the church at Rome, what are Priscilla and Aquila doing there? (3) In these verses, Paul sends personal greetings to Epaenetus, "who was the first convert to Christ from Asia" (16:5). If this personal greeting is directed to the church at Rome, what is the first convert from Asia doing there? Surely, he's much more likely to live at Ephesus. (4) In these verses, Paul inserts a warning concerning false teachers (16:17-20). If this warning is directed to the church at Rome, why hasn't Paul given the issue some attention in this letter? His warning appears to be more in keeping with the situation at Ephesus (Acts 20:28-31).

---

[1] Bruce, *Romans*, 254.

Having explained the four reasons for viewing chapter 16 as an appendix to the Ephesians, F.F. Bruce gives four arguments in support of accepting chapter 16 as part of Paul's letter to the Romans.[2] (1) If this chapter is intended for the church at Ephesus, would Paul have set apart twenty-six people for special greeting in a church where he knew just about everyone? Wouldn't he have been concerned that such an approach might offend those not mentioned? Assuming this greeting is directed to the church at Rome, how do we explain Paul's familiarity with so many people in a place he's never visited? Perhaps he had met these twenty-six individuals in other places during the course of his travels. He had received word that they were residing at Rome. And so, he greets them. (2) Most of the names in these verses are found on ancient inscriptions at Rome. That can't be said for Ephesus. (3) Paul's reference to "all the churches of Christ" in 16:16 includes those churches whose delegates were joining Paul in conveying their offering to the church at Jerusalem. Ephesus is one of those churches (Acts 20:4). Why then would Paul send a greeting to Ephesus from Ephesus? (4) Paul's warning in 16:17-20 is simply an attempt on his part to put the Roman Christians on their guard. If there had been problems at Ephesus, Galatia, and Corinth, then it was just a matter of time before there would be problems at Rome.

In short, I accept these verses as part of Paul's epistle to the Romans. I see no reason for concluding otherwise. Before proceeding, I need to remove a couple of potential stumbling blocks in the text.

The first concerns the mention of Tertius in 16:22. He claims to have written this letter. But I thought Paul wrote it. He did. Tertius is a scribe (secretary), who writes while Paul dictates. This is Paul's common practice. "I, Paul, write this greeting with my own hand" (1 Cor. 16:21; Col. 4:1; 2 Thess. 3:17).

The second concerns the absence of 16:24 from the ESV and NIV. It's included in the AV. It's in parentheses in the NASB. Was it present and then deleted, or was it absent and then added? We don't know, but it doesn't make any difference. There are thousands of ancient NT manuscripts. They differ at times due to copyist mistakes. Substantial variants affect merely .001% of the NT. In other words, they never alter the text's meaning.

Are these verses profitable?

We have the Holy Spirit's testimony that they are (2 Tim. 3:16). But, in

---

[2] Bruce, *Romans*, 255-57.

FINAL GREETINGS (16:1-24)

discerning how, we must be careful to make a distinction between verses that are *prescriptive* (stating what should be done) and verses that are *descriptive* (describing without expressing judgment). In most of this epistle, Paul's words are prescriptive, in that he's explaining truths or giving commandments. For example, his explanation of the doctrine of justification is prescriptive. It's still valid today. His commandment to love without hypocrisy is prescriptive. It's still valid today. In some parts of this letter, however, Paul's words are descriptive. He isn't explaining truths or giving commandments. He's simply describing events or circumstances as they are. We can't take these verses as prescriptive. For example, the fact that Paul plans to visit Spain doesn't mean that we should plan to visit Spain. The fact that Paul urges the Roman Christians to strive in prayer on his behalf doesn't mean that we should strive in prayer on his behalf. The fact that Paul tells the Roman Christians to receive Phoebe doesn't mean that we should receive Phoebe. The fact that Paul tells the Roman Christians to greet one another with a kiss doesn't mean that we should greet one another with a kiss.

This distinction between *prescriptive* and *descriptive* portions of Scripture is important. Why? It helps us to avoid wrong conclusions. Again, by way of example, are we to conclude from what Paul says in 16:16 that we should greet one another with a kiss? Is this prescriptive or descriptive? We must be certain that what we hold to as non-negotiable is based upon prescriptive (not descriptive) portions of God's Word. If we're going to call something doctrine, and define ourselves by it, and disagree with others over it, then we better make certain that it's actually prescribed in the Bible.

How are these verses profitable?
And so, in 16:1-24, we have a descriptive portion of Scripture. We must interpret it accordingly. When we do, we see that there are several principles that we can apply to ourselves. We see, for example, the importance of hard work. Paul acknowledges this quality in various individuals (16:1, 3, 6, 9, 12). We also see the importance of Christian fellowship. Paul identifies some as his "fellow" workers and others as his "fellow" prisoners (16:3, 7, 9). And we see the importance of brotherly love. Paul refers to Epaenetus, Ampliatus, Stachys, and Persis as his "beloved" (16:5, 8, 9, 12). But I want to focus on five details that are worthy of imitation.

We see a church

Paul names twenty-six people in his greetings. Clearly, he knows who belongs to this church. This means there must have been some way of recognizing church members.

This is implied throughout the NT. Paul recognizes elders and deacons in each church (Phil. 1:1). These offices assume church membership. They're pointless unless people know who belongs. Peter exhorts elders to "shepherd the flock of God that is among [them], exercising oversight" (1 Peter 5:2). How can they do that without knowing who constitutes the flock? Moreover, Paul speaks of church discipline, culminating in expulsion from the church: "Purge the evil person from among you" (1 Cor. 5:13). This command assumes church membership. It makes no sense unless people are part of the church.

Therefore, we use the term "membership" to describe what's clearly assumed in the NT—that is, the formal organization of a community of believers in a particular place.

This isn't the way everyone thinks. I hear the following from far too many professing believers. "I think I can attend a church indefinitely without making any formal commitment to it." "I think I can follow Christ without formally identifying myself with a church." "I think I can submit to Christ without ever submitting to a church." "I think I can gather with a church whenever it suits me." "I think the church is a service provider, which exists for the sole purpose of meeting my needs." "I think I can make major life decisions without considering the ramifications for the church." "I think I can live without assuming any responsibility for the spiritual or material welfare of other believers in the context of a church."

If you think in any of these ways, you misunderstand God's plan. Christ has established the local church as his authority on earth for the purpose of giving shape to the Christian life.[3] (1) The church is God's plan for *service*. Membership tells us who we're responsible to love, edify, correct, and encourage. (2) The church is God's plan for *discipline*. Membership tells us for whom we're accountable to discipline wisely and lovingly. (3) The church is God's plan for *discipleship*. Membership puts our claim to follow Christ into a real-life setting where authority is actually exercised over us. (4) The church is God's plan for *evangelism*. Membership puts the rule of Christ on display for the

---

[3] Jonathan Leeman, *Church Membership* (Wheaton: Crossway, 2012), 79-81.

watching world. In so doing, it invites the nations to take notice.

We see a diverse church
Paul mentions twenty-six people. They differ in ethnicity: Jews and Gentiles. They differ in gender: men and women. They differ in class: slaves and masters. They differ in culture: Latin and Greek. Racial tension is all over the news these days. The church must be different from the world. How? The gospel means that we're "in Christ" (16:2, 3, 7, 8, 9, 10, 11, 12, 13), and this identity crushes our superiority complexes and inferiority complexes.

We see a loving church
Paul refers to four individuals as his "beloved" (16:5, 8, 9, 12). This is reminiscent of his command back in 12:10, "Love one another with brotherly affection." This is the love of a family that grows with familiarity. Despite differences, disagreements, and disappointments, there's devotion.

We see a giving church
Paul refers to those who risked their neck for him (16:3-4). He refers to those who host the church in their homes (16:5, 14, 15). This takes us back to his command in 12:10, "Outdo one another in showing honour." We're to give our attention to how we can help others rather than be helped by them. We're to expend our energy to edify others rather than be edified by them.

We see a serving church
Paul acknowledges this quality in various individuals (16:3, 6, 9, 12). Again, it points back to his command in 12:11, "Do not be slothful in zeal, be fervent in spirit, serve the Lord." Each of us possesses at least one spiritual gift. God commands us to use it in the context of the church for the spiritual good of the other members of the body.

Conclusion
A man, seeking a perfect church, approached C.H. Spurgeon to ask him about the Metropolitan Tabernacle. Spurgeon replied, "My church is not the one you're looking for. But if you should happen to find such a church, I beg you not to join it, for you would spoil the whole thing."[4] The church at Rome

---
[4] Source unknown.

wasn't a perfect church. There is no such thing as a perfect church. Each local church is a gathering of imperfect people who are committed to one another because of their love for Christ. Our calling is to seek one another's good, for the edification of all.

88
Doctrinal Discernment (16:17-20)

There's a tidal island off the northeast coast of England, called *Lindisfarne*. The causeway is flooded twice per day. When the tide is out, it's possible to walk or drive across the causeway to the island. At different points along the way, there are refuge boxes with warning signs: "If you see water, climb up!" The tide comes in so quickly, that there's no time to make it to the other side of the causeway. Each year, at least one car is stranded in the tide. Why? The driver ignored the warning signs. We ignore warning signs to our peril. The same is true in the context of the church.

One of parents' many responsibilities is to teach their children to discern. They need to learn to identify hazards. They need to look both ways before crossing the road. They need to stay away from the water's edge. They need to keep their fingers out of the light sockets. "This is good; that isn't." "This is safe; that isn't." "This is beneficial; that isn't." If they reach sixteen years of age without learning how to discern, they're immature (and in danger).

It works the same way in the church. When we become Christians, we need to learn to discern—to judge between what's good and evil, true and false, right and wrong. That's Paul's focus in 16:17-20.

A twofold appeal (16:17)
"I appeal to you, brothers, to watch out for those who cause divisions and create obstacles contrary to the doctrine that you have been taught; avoid them." The word "appeal" conveys urgent affection. This is the third time Paul uses the phrase (12:1; 15:30). When we put these three texts together, we hear a call to consecration, prayer, and discernment. If you're floundering spiritually, there's a very high probability your condition stems from a lack of one of these three. I encourage you to remember from where you have fallen. Here, Paul appeals to his readers to do two things.

First, they must "watch." We don't know what "divisions" and "obstacles" Paul has in mind. He's likely referring to any teaching that undermines his explanation and application of the gospel as found in chapters 1-15. He's telling his readers to hold fast to the "doctrine" they've been taught.

Second, they must "avoid." If they identify someone who's causing "divisions" and creating "obstacles" by departing from sound doctrine, they're to shun that person. This isn't an excuse to be rude. It's a commandment to stop listening to such an individual.

How do we reconcile Paul's hard line with what he has said in chapter 14? Do you remember? Paul exhorts his readers not to quarrel over "opinions," but to welcome those who differ (14:1). But, here, he tells them to avoid those who differ. How do we resolve this? There, Paul speaks of non-essentials—matters of conscience to which the Bible doesn't speak directly or definitively. In such cases, the most important thing isn't winning an argument, but maintaining unity. Here, Paul speaks of essentials. There are acceptable and unacceptable divisions. The dividing line is doctrine. There's "a standard of teaching" (6:17) and "an analogy of faith" (12:6). This body of doctrine must not be compromised.

A twofold reason (16:18-19)

"For such persons do not serve our Lord Christ, but their own appetites, and by smooth talk and flattery they deceive the hearts of the naive. For your obedience is known to all, so that I rejoice over you, but I want you to be wise as to what is good and innocent as to what is evil." Here, Paul gives two reasons why vigilance is so important.

The first is the threat of deception. Those who depart from the "doctrine" aren't making an intellectual error, but serving their own "appetites" (bellies). In other words, they depart from sound teaching because they crave something—power, control, wealth, approval, fame, success, etc. Thus, they employ "smooth talk" and "flattery" (eulogy—blessing) in order to deceive the hearts of the "naïve" (unsuspecting). They're nice, pleasant, and friendly. Their ideas seem plausible.

The second reason is the danger of disobedience. The church at Rome has a reputation for obedience. What will happen if they fall prey to the deception of these false teachers? It will lead to disobedience, and their reputation will be ruined. And so, they must "be wise as to what is good and innocent as to what is evil." How do we know the difference between good and evil? We know the difference by studying the will of God as found in the Word of God (12:2, 9).

A twofold hope (16:20)

Paul's charge in 16:17-19 is a little daunting. He knows it. And so, he gives a little encouragement: "The God of peace will soon crush Satan under your feet. The grace of our Lord Jesus Christ be with you." I want you to notice three details in the promise.

First, God will crush Satan. This promise has an OT context (Gen. 3:15). Christ crushes Satan in three stages. (1) The first was at his crucifixion. "He disarmed the rulers and authorities and put them to open shame, by triumphing over them in him" (Col. 2:15). (2) The second is during his exaltation. "He seated him at his right hand in the heavenly places far above all rule and authority and power and dominion" (Eph. 1:20-21). (3) The third will be at his return. "Then comes the end, when he delivers the kingdom to God the Father after destroying every rule and every authority and power" (1 Cor. 15:25).

Second, God will soon crush Satan. "The night is far gone; the day is at hand" (13:12). The Bible divides history into "this age" (night) and "the age to come" (day). Christ inaugurated "the age to come" at his first advent. It overlaps with "this age." The next event in God's plan of redemption is Christ's return. It could happen at any moment. The eternal kingdom is going to break into human history at any moment. "With the Lord one day is as a thousand years, and a thousand years is one day" (2 Peter 3:3-4).

Third, God will soon crush Satan under your feet. He says "our feet" because we're in Christ (Eph. 1:22).

> The Prince of Darkness grim, we tremble not for him;
> his rage we can endure, for lo, his doom is sure;
> one little word shall fell him.[1]

This victory (as with all the blessings of salvation) flows to us through our union with Christ. Our life is intertwined with his, meaning his wisdom is ours to direct us, his power to protect us, his mercy to assist us, his grace to forgive us, and his faithfulness to encourage us. To engage in spiritual warfare is (above all else) to live daily in the reality of what it means to be in Christ.

Conclusion

"Be wise as to what is good and innocent as to what is evil." That is a command that we need to take to heart in our day. We need to watch for those who

---

[1] Martin Luther, "A Mighty Fortress is our God" in *The Hymnal for Worship and Celebration*, 26.

teach an unbiblical view of man. "All are under sin" (3:9). We need to watch for those who teach an unbiblical view of the gospel. "We are justified by his grace as a gift through the redemption that is in Christ Jesus" (3:24). We need to watch for those who teach an unbiblical view of sanctification. "Thanks be to God, that you who were once slaves of sin have become obedient from the heart to the standard of teaching to which you were committed" (6:17). We need to watch for those who teach an unbiblical view of God. "Oh, the depths of the riches and wisdom and knowledge of God! How unsearchable are his judgments and how inscrutable his ways!" (11:33).

89
The Only Wise God (16:25-27)

I began this series of studies with the following words from F.F. Bruce: "There is no saying what may happen when people begin to study the letter to the Romans." Here is truth, to make us wise. Here is light, to guide our way. Here is hope, to calm our fears. Here is joy, to ease our sorrows. Here is water, to quench our thirst. Here is food, to satisfy our hunger.

Paul brings his epistle to a close, declaring,

> Now to him who is able to strengthen you according to my gospel and the preaching of Jesus Christ, according to the revelation of the mystery that was kept secret for long ages but has now been disclosed and through the prophetic writings has been made known to all nations, according to the command of the eternal God, to bring about the obedience of faith—to the only wise God be glory forevermore through Jesus Christ! Amen (16:25-27).

What does it mean to "strengthen"? The term is *sterizo*: "to fix, to set, to establish, to make fast." Abraham says to the rich man: "Between us and you a great chasm has been fixed" (Luke 16:26). It's the same word. And so, to be strengthened is to be fixed in place—immovable. The term also conveys the idea of determination. Luke writes, "When the days drew near for him to be taken up, he set his face to go to Jerusalem" (Luke 9:51). Jesus "set" his face, meaning his decision was established and there wasn't anything that could change his mind. To be strengthened is to be established or determined.

The source of spiritual strength
Paul says we're strengthened by "him who is able." In other words, he ascribes our immovability to God's power. That's confirmed throughout Scripture. "God is able to make all grace abound to you, so that having all sufficiency in all things at all times, you may abound in every good work" (2 Cor. 9:8). "Now to him who is able to do far more abundantly than all that we ask or think, according to the power at work within us" (Eph. 3:20). "I am not ashamed, for I know whom I have believed, and I am convinced that he is able

to guard until that Day what has been entrusted to me" (2 Tim. 1:12). "He is able to save to the uttermost those who draw near to God through him" (Heb. 7:25). "Now to him who is able to keep you from stumbling and to present you blameless before the presence of his glory with great joy" (Jude 1:24).

Our God "hangs the earth on nothing ... He binds up the waters in his thick clouds ... He covers the face of the full moon ... He has inscribed the boundary between light and darkness ... Behold, these are but the outskirts of his ways, and how small a whisper do we hear of him" (Job 26:7-14). This magnificently omnipotent God is our God. As J.I. Packer states, "God's dominion is total: He wills as he chooses and carries out all that he wills, and none can stay his hand or thwart his plans."[1] Therefore, we're certain that God will establish us. We're confident that "the work which his goodness began, the arm of his strength will complete."[2]

The means of spiritual strength
God strengthens us according to,

> The gospel and the preaching of Jesus Christ, according to the revelation of the mystery that was kept secret for long ages but has now been disclosed and through the prophetic writings has been made known to all nations, according to the command of the eternal God, to bring about the obedience of faith.

Please notice what Paul says about the gospel. (1) It was *concealed*: it "was kept secret for long ages." The gospel is certainly in the OT, but it wasn't fully made known to those who lived at that time (1 Peter 1:10-12). (2) It is *revealed*: it "has now been disclosed and through the prophetic writings has been made known." The gospel is rooted in the OT. That's why there are sixty-four quotations from the OT in this epistle. (3) It is *proclaimed*: it has been made known "to all nations, according to the command of the eternal God." The gospel has gone forth into the whole world. This means that God determined when this full revelation of the gospel would be made. (4) It is *obeyed*: it has been made known "to bring about the obedience of faith" (16:26). The gospel commands people to place their faith in Christ.

But how exactly is the gospel the means of spiritual strength? We've seen

---

[1] Packer, *Concise Theology*, 33.
[2] Augustus Toplady, "A Debtor to Mercy Alone" in *Hymns of Worship and Remembrance*, 326.

The Only Wise God (16:25-27)

how in this epistle.

The gospel strengthens by remedying our greatest ailment. "There is therefore now no condemnation for those who are in Christ Jesus" (8:1). For those who are in Christ, the verdict is changed from guilty to innocent, and the sentence is changed from death to life. Our condition is changed from condemnation to justification. This is freedom.

The gospel strengthens by satisfying our greatest longing. "The Spirit himself bears witness with our spirit that we are children of God" (8:16). We approach God as our reconciled Father. He isn't a terrifying God but a loving God. He isn't a condemning God but a pardoning God. He isn't a threatening God but an accepting God. Our peace with God is such that he loves us as if we had never been the object of his wrath.

The gospel strengthens by imparting hope for eternity. "We groan inwardly as we wait eagerly for adoption as sons, the redemption of our bodies" (8:23). At that time, God will make us spiritually glorious (1 Cor. 13:12). This means that he will renew his image in us. Every thought, impulse, and desire will terminate in Christ. Our love for him will burn so intensely that it will bring our hearts into perfect alignment with God's will. At that time, God will also make us physically glorious (1 Cor. 15:42-43). Our bodies will be "imperishable," "glorious," "strong," and "spiritual." This doesn't mean that our bodies will be nonphysical, but that our bodies will be fully conformed to the life given by the Holy Spirit. Our bodies will be more disposed to spiritual uses.

The gospel strengthens by assuring us that God is for us. "What then shall we say to these things? If God is for us, who can be against us?" (8:39). God is a perfect being. He's like a sphere whose centre is everywhere and whose circumference is nowhere. He isn't shut in, or shut out, of any space. He isn't far from us, yet he's far above and beyond us. He is our God!

> My name from the palms of his hands, eternity will not erase;
> Impressed on his heart it remains, in marks of indelible grace.
> Yes, I to the end shall endure, as sure as the earnest is given;
> More happy, but not more secure, the glorified spirits in heaven.[3]

---

[3] Augustus Toplady, "A Debtor to Mercy Alone" in *Hymns of Worship and Remembrance*, 326.

The result of spiritual strength

What does this spiritual strength look like in our lives? It means we're established in *faith*: "we sent Timothy, our brother and God's co-worker in the gospel of Christ, to establish and exhort you in your faith" (1 Thess. 3:2). It means we're established in *holiness*: "So that he may establish your hearts blameless in holiness before our God and Father, at the coming of our Lord Jesus with all his saints" (1 Thess. 3:13). It means we're established in *good works*: "Now may our Lord Jesus Christ himself, and God our Father, who loved us and gave us eternal comfort and good hope through grace, comfort your hearts and establish them in every good work and word" (2 Thess. 2:16-17). It means we're established in *heart*: "You also, be patient. Establish your hearts, for the coming of the Lord is at hand" (James 5:8). It means we're established in *truth*: "Therefore I intend always to remind you of these qualities, though you know them and are established in the truth that you have" (2 Peter 1:12).

Conclusion

"To the only wise God be glory forevermore through Jesus Christ! Amen" (16:27). I can't imagine a more fitting conclusion to this epistle, or a more fitting conclusion to this series of studies.

> To God be the glory great things he has done,
> So loved he the world that he gave us his Son,
> Who yielded his life an atonement for Sin,
> And opened the life-gate that all may go in.
>
> Praise the Lord, Praise the Lord, let the earth hear his voice,
> Praise the Lord, Praise the Lord, let the people rejoice.
> O come to the Father through Jesus the Son,
> And give him the glory, great things he has done![4]

---

[4] Fanny Crosby, "To God Be the Glory" in *Hymns of Grace*, 19.

About the Author

Stephen Yuille resides in Cambridge, Ontario, with his wife Alison, and their daughters Laura and Emma. He is the Vice President of Academics at Heritage College & Seminary. He also serves as an Associate Professor of Biblical Spirituality at The Southern Baptist Theology Seminary in Louisville, Kentucky.

Bibliography

Albenese, Catherine. *Nature Religion in America: From the Algonkian Indian to the New Age*. University of Chicago, 1990.

Alexander, Archibald. *Biographical Sketches of the Founder and Principal Alumni of the Log College*. Philadelphia: Presbyterian Board of Education, 1851.

Alleine, Joseph. *A Sure Guide to Heaven*. Edinburgh: Banner of Truth, 1989.

Athanasius. *A Library of Fathers of the Holy Catholic Church, Anterior to the Division of East and West*. Oxford: John Henry Parker, 1843.

Augustine. *The Confessions of Saint Augustine*. London: Collier Books, 1969.

Baxter, James S. *The Master Theme of the Bible: Grateful Studies in the Comprehensive Saviorhood of Our Lord Jesus Christ*. Wheaton: Tyndale, 1973.

Baxter, Richard. *The Practical Works of Richard Baxter*. 1846. Reprint, Morgan: Soli Deo Gloria, 2000.

———. *The Saints' Everlasting Rest*. New York: American Tract Society.

Beeke, Joel. *Overcoming the World: Grace to Win the Daily Battle*. Phillipsburg: P&R Publishing, 2005.

———. *Puritan Evangelism: A Biblical Approach*. Grand Rapids: Reformation Heritage Books, 1999.

Blamires, Harry. *The Christian Mind: How Should a Christian Think?* Ann Arbor: Servant, 1963.

Blanchard, John. *The Beatitudes for Today*. Epsom: Day One Publications, 1999.

Boice, James M. *Genesis 1-11*. Grand Rapids: Baker Books, 2002.

———. *Romans: The New Humanity*. Grand Rapids: Baker Books, 1995.

Boice, James M. and Ryken, Philip G. *The Doctrines of Grace: Rediscovering the Evangelical Gospel*. Wheaton: Crossway Books, 2002.

Bolton, Robert. *The Four Last Things: Death, Judgment, Hell, Heaven*. 1830. Reprint, Pittsburgh: Soli Deo Gloria, 1994.

Bonar, Horatius. *Words to Winners of Souls*. Phillipsburg: P&R Publishing, 1995.

Bridges, Jerry. *The Discipline of Grace*. Colorado Springs: NavPress, 1994.

Bruce, Frederick F. *Tyndale NT Commentaries: Romans*. Grand Rapids: Wm. B. Eerdmans, 1988.

Bunyan, John. *The Fear of God*. Morgan: Soli Deo Gloria, 1999.

_____. *The Miscellaneous Works of John Bunyan*. Vol. 10. Oxford: Clarendon Press, 1988.

_____. *The Pilgrim's Progress*. Uhrichsville: Barbour Publishing, 2005.

Calvin, John. *Calvin's Commentaries*. Vol. 19, *Commentaries on the Epistle of the Apostle Paul to the Romans*. Grand Rapids: Baker Books, 2003.

_____. *Institutes of the Christian Religion*. Vol. 1. Philadelphia: Westminster Press, 1960.

Charnock, Stephen. *The Existence and Attributes of God*. Vols. 1 and 2. Grand Rapids: Baker Books, 1990.

Comfort, Ray. *God Has A Wonderful Plan for Your Life: The Myth of the Modern Message*. Bellflower: Living Waters Publications, 2010.

DeYoung, Kevin. *The Hole in our Holiness: Filling the Gap between Gospel Passion and the Pursuit of godliness*. Wheaton: Crossway, 2012.

Drummond, Lewis A. *Spurgeon: Prince of Preachers*. Grand Rapids: Kregel Publications, 1992.

Edwards, John. *Charity and Its Fruits*. Edinburgh: Banner of Truth, 2000.

_____. *Religious Affections*. Minneapolis: Bethany House Publishers, 1996.

_____. *The Works of Jonathan Edwards*. Vol. 1. Peabody: Hendrickson, 1998.

Flavel, John. *The Works of John Flavel*. Vol. 1. London: Banner of Truth, 1968.

Gilbert, Greg. "The Gospel: God's Self-Substitution for Sinners," in *Don't Call It a Comeback*, ed. Kevin DeYoung. Wheaton: Crossway Books, 2011.

Godfrey, Robert. "Martin Luther," in *Great Leaders of the Christian Church*. Edited by John D. Woodbridge. Chicago: Moody Press, 1988.

Gouge, William. *Domesticall Duties*. London, 1622.

Gurnall, William. *The Christian in Complete Armor: A Treatise of the Saints' War Against the Devil*. Vol. 1. Edinburgh: Banner of Truth, 1995.

Hasker, William. *Providence, Evil and the Openness of God*. New York: Routledge, 2004.

Hendriksen, William. *New Testament Commentary: Galatians and Ephesians*. Grand Rapids: Baker Books, 1987.

Hughes, R. Kent. *1001 Great Stories and Quotes*, Wheaton: Tyndale, 1988.

Innes, Taylor. *John Knox*. Edinburgh: Oliphant, Anderson & Ferrier, 1896.

Johnson, Terry. *When Grace Transforms: The Character of Christ's Disciples Put Forward in the Beatitudes*. Ross-shire, UK: Christian Focus, 2008.
Josephus, Flavius. *The Antiquities of the Jews* in *Josephus: The Complete Works*. Nashville: Thomas Nelson, 1998.
Leeman, Jonathan. *Church Membership*. Wheaton: Crossway, 2012.
Lewis, Clive S. *Abolition of Man*. New York: HarperCollins, 2000.
_____. *Mere Christianity*. New York: MacMillan, 1943.
_____. *The Last Battle*. New York: HarperCollins, 2000.
_____. *The Lion, the Witch, and the Wardrobe*. New York: HarperCollins, 1994.
Lloyd-Jones, Martyn. *Romans 3:20-4:25*. Grand Rapids: Zondervan, 1971.
_____. *Romans 7:1-8:4*. Grand Rapids: Zondervan, 1973.
_____. *Studies in the Sermon on the Mount* Grand Rapids: Wm. B. Eerdmans, 1962.
Luther, Martin. *Commentary on Romans*. Grand Rapids: Kregel, 1976.
_____. *The Bondage of the Will*, in *Martin Luther's Works*. Edited by H. T. Lehmann. Philadelphia: Fortress Press, 1960.
_____. *The Freedom of a Christian*, in *Reformation Writings of Martin Luther*. London: Lutterworth Press, 1952.
MacDonald, William. *Alone in Majesty*. Nashville: Thomas Nelson, 1994.
_____. *My Heart, My Life, My All*. Grand Rapids: Gospel Folio Press, 1997.
_____. *The Forgotten Command: Be Holy*. Kilmarnock: John Ritchie, 1993.
Mahaney, Charles J. *Christ Our Mediator*. Sisters: Multnomah Publishers, 2004.
_____. *The Cross Centered Life*. Sisters: Multnomah Publishers, 2002.
Manton, Thomas. *An Exposition on the Epistle of James*. London: Banner of Truth, 1968.
_____. *The Complete Works of Thomas Manton*. Vol. 2. London: James Nisbet, 1870-75. Reprint, Birmingham, AL: Solid Ground Christian Books, 2008.
Moule, Handley. *Thoughts on Union with Christ*. London: Seeley & Co., 1885.
Murray, Iain. *David Martyn Lloyd-Jones: The Fight of Faith 1939 to 1981*. Edinburgh: Banner of Truth, 1990.
_____. *Revival and Revivalism: The Making and Marring of American Evangelicalism 1750-1758*. Edinburgh: Banner of Truth, 1994.

_____. *The Puritan Hope: Revival and the Interpretation of Prophecy* Edinburgh: Banner of Truth, 1998.

_____. *Wesley and Men Who Followed*. Carlisle: Banner of Truth, 2003.

Murray, John. *Redemption Accomplished and Applied*. Grand Rapids: Wm. B. Eerdmans, 1955.

_____. *The Epistle to the Romans*. Grand Rapids: Wm. B. Eerdmans, 1997.

Owen, John. *The Death of Death in the Death of Christ*. Vol. 1. Carlisle: Banner of Truth, 1999.

_____. *The Works of John Owen*. Edinburgh: Banner of Truth, 1977.

Packer, James I. *A Quest for godliness: The Puritan Vision of the Christian Life*. Wheaton: Crossway Books, 1990.

_____. *Concise Theology*. Wheaton: Tyndale House, 1993.

_____. *Keep in Step with the Spirit: Finding Fullness in Our Walk with God*. Grand Rapids: Baker Books, 1984.

_____. *Knowing God*. London: Hodder and Stoughton, 1975.

_____. *Rediscovering Holiness*. Ann Arbor: Servant Publications, 1992.

Perkins, William. *The Works of William Perkins*. Vol. 3. London: John Legate, 1631.

Pink, Arthur W. *The Attributes of God*. Grand Rapids: Baker Books, 1975.

_____. *The Doctrine of Human Depravity*. Pensacola: Mt. Zion Publishers, 1952.

_____. *The Sovereignty of God*. London: Banner of Truth, 1961.

Pinnock, Clark, Richard Rice, John Sanders, William Hasker, and David Basinger. *The Openness of God: A Biblical Challenge to the Traditional Understanding of God*. Downers Grove: InterVarsity, 1994.

Piper, John. "Are There Two Wills in God?" in *Still Sovereign: Contemporary Perspectives on Election, Foreknowledge, and Grace*. Edited by Thomas Schreiner and Bruce Ware. Grand Rapids: Baker Books, 2000.

_____. *The Pleasures of God*. Sisters: Multnomah Publishers, 2000

Plumer, William. *The Grace of Christ; or, Sinners Saved by Unmerited Kindness*. Philadelphia: Presbyterian Board of Publication, 1853.

Rupp, Gordon E. and Benjamin Drewery, eds. *Documents of Modern History*. London: Edward Arnold, 1970.

Ryle, John C. *Practical Religion*. London: James Clarke & Co., 1959.

Sanders, John. *The God Who Risks: A Theology of Providence*. Downers Grove: InterVarsity, 1998.

Shepard, Thomas. *The Parable of Ten Virgins*, in *The Works of Thomas Shepard*. Vol. 2. Ligonier: Soli Deo Gloria, 1990.

Sproul, Robert C. *Lifeviews: Understanding the Ideas that Shape Society Today*. Old Tappan: Fleming H. Revell, 1986.

_____. *Loved by God*. Nashville: Word Publishing, 2001.

_____. *The Holiness of God*. Wheaton: Tyndale House, 1998.

Stevenson, Robert L. *Dr. Jekyll and Mr. Hyde*, in *Robert Louis Stevenson: Four Complete Novels*. New York: Gramercy Books, 1995.

Stott, John. *The Message of Romans: God's Good News for the World*. Downers Grove: InterVarsity, 1994.

Swinnock, George. *The Works of George Swinnock*. Vols. 1 and 4. Edinburgh: Banner of Truth, 1992.

Thomas, Derek W. H. *How the Gospel Brings Us All the Way Home*. Orlando: Reformation Trust, 2011.

Thomas, I. D. E. *A Puritan Golden Treasury*. Edinburgh: Banner of Truth, 2000.

Vaughan, Charles J. *St. Paul's Epistle to the Romans*. New York: Macmillan, 1885.

Vos, Geerhardus. *Biblical Theology: Old and New Testaments*. Edinburgh: Banner of Truth, 1992.

Ware, Bruce. *God's Greater Glory: The Exalted God of Scripture and the Christian Faith*. Wheaton: Crossway Books, 2004.

_____. *God's Lesser Glory: The Diminished God of Open Theism*. Wheaton: Crossway Books, 2000.

Warfield, B. B. *The Inspiration and Authority of the Bible*. Phillipsburg: P&R Publishing, 1979.

_____. *The Works of B. B. Warfield*. Grand Rapids: Baker Books, 2003.

Watson, Thomas. *A Body of Divinity*. 1890. Reprint, London: Banner of Truth, 1958.

_____. *All Things for Good*. Carlisle: Banner of Truth, 1994.

_____. *The Mischief of Sin*. 1671. Reprint, Pittsburgh: Soli Deo Gloria, 1994.

Wells, David. *God in the Wasteland: The Reality of Truth in a World of Fading Dreams*. Grand Rapids: W. B. Eerdmans, 1994.

White, James. *The God Who Justifies: The Doctrine of Justification*. Minneapolis: Bethany House, 2001.

Whitney, Don. *Spiritual Disciplines for the Christian Life*. Colorado Springs:

The Obedience of Faith

NavPress, 1991.

Scripture Index

Old Testament

Genesis
- 1:31 .... 46, 233
- 1:1-2 42
- 1:1-3 42
- 2:1 233
- 2:17 .... 33, 220
- 2:20 169
- 2:23-24 168
- 3:5 159
- 3:15 .... 11, 46, 112, 160, 233, 483
- 3:17 233
- 3:19 162
- 4:25 162
- 4:26 .... 162, 163
- 4:10-15 161
- 4:16-24 161
- 4:1-7 160
- 4:8-9 161
- 6:5 .... 184, 374, 412
- 6:6 372
- 6:8 98
- 6:8-9 113
- 9:6 .... 403, 411
- 12:1-3 12
- 14:23 124
- 14:19-20 123
- 15:1 123
- 15:2 .... 124, 125
- 15:4 124
- 15:5 125
- 15:6 .... 93, 110, 115, 119, 125
- 15:1-6 .... 123, 125, 126
- 16:2 126
- 17:5 120
- 17:7 311
- 17:8 119
- 18:25 75
- 22:2 275
- 22:12 .... 275, 372
- 25:29-34 293
- 27:18-29 293
- 27:6-17 293
- 41:28 366
- 42:36 261
- 50:20 .... 261, 268
- 50:19-20 375

Exodus
- 3:6 98
- 3:17 152
- 4:21 375
- 9:16 .... 298, 312
- 16:10 314
- 20:3 152
- 20:13 422
- 20:14 422
- 20:15 422
- 20:17 422
- 20:1-17 419
- 20:13-17 422
- 33:18 298
- 33:19 .... 298, 312
- 40:34 314

Leviticus
- 1:13 382
- 4:3 215
- 18:5 324
- 19:18 420

Numbers
- 8:8 215
- 12:8 98

23:19 .... 333, 354
Deuteronomy
3:24 235
6:3-5 421
9:10 151
9:27 51
10:19 328
10:12-13 421
18:18 213
29:29 335
30:12-14 .... 324, 327
32:21 328
32:35 405
32:43 .... 405, 446
Joshua
10:13 366
Judges
14:1-4 375
Ruth
1:20 236
1 Samuel
13:14 98
15:29 373
16:14 367
17:8-11 103
2 Samuel
7:14-15 314
1 Kings
4:21 .... 120, 226
12:15 412
17:6 367
19:10-18 335
19:1-4 335
1 Chronicles
21:1 375
21:27 367
29:11 .... 370, 439
2 Chronicles
16:9 358
18:13 395
Ezra
7:10 .... 8, 395
Esther
5:9 398
5:13 398
Job
1:6 275
4:18 359
5:9 257
5:13 362
9:2 60
9:4 21
11:7 359
12:13 359
14:5 .... 163, 368
19:25-27 243
19:26-27 231
21:22 362
23:13 254
23:13-14 469
26:7-14 486
31:4 358
33:4 42
37:5 .... 46, 162
37:16 357
37:23 21
41:11 355
42:2 273
Psalms
2:6-7 213
4:2 466
10:18 328
15:1-2 436
16:11 .... 133, 136, 288, 451
17:15 231
18:49 446
19:1 42
19:4 328
19:7-10 7
25:6 75
32:1-2 .... 93, 119, 462
33:6 .... 36, 42
33:11 .... 354, 359
34:2 71
34:18 255
37:9 119
37:11 119
37:22 120
37:29 120
37:34 120
39:6 215
48:14 .... 141, 451
49:17 288
51:5 184

51:10 82
62:9 74
89:14 75
90:8 358
90:12 423
103:8 32
103:14 358
104:24 360
104:30 42
110:4 213
116:12 468
117:1 446
119:71 264
119:99 363
119:162 331
139:14 360
144:15 .... 141, 451
145:3 46
145:3-9 161
145:5 355
145:8 46
145:9 46
145:17 75
145:2-3 10
145:4-7 46
148:5 42

Proverbs
5:4 261
9:10 363
13:13 7
15:11 40
16:4 369
16:6 181
16:9 470
19:21 .... 356, 470
21:1 417
21:30 359

Ecclesiastes
5:15-16 288
8:8 163
12:8 236
12:14 40

Isaiah
1:9 313
6:5 392
8:14 319
10:15 328
10:16 328
10:20 328
10:21-23 313
10:5-6 368
11:10 446
11:6-9 234
14:24 356
27:9 353
28:16 ....321, 325
29:10 340
30:10 82
40:8 354
40:13 356
40:14 359
40:22 295
40:12-14 355
42:6-7 213
43:6 223
43:7 42
43:25 116
44:22 116
44:6-7 .... 253, 257
45:22 101
45:6-7 368
46:10 162
46:9-10 .... 254, 357
50:1-3 63
52:5 63
52:7 328
53:1 328
53:6 116
53:12 445
59:17 405
59:20 352
59:20-21 353
60:21 42
61:3 42
65:1 328
66:2 204
66:20 461

Jeremiah
6:14 203
16:17 358
17:9 184
27:6 412
31:33 451
31:34 352

31:31–33 420
31:33–34 132
50:31 274
Ezekiel
11:5 358
18:23 ..... 255, 306
28:2 362
36:26–27 ..... 67, 420
Daniel
1:8 431
2:21 412
2:22 362
4:25 123
4:35 450
4:34–35 124
11:32 370
Hosea
1:10 312
1:4–9 312
2:23 312
Joel
2:32 325
Amos
3:6 32
Nahum
1:2 405
Habakkuk
1:5 336
1:6 375
2:4 ..... 29, 93, 143
Malachi
1:11 13
1:2–3 286
3:6 162
3:16 254

Scripture Index

New Testament

Matthew
1:1112
3:17 .... 139, 213
5:3 204
5:5 120
5:8 .... 133, 136, 242
5:28 440
5:29 181
5:45 304
5:44–45 225
6:21 222
6:32–33 227
7:11 223
7:23 255
8:12 288
9:13 114
9:35 149
10:29–31 223
10:38–39 232
11:28 249
12:34 .... 80, 342
12:37 80
12:40 130
16:24 452
16:26 232
16:27 55
17:2 387
18:3 16
19:5 397
19:28 233
22:14 251
22:36–40 .... 152, 419
22:37–40 421
22:41–45 130
23:25–28 64
25:41 288
28:18 .... 213, 471
28:19–20 465

Mark
1:5 149
4:39 366
7:20–23 221

9:2–3 387
10:47–48 331
12:30 69

Luke
3:15 149
4:18–19 213
6:36 225
9:51 485
11:21–22 214
12:33 133
16:26 485
18:10–13 64
18:11–12 320
23:28–30 100
24:12 245
24:44 9
24:44–45 214

John
1:12 227
1:14 214
1:18 214
1:29 .... 10, 13, 105
3:16 105
3:26 149
3:14–15 98
4:10 20
5:25 179
5:26 162
6:27 213
6:35 .... 259, 307
6:39 252
6:40 242
6:44 .... 249, 259, 270, 307, 342
6:45 251
6:65 .... 82, 270, 307
6:37–40 308
6:70–71 375
8:2 149
8:34 .... 5, 152, 160
8:36 5
8:56 112
8:43–44 79

The Obedience of Faith

9:3	368
10:3	259
10:11	213
10:14	255, 258
10:27	251
10:14–17	105
12:31	386
12:32	149
15:3	171
15:5	170, 190, 342
15:15	214
15:16	197
15:25	93, 246
15:1–5	170, 393
15:15–16	190
15:18–20	230
17:2	258
17:9	258, 386
17:14	386
17:17	171, 388
17:22	315
17:24	245, 258
17:26	269, 305
19:10	412
20:21	6

Acts

1:14	399
2:17	149
2:23	254, 268, 375
2:36	130
2:42	399
4:12	146, 196
5:29	413
7:52	75
10:12	149
13:48	259
13:38–39	259
14:17	304
14:16–17	10, 13
15:24	429
15:29	429
15:23–29	429
16:14	249
17:25	162
17:26	367
17:28	367
17:22–23	47
17:24–25	45
18:25	398
18:26	475
19:11–12	463
20:4	476
20:28–31	475
21:17	469
21:30	469
22:15	149
22:22	469
23:10–16	469
25:11–12	469

Romans

1:18–32	41, 47
2:4	304
3:19	255
3:24	276
3:20–4	95, 493
4:18–22	125
4:20–21	333
4:7–8	462
5:1	111, 441
5:5	269, 305
5:1–2	442
6:21	181
6:23	163
7:1–8	493
8:7	249, 342
8:8	249
8:18	244
8:26	362
8:28	362, 375, 453
8:14–17	275
9:3	22
9:4	313, 314
9:5	313
9:15	258
9:16	258, 342, 369
9:26	315
10:2	317
10:13	421
11:33	252, 453
11:36	42
11:33–36	355
12:1	394
12:3–8	394
13:14	221

Scripture Index

1 Corinthians
1:20 385
1:25 362
1:30 .... 185, 251
2:14 .... 78, 249, 342
3:1 222
3:3 222
3:17 387
3:18 385
3:22–23 277
3:6–7 330
4:5 60
4:7 .... 252, 259, 296, 310, 468
5:7 94
5:13 478
5:1–5 433
6:12 .... 387, 428
6:19 428
6:9–10 .... 436, 440
8:6 42
9:16 .... 10, 22
9:24 181
9:27 .... 221, 387
10:23 428
10:31 428
12:13 .... 168, 169
13:12 .... 243, 487
13:1–3 402
15:10 465
15:14 130
15:17 130
15:22 149
15:25 483
15:28 231
15:45 .... 148, 219
15:42–43 .... 243, 487
15:9–10 22
16:13 221
16:19 475
16:21 476
16:7–8 174

2 Corinthians
3:2 149
3:14 352
3:18 387
4:4 385
4:16 220

4:17–18 231
5:17 186
5:21 .... 215, 251
6:18 223
8:1–9 467
9:8 485
11:25–26 303
12:2 463
13:11 473

Galatians
1:4 385
1:14 202
1:11–12 8
1:15–16 8
1:6–9 433
2:10 467
2:20 .... 6, 170, 251
3:6 115
3:13 214
3:16 .... 292, 311
3:24 .... 155, 420
3:27 175
3:29 311
3:13–14 107
4:4–5 .... 106, 420
5:6 118
5:16 221
5:22 459
6:10 400
6:14 386

Ephesians
1:3 .... 17, 259, 296
1:4 342
1:5 223
1:6 258
1:8 361
1:10 234
1:11 .... 45, 359, 361, 453
1:13 154
1:18 .... 243, 387
1:22 483
1:23 169
1:19–20 132
1:20–21 483
1:5–6 .... 223, 342
2:1 179
2:2 385

503

2:3	99, 134, 227
2:6	17
2:8	88, 259
2:10	197
2:13	105
2:18	256
2:19	106
2:11–22	313
2:13–18	314
2:19–22	314
2:4–5	132
2:8–10	115
2:8–9	17, 55
3:8	22
3:10	245, 361
3:19	281
3:20	240, 485
4:1	251
4:6	42
4:18	184
4:23	243
4:24	413
4:1–13	394
4:17–19	271
5:1	224, 227
5:8	186, 227
5:14	65
5:23	169
5:25	169
5:29	171
5:30	169
5:32	169
5:22–24	393
5:25–26	388
5:25–32	169, 393
5:26–27	170, 191
5:30–31	168
5:6–10	34
6:10	181
6:21	149

Philippians

1:1	478
1:8	18
1:29	259
2:5	401
2:8	401
2:15	225
2:3–4	398
3:3	68, 70
3:6	202, 320, 419
3:9	320
3:13–14	244
3:20–21	135, 231, 244, 399
4:7	240

Colossians

1:9	387
1:16	42
1:20	134, 234, 315, 441
1:25	22
1:13–14	94
1:15–17	42
1:16–17	149
1:3–4	17
2:15	483
2:23	181
2:11–13	67
3:4	135
3:5	440
3:10	243, 413
3:11	105
3:12	402
3:14	402
3:24	244
4:2	399

1 Thessalonians

1:2–3	17
2:12	244
2:3–4	329
3:2	488
3:6	18
3:13	488
4:17	231
5:8	422
5:9	258
5:22	181
5:23–24	171

2 Thessalonians

1:7–8	52
2:13	251, 255, 259, 294
2:13–14	251
2:16–17	488
3:16	473
3:17	476

1 Timothy
- 1:13 .... 5, 467
- 1:14 467
- 1:15 19
- 1:15–16 21
- 2:1 149
- 2:2 416
- 2:4 255
- 4:7 181
- 5:21 .... 245, 255
- 6:16 .... 242, 354
- 6:15–16 45

2 Timothy
- 1:12 486
- 2:10 252
- 2:19 .... 258, 342, 358
- 3:5 347
- 3:10 230
- 3:16 .... 7, 475, 476
- 3:14–15 8
- 3:16–17 329
- 4:14 406

Titus
- 1:15 184
- 2:13 230
- 2:14 56
- 2:11–12 386

Hebrews
- 1:3 .... 257, 360, 450
- 2:10 223
- 2:17 215
- 3:1–6 106
- 3:5–6 8
- 4:13 358
- 6:18 454
- 6:19 454
- 7:25 .... 279, 486
- 7:21–25 213
- 8:11 149
- 9:5 94
- 9:24 279
- 10:4 95
- 10:6 215
- 11:1 121
- 11:3 .... 42, 43
- 11:4 161
- 11:6 .... 43, 259
- 11:12 .... 121, 131
- 11:19 131
- 12:6 .... 224, 263
- 12:9 227
- 12:16 217
- 12:29 288
- 13:8 354

James
- 1:17 .... 16, 354, 369
- 1:18 171
- 1:25 329
- 1:22–25 8
- 1:2–3 181
- 2:19 115
- 2:21 116
- 2:23 .... 98, 115
- 2:22–23 116
- 3:14 81
- 3:16 .... 81, 402
- 3:5–6 80
- 4:1 81
- 4:4 386
- 4:14 .... 162, 367
- 4:13–15 469
- 5:8 488
- 5:11–12 453

1 Peter
- 1:6 181
- 1:12 245
- 1:16 225
- 1:22 397
- 1:23 171
- 1:10–12 486
- 1:18–19 94
- 2:9 22
- 2:12 405
- 2:22 215
- 3:18 .... 141, 451
- 3:20 12
- 4:12–16 230
- 5:2 478
- 5:4 133
- 5:7 256

2 Peter
- 1:10 251
- 1:12 488
- 2:9 362

3:13 .... 133, 234
3:18 177
3:3-4 483

1 John
1:8 .... 82, 180
2:15 386
2:16 386
3:1 .... 269, 293, 305
3:2 231
3:3 244
3:14 186
3:20 356
3:24 226
3:11-12 161
3:2-3 226
4:12 226
4:16 304

4:20 401

Jude
1 24
3 394
24 486

Revelation
1:17-18 176
3:17 203
3:12-13 164
4:11 .... 42, 366
14:11 288
18:20-21 164
19:7-9 197
20:12 55
21:1 234
21:4 .... 133, 136